RONALD RUDIN

Making History in
Twentieth-Century Quebec

UNIVERSITY OF TORONTO PRESS
Toronto Buffalo London

© University of Toronto Press Incorporated 1997
Toronto Buffalo London
Printed in Canada

ISBN 0–8020–0853–4 (cloth)
ISBN 0–8020–7838–9 (paper)

Printed on acid-free paper

Canadian Cataloguing in Publication Data

Rudin, Ronald
Making history in twentieth-century Quebec

Includes bibliographical references and index.
ISBN 0-8020-0853-4 (bound)   ISBN 0-8020-7838-9 (pbk.)

1. Quebec (Province) – Historiography.   2. Historians –
Quebec (Province).   I. Title.

FC2909.R84 1997   971.4'007'2022   C97-931223-X
F1024.R84 1997

This book has been published with the help of a grant from the Humanities
and Social Sciences Federation of Canada, using funds provided by the Social
Sciences and Humanities Research Council of Canada.

University of Toronto Press acknowledges the financial assistance to its
publishing program of the Canada Council for the Arts and the Ontario Arts
Council.

TO DAVID

Contents

Preface

This book began with my efforts to become an Irish historian. During the 1970s and 1980s I wrote a number of books and articles that adhered to what I describe throughout this volume as the revisionist interpretation of Quebec history. In short, this meant that I was writing from a point of view that saw the course of Quebec history as largely indistinguishable from that followed by other Western societies. By the end of the 1980s, however, I was beginning to feel uncomfortable with this interpretation, which seemed to try too hard to deny those features of the past that distinguished Quebec from comparable societies. At roughly the same time, I was invited to attend a conference in Dublin which brought together academics from Quebec and Ireland. In the course of lengthy conversations with my Irish counterparts I began to realize that Irish historical writing had gone through a similar transformation, with Ireland's distinctiveness having been pushed aside in favour of an emphasis on its normalcy.

I returned to Canada with the rather nebulous idea of trying to compare aspects of Irish and Quebec history, and as I began to work my way through the Irish literature I started to see what my colleagues in Dublin had meant when they talked about contemporary Irish historians disavowing certain features of the past. In book after book, I discovered the efforts of historians intent on minimizing the significance of such forces as Catholicism and colonialism in the Irish experience. These historians even attempted to marginalize Ireland's legacy of violence. This process of denying aspects of the past seemed to parallel the efforts of revisionists in Quebec, but what was different in the Quebec context was the relative absence of reflection about the way in which historical writing mirrored certain characteristics of the larger society. While in Ireland there were studies suggesting the link, for instance, between denial of a violent past and hope for an end to violence in Northern Ireland, little such reflection existed in Quebec. And so, while I had begun the process of reading Irish history as a means of leaving Quebec history behind, I found myself drawn back to it in a process that ultimately led to this volume, which considers the relationship between historical writing and the larger society in twentieth-century Quebec.

As befits a book focusing on Quebec, it is necessary to deal with a few linguistic matters at the outset. This is a work that pertains almost exclusively to French-speaking historians and their relationship to the francophone population of Quebec. Accordingly, the reader will find relatively few references to English speakers who have written about Quebec's history. In making this decision, I have meant no slight to those such as Mason Wade, Ramsay Cook, Brian Young, and Allan Greer, to name only a few, who have contributed much to our understanding of Quebec's past. Rather, I based my decision on the fact that this book is, to a considerable degree, oriented towards assessing the relationship between historical writing and social change within French-speaking Quebec. I am not one of those who would argue that only the members of a given group can write about that group's experience. Nevertheless, I do believe that, to a certain degree, English speakers have approached the writing of Quebec's history as outsiders. Since my interest here is rather to view how 'insiders' have studied that past, I have looked almost exclusively at francophone authors.

Along the way, I have considered how historians in Quebec were affected by others in the profession, particularly those in France and the United States. The reader will notice, however, that there are relatively few references to English Canadians, who exercised remarkably little influence over the individuals under study here. English-Canadian historians and their French-language counterparts followed very different paths, having been shaped both by distinctive approaches to history and by different pressures from the societies in which they lived. Accordingly, I have engaged in relatively little direct comparison between these two groups.

Further to linguistic matters, the reader should also be aware that I have generally used the term 'Quebecer' without a modifier to refer to the province's francophone majority. As an English speaker who considers himself as much a Quebecer as someone whose family came to the province in the seventeenth century, I am not entirely happy about this decision. However, readers would be appropriately annoyed if they had to endure the cumbersome 'French-speaking Quebecers' for three hundred pages. Lastly, on the linguistic front, I have translated all the French quotations in the text into English. Given the nature of this book, with its frequent reference to both the private papers and the published works of historians who wrote primarily, if not exclusively, in French, I decided that too much of the text would have become inaccessible to too many readers had I left the quotes in their original form.

As for technical matters of a different sort, the more adventurous reader may notice that I have included a fair amount of explanatory material in the notes, which are, I regret, at the back of this book. I left this material separate from the body of the text so as to allow the central argument to come across as clearly as possible. The explanations in these notes are a bit tangential, but not irrelevant, to my argument, and I can only hope that some readers will put up with the inconvenience of flipping to the back to consult this material. As for the more conventional notes, which point to the sources that I have employed, I have complied with the University of Toronto Press's house style, which itself requires a few words of explanation. Very brief references have been provided for works that are frequently cited and can be found in the bibliography. For less frequently cited material I have provided fuller references in the notes.

Many of the notes refer to the private papers of the historians under study here, and these documents could not have been consulted without assistance from various quarters. The papers of Abbé Groulx, housed at the Centre de recherche Lionel-Groulx, were put at my disposal cheerfully by François David. Jean Roy, former president of the Institut d'histoire de l'Amérique française, allowed me to be the first researcher to look at that institution's archives. Denis Plante aided me in my perusal of the various collections of the archives of the Université de Montréal, while Lucie Pagé helped me during my visits to the archives of the Centre de recherche en civilisation canadienne-française (CRCCF) at the University of Ottawa. Lilianne Frégault graciously permitted me to consult and cite from the Frégault collections deposited at the CRCCF. The Hector Garneau papers, also deposited at the University of Ottawa, were put at my disposal with the permission of Pierre Savard. Marcel Trudel generously allowed me to cite from some of his personal correspondence, while Blair Neatby of Carleton University was kind enough to provide me with some of his personal files.

The funds to carry out the research for this project came from the Social Sciences and Humanities Research Council of Canada, to which body I am most grateful. Since a reader somewhere will probably ask why I did not use any of these funds to interview some of the historians discussed in this book, I would like to respond to the question in advance. While I considered speaking with some of these people at various stages in the process, I finally came to the conclusion that such a process would probably have added little to the rich record that these historians had already left regarding their views of the past. Many of the living historians have written either memoirs or reflections on their careers, and most have already been interviewed. In particular, I found the interviews prepared for the Radio-Canada series *Écrire l'histoire au Québec* very helpful. With this wealth of material at my disposal, I found little reason to seek out historians who have already had ample opportunity to put their points of view on the record.

While I may not have formally interviewed the historians who figure as subjects in this book, I would like to think that the project has benefited from my long conversations with colleagues on both sides of the Atlantic such as Cormac O Gráda of University College, Dublin, whose insights regarding Irish historiography have influenced my thinking about Quebec historical writing. George Huppert of the University of Illinois at Chicago was the first to hear many of my ideas over espressos when we were both on leave in Paris. Some of these ideas ultimately found their way into an article published in the *Canadian Historical Review* in 1992, a French translation of which appeared in 1995 in the *Bulletin d'histoire politique* thanks to the efforts of the journal's editor, Robert Comeau. I am also grateful to Robert for having organized a colloquium focused on my perspective on recent Quebec historical writing, which pushed me to refine some of my ideas. Gerry Hallowell of University of Toronto Press also facilitated the project by expressing interest in this manuscript when it was little more than a collection of vague ideas. His support and encouragement helped me through those moments when the academic author wonders if the project at hand will ever end.

Closer to home, I was aided by my colleagues at Concordia, Shannon McSheffrey, Diana Pedersen, and Mary Vipond, who put up with my droning on for years about the issues discussed in these pages. I am particularly appreciative of the time invested by my colleague Graham Carr, who read parts of the manuscript. Lastly, at Concordia, my thanks go out to the students who have taken my graduate-level course on Canadian historical writing over the past few years and who have pushed me to think through some of the ideas that I wanted to develop in this book. At home, I was aided once again, in ways too numerous to list, by my best friend, my wife, Phyllis, editor and critic par excellence. This is the first time that I have had the opportunity to say something in print about our son, David, to whom the volume is dedicated. His presence has made this project take longer than might otherwise have been the case; of course, I would not have wanted it any other way.

François-Xavier Garneau

Hector Garneau

Lionel Groulx, 1920

Lionel Groulx, 1946

Thomas Chapais

Gustave Lanctot

Robert Rumilly

Arthur Maheux

Faculty and students, history department, Université de Montréal, c. 1948.
The professor at the head of the table (second from right) is Guy Frégault; next
to him (partially hidden, to the left) is Maurice Séguin.

Maurice Séguin

Michel Brunet (left) and Lionel Groulx, 1965, on the fiftieth anniversary of the beginning of Groulx's career as a university professor.

Professors (top row) and graduates (second row) of Université Laval, 1950. The professor second from the right is Arthur Maheux, and the one at the far right is Marcel Trudel. The student at the far left is Claude Galarneau, and at the far right, Fernand Ouellet.

Marcel Trudel

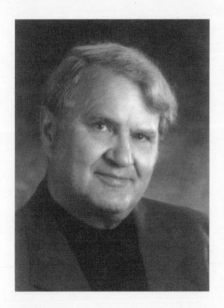

Fernand Ouellet

Jean Hamelin

MAKING HISTORY IN TWENTIETH-CENTURY QUEBEC

Introduction

The point has often been made that history occupies a privileged place in Quebec culture. The motto of the province – 'Je me souviens' (I remember) – is but one indicator of this reverence for the past. Another is the special status still reserved in Quebecers' collective memory for Abbé Lionel Groulx, the first full-time university professor of Quebec history, more than twenty-five years after his death.[1] In spite of this interest in the past, however, no single volume has yet been dedicated to a comprehensive analysis of Quebec historical writing over the course of the twentieth century. During this period historical writing was increasingly carried out, throughout much of the Western world, by people who viewed themselves as professionals engaged in a 'scientific' endeavour. In most countries, the late nineteenth and early twentieth centuries saw both the establishment of history as a separate discipline in universities and widespread acceptance of the idea that historical writing, at its highest level, was a profession to be carried out by experts with appropriate credentials – increasingly, the PhD.

The growth of a historical profession could not prevent 'amateurs' from continuing to write for popular audiences. Nevertheless, the twentieth century witnessed the growth of the idea that the past could be known 'as it really was,' free of the biases of the historian, if only proper, scientific methods were employed. Accordingly, this century has constituted the time frame for such assessments of the profession as Peter Novick's *That Noble Dream*, which examined the 'objectivity question' in the American context and Carl Berger's *Writing of Canadian History*, which dealt with the situation in English Canada. Though English Canada allegedly has an underdeveloped historical consciousness, Berger's volume has been available for roughly twenty years, while French-speaking

Quebec, supposedly preoccupied with its past, has not yet seen a volume dealing with the development of its historical profession.

The volume that follows is designed to fill this historiographical void by exploring how Quebec's historical writing was moulded both by forces within Quebec society and by changing currents of thought within the larger historical profession. Like Berger's work, it is based on a reading of the publications of the historians in question, as well as their private papers. Moreover, just as Berger was careful to warn readers that his study was 'deliberately selective [and] ... not intended as a comprehensive inventory and bibliography of the literature or as a biographical dictionary of historians,' so too this volume concentrates on historians who, collectively or individually, helped to alter the way in which Quebec's history was approached by those who studied and wrote about the subject for a living. Lastly, I share Berger's belief that historical writing can 'reveal a good deal about the intellectual climate in which it was composed.'[2]

For all the similarities between Berger's approach and my own, however, I also fundamentally differ with him on several counts. For instance, I do not accept his assumption, implicit in *Writing of Canadian History*, that historians across the twentieth century have been united by their search for the truth. This faith in their common purpose allowed him to emphasize the way in which each generation generally built on the accomplishments of that which preceded it. Accordingly, even when a group struck out in new directions, as was the case with the historians of the 1970s and 1980s discussed in a new chapter added to the second edition of his work, Berger insisted that they owed a debt 'to those who had gone before.'[3] This debt reflected the shared objective of all historians to understand the past as it was. Accordingly, Berger did not want his book to leave an 'exaggerated impression of relativism [because] a work such as this one simply could not be written without a faith in the ability of the historical imagination to penetrate a segment of the thought of the past and to understand it, however tentatively and incompletely, on its own terms.'[4] He even held out high hopes for historiographical analysis in this regard, arguing that it was useful to help historians keep 'hidden and unsuspected factors behind any national tradition of historical writing ... neutralized and under control.'[5]

There was something celebratory in Berger's insistence that historians were capable of repressing their subjective instincts and improving their techniques so as to develop a 'better' understanding of the past. In this regard, however, Berger was in good company. As Peter Novick has observed, few historians are prepared any longer to talk about what Herbert Butterfield called 'the Whig interpretation of history [which] ... emphasize[d] certain principles of progress in the past and produce[d] a story which is the ratification if not the glorification of the present.' This disinclination to view the past as the great march forward of progress has not, however, prevented historians from seeing their own discipline in precisely such terms. As Novick has put it, the Whig interpretation 'survives anachronistically in historiography.'[6]

This Whiggish view of historical writing certainly continues, at least implicitly, in Quebec, where most historiographical analysis over the past twenty-five years has amounted to a celebration of the field's liberation from historians whose biases had prevented the development of a truly 'objective' view of the past. Throughout the first seven decades of the twentieth century, historical writing in Quebec was dominated by individuals – as varied in their methods and political views as Abbé Groulx and Fernand Ouellet – who emphasized the distinctiveness of the francophone experience and who, by and large, were not overly bothered if they wore their political views on their sleeves. This situation changed quite radically during the course of the 1970s and 1980s, as the field came to be dominated by a new generation, to which I refer throughout this study as 'revisionists.'

The revisionists, whose ranks included Paul-André Linteau, Jean-Claude Robert, and Normand Séguin, to name only a few, insisted that French-speaking Quebecers had long been a people with a 'normal' past.[7] These historians played down the influence of Catholicism or of resistance to capitalism – aspects of Quebec's experience that might have placed francophones outside the mainstream of western developments – and concentrated instead on the way in which Quebecers had been secular, materialistic, and urban since early in their history, much like their neighbours in North America. To the revisionists, nearly all aspects of Quebec's experience could be explained by reference to structural developments germane to much of the Western world.

By integrating Quebecers into larger Western developments, the revisionists desensationalized the writing of Quebec history. While their predecessors had dwelled on the distinctive traits of Quebecers in order to make political points of one sort or another, the revisionists eschewed explicit political commentary so as to give their work the appearance of 'objectivity.' In order to further this self-image they have engaged in considerable historiographical analysis that has further distanced them from their overly subjective and not always sufficiently 'scientific' predecessors. Accordingly, most assessments of the field over the past twenty-five years have been aggressively hostile towards the work of Lionel Groulx, who dominated historical writing in Quebec until the end of the Second World War. Neither Serge Gagnon nor Jean Lamarre, who have written extensively on the subject, have made any reference to Groulx's interest in developing a 'professional' historical community in Quebec or to the way in which he altered his views from time to time in the face of new evidence that came to light or new techniques with which he became familiar.[8]

Commentators such as Gagnon and Lamarre were more positively inclined towards the historians who emerged after 1945, particularly those such as Guy Frégault, Michel Brunet, and Maurice Séguin, under whose influence historical writing allegedly became 'more objective.'[9] Gagnon and Lamarre were impressed not only by the professional credentials of Frégault and his colleagues, all of whom had doctorates, but also by their interest in using their expertise to advance a nationalist program. By contrast, Fernand Ouellet, another postwar historian, has been singled out for particular abuse, not because of any lack of professional competence, but rather because of his preoccupation with the shortcomings of Quebecers. Gagnon, for instance, criticized Ouellet because his work was marred by the way in which 'ideology has discreetly slipped in behind a screen of words, turns of phrase, and circumlocution.'[10] By the 1970s, however, the revisionists had finally emerged, and Quebec history had firmly passed 'from hero worship to serious analysis.'[11] Accordingly, the great march from Groulx's subjectivity to revisionist objectivity had come to a successful conclusion.

The revisionist perspective on Quebec historiography, which shares much with Berger's view of the situation in English Canada, is at odds with the one that will be developed in this book. As will soon become apparent, I am not convinced that historical writing at the end of the twentieth century is inherently any 'better' than that produced earlier in the century; nor for that matter do I believe that there is such a thing as a truly 'objective' view of the past that can distinguish the work of someone such as Lionel Groulx from that of late-twentieth-century historians such as Paul-André Linteau. My thinking on these issues has been greatly influenced by Peter Novick, who was doubtful about the Whiggish view of historical writing precisely because of his own reservations about the historian's search for objectivity.

Novick's study of the way in which historians in the United States have dealt with the concept of objectivity was in its own right a response to attacks on the scientific pretensions of professional historical writing. At various moments throughout the twentieth century, there have been historians who have doubted the possibility of developing a truly objective view of the past. While these relativists, such as Charles Beard and Carl Becker in the United States, were convinced that historians' biases shaped their interpretations, they still believed that there was some intrinsic merit in trying to work through the relevant sources to develop a well-documented, if not final, explanation.

This larger faith in the value of research and the scientific pretensions of historical writing has been challenged over the past quarter-century, however, by critics such as Hayden White and Dominick LaCapra, who have argued that there was frequently relatively little to distinguish historical writing from other representations of the past, such as those that one might find in fiction. These critics refused to take the historian's search for the 'truth' seriously, arguing that 'when it comes to the historical record, there are no grounds in the record itself for preferring one way of constructing its meaning over another.' In the final analysis, it became more important to look at the literary form of the historian's text than to judge the adequacy of the sources employed or the internal logic of the argument presented.[12]

Novick did not respond by insisting, as Berger might have, that historians had been relatively successful in their search for objectivity. While he suspected that most historians throughout the twentieth century believed that it was important to play the role of 'a neutral, or disinterested judge,' he was sceptical as to whether many really acted in such a manner. Accordingly, he argued that the belief that objective history was attainable 'promotes an unreal and misleading distinction between, on the one hand, historical accounts "distorted" by ideological assumptions and purposes; on the other, history free of these taints. It seems to me that to say of a work of history that it is or isn't objective is to make an *empty* observation.'[13]

One might conclude from this disclaimer that Novick was prepared to accept any historical account as legitimate because perfect objectivity was unattainable. In fact, however, he responded to those who would consign history to the ranks of fiction by noting that the pursuit, if not the attainment, of historical objectivity was a form of '*salutary nonsense*'; it was undefinable and unachievable, but just the same it provided some direction for historians.[14] As several commentators have observed, Novick indicated his own faith in the value of trying to get close to some well-documented, reasoned truth by producing a 650-page monograph grounded in years of painstaking research.[15]

In spite of his own example, several of Novick's critics felt that he had been too categorical in doubting the historian's ability to develop an objective view of the past, in the process leaving the door open for propagandists masquerading as historians. In particular, Thomas Haskell argued that Novick's assumption that personal values were at odds with objectivity confused the issue. To Haskell, there was nothing wrong with historians having preconceived ideas; the question was whether, when faced with evidence that contradicted their beliefs, they ignored the facts or changed their conclusions. Trying to bolster his own belief in the historian's ability to describe the past objectively, Haskell asserted that 'most historians would indeed say that the historian's primary commitment is to the truth, and that when truth and "the cause," however defined, come into conflict, the truth must prevail.'[16]

Haskell's position was, of course, little more than an article of faith, a proposition incapable of empirical verification. In terms of the Quebec context, one would like to know, for instance, whether Abbé Groulx, when he made one of his frequent trips to the archives, was prepared to overlook evidence that contradicted his deeply held views regarding Quebec history; or to put the question somewhat differently, one would like to know whether he was any more likely than his successors to push aside evidence that was at odds with his views.

My research suggests that nearly all the historians considered in this study believed, at least in a vague way, in the principle that historical conclusions were valid only if supported by documentary evidence. Moreover, I suspect that most would have been troubled had they found evidence diametrically opposed to their preconceived views, which were shaped by the society in which they lived. Beyond that, we will never know what they would have actually done at the moment of truth. I tend to share Novick's belief that consciousness of the existence of a struggle for objectivity, even if the ideal was rarely attained, is a worthwhile goal, one that was probably shared by most of the historians to be considered here. In other words, as practitioners of a 'scientific' history that needed to be supported by appropriate evidence and as soldiers in the inevitably lost battle for objectivity, the various Quebec historians of the twentieth century whose careers will occupy these pages differed little among one another. This is not to say, however, that these historians were totally indistinguishable. While they may not have differed all that much on the issue of objectivity, they approached the past in very different ways, largely in response to the forces, both intellectual and social, with which they came into contact.

As we shall see, Quebec historical writing was moulded both by developments within the profession, such as the emergence of new techniques and changing perspectives on the concept of objectivity, and by forces within Quebec society, such as urbanization and the rise of a powerful Quebec state. Quebec's historians, from the time of Groulx to the present, have been sensitive to changes within their discipline, but those who have written about the subject have paid relatively little serious attention to these influences. Serge Gagnon, for instance, tried to understand early-twentieth-century writing without considering 'the influence of foreign authors.'[17] Jean Lamarre was interested more in establishing the influence of Maurice Séguin on his contemporaries at the Université de Montréal than in tracing the European influences on the first generation of university-trained historians.

At the same time that Séguin and his colleagues were holding sway in Montreal, Marcel Trudel, Fernand Ouellet, and Jean Hamelin were developing a very different view of Quebec's past at the other French-language university, Laval in Quebec City. To be sure, some commentators have noted the impact of the Annales approach on these historians, but generally they have done so cursorily, failing to recognize the varieties in this French approach to the discipline and the way in which only certain strains left their mark in Quebec.[18] In short, there has been little serious effort to ground Quebec historical writing within the larger discipline.

In a similar fashion, there has been only the most casual attempt to associate this writing with the larger society within which it developed. As we shall see, over the past twenty years revisionist historians have been insisting on Quebec's insertion into the mainstream of developments across the Western world. To use their favourite expression, Quebec had long been a 'normal' Western society, whose history provided considerable evidence of the forces of modernity. However, at the same time that the revisionists were focusing on the province's modernity, they were also insisting that most of its historical writing up to the Second World War, if not up to the Quiet Revolution, had been profoundly primitive. They did this, in part, to disassociate themselves from historians such as Groulx whose attitudes, such as his anti-semitism, were both disagreeable to late-twentieth-century sensitivities and potentially at odds with the revisionists' insistence on the liberalism of the larger society.

Since they had locked themselves into an untenable situation, insisting on both the 'normal' development of their society and the abnormally slow development of its historical writing, the revisionists generally took the easy way out. They engaged in little serious analysis of the relationship between historical writing and the society in which it was conceived, in part because such analysis might have challenged their assumptions about the long-standing modernity of Quebec. Rather, they simply asserted that earlier writing had been primitive, in the process giving their own work impeccable scientific credentials.

The current volume, with its emphasis on historical writing, cannot deal exhaustively with the claims of the revisionists regarding the 'normalcy' of Quebec's past. Nevertheless, by using historical writing as a mirror of the larger society, I do hope to raise some questions about the way in which the revisionists have conceptualized the history of twentieth-century Quebec. In place of their insistence on its constant march towards modernity, we shall see the intermingling of newer and older influences, in both society and historical writing, throughout most of the century.

In the chapters that follow, then, I have no intention of charting the steady 'progress' of historiography in twentieth-century Quebec; nor do I intend to heap abuse on those who have tried, more or less conscientiously, to explain Quebec's past. I share Novick's apprehension that his book would be read wrongly because of his refusal to accept the 'celebratory tone of most of the disciplinary histories of history.' Novick feared that his 'attempt at detachment [might] be read as hostility, on the grounds that the alternative to affirmation must be negativism.'[19] My interest, simply put, is to consider the historians who have plied their trade during this century by examining both their published works and their private papers. I hope to show how their conceptions of Quebec's history were moulded by developments within both their discipline and their society.

In the process, I think that I have arrived at a view of Quebec historical writing which, if graphed, would resemble a horizontal line, rather than a constantly rising curve. By and large, Quebec historians, like their counterparts throughout the West, produced works that reflected both professional standards and local circumstances. Along the way, they came up with changing conceptions of the past, but I would not be prepared to argue that some views were intrinsically better than others. Rather, historians simply used the tools at their disposal at any given time to develop views of the past that seemed to make sense in a particular social and political context.

While Quebec historical writing has dramatically changed during the twentieth century, notions of constant improvement seem somehow out of place. To reinforce my break with the triumphant tone of much Quebec historiographical writing, I have departed from the standard periodization, which usually posits a pre-professional era, dominated by Lionel Groulx, which came to an end after the Second World War, when a new generation of lay professionals emerged on the scene.

Instead, in this volume Groulx will play a central role in much of the first three chapters, which consider aspects of historical writing in Quebec from the start of the century up to the early 1970s. In the first chapter, we shall see Groulx as a rather inept amateur who was clearly in over his head on becoming a university professor in 1915. Nevertheless, by 1925, where the first chapter ends, he had begun to produce works of a certain sophistication and had organized the first conference of Quebec historians. In chapter 2, which follows the discipline up to Groulx's retirement from the Université de Montréal in 1949, we shall see a historian whose work continued to evolve and who was deeply involved in creating the infrastructure for a true profession. Through the 1940s he helped establish a formally constituted department of history at his university and created, outside the university, both a professional association of and a professional journal for Quebec's historians. In chapter 3, we shall see a retired professor who, up to his death in 1967, continued to write works in which his views on the past evolved in step with changes in both his society and the larger profession.

In making Groulx into a 'normal' historian, instead of the anachronistic figure that he has become in most accounts of Quebec historical writing, I am not intent on turning him into someone who was consistently producing works that were getting closer to the 'truth' about the past. Rather, I am interested in showing him to have been a fairly accurate mirror of both the larger profession to which he belonged and the society in which he lived.

Moreover, I would not want anyone to see Groulx as the embodiment of the Quebec historical community during the period covered by the first three chapters. While he was clearly the most important figure over the first half of the twentieth century, we shall see him in the company of such historians as Thomas Chapais and Gustave Lanctot, in chapter 1, and along with such lay professionals as Guy Frégault, Maurice Séguin, Michel Brunet, and Marcel Trudel in chapters 2 and 3. While these highly trained individuals are usually lionized for the way in which they broke with Groulx, we shall see that the ties between the maître and his successors dissolved very slowly. These links endured as long as they did because Groulx and his successors, in spite of their very different perspectives on the past, were engaged in producing works that reflected both the larger profession's notions of 'science' and the demands of the more immediate society.

In the same spirit, we shall also see the similarities between the Montreal historians (Frégault, Séguin, and Brunet), who provide much of the focus for chapter 3, and the Laval historians (Trudel, Ouellet, and Hamelin) who occupy centre stage in chapter 4. While most previous writing on the subject has emphasized what divided the two groups of post-1945 historians, I shall argue that both were trapped between a concern for the 'truth' and the demands of their own society. Without denying the differing conceptions of the past offered by these historians, we can see that there was less to divide them than is usually admitted.

Moreover, as chapter 5 shall reveal, there was less to distinguish the revisionists from their predecessors than most Quebec historians have been prepared to concede. Most analysis of revisionist writing has come from the revisionists themselves, who, not surprisingly, have used the opportunity to tout their own 'scientific' credentials. Their insistence on the normalcy of Quebec, itself a reflection of their society in the late twentieth century, constituted a new and significant departure from previous writing. Nevertheless they, much like their predecessors, were involved in the battle of balancing the demands of profession and society.

All the historians discussed in this volume were bedevilled, in one way or another, by these conflicting demands. While historians such as Groulx, Frégault, Ouellet, and Linteau all approached the past from different perspectives, shaped largely by the changing society in which they lived, they were also influenced by developments within the larger profession to which they belonged. The conflicting demands of profession and society linked these Quebec historians to one another and to their counterparts across much of the Western world. In the final analysis these historians were 'normal,' which is fitting, since, as we shall see below, the concept of normalcy has proven an important one to Quebec historians during much of this century.

1

Not Quite a Profession: The Historical Community in Early-Twentieth-Century Quebec

I

While the exact timing varied from nation to nation, in most parts of the Western world the late nineteenth and early twentieth centuries saw some fundamental changes in both the nature of historical writing and the circumstances under which it was produced. Descriptions of the past had long been the work of individuals who hardly thought of themselves as professionals even though they may have been conscientious researchers. These practitioners, such as Francis Parkman and George Bancroft in the United States and François-Xavier Garneau in Quebec, had little interest in communicating any 'objective' description of the past, preferring instead to advance a particular cause.[1] Quite aside from what these nineteenth-century historians thought about the function of history, they also tended to practise their trade outside the university, thus adding to the impression that they were amateurs speaking to a general audience.

Around the turn of the century, however, the situation was beginning to change quite radically. Though the establishment of formal history departments occurred in certain places earlier than in others, universities in most Western nations were by then hiring full-time professors to teach history. Even more significant, most nations experienced the arrival of Germanic notions of history as an objective science, though the lessons to be drawn from Germany were interpreted differently from place to place. Nevertheless, by early in the twentieth century there was a reasonably widespread idea that the historian's primary obligation was to communicate some sort of 'objective' truth. The historians of the time may have found no contradiction between this search for objectivity and the advancement of certain more subjective goals, but what separated them from their predecessors was their sense that they were engaged in an activity that had scientific pretensions. In line with this new self-image came the founding of professional associations, creation of professional journals, and the demand for appropriate credentials, namely the PhD, for entry into the guild.[2]

By and large, the institutional aspects of these changes did not affect the writing of Quebec history until the 1940s. That decade saw the setting up of history departments in the province's two French-language universities, the beginning of a professional association of Quebec historians, the launching of a professional journal of Quebec history, and the hiring of the first professor with a PhD in the field. Accordingly, there can be little doubt that the institutional framework for historical scholarship came late to Quebec by almost any standard of comparison. To some extent, this lag was a reflection of the generally slow development of universities within francophone Quebec during the first half of the twentieth century – a situation that reflected both the power of the Catholic church and the distance of francophones from positions of influence in the economy.

Though the church ran the French-language universities, it was wary about encouraging the 'scientific' development of both the Université Laval, established in 1852, and the Université de Montréal, which began in 1876 as a branch of Laval and became independent in 1920. Clerical leaders saw some danger in transforming the university into an institution dedicated more to establishing the 'truth' than to propping up a particular social order. By the early twentieth century, however, these leaders found themselves with little choice but to make some tentative steps in the direction of providing a more 'scientific' education to the population.

By that time, many Quebecers were moving to the cities, spurred by the industrialization that had been transforming society since the middle of the previous century. As Quebec became more urban and industrial, it also fell more firmly under the control of large firms, which were almost invariably run by English speakers. In the process, French speakers, whose role as owners had long been been restricted to small and medium-sized concerns, found their influence reduced even further. Accordingly, by the close of the Second World War francophones probably controlled even less of Quebec's economy than they had earlier in the century.

While this marginalization of French speakers made them sceptical about the likelihood of success in business, it also fuelled support for institutions dedicated to preserving something of the old order and improving francophones' position within the new. The caisses populaires and the Catholic trade unions emerged in precisely this context in the first decades of the century. Both were supported energetically by the clergy and designed to revive the sagging fortunes of the traditional elite of French-speaking Quebec, made up of the clergy, liberal professionals, and small business people. At the same time, these new institutions were also dedicated to providing Quebecers with the means – credit in one case and a bargaining agent in the other – to function in the modern world.[3]

The university began, in a similar fashion, to shed its earlier distance from the 'scientific' world. Marcel Fournier, in his study of the role of scientific ideas in twentieth-century Quebec, has shown how the clerical authorities had been somewhat insulated from the pressures of the larger economy by the distance of francophones from positions of power. Marginal economic status of French speakers made accumulation of scientific knowledge less pressing than was the case in English Canada or the United States, where 'practical' knowledge was more likely to pay dividends. As Fournier has explained, French-speaking leaders, 'threatened by an industrial society which had been imposed by out-siders, were sceptical about embracing cultural values that placed a premium upon the pursuit of practical knowledge that might facilitate industrialization.'[4]

In the end, much like the caisses populaires and the Catholic trade unions, both inspired by Catholic social thinking of the time, the univer-sities had little choice but to respond to social and economic changes facing early-twentieth-century Quebec. The men who emerged to lead the universities reflected the same concern for bridging the gap between the older and newer orders that was evident in the other Catholic institu-tions. Fournier pointed to the case of Frère Marie-Victorin, selected in 1920 to oversee teaching of the natural sciences in the Université de Montréal's new faculty of science, even though he had little formal training. He was no doubt seen as a safe choice in light of his remark only a few years earlier that he was a 'Christian professor' who did not believe either 'that science could be totally objective' or that it was worth pursuing 'science for science's sake.'[5] Fournier has similarly character-ized Édouard Montpetit, secretary-general of the newly independent Université de Montréal, as the embodiment of that institution because of his commitment 'to both a clerico-nationalist and a liberal ideology.'[6] In the same context, Père Georges-Henri Lévesque was inspired to establish the School of Social Sciences at Laval in the late 1930s to provide a modernizing society with much-needed services and the church with the means for perpetuating its place in that society.[7]

Fournier, along with a number of other historians and sociologists, has, over the past twenty years, emphasized the modernity of Quebec's early-twentieth-century intellectual world in order to lay to rest notions of its backwardness up to the eve of the Quiet Revolution.[8] Without denying the gap that may have existed between Quebec and other parts of the Western world in terms of embracing the scientific approach, these authors have tried to qualify the extent of this alleged backwardness and to place it in the context of other 'societies whose development depended largely upon outside sources of both entrepreneurship and capital.'[9] Curiously, however, authors such as Fournier have consistently failed to make any reference to the early development of history as a scientific discipline in Quebec. While Fournier reproduced Claude Ryan's oft-cited reference to Marie-Victorin, Montpetit, and Groulx as the 'three great intellectual figures' of their generation, he gave serious treatment to only the first two.[10] Yves Gingras similarly marginalized Groulx by observing that there were two paths available to the youth of Quebec – that of Marie-Victorin, committed to the 'modernization of Quebec's institutions,' and that of Groulx, about whom Gingras had little to say other than to compare him negatively to Marie-Victorin, who was firmly committed to scientific research.[11] Fournier and Gingras came to their conclusions even though, as we shall see, Groulx helped lay the groundwork for the professional historical discipline that would emerge in the 1940s.

While history may have emerged as a scientific endeavour more slowly in Quebec than in other Western societies, it did not stagnate over the first half of the century; nor did it particularly suffer by comparison with other disciplines within Quebec that have received considerable, generally positive attention. To be sure, history emerged as an autonomous discipline somewhat later than other more 'practical' fields, which had supporters lobbying university administrators, eager to make their Catholic institutions relevant to the new order. However, none of this explains the scant attention that has been paid to the emergence of a historical profession in Quebec over the first half of the twentieth century.

This curious neglect reflects the general discomfort on the part of Quebec's intellectuals with the legacy of Lionel Groulx, the most significant French-speaking historian up to the 1940s. In particular, over the past thirty years, as Quebecers have tried to give themselves the image of a people who have long been 'modern,' Groulx has become something of an embarrassment because of his social and political views.[12] While, as we shall see, Groulx was a prolific historian, he also wrote and spoke at great length about what he saw as the great problems of his times. He never made much of a secret of his fears about the perils that the twentieth century held for French-speaking Quebecers. He saw Catholicism as the cornerstone of this society, but he worried that such forces as industrialization, immigration, Confederation, and British imperialism might lead to the assimilation of his people. Accordingly, he spent a considerable part of his life campaigning for various causes that are, for good reason, not particularly popular today. Groulx was occasionally sceptical about the virtues of democracy and hostile to the arrival of newcomers in Quebec – a point made at some length in Esther Delisle's *The Traitor and the Jew*, which focused on Groulx's anti-semitism between the wars.[13]

Delisle's work, because it touched on the honour of one of Quebec's cultural icons, produced considerable controversy. Some writers, such as Jean Éthier-Blais, rushed to Groulx's rescue, seeing him as an individual who had merely reflected the values of his times and had meant no ill will towards anyone; others, such as Mordecai Richler, used the opportunity to attack anyone with nationalist inclinations.[14] While both Éthier-Blais and Richler were prolific authors who had written much about Quebec society, neither was a major figure within the province's university community, and neither had any particular interest in discussing Groulx's significant role as an early member of that community.

In fact, what was particularly interesting about the debate over Delisle's book was the conspicuous absence of active researchers such as Marcel Fournier, who might have indicated that there was more to Groulx's legacy than a collection of disagreeable social and political views. Even more conspicuously absent were the leading Quebec historians, who might have spoken about Groulx's contribution to Quebec's historical profession, were it not for the fact that they had long since decided to disassociate themselves from Groulx.[15]

Paralleling Fournier's refusal to view Groulx as an agent of scientific thought early in the century, historians have tended to cut him off from the 'real' professional developments that came only at mid-century. Serge Gagnon, for instance, managed this by dividing his analysis of Quebec historical writing over the nineteenth and twentieth centuries into two volumes, with 1920 serving as the watershed.[16] Groulx figured prominently in the first volume, which emphasized the primitive nature of Quebec historical writing, while the second paid scant attention to the priest-historian, reserving most credit for professionalization to a number of laymen who emerged after 1945.

In a similar spirit, Jean Lamarre has more recently argued that 'the late development of the infrastructure to support historical writing' ensured that such efforts would remain largely unchanged from the mid-nineteenth century up to the 1940s.[17] For Lamarre, the pre-professional era extended from the publication in 1845 of François-Xavier Garneau's *Histoire du Canada*, the first significant work dedicated to the history of French speakers, to the relevant institutional transformations roughly a century later. Throughout this period, he found no evidence of historians' changing the way in which they approached historical research and scarcely any greater shift in their description of the past. The 1940s saw the emergence of a new generation of historians dedicated to 'an objective interpretation.' Accordingly, as Lamarre noted, it would be difficult to 'imagine a more radical break with the past.'[18]

This same conclusion that Groulx was an ideologue masquerading as a historian was evident in a recent volume dealing with the ways in which Quebecers have constructed their collective memory. When it came to the role of Groulx, the authors, both historians, dismissed him for having been too willing to sacrifice 'a scientific approach to history in order to promote his nationalist ideology.'[19] Given this general distancing of Quebec's historians from Groulx, it is not entirely surprising that a recent high-school textbook mentioned Groulx 'more as a nationalist leader than as an historian.'[20]

This marginalizing of Groulx, and by extension of the historical community over the first half of the twentieth century, has had more to do with the priest's extra-historical activities than with his view of the discipline, which has received relatively little attention. There is no reason why anyone, historians included, should make apologies for Groulx's social and political views. At the same time, however, by dismissing Groulx as a figure not to be taken seriously, observers have tended to ignore his historical scholarship, in the process leaving the impression that there was no historical profession in Quebec prior to the 1940s.

Both this chapter and the following one are designed to place Groulx back into the picture and to point to the professional aspects of historical writing in early-twentieth-century Quebec. As we shall see, Groulx was a poorly trained historian when he became the first full-time university professor of Quebec history. Over time, however, he did what he could to equip himself with the tools needed to be a 'scientific' historian. Somewhere along the way he absorbed the notion that the professional historian needed to be open to new ideas and new evidence, and so his interpretation of Quebec's past changed significantly during his long career.

Moreover, Groulx played a crucial role in encouraging colleagues to follow the path of serious research. While historians such as Thomas Chapais, Hector Garneau, and Gustave Lanctot will appear from time to time over the next two chapters, Groulx stood out for the way in which he helped establish the institutional framework to permit others to improve their studies. Ultimately, by the 1940s, he was instrumental in creating both the professional association and the professional journal for Quebec historians. As early as 1925, however, he organized the first conference of Quebec's historians – the Semaine d'histoire held at Montreal. As we shall see, Groulx used this meeting to bring together individuals of various backgrounds, political persuasions, and methodological sophistication. It would probably be an overstatement to view this event as marking the birth of the profession in Quebec; too many participants had a view of history that was far from professional. Nevertheless, it did reveal the existence of a community of Quebecers who had more than passing interest in understanding the past through use of the techniques of the modern historian. Because of its significance, this chapter closes with a discussion of the Semaine d'histoire.

I shall pay relatively little attention, either in this chapter or in the next, to Groulx's wide-ranging social and political activities, or even to his career as a teacher or as a communicator of history to a mass audience. These aspects of his career have been dealt with at great length by others and in his own mind were quite separate from his notion of the proper role for the truly professional historian.[21] For instance, on one occasion he distinguished between 'those who write history and those who teach it. The first needs to be completely free to develop an objective view of the past based upon the use of appropriate historical methods. By contrast, the history professor, especially if he is teaching young children, must never forget the historical and political context in which French Canadians have had to live. The young need to understand their past in order to recognize the fragility of their nation. While the teacher should never distort the past, he needs to focus upon those facts which might encourage a sense of patriotism.'[22]

My relative neglect of Groulx's political causes should not be seen as an implicit apology for his views; nor should the emphasis on his interest in a scientific approach to the past be construed as making him more 'modern' than he really was. Like his counterparts in other academic disciplines, such as Édouard Montpetit and Frère Marie-Victorin, Groulx was part of what Marcel Fournier has called 'the new generation of intellectuals which embraced scientific rationality without rejecting a more traditional culture which conveyed a central role to religion.'[23] In this chapter and the next I shall try to place Groulx and his colleagues in the context of larger developments within both Quebec's burgeoning intellectual world and the historical community that extended beyond the province's borders.

II

The teaching of Quebec's history assumed what turned out to be a permanent place in the twentieth-century university with Groulx's appointment as part-time lecturer at the Montreal branch of the Université Laval in 1915. As he himself observed, this was a far cry from a full-time university appointment, because funds did not exist for such a position.[24] Instead, he was paid $50 to offer five evening lectures to a public audience, which consisted presumably of more outsiders than university students. Nevertheless, this was the first formal teaching of Canadian history in the Laval system since Abbé J.B.A. Ferland had offered a comparable series at Quebec City in the 1860s. In the interim, various priests and laymen on the staff of the two branches had offered lectures from time to time, but there had been no formal and regular instruction in the half-century between Ferland and Groulx. As Groulx put it in his memoirs, the teaching of Canadian history at the university level had 'effectively been abandoned over the previous half century ... During this period, historical writing became the responsibility of amateurs, a few of whom were excellent researchers, well versed in historical methods. Others, however, were totally unprepared to understand the past, with the result that they obscured as much as they explained about the history of their people.'[25]

In fact, however, Groulx was also 'totally unprepared to understand the past' when he began his lectures in the fall of 1915. Born in 1878, he was ordained as a priest in 1903, the year he began teaching full-time at the collège classique at Valleyfield, where he was responsible for courses in Latin and literature. His interest in teaching was, from the start, closely linked to his own hopes for French-speaking Quebecers. The journal that Groulx kept during this period reflected his fears for the future of his people in the face of the English-speaking, Protestant world that surrounded them. He wanted to do everything he could to defend his 'cherished Canada which was under attack from that curse that we call modern liberalism; when I see the way in which the Catholic church is being persecuted in Canada, I feel the urge to enter the fray, to join those who are willing to fight a holy war in defence of my nationality and my religion.'[26]

The early twentieth century was certainly a troubling time for a young man such as Groulx. There were, for instance, dangers emanating from the two powers to which Quebec had been linked. On the one hand, France was then controlled by republicans with little sympathy for the role of the Catholic church in the larger society. On the other hand, Britain was beginning to make demands on Canada for assistance in its imperial adventures. British imperialism was particularly distasteful for someone such as Groulx, since it manifested itself within Canada in the attack on the rights of French-speaking Catholics outside Quebec. This attack even had its counterpart within Quebec in the growing influence of large corporations, which, in the midst of the steady urbanization of Quebec society, were concentrating power in the hands of men who were almost invariably English-speaking and Protestant.

In response to these challenges, a number of movements arose in early-twentieth-century Quebec to defend a French-Catholic identity within the province, if not across all of Canada. In this context, for instance, Alphonse Desjardins established the first caisse populaire in 1900 in order to revive the role of Catholicism in the province and to challenge English-Protestant economic control. In addition, a number of organizations arose, less committed to direct action than Desjardins's caisses, but designed to increase the awareness of Quebecers, particularly young men, to the dangers that were afoot. As Groulx put it some years later, he had been swept up in this movement, inspired by Henri Bourassa, which manifested itself over the first decade of the new century in the establishment of both the Ligue nationaliste and the Association catholique de la jeunesse canadienne-française.[27]

Groulx quickly recognized that he could best contribute to the nationalist movement through teaching. Accordingly, he set out to encourage the youth to join him in his crusade to preserve 'our religion and our nation.'[28] History did not figure, however, among the subjects that Groulx taught in his first years at Valleyfield, even though he had displayed considerable interest in the subject during his student days, searching for lessons from the past that might inspire patriotism among French speakers. Looking outside Quebec, he was particularly fond of Catholic leaders such as Daniel O'Connell, who in the early nineteenth century had provided Catholics in Ireland with full political equality within the United Kingdom. In 1895 Groulx confided to his journal: 'Illustrious O'Connell, oh how I admire you. You are my greatest hero; a young man of means could have no higher calling than to follow in your footsteps.'[29] In a similar fashion, he looked to Quebec's past to admire the deeds of great men such as Louis-Joseph Papineau and George-Étienne Cartier. As Groulx observed: 'The biography of a great man cannot help but fill us with enthusiasm.'[30]

From these remarks, there is little to indicate that Groulx's early interest in history had anything to do with the emergence of the discipline along scientific lines. Rather, nationalist concerns led to his decision in 1905 to add two hours per week of history lessons to an already full schedule at Valleyfield. Groulx was motivated by his 'bad memories of the totally inadequate teaching of the history of [his] country that [he] had received in [his] collège classique. The textbooks, in particular, were totally inadequate. In fact, it was common to use books that had been prepared for much younger students.'[31] In 1908, only a few years after he had begun teaching history, Groulx complained to his close friend Emile Chartier that the manuals then in use were so 'devoid of nationalism that the history of our country was no more lively, no more interesting than that of the Hindus.'[32]

To fill this void, Groulx began the preparation of a *Manuel d'histoire du Canada* over the course of 1905–6, which, though it represented his first effort at providing an overview of the subject, has received curiously scant attention by historians.[33] He concluded the *Manuel* with a call for historians to 'be more conscientious in their use of historical methods,' but there is relatively little in this work to suggest that Groulx would later become a conscientious researcher, well attuned to larger debates regarding the nature of historical writing.[34] Rather, the value of the *Manuel* is the way in which it allows us to see Groulx's early conceptualization of the field and how his approach deviated from the conventional wisdom of the time. While Quebec historiography at the turn of the century provided Groulx with two different paths to follow – one represented by François-Xavier Garneau, and the other by Abbé Ferland – the young priest carved out a place of his own by developing a synthesis of the two.

Groulx made it clear from the very start of the *Manuel* that he owed a considerable debt to Garneau, whom he ranked 'among the founders of the French-Canadian race.'[35] In preparing his history courses to inspire young Quebecers to be true to their roots, Groulx identified with Garneau, who had begun his *Histoire du Canada* in the immediate aftermath of the Rebellions of 1837–8 to provide encouragement for a defeated people. At

the same time, however, Groulx was put off by what he described as
Garneau's questionable views regarding the role of religion in Quebec
society.[36] Even though Garneau's *Histoire*, which first appeared in 1845,
had gone through four editions by the time that Groulx began teaching
history in 1905, the work still bore the imprint of a man who had been, at
best, doubtful about the role of Catholicism in Quebec society.

While Garneau toned down his views in this regard over the course of
the three editions for which he was personally responsible, he never
abandoned them altogether. Garneau insisted to the very end that the
first bishop of Quebec, Mgr de Laval, had been both 'uncompromising
and domineering' and that New France would have been a more viable
colony if the Huguenots had been allowed to settle there.[37] Curiously,
however, commentators such as Serge Gagnon have tended to ignore
these examples of Garneau's unwillingness to tailor his *Histoire* in response to clerical pressure.[38] In Gagnon's case, this was part of a larger
strategy of denying any legitimacy to Quebec historical writing until the
arrival of the lay-professionals in the 1940s.

In spite of Garneau's views regarding religion, Groulx was still attracted by his 'clear-sighted patriotism.'[39] What united Garneau's *Histoire*
with Groulx's *Manuel*, and, as we shall see, what distinguished them
from intervening writers, was their insistence that French-speaking
Quebecers had been left to their own devices, to make their way in the
world, with little sympathy from either France or Britain. Both men were
convinced that the French had been totally uninterested in the fate of the
Canadiens, the French-speaking inhabitants of the St Lawrence valley,
who in the final analysis had been abandoned during the Seven Years'
War. In terms of the last days of New France, they both contrasted the
treachery of Montcalm, the French general, with the genuine patriotism
of Vaudreuil, the Canadien governor. As Groulx wrote in a section of his
Manuel entitled 'Animosité entre Canadiens et français' ('The Hostility
between the Canadiens and the French'), the Canadiens had been 'ruined
by their mother country.'[40]

Garneau and Groulx also shared a similar attitude towards the British,
whom they described as having arrived on the banks of the St Lawrence
as merciless conquerors. Garneau saw the Canadiens as victims of oppression, who in the immediate aftermath of the Conquest had nothing
to look forward to but 'suffering and humiliation.'[41] As for Groulx, the
arrival of the British constituted 'an invasion of barbarians'; here was 'a
conqueror who would use all the means at his disposal to annihilate the
Canadiens as a race. '[42] This annihilation, of course, never took place, but

not because of any goodwill on the part of the British. To both Garneau and Groulx, national survival had been facilitated by the American Revolution, which had placed the Canadiens in an advantageous bargaining position, leading in fairly short order to the passage of the Quebec Act and, subsequently, the establishment of parliamentary democracy in Lower Canada. As Groulx wrote, 'The American Revolution turned out for us to have been a providential event.'[43]

Once integrated into the British regime, the Canadiens then worked peacefully to improve their lot. From this perspective, neither Garneau nor Groulx saw the Rebellions of 1837–8 as particularly significant. Both men blamed them on British intransigence and insisted that there had been no 'general uprising of the people.'[44] When affairs returned to normal, the Canadiens successfully worked within the system and tasted power with the arrival of responsible government in the 1840s. Garneau's narrative ended there, but Groulx carried on in the same vein, viewing Confederation as the end of 'the era of our struggles to secure our rights as a people. Today we are on an equal footing with our fellow citizens of a different race.'[45] By and large, Groulx ended the *Manuel* on an upbeat note that reflected the early-twentieth-century faith of leaders such as Henri Bourassa that Confederation had been a pact between two peoples and that, through persistence, the rights of French speakers could be secured. Accordingly, in 1905 Groulx could still observe that Confederation had encouraged 'the brotherhood of two races.'[46]

At the same time, however, Groulx also presented a different message regarding the future of Confederation – one not unlike that being promoted by Bourassa's nemesis, Jules-Paul Tardivel, who had doubts about the capacity of Canada to respond to the needs of a French-speaking, Catholic people.[47] Groulx observed, not unlike certain contemporaries in English Canada, that Confederation was 'a geographical and political absurdity.' He envisioned the dissolution of Canada and the reorganization of the territory in a way that would recognize 'the power of racial identity and the dictates of geography.' Without being very specific, he made reference to the possible emergence of a new 'unit, distinct and compact,' taking in not only Quebec but also French-speaking parts of Ontario and the Maritimes.[48] Groulx even hoped that one day he might see 'an independent French state,' but to achieve that goal Quebecers required a real 'homme d'état' who would lead them to the promised land. He ended the *Manuel*: 'Canada has never had a real leader of the likes of García Moreno.'[49]

Groulx's closing reference to García Moreno suggests that in 1906 the young professor was more sceptical about the value of British parliamentary institutions than Garneau had been. Gabriel García Moreno had been the president of Ecuador twice during the 1860s and 1870s, but neither time did he secure power through constitutional means. In 1860 he emerged as the political master of his nation following the overthrow of the previous regime. He retained power until 1865, when he stepped down to comply with the Ecuadorian constitution, which forbade a president from succeeding himself. Unhappy with his handpicked successors, García Moreno once again used force to regain the presidency in 1869. Having now altered the constitution to make it possible to succeed himself, he was prepared to begin a third term in 1875 when he was assassinated only three days before his inauguration.

Groulx was prepared to overlook the means that García Moreno had employed to secure power because they had been used in the name of Catholicism. The Ecuadorian claimed to have entered politics in the 1850s only to counter the liberalism that had been evident in Europe in 1848 and which had now spread to his own country. Accordingly, even before seizing power he had tried to reverse an order to expel the Jesuits from his country, though to no avail. Once in power, he not only recalled the Jesuits but also worked out a Concordat with the Vatican, by which Ecuador would be a truly Catholic state. Henceforth, Catholicism was to be the only religion practised in the country; non-Catholics would be denied citizenship. Given such activities, the circumstances of García Moreno's death made him a martyr to those, such as Groulx, who were prepared to welcome the rise of a strong man committed to promoting Catholicism as a means of both challenging the forces of liberalism and strengthening national identity.[50]

Groulx's embrace of García Moreno both set him apart from Garneau and showed his affinity with a completely different tradition of Quebec historical writing, best represented by Abbé Ferland, described by Groulx as having been, along with Garneau, his major source of inspiration.[51] Ferland provided Groulx with the positive depiction of the Canadiens' Catholic roots that was missing in Garneau. In his *Cours d'histoire du Canada*, published in 1861, Ferland focused entirely on New France, a colony moulded by the 'considerable and positive influence' of Catholicism.[52] However, while Groulx may have shared Ferland's Catholic faith, he departed from the nineteenth-century historian when it came to evaluating the role of the French and British empires. Unlike Groulx, Ferland retained a certain respect for French colonial rule, to a considerable degree because he saw France as the 'eldest daughter of the church.'[53]

Moreover, while Groulx viewed the British as rulers who had acted benevolently only when they had no other option, Ferland was much more positive. Writing several years after the publication of his *Cours d'histoire*, Ferland sang the praises of British rule, which had allowed 'the Catholic clergy and the rural population greater freedom than they had been granted before the Conquest.'[54] Groulx reacted violently against the idea that the Conquest had been a providential act, noting in his *Manuel*, 'We must fight against the teaching of a school of thought that insists that our rights came from the generosity of the English. This point of view is simply an historical error.'[55]

Groulx insisted on this point to counter the ongoing support for Ferland's characterization of the past in early-twentieth-century Quebec, thanks to the writings of Thomas Chapais, who would play a significant role in the evolution of the Quebec historical profession. By the time Groulx began teaching history at Valleyfield, Chapais had already been a lawyer, journalist, and cabinet minister in several Quebec governments; he was also a member of the legislative council, a position that he had held since 1892. These occupations had not prevented him from writing about Quebec's history during the 1880s and 1890s. In speeches, in a series of newspaper columns that began to appear in *La Presse* in 1897, and in a biography of Jean Talon, Chapais presented a view of Quebec's past that shared elements of Ferland's conception. The Catholic church was the major formative influence in this narrative, while the two imperial powers, though not without faults, were generally well intentioned. As for the British, Chapais followed in Ferland's footsteps by crediting the Conquest with having sheltered the Canadiens from the French Revolution.[56] This belief in the providential effects of the Conquest was not entirely surprising from a man whose father and father-in-law had both been fathers of Confederation.

Groulx simply could not accept the notion, advanced by both Ferland and Chapais, that the Canadiens' fate had been determined by what others had done for them. Rather, in the spirit of Garneau, the young professor viewed the Canadiens as 'a self-made nation ... First there were the Canadiens and the French; later the Canadiens and the English.'[57] If only Garneau had been more respectful of the role of the church in Quebec history, Groulx would have been his unqualified supporter. Groulx could still rate Garneau, even with that failing, as superior to all who followed him.[58] In assembling his *Manuel*, Groulx combined small doses of Ferland and Chapais with a large infusion of Garneau, and in so doing created a new framework for studying Quebec's history. Jean-Pierre

Gaboury oversimplified the situation when he observed that 'the priest-historian was loyal to the tradition set by the French-Canadian historians who had preceded him.'[59] By identifying Groulx with a single school of historical writing, Gaboury missed the way in which the priest had created a new synthesis that viewed the Canadiens as a Catholic people prepared to do what was necessary to retain their identity. Because it was never published, the *Manuel* influenced only a relatively small number of Quebecers. Nevertheless, this first outline of Groulx's conceptualization of the history of Quebec reflected the challenges facing French speakers at the time and suggested a new paradigm for Quebec historical writing in the twentieth century.

III

Groulx would eventually change the nature of historical debate in Quebec by expanding on and communicating the point of view that first appeared in the *Manuel*. Little in the study, however, indicated that Groulx was either aware of or interested in larger debates taking place throughout the Western world regarding the scientific pretensions of the historical profession. This was to change, however, when Groulx set out for a sojourn in Europe in the fall of 1906. As he noted poignantly in his memoirs, 'Every day I was feeling more and more inadequate. I felt inadequate both as a professor and as a spiritual advisor to my students. I wanted to know more about philosophy, theology, and literature. I simply wanted to learn more about culture.'[60] His travels took him first to Rome, but before his return to Canada in 1909 he also spent considerable time in France and Switzerland.

These years had a profound impact on Groulx's thinking. In particular, his arrival in France in 1907 brought him face to face with the forces of liberalism, which had led France to break diplomatic relations with the Vatican in 1904, which had definitively separated church and state in 1905, and which had re-established Alfred Dreyfus as an innocent man in 1906. Given the considerable hostility towards the religious orders, Groulx's memoirs record his painful recollection of a France he could not entirely love: 'I could not love its religious waywardness, and I could not love its politics ... In the Paris of 1907 I had more than sufficient opportunity to get a taste of the anticlericalism that was in the air ... I was staying at the Séminaire d'Issy-les-Moulineaux (near Paris) where all of the priests were required to wear the cassock. As a result it was impossible to visit Paris without having to endure insults and hissing both from children and older passers-by, some of whom were well-dressed men. The anticlericalism of early twentieth century Paris deeply hurt me.'[61]

In addition to observing the violent clashes between defenders of a thoroughly secular republic and supporters of a truly Catholic France, Groulx also observed a society that was in turmoil on other grounds. For instance, 1906, the year of his arrival in Europe, saw over 400,000 French workers take part in more than 1,300 strikes. This assertiveness culminated in a May Day unlike any other, with widespread agitation for the eight-hour working day.[62] Not surprisingly, when Groulx returned to Canada, he was more determined than ever to defend his people from the forces plaguing France. As Nathalie Rogues has observed, 'The situation in Europe deeply troubled Groulx ... He came back home with a greater love for both his church and his nation ... He became much more nationalistic during his trip and returned with greater sympathy for the forces of the right.'[63]

Groulx's trip to Europe was well timed in terms of shaping his view not only of Quebec society but of history as a discipline. While, as Pierre Trépanier has noted, Groulx may have attended only one public meeting of Charles Maurras's Action française movement, it is hard to avoid the conclusion that Groulx was in some way attracted by its message, which rejected the secular tendencies of the third republic.[64] Groulx may or may not have been seduced by Maurras's call for a return to a monarchy, but the young priest was very much interested in the efforts to reinvigorate the French nation by marginalizing foreign elements and stressing its Catholic roots. Yet Groulx, the historian, was influenced also by those in revolt against the dominant form of historical thinking in France, which was, in its own right, closely linked to the secular republic.

Over the last third of the nineteenth century, the French historical profession established itself in the universities under the influence of individuals who hoped to define their discipline along scientific lines. The manifesto for this new approach to the French past was published in 1876 by Gabriel Monod in the new journal the *Revue historique*. Monod affirmed that he would publish only works 'in which each statement was supported by evidence, with notes referring to the sources. There was no room for either vague generalities or oratorical flourishes.'[65] In the decades to follow, large numbers of history professors were hired who, by and large, subscribed to 'l'école méthodique.'[66] Ultimately, this method was codified by Charles Langlois and Charles Seignobos in their *Introduction aux études historiques*, which was based on their course at the Sorbonne on historical methodology. The authors emphasized historians' careful examination of documents so as to present the past 'exactly as it was': 'The aim of history is not to please, nor to give practical maxims of conduct, nor to arouse the emotions, but knowledge pure and simple.'[67] As Alice Gérard has remarked, they concentrated on 'political history, individual events, and chronological order.' In the process, they seemed 'to marginalize the role of imagination and literary skill in historical writing.'[68]

By the time Groulx arrived in Europe, this allegedly value-free view of history was under heavy attack for the way in which it was linked to the interests of the third republic. While Langlois and Seignobos claimed that they were above allowing their discipline to be used for political purposes, they hardly concealed their interest in disseminating 'facts' that might generate sympathy for the secular republic. Accordingly, the facts of French history that they stressed tended to trace the roots of the third republic back to the French Revolution. In this spirit they helped justify the establishment of Bastille Day as the French national holiday, even though the revolution's republican and anti-clerical connotations would not be appreciated by all. William Keylor has observed that the historians of the 'école méthodique' appeared remarkably oblivious to 'the incompatibility between history's professed commitment to scientific objectivity and the services that it was expected to render to the program of patriotic instruction.'[69]

By the early twentieth century, opposition to the 'école méthodique' was beginning to take shape, and not always in the tranquility of the university. Because of his identification as a Dreyfusard, Seignobos 'occasionally had to be rescued from anti-semitic mobs that invaded his classroom.'[70] An even more significant public demonstration of disenchantment with the French historical establishment came in 1905, when the Action française movement orchestrated what came to be known as 'La bagarre de Fustel' (the squabble over Fustel) to celebrate the seventy-fifth anniversary of the birth of the historian of the ancient and medieval periods Fustel de Coulanges, who had died in 1899.

Charles Maurras played a central role in commemorating the life of a historian who had accepted certain of the 'scientific' notions of the 'école méthodique,' but who had not entirely embraced the secular and republican tone of the work of the historical establishment. While Fustel endorsed 'the golden rule that history had to be based upon a critical reading of documents,' he also insisted on the central role of religion in history and denied the significance of Germanic influences on early French society.[71] Fustel was cast in the role of the true patriot who had

had difficulty in winning a chair at the Sorbonne because he was 'suspected of monarchist and clerical views.'[72] His 'scientific' orientation, however, was never denied. Accordingly, the organizers of the Fustel celebrations proclaimed: 'In France, science must be nationalistic, and nationalism must be based upon scientific inquiry,' a formulation very similar to that embraced by such early-twentieth-century Quebecers as Édouard Montpetit.[73]

Groulx picked up some of this reaction to the political message, if not the historical methods, of Langlois and Seignobos when he spent the summer of 1907 at the Université de Fribourg in Switzerland. Nathalie Rogues has noted that in all of his travels in Europe, 'only the very Catholic university in Fribourg reassured him and left him with a fond memory.'[74] Some have claimed that Groulx's contentment at Fribourg, where he also spent some time in late 1908 and early 1909, was a function of the extremely conservative, even racist, view of the world that was communicated to him there.[75] Be that as it may, Groulx received his first formal training as a historian by attending a two-week summer course taught by Père Pierre Mandonnet, a medievalist, whose view of history has been preserved in Groulx's careful notes.

Mandonnet apparently went on at great length about the conscientious analysis of historical documents: 'The historian who has not lived with his documents, who has not manipulated and analyzed them, is a bad historian.'[76] Mandonnet also saw, however, that the historian had the responsibility to place the facts that he uncovered in some logical sequence, thus reflecting the widespread impatience, evident even in the 'Bagarre de Fustel,' with the rather arid approach of the 'école méthodique.' According to the Fribourg professor, the historian was responsible for explaining why man did what he did; otherwise 'there was no truly scientific history, but only historical information.' Mandonnet, while granting an important place to religion, was not prepared to see the hand of God behind all historical developments. As he wrote: 'It is impossible to explain everything in providential terms because we simply do not know the intentions of God.' Mandonnet showed his kinship with some of the opponents of Langlois and Seignobos when he remarked that in history 'revolutions always constitute a step backwards.'[77]

When Groulx returned home in 1909, he was one of the few Quebecers to have been exposed to modern notions of history as a discipline. If he came away from Europe with an even stronger sense that history could be used to advance a particular conception of the world, he also returned with the idea, which he had not had in 1906, that there were certain rules concerning use of documentation that had to be respected. In the short term, however, Groulx had relatively little opportunity to apply this newfound training. He returned to his teaching at Valleyfield, using whatever free time remained to participate in nationalist organizations. He made a few alterations to his manual, but he showed little inclination to do the archival work that was central to scientific history.

IV

In the early 1910s, while Groulx was otherwise occupied, the modern approach to historical writing was being advanced by a French speaker whose political vision was quite different from his. In 1913 Hector Garneau, grandson of Quebec's *historien national*, published a new edition of *Histoire du Canada*, which he claimed would be true to the relatively liberal interpretation of the first edition.[78] Hector, a lawyer and journalist by profession, provided some indication of the extent to which he was at odds with the version of the *Histoire* widely accepted since the 1860s when he remarked in 1911 that his grandfather 'was a liberal in terms of his temperament, his way of thinking and his general view of the world ... When Garneau had the opportunity to identify the writers who had influenced him the most, he began by recognizing his debt to Voltaire.'[79] In 1912, at the unveiling of a statue to his grandfather in Quebec City, Hector distinguished himself as the only French speaker failing to refer to the place of Catholicism in François-Xavier's work.[80]

As we saw earlier, François-Xavier Garneau, much to Lionel Groulx's dismay, never entirely abandoned his jaundiced view towards the church. Nevertheless, Hector set out to revise the fourth edition of *Histoire du Canada*, which was generally acceptable to clerical authorities and had been in circulation since the 1880s, by reinserting some of the more strident claims of his grandfather's original version. For instance, in his fifth edition of the text, Hector reinstated his grandfather's remark from the 1840s that New France would have been better off if the ban on Huguenot emigration had fallen instead on Catholics, since the former were interested in going to the St Lawrence valley, while the latter were content to stay at home.[81] In still other cases, however, Hector added evidence that made the judgment against the clergy much harsher than his grandfather's. For instance, in all the previous editions Bishop Laval had been referred to as having been 'uncompromising and domineering,' but in Hector's rendition this point was reinforced by an appendix that chronicled the mean-spiritedness of the bishop. Hector noted, among other actions, Laval's insistence that two young men be whipped for saluting the governor prior to saluting the bishop.[82]

Hector employed many such appendices in reworking his grandfather's text. In all, he provided two thousand notes and two hundred appendices to indicate his own commitment to the principles of modern historical writing. As he observed in his introduction to the 1913 text: 'We have done everything possible to introduce both the modern scientific approach and the newest discoveries about the past. The sources for all documents have been provided in the notes which also contain discussions of the issues at hand. We have also included a bibliography as well as numerous appendices in which additional information has been provided.'[83] In effect, this was the first work pertaining to Quebec history that so clearly bore the trademarks of modern scientific scholarship, and it is significant that few of those who examined Hector's work were critical of his efforts in this regard. Reviewers from France led the way in praising him for having merged 'the simplicity of the original text with both additional documentation and the trappings of modern historical scholarship.'[84] Yet another commentator from France pointed at the way in which Hector had taken 'an outdated work' and had 'brought it up to date' by turning his grandfather's history into 'a modern piece of scholarship based upon scientific methods.'[85]

Quebecers were no less enthusiastic about the technical improvements. One reviewer noted that the new version was 'a modern work which was faithful to the scientific standards demanded by a Seignobos.'[86] Henri Bourassa, writing in Le Devoir, gave Hector full marks for having added 'a large number of notes and references,' and in a personal letter, Paul Bruchési, archbishop of Montreal, offered congratulations for 'a superb volume ... greatly enhanced by the inclusion of notes and appendices of great value.' Quite aside from these technical matters, however, there was considerable consternation, particularly from clerical quarters, about Hector's secular tendencies, in particular his emphasis on his grandfather's links to Voltaire and his decision to return to the first edition of the Histoire, which even his grandfather had reconsidered, albeit under some considerable pressure, prior to his death. Bourassa was particularly unhappy with Hector's decision to return to his grandfather's critique of the ban against Protestant emigration to New France, while Archbishop Bruchési objected to the condemnation of Bishop Laval.[87]

Adversaries such as these made life difficult for Hector Garneau over the next three decades, as they insisted that he publish a more clerically correct version of his grandfather's work. Much of this story took place after 1925 and will be discussed in the next chapter. In the short term, however, Hector had to put up with such inconveniences as the temporary blocking of his election to the Royal Society of Canada because he had dared to offer a view on such issues as 'the exclusion of the Huguenots' that did not coincide with that of some clerical leaders.[88] None of Hector's critics, however, particularly objected to his introduction to Quebec of the new methods of historical writing. Much like the organizers of the 'Bagarre de Fustel' in France, these critics accepted the new style of historical writing, even if they did not appreciate the message being communicated. In fact, at roughly the time that critics such as Henri Bourassa were offering their judgment of Hector's work, a series of events began to unfold that would ultimately lead to Lionel Groulx's first effort to employ these modern methods himself.

This chain of events began innocently enough in September 1913 with an editorial in *Le Devoir*, in which Bourassa stressed the need for a better understanding of Canada's past. Along the way, Bourassa remarked: 'We have to face up to the fact that history is not taught to the youth of Canada in a manner that would allow them to understand the rights and duties of the Canadian people. In most schools, both French and English, history is taught very badly when it is taught at all.'[89] In response to this blanket condemnation, Bourassa received a number of rejoinders from priests who, in fact, had been teaching Canadian history in Quebec's collèges classiques for some time. The first came from Groulx, who pointed out to Bourassa that 'over the past ten years the teaching of history has been completely revised, renewed. It would not be an exaggeration to say that it has been reborn in our colleges.' To be sure, there was no universally accepted textbook for use in the collèges, but Groulx observed that numerous professors, himself included, had created manuals for their students. In a blatant act of self-promotion Groulx described how he had prepared a work of 900 pages (in fact there were only 420 pages), which contained 'elements of the works of all of our best historians.'[90]

Having placed himself in the limelight, Groulx was then encouraged to publish his manual. As he recalled in his *Mémoires*, 'I was incredibly embarrassed. This manual, which I had put together in my free moments, had some glaring defects. Its only value was that it was better than nothing ... I was badly advised by my friends who encouraged me to improve the manual by going off to the Public Archives in Ottawa. Not knowing any better, I believed that in a relatively short period of time I might collect enough information to put the manual in a form that would make it suitable for publication.'[91] Groulx proceeded to drop his teaching responsibilities in December 1913 to try out the techniques of Père Mandonnet and Hector Garneau for himself, but he was soon to find out that there was more to the job than simply reading old documents. 'Left to my own devices, with no one to guide me, I found myself completely overwhelmed by the endless examination of dossiers ... Without realizing it at the time, this was my introduction to serious historical research. After a few weeks I had to admit that I was simply not equipped to carry out the task at hand.' The beginner was at a loss as to where he should even start such a monumental task, so that 'towards the end of January 1914, [he] returned to Valleyfield, taking with [him] his dashed hopes.'[92]

Groulx was not exaggerating the futility of his first research trip, which produced little more than failed attempts to recast the 1905 *Manuel*.[93] Nevertheless, Groulx, along with Hector Garneau, had indicated on the eve of the First World War that an older style of history, whose sole intent was to provide moral or political lessons, was in decline in Quebec. Their work showed that by the mid-1910s, just as Quebec history was about to be firmly established in the university, a new view of historical method was emerging alongside Groulx's suggestion of a new way to conceptualize Quebec's past.

V

To understand the circumstances that led ultimately to Groulx's appointment as the first full-time Canadian historian in a Quebec university, we have to return once again to Henri Bourassa's editorials in the fall of 1913 regarding the teaching of history. Not content to assess the situation in the collèges classiques, Bourassa also commented on history teaching at the university level in light of *'the new problems that are on the rise.'* Bourassa was concerned in particular with the efforts of 'powerful financial interests which have tried to redefine the nature of Canadian nationalism.' In the face of demands for Canadians to take on the responsibilities of the British Empire, Bourassa wondered if 'the youth of the ruling classes know enough about their history to respond to this challenge.' History had to become part of the the curriculum of the university, which he saw as 'the nursery for the development of the ruling class. We have to recognize the importance of history in developing young men capable of assuming leadership roles ... The English-Canadian universities have understood this lesson ... It is now time for us to make up for lost time and establish a chair in Canadian history at the Université Laval. We need to have our youth exposed to the truth about the past, without concern for the criticism of politicians and exploiters.'[94]

One person who was particularly taken by Bourassa's critique in this regard was Archbishop Bruchési, who was responsible for the Montreal branch of the Université Laval. Groulx had come to Bruchési's attention through his letter to *Le Devoir*, and the two apparently chatted briefly in the fall of 1913 about the woeful ignorance of Quebecers regarding their own history. Nothing more came of this discussion until the fall of 1915, by which time Groulx found himself in Montreal, having decided that he had had enough of teaching at Valleyfield. Not knowing exactly what he would do in Montreal, Groulx presented himself to the archbishop, fearful that he would end up as a parish priest, far away from the world of teaching and, to some degree, research that he had come to know. Groulx had no reason to worry in this regard, however, because Bruchési had already decided to employ Groulx in the reorganization of the university, with an eye towards 'making its curriculum more nationalistic.'[95]

Bruchési led Groulx to believe that this reorganization was not imminent, but only weeks after their initial meeting in September 1915 Groulx was informed that the war had resulted in one of the university's professors returning to his native France. The departing instructor had been responsible for twenty 'conférences publiques' – that is, lectures open to the general public. Bruchési called on Groulx to offer ten of them, to which Groulx replied with an offer of five. The archbishop immediately accepted Groulx's proposition, noting: 'You will present your first lecture on 3 November, and I will be there to preside over the event.' As Groulx commented in his memoirs, 'And that is how, in the French Canada of 1915, one became a professor of Canadian history in a Quebec university.'[96]

Groulx's first lecture became a major public event. It was widely publicized in *Le Devoir* almost from the moment that the series was established, and on the morning of the lecture the same newspaper ran a long interview with Groulx in which he explained what he would be saying. This marketing campaign apparently succeeded, since 1,200 people turned out to hear the new professor. Even more significant, the initial lecture was warmly received by the university. On the following morning, the vice-rector, Mgr Gaspard Dauth, asked Groulx to teach a number of courses at the École des hautes études commerciales. As Dauth told him: 'The Faculty of Arts has no budget to pay you, so we had to look around to find a way for you to support yourself.'[97] The administration's opinion of Groulx's worth had not changed by the end of the lectures in spring 1916, and he was invited to present his public lectures on a regular basis.[98]

Between 1915 and 1921 Groulx presented six series of lectures dealing exclusively with Quebec history prior to Confederation. His general argument was roughly the same as that which he had developed a decade earlier at Valleyfield in his *Manuel*. Much like Garneau, and in opposition to contemporaries such as Thomas Chapais, Groulx depicted a people who owed little to either of the empires that had dominated its history. In terms of the French regime, he found a homogeneous population with a distinctive identity which had not been particularly well treated by the colonial rulers in Paris. He cautioned francophones against being overly nostalgic about a France that had been untroubled by the ceding of Quebec to the English.[99] As for the English regime, which provided the focus for five of the six series of lectures, he constantly stressed that whatever gains had been made by the time of Confederation had been the result of French-Canadian determination, not British generosity. He noted in the final lecture to his first series of talks: 'The freedom that we enjoy was won by hard work and was not a gift from the conqueror. Accordingly, it is time for us, once and for all, to stop talking about a liberal and nurturing England which treated us better than we deserved. Should the day come when, due to our complicity, this ridiculous view of the past gains a certain credibility, we might as well topple the statues of our great leaders from their pedestals, for this will be the undoing of our history.'[100]

Groulx made no particular effort in these lectures to appear as if he were a detached observer. He took up his university position in the immediate aftermath of the curbing of French-language rights in Ontario and in the midst of the First World War, and he hoped that the lessons of history would steel the resolve of his compatriots in the face of the challenges that they faced. By way of introduction to the published version of one series of lectures, he noted: 'We should never confuse impartiality with neutrality. The writing of history carries with it heavy consequences. Accordingly, we need to write history from a Catholic and French-Canadian perspective. The historian ought to work and to think with the benefit of his personality. If he tries to be 'neutral' ... he sacrifices part of what it means to be human.'[101]

Because Groulx believed that history should communicate a message to the larger population, it has been easy enough for his critics to assume that he was uninterested in questions of method. In this context, Jacques Mathieu, writing in the early 1990s, viewed Groulx as representative of a generation of Quebec writers for whom passionate belief in an idea was an acceptable substitute for a careful marshalling of evidence.[102] However, Groulx's actions during his early years as a university professor suggest another interpretation. He recounted in his memoirs that he was painfully conscious from the time that he was hired in 1915 that he had much catching up to do in his development as an historian. Up to then his formal training had amounted to little more than his summer course at Fribourg, and he later regretted that he had passed up an opportunity to study at Oxford, where he might have received a real 'initiation to the historical profession.'[103] Instead, he remained in Quebec, where he immersed himself in 'manuals dealing with historical methodology, including the great work of [Langlois and] Seignobos which seemed far too mechanical for [his] tastes.' In addition, he devoted himself to 'systematically reading the works of the great historians.' By his account, he worked his way through authors ranging from Thucydides, to Thierry, to Fustel de Coulanges.[104]

During these years Groulx also achieved a measure of success in archival research, in contrast with his dismal failure as a researcher while still a professor at Valleyfield. He made regular trips to both Ottawa and Quebec City, the fruits of which are evident in the published versions of his early lectures. Each of these volumes contained substantial bibliographies, and several provided references to archival material that he had collected. His empirical side was evident when he complained in the introduction to his volume on Confederation that the sources became harder to unearth as one came closer to the present. 'Some of the most important evidence was simply not available. Diaries, personal correspondence and classified documents remain buried in the archives of the relevant families with the result that some questions cannot be answered.'[105] Not content with Canadian sources, Groulx also spent part of a sabbatical during the academic year 1921–2 in Paris and London, collecting material from archives, where he experienced 'the joys of research.'[106]

The tentative arrival of modern historical scholarship in Quebec by the early 1920s was evident, however, not only in Groulx's respect for many of the canons of the discipline, but also in his membership in a historical community that was starting to take shape in the province. Most of the members operated outside the university milieu, where there was only one other regular professor of Canadian history. Thomas Chapais had received a position at the Quebec City campus of the Université Laval in 1916 to offer the sort of public lectures that Groulx had begun in

Montreal the previous year. Chapais was hardly a newcomer to Laval, where he had been teaching courses from time to time since 1907.[107] As with Groulx's appointment in Montreal, however, Chapais was now going to present 'a course on the history of Canada on a regular and permanent basis' in Quebec City.[108]

Just as Groulx's early lectures reflected the ideas that he had developed at Valleyfield, so too were Chapais's lectures consistent with a view of Quebec history that he had long been promoting – and which Groulx had long been attacking. Chapais offered four series of lectures between 1916 and 1920 and another four between 1926 and 1930, which, focusing on the period from the Conquest to the Union of the Canadas, covered much of the same territory considered by Groulx. Unlike his colleagues, however, Chapais was an unrepentant apologist for the two empires that had shaped Quebec. While Groulx cautioned Quebecers to avoid excessive nostalgia for France, Chapais spoke of a 'mother country' that deserved respect for having sent to Canada 'its teachers, its administrators, its talented women, its religious leaders, and its heroes.'[109]

As for the arrival of the British, Chapais stressed that 'Providence had decreed this change in sovereignty.'[110] True to this spirit, and quite contrary to Groulx's view of affairs, Chapais interpreted all constitutional gains as proof of British goodwill. For instance, he bristled at the notion that the British had been pushed into the Quebec Act out of fear of losing Quebec to the Americans. Ever the defender of British rule, Chapais asked: 'Why should we begrudge giving recognition to the British for the generosity of their actions?'[111] Even Chapais's decision to embark on a new set of lectures in the mid-1920s was linked to his interest in putting British rule in the best possible light. His first set from the late 1910s concluded with the imposition of the Union of the Canadas – not necessarily the best way to convince Quebecers of the blessings of the Conquest. Chapais admitted as much in 1926 when he noted that 'in 1840 prospects were rather bleak ... This was not a good point at which to interrupt the course. We need to continue up to the point when we finally received the right to participate in the governing of our country.'[112]

In describing Quebec's history in such a manner, Chapais added little to the way in which the past had been explained by numerous nineteenth-century historians, including Abbé Ferland, his predecessor at Laval. Nevertheless, unlike Ferland, Chapais's published lectures indicated considerable archival work. True to the spirit of the 'école méthodique,' Chapais criticized Ferland for faulty documentation and more generally stressed the need for a critical eye in 'understanding and interpreting' historical sources.[113] Much like Groulx, however, he was not prepared to view history simply as the collecting of well-documented facts. In a 1924 address to the Royal Society of Canada, he remarked: 'Analyzing the sources and spending a considerable amount of time in the archives is not what makes a piece of scholarship into a work of art.'[114] In the same speech, he reflected Groulx's own conviction that historians should advance a particular point of view on the basis of a careful examination of the relevant documentation. 'While the historian needs to be impartial, this does not mean that he has to abandon all of his emotions ... Art and science, truth and beauty, these are the two paths followed by the historian.'[115]

In the eyes of many, Chapais's view of Quebec's past was contradicted by the conscription crisis of the First World War, which hardly made British rule appear as if it had been sent from heaven. Indicating a certain general incomprehension of current affairs, Chapais chose to lecture on the day after the conscription riots in Quebec City, even though 'the local residents had been asked to stay at home in the evening.'[116] Perhaps because of his political views, Chapais attracted relatively few Quebecers to his lectures in the years immediately following the war. The superior of the Séminaire de Québec, which ran the Quebec City campus of Laval, wrote in regard to one of his lectures in December 1918: 'Aside from those who were obliged to attend, very few people were present. Most people probably preferred going either to the cinema or the theatre.'[117] There were so few at a lecture in early 1919 that instead of introducing his talk '"Mesdames et Messieurs," [Chapais] could just as easily have said "Madame" because only Mme Chapais was there.'[118]

Groulx's numerous attacks against the 'providential' interpretation of the Conquest were poorly veiled criticisms of Chapais. In a commentary written after Chapais's death in 1947, the Montreal professor criticized his Quebec City counterpart for having failed to 'follow in the footsteps of Garneau.'[119] In that same commentary, however, Groulx also praised Chapais because 'he [had been] tolerant of interpretations of the past that differed from his own. In this discipline in which only amateurs believe that they have the sole correct explanation, Chapais was not so sure of his opinions that he believed himself to be infallible.'[120] Groulx was not simply going out of his way to speak kindly of the dead, however, because there is evidence that the two historians felt a kinship by dint of their membership in a common 'profession.' In 1921 Groulx sent Chapais a copy of his most recently published lectures, noting, 'You will observe that on certain questions, we have a fundamental difference of opinion ...

Since I have the highest admiration for both your talent and your integrity, I know that we can always have a civilized discussion.'[121] Chapais responded philosophically and without the slightest hint of bitterness, commenting that 'differences of opinion are inevitable.'[122] The Laval professor spoke kindly of his Montreal counterpart in 1934 in writing a letter in support of Groulx's application for a Carnegie fellowship: 'I have the highest esteem and the most sincere admiration for this distinguished professor. His writings have made him one of our most important historians. He is a scholar of the first order who is worthy of the support of your committee.'[123]

Because of their substantial political differences, it has become commonplace for Groulx and Chapais to be depicted as enemies. Serge Gagnon, for instance, has referred to Groulx as 'the official critic' of Chapais's work.[124] In stressing political matters, however, one misses the bonds that united them as early members of a fledgling historical community dedicated to conscientious use of source material.

Groulx was linked also to Gustave Lanctot by a certain professional, if not political affinity.[125] Lanctot was arguably the best-trained historian in Quebec up to the start of the Second World War. He studied history at both Oxford and the Université de Paris, receiving a doctorate from the latter institution in 1919, thus making him one of the first French-speaking Quebecers with a PhD in history.[126] Both prior to and after his service in the First World War, Lanctot was employed in the Public Archives of Canada, where he was made head of the French section in 1918 and dominion archivist in 1937. Following his retirement from the archives in 1948, Lanctot wrote a number of lengthy works, including a multi-volume history of New France as well as books dealing with Montreal in the age of Maisonneuve and Canada during the era of the American Revolution.

In the early 1920s, however, Lanctot's publications were largely critiques of the works of others, and in this regard he paid particular attention to those of Abbé Groulx. Much like Chapais, Lanctot could not accept Groulx's negative attitude towards both the French and the British empires.[127] Unlike Chapais, however, Lanctot believed that it might be possible, if one only properly collected the relevant documents, to discover the objective 'truth.' Perhaps reflecting his education at the university of Langlois and Seignobos, Lanctot observed, as part of a review of Groulx's *Lendemains de conquête*, that historians were engaged in a scientific endeavour as they set out to compile 'the bible of a people.' He insisted that 'science should never be influenced by political opinions.'

Accordingly, Lanctot was particularly critical of the way in which Groulx's predetermined notions had warped his work. 'When he studies a document, he does not look for information, but for evidence to support his preconceived views.' Given Lanctot's emphasis on the document as the building block of all historical writing, he concluded the review with a critique of Groulx's footnotes, which were 'based upon no discernible system.'[128]

However, Lanctot, much like his Parisian teachers, had difficulty in recognizing that his own concentration on the technical aspects of historical writing did not free him from having a point of view. The archivist hardly appeared politically neutral when he attacked Groulx for supporting 'the new crusade ... which seeks to establish something like the Great Wall of China around the St-Lawrence valley in order to keep outside influences at bay.'[129] Lanctot seemed equally oblivious to the conflict between objectivity and interpretation in his writings in praise of François-Xavier Garneau, whom he depicted as the 'the first of our historians with a scientific perspective upon the discipline.'[130] From Lanctot's viewpoint, Garneau, unlike Groulx, whenever he was faced with the choice between advancing a cause and presenting the 'truth' always opted for the latter.[131] This search for the truth, however, had not prevented Garneau, by Lanctot's own admission, from supporting certain 'liberal Catholic' principles. Lanctot did not seem unduly bothered by the way in which these concepts might have influenced Garneau's view of the church in Quebec history.[132] Lanctot revealed his own values, even if he would not admit their existence, in taking Groulx to task for sins that he forgave in Garneau.

The differences between Groulx and Lanctot did not prevent the two from having relatively cordial relations, based on certain shared notions of historical scholarship. Just as Groulx and Chapais saw each other as kindred spirits interested in bringing 'modern' notions of historical writing to Quebec, Groulx and Lanctot had enough in common to allow the former to support the latter's candidacy in 1926 for membership in the Royal Society of Canada.[133] Groulx's esteem for Lanctot had been similarly evident a year earlier, when he asked him to help organize and to participate in the first conference dedicated to Quebec's history.

VI

The Semaine d'histoire du Canada was a significant, and heretofore curiously neglected, event, which for the first time brought together

Quebecers who shared a common interest in studying the past. Over five days in the autumn of 1925 twenty-four lectures were presented to eight thousand people.[134] It would clearly be an exaggeration to call this the first professional conference of Quebec historians; as we shall see, the approach of many of the speakers was far from professional. Nevertheless, the event did indicate the existence of a community of individuals interested in the study of Quebec's past. As Henri d'Arles noted, 'This was the first time that a conference was held in Quebec devoted entirely to various issues relevant to the study of the important field of history.'[135]

The conference was modelled after the numerous Semaines sociales that had been held since 1920 under the auspices of the Jesuit-led École sociale populaire. Each Semaine sociale brought together experts for a week to give talks on a particular theme, such as colonization or the family, to those with more than a passing interest in the subject.[136] In organizing the Semaine d'histoire in 1925, Groulx followed the Semaine sociale format in assembling experts in the field. There is little evidence, however, that he was interested in selecting only individuals who were advocates of a particularly 'Catholic' view of history as a discipline. In 1924 he wrote to the Société historique de Montréal asking it to sponsor the conference, in which specialists would give 'a series of lectures dealing with various topics. One lecturer, for instance, might present an inventory of archival sources in order to help historians provide appropriate documentation for their studies ... In addition, there would be lectures dealing with various technical and methodological issues in history.'[137]

The lectures, some presented by clerics and others by laymen, indicated a wide variety of approaches to the discipline. There were those such as Lanctot who stressed the scientific side of the historical profession. In a similar fashion, Père A.M. Mignault remarked that 'the historian must try to provide a reasoned view of the past based upon the documentation which has survived.'[138] Moreover, Abbé H.A. Scott ended his presentation with a call for the writing of history 'based upon a love for the truth which is the basis for any real work of science.'[139] Presumably, the scientific pretensions of history would also have been stressed by the much-maligned Hector Garneau, had he accepted his invitation to participate.[140] There were, however, participants who were more interested in promoting Catholicism than in troubling themselves over questions of evidence. Leading the way in this regard was Père G. Simard, who wondered: 'Is it really necessary to prove that providence is at the root of most events? ... The history of the Catholic church opens one's eyes to the ways in which providence and the hand of God touch all human affairs ... We have an obligation to return our history to its Catholic roots.'[141]

Somewhere in between these two extremes were participants such as Thomas Chapais and Lionel Groulx. The Laval professor observed that Garneau deserved high praise for the way in which he had striven to make his documentation 'as complete as possible.' Chapais insisted, however, that the historian had the right to advance his own view of the world: 'The historian has a heart, and no rules can prevent his emotions from influencing his work.'[142] Groulx observed that he was unprepared to see in the history of Quebec any 'absolute determinism,' but insisted that 'in history there are always two great actors: man and God.'[143]

There was similarly a considerable diversity of political opinion among the participants at the Semaine d'histoire. At one extreme, there was Groulx, whose presentation characterized the dominion government as the arm of English-speaking, businessmen interested only in advancing the concerns of 'the dominant race.'[144] Sympathetic to Groulx's view of the present, *Action française* hoped that the Semaine d'histoire would strengthen an appreciation of the past that would provide a path towards liberation.[145] By contrast, *La Presse* believed that the study of history would lead to greater understanding of what united French and English-speaking Canadians. It hailed the staging of the Semaine d'histoire because 'it is by the careful study of history that we will manage to cultivate within Confederation the spirit of "bonne entente" that we have spoken about for so long.'[146]

Indeed, there was support for a less conflictual view of Quebec's past in the presentation to the Semaine d'histoire by Mgr Emile Chartier, vice-rector of the Université de Montréal and Groulx's close friend since early in the century. Chartier offered a diatribe against 'the combative history of some of our historians' who claimed that English speakers had consistently and self-consciously acted in an 'infamous manner.' By advancing their own personal opinions, Quebec historians had failed to develop an 'impartial' perspective on the past. According to Chartier, the historian had the responsibility to understand the motives of people, such as the English conquerors, who had come from a different background and who had lived in a different time; it was not the historian's responsibility to pass judgment on such individuals. Chartier found that it was especially crucial to cultivate 'an appreciation of cultural differences' in a country such as Canada, if two different 'races' were to live together.[147]

Abbé Groulx and his supporters should not have been surprised by Chartier's presentation. After all, earlier in 1925 Émile Bruchési, writing in *Action française*, had taken Chartier to task for having advocated, in the spirit of bonne entente, a general policy of bilingualism across Canada, which would have had 'disastrous consequences ... Were our people, a small minority in North America, to become bilingual, it would be the beginning of a process of rapid assimilation.'[148] Commentaries in the same journal criticized Chartier for his presentation to the Semaine d'histoire in which he seemed to apologize for the actions of English speakers since the Conquest. In an overview of the conference, Albert Lévesque singled out Chartier for having offered 'a classic plea for loyalty to the conqueror.'[149] In the same spirit, Henri d'Arles wrote: 'According to [Chartier], we should write our history from an English, instead of a Canadian point of view.'[150]

Indicating his own dismay over Chartier's talk, Groulx refused to have his contribution to the conference published in the proceedings along with that of his old friend. Groulx understood that Chartier's condemnation of 'the combative history of some of our historians' was pointedly aimed at him. He claimed, however, that his refusal to allow the publication of his talk was not because he minded criticism per se. Rather, he remarked that he was offended by being attacked at a conference that he had largely organized.[151] One suspects, however, that there was more calculation behind the actions of both Groulx and his colleagues at *Action française*. After all, why such a well-orchestrated attack against Chartier, when others such as Thomas Chapais presented, as one would have expected, a similarly favourable interpretation of the actions of the British conquerors without any particular reaction?

Groulx may have felt resentment at being publicly attacked by someone with whom he had been very close as a young man.[152] More generally, however, what differentiated Chartier from Chapais in the eyes of the critics associated with *Action française* was the sense that the Université de Montréal administrator lacked Chapais's professional credentials. Émile Bruchési, for instance, argued that modern historical scholarship was based on the need 'to consult and to analyze the relevant documents,' and in this regard Chartier was found wanting. Moreover, Bruchési complained that Chartier did not understand that the historian, once he collected his material, then needed to impose an interpretation on it: 'The historian does not play the role of a phonograph which produces whatever sounds are imprinted upon the record. The historian has a soul which responds to the circumstances of his times and his people, and he has no choice but to be loyal to the direction that his soul provides. The historian should tell the truth, but he cannot hope to be neutral.'[153] In the same spirit, Henri d'Arles complained that 'Chartier is not really known as an historian.' Because he was not 'a professional in this difficult discipline,' Chartier could not understand that 'history is both a science and an art. The historian must bring these qualities together to be worthy of the name.' Placing his critique in the context of larger debates within the historical profession, d'Arles linked Chartier's approach with that of Langlois and Seignobos, whose work gave historians guideposts that were both 'erroneous and absurd,' because they focused on description at the expense of analysis.[154]

Whatever those connected with Groulx thought of the work of Chapais or Lanctot, they never doubted that the two men were well versed in both the technical matters related to historical research and the literature relevant to the evolution of the discipline. In short, Chapais and Lanctot, along with Groulx and even Hector Garneau, were part of the community of historians that had begun to take shape in Quebec by the 1920s, and to which most of the participants at the Semaine d'histoire, Chartier excluded, could claim membership.

VII

The Semaine d'histoire was the logical culmination of the growing interest of Quebecers in modern approaches to historical writing. While it may not have been a late-twentieth-century–style professional conference, it certainly suggested that there was more than passing interest in larger developments in the discipline. Moreover, the event deserved more than the dismissive treatment accorded it by Serge Gagnon, who found it indicative of just 'how far French Canadians were from Western standards of scholarship in the period just after the First World War.'[155] Gagnon managed to come to this conclusion by focusing on the presentation of Abbé Georges Courchesne, to the exclusion of the other twenty-three lectures.

Gagnon bemoaned Courchesne's rejection of the Seignobos approach to the discipline, seemingly oblivious to the fact that reservations regarding Seignobos were widespread both in Quebec and in France, and among historians of differing ideological persuasions. Moreover, Gagnon rather conveniently ignored passages from Courchesne's lecture that indicated a less categorical rejection of the scientific pretensions of history. In a speech dealing with the teaching of history at the university level, Courchesne touted the discipline as one that could assist in 'the development of critical analysis and logical thinking.' More generally, history was crucial to the cultural development of students, so that they might assume their 'responsibilities among the elite of our society.'[156]

In a completely different context, Gagnon stressed the primitive nature of Quebec historical writing at the time by focusing on the obscure writings of Frère Alexis de Barbezieux, who, for good reason, was not invited to speak at the Semaine d'histoire. It is difficult to argue with Gagnon's dismissive attitude towards Frère Alexis, who once claimed that his only qualification was 'the desire to be of service to others' and who insisted that 'the conscientious historian cannot help but discover, sooner or later, that Providence plays a positive and paternal role in human affairs.'[157] Gagnon was arguing beyond his evidence, however, in insisting that Frère Alexis was representative of the complete absence of 'scientific standards' among Quebec historians prior to the 1940s.[158] Most of the contributors to the Semaine d'histoire, Abbé Groulx included, would have rejected Frère Alexis's point of view.

While Gagnon went too far to one extreme in his categorical rejection of the scientific claims of Quebec historians by the early 1920s, one can also go too far in the other direction, seeing in Abbé Groulx and his contemporaries a greater degree of sophistication than their work warranted. For instance, in his introduction to a reprint of one of Groulx's early series of lectures at the Université de Montréal, Jean-Pierre Wallot observed: 'Groulx was still at the start of his career upon publishing *Lendemains de conquête* in 1920. Already, however, he was offering a modern orientation to the field, far in advance of a descriptive approach.' Wallot went on, however, to overstate his case, comparing Groulx at this stage of his career with other historians such as Marc Bloch, Fernand Braudel, and Christopher Hill.[159] While Groulx recognized the role of man in history, unlike Frère Alexis, he also gave some credit to Providence, unlike Bloch, Braudel, and Hill.

The Quebec historians of this period defy easy classification as either 'modern' or 'primitive.' Rather, as the Semaine d'histoire indicated, they were a reasonably diverse lot, who by and large paralleled Groulx's ambiguity regarding whether history was a science or an art and whether man or Providence had the upper hand in determining the destiny of Quebecers.[160] This ambiguity reflected the fact that Groulx and many of his colleagues were bridging the gap between an older style of history, dedicated to providing stories designed to prop up the traditional social order, and a newer style, based on certain 'scientific' principles. Groulx was in the mainstream of Quebec thinkers of the early twentieth century, such as Frère Marie-Victorin, Édouard Montpetit, and Alphonse Desjardins, all of whom saw something worth preserving in the more traditional society that was under attack. They were also prepared, however tentatively, to use the tools of modern society to improve the lot of their people.

In precisely the same context, the journal *Action française* was established in 1917, both to oppose certain of the modernizing tendencies of the new century and to encourage French speakers to participate in the modern world. On the one hand, the journal's inaugural issue encouraged Quebecers to be vigilant in the defence of 'our rights, our traditions and our language.' On the other hand, as Andrée Fortin has observed, 'Edouard Montpetit's introduction to the first issue of *Action française* had a very modern tone. Montpetit began with the dramatic declaration: "Let us train our men; let us develop our skills."'[161] In 1924 this sentiment was echoed by the president of the recently established Association canadienne-française pour l'avancement des sciences (ACFAS), which grouped together, much like the learned societies of today, the university disciplines committed to the scientific approach. As Léo Pariseau stated, the role of ACFAS was to encourage science '"For the race, by the university."' Once more, the 'race,' having survived from the traditional world, was to be bolstered by the tools of science that were being developed in the modern university.[162]

Much like a journal such as *Action française* or an organization such as ACFAS, the Semaine d'histoire was designed to encourage the spread of modern ideas – in this case ideas regarding the scientific approach to historical writing – among educated Quebecers. In addition to those who attended Groulx's conference of historians in 1925, an even larger number came into contact with the presentations by way of the published proceedings, which were aimed at educating 'the elite of our nation.'[163] Nevertheless, in spite of the apparent success of the Semaine d'histoire, most accounts of intellectual life in early-twentieth-century Quebec tend to minimize the scientific credentials of the historians of the time. For instance, while Yves Gingras has argued that the establishment of ACFAS reflected the existence, even in the 1920s, of 'a modern, urban view of Quebec,' he insisted that historical writing was still stuck in 'a tradition dedicated to little more than hero-worship' as late as the 1950s.[164] In the final analysis, Montpetit, Marie-Victorin, and the founders of ACFAS were not as unambiguously 'modern' as Gingras and others would suggest; nor were Groulx and his colleagues as primitive as most commentators have argued. Rather, they all formed part of a French-speaking Catholic elite that was looking for ways of living with feet in both the older and the newer worlds.

2

Nuts and Bolts: Lionel Groulx and the Trappings of a Profession

I

Between the two world wars Quebec's universities saw the rise of lay professionals in nearly every academic discipline. In most accounts of these disciplines, the pioneers in the various fields – individuals such as Frère Marie-Victorin and Père Georges-Henri Lévesque – had given way by the end of the Second World War to a new generation, which had travelled outside Quebec to secure proper training and had then returned to pass its skills on to other Quebecers as the universities rapidly expanded. This second generation, represented by such diverse figures as Léon Dion, Fernand Dumont, Jean-Charles Falardeau, Albert Faucher, and Maurice Lamontagne, encouraged larger changes in Quebec society and was closely connected with the political and social developments that began during the postwar period and continued into the 1960s.[1] Nevertheless, the bases for the disciplines had been laid by 1939, thus leading Marcel Fournier to refer to the interwar years as 'the crucial period.'[2] From Fournier's perspective, the second generation did not introduce scientific methods to Quebec's universities but rather built on the work of its predecessors, who had already done so.

By contrast, the literature about Quebec's historical community during the interwar period, while emphasizing the rise of the lay professionals, has given little credit to those who preceded them. By and large, it creates the impression that the historians who were hired in the 1940s, with PhDs in hand, were the first Quebecers to have taken historical writing seriously. In this spirit, Serge Gagnon hailed the arrival of Marcel Trudel at Laval as allowing 'the introduction of the scientific theory of history – a theory that devotees of clerico-conservatism regarded as an intellectual practice bordering on atheism.'[3] In a similar fashion, Jean Lamarre, writing about the Université de Montréal historians Michel Brunet, Guy Frégault, and Maurice Séguin, credited them with 'giving historical research a truly scientific character so that it might be distinguished from the works of literature and the exercises in propaganda which had previously dominated the scene.'[4] In the same spirit, Jean Blain has found that until the passing of Lionel Groulx from the university scene in the late 1940s Quebec's historical writing had nothing to offer the serious student.[5]

This position is defensible only if one ignores the Semaine d'histoire of 1925 and other developments with which Lionel Groulx was closely connected. As we shall see in this chapter, Groulx's own view of the past evolved quite dramatically in the quarter-century following the Semaine d'histoire. Moreover, during this period he largely retained the respect of the younger lay professionals, who generally referred to him as their 'maître,' an expression of respect that indicated that Groulx was not only their teacher but also a guru of sorts. These links between the two generations were best symbolized in the establishment by Groulx and his younger followers of the trappings of a historical profession in Quebec with the creation of the Institut d'histoire de l'Amérique française in 1946 and the Revue d'histoire de l'Amérique française in the following year.

Many of Groulx's activities during this period revealed a historian who had kept up to date with the major developments in his profession. However, Groulx, much like his Quebec counterparts in other fields, was occasionally only a lukewarm supporter of scientific research. Groulx's less scientific side was evident, for instance, in his apparent satisfaction with the publication in 1944 of a new edition of François-Xavier Garneau's Histoire du Canada, in which Hector Garneau backtracked on many of the substantive and technical improvements that he had introduced thirty years earlier. As well, Groulx came across as somewhat less than fully cognizant of modern historical techniques in his role as organizer of a second Semaine d'histoire in 1945 – a conference that did not entirely reflect the changes in historical writing, on both sides of the Atlantic, since 1925.

If Groulx's own career during this period indicated considerable, if not complete, sympathy for 'modern' ideas, he was only reflecting certain larger trends within Quebec society. For instance, his personal voyage towards a greater, albeit qualified, appreciation of the value of scientific methods paralleled changes taking place within such institutions as the caisses populaires and the Catholic trade unions. As we saw in the previous chapter, these organizations had been established, to a considerable degree, to isolate Quebecers from such twentieth-century developments as massive immigration and centralized bureaucratic control. While neither entirely abandoned its nationalistic mandate, by the end of the Second World War both had become more open to Quebecers who neither spoke French nor professed Catholicism. Moreover, both had been reorganized so as to concentrate power in head offices with a mandate to manage affairs in a modern, rational manner.[6] Much like Groulx, the caisses and the Catholic trade unions retained a commitment to the betterment of a people defined by their religion and their language, but this goal did not necessarily conflict with an embrace of modern modes of behaviour.

Groulx's historical writing and his other activities to establish a historical profession in Quebec between 1925 and 1950 reflected his ties to both 'science' and the 'nation.' There is little evidence that his young protégés were particularly bothered by this mixture of influences, which placed Groulx in the mainstream of both the larger historical profession and Quebec's intellectual life. Because the younger historians shared so much of Groulx's view of the past, there is good reason to avoid the Whiggish notions of constant improvement in historical writing that tend to creep into historiographical analysis whenever professionals emerge to replace relative amateurs such as Groulx.[7] The priest-historian and his young followers were united by certain notions of 'scientific' research, which may have been more highly developed in the generation that came in during the 1940s. Nevertheless, the technical improvements introduced by Frégault and his peers could not entirely eliminate the role of the historian in reconstructing the past based on his own view of the world. For Groulx, as for his successors, there was no escape from the inherently subjective nature of all historical writing.

II

Lionel Groulx was even more clearly the focus of the small community of Quebec historians over the twenty years following the first Semaine d'histoire than had been the case prior to 1925. Following Thomas Chapais's retirement in 1930, Groulx was effectively the only university professor of Quebec history in the province, a situation that did not really change until the hiring of Guy Frégault at the Université de Montréal in 1943. Accordingly, when the University of Ottawa needed to find someone to provide a series of lectures on Canadian history, Groulx stepped in to fill the void over the course of 1933–4, and when the Société St-Jean-Baptiste of Quebec City wanted to supplement the meagre offerings at Laval, particularly after Chapais retired, Groulx consented to offer public lectures outside the university between 1937 and 1941. When Groulx first agreed to accept the Quebec City offer, he did so only after consulting with his friend Abbé Albert Tessier, who had stepped in to fill Chapais's shoes. It is unlikely, however, that Groulx would have been so considerate had the Laval lecturer at the time been Abbé Arthur Maheux, who replaced Tessier in 1938.

Groulx always indicated considerable respect for Chapais as a historian, even though he did not share the Laval professor's conception of Quebec's past. As we have seen, on Chapais's death in 1947, Groulx agonized over writing an assessment of the former's life, fearing that it would be overly negative towards someone who had approached the discipline in a professional fashion. Towards Maheux, however, who shared Chapais's belief in the providential role of the Conquest and who campaigned during the Second World War for cordial relations between francophones and anglophones, Groulx did not indicate the slightest hint of professional respect. Writing to Abbé Tessier, Groulx predictably complained about Maheux's penchant for ignoring the sins of the English conquerors. More significantly, however, he went on to condemn his lack of professionalism: 'What are we supposed to think about a history professor who hardly ever sets foot inside a building housing archival collections?'[8]

Maheux's unwillingness to engage in archival research did not stop him, however, from either lecturing or writing about Quebec history, in both cases distinguishing himself more by the strength of his anglophilia than by any new insight. The superior of the Séminaire de Québec, commenting in 1941 on the close of a series of Canadian history lectures given by Maheux at Laval, noted that the professor had made 'certain statements about the nature of history teaching in our colleges which created quite an uproar. He insisted that this teaching was so anti-English that it could not help but make our youth feel hatred towards England.'[9] In the published version of the same lectures, which appeared as *Ton histoire est une épopée*, Maheux emphasized the way in which the English had been the best of conquerors when compared with real barbarians such as Mussolini and Hitler. Accordingly, Maheux characterized the period of the Conquest as having been 'idyllic.'[10] As one of the more moderate of Maheux's critics observed: 'The author raises questions about our difficulties, but he offers no solutions. He is so preoccupied with sugar-coating our history that he ends up discussing the problems of other people at length. When it comes to dealing with the various calamities that have marked our own history, he either glosses over them or ignores them altogether.'[11]

Maheux returned to many of the same themes a few years later when, as a means of encouraging unity in the midst of war, he published another series of lectures, *Pourquoi sommes-nous divisés?* (Why Are We Divided?). Once again, he insisted that Canadian unity was constantly being undermined by the teaching of history in Quebec in a fashion that encouraged hatred. Groulx, correctly perceiving Maheux's comments as directed towards him, responded with a pamphlet of his own – *Pourquoi nous sommes divisés* (Why We Are Divided). Groulx's brochure, much like Maheux's lectures, had more to do with political issues than with the way in which history should be studied. Nevertheless, Groulx did make the effort to argue that he had always tried to present 'objective and accurate history.' A copy of Groulx's pamphlet, annotated by Maheux, has survived, and while the latter made well over one hundred comments in the margins, he had nothing to say in response to Groulx's passing comment about historical method, perhaps because Maheux did not think in such terms.[12]

Years after the end of the war, Maheux wrote to a friend complaining about Groulx's historical writing, noting that it contained 'many errors regarding facts and dates. Gustave Lanctot tells me that he could write a complete book dealing with the mistakes of M. Groulx. In any event, I have never written about these problems, and I have only spoken about them in private, but never in public.' One wonders, however, if Maheux chose not to engage in public debate about historical practices because of his own limitations in this area.[13]

More prolific but no more insightful than Maheux was Robert Rumilly, who published ten volumes on Quebec history in the 1930s, before embarking in 1940 on his *Histoire de la province de Québec*, which, when finished, comprised forty-one volumes, containing ten thousand pages. Rumilly had no training as a historian, and never held a teaching position of any kind, earning his living through much of the 1930s and 1940s in various capacities with the dominion government in Ottawa. Accordingly, much like Maheux, Rumilly did not distinguish himself either by dedication to archival research or, more generally, by any appreciation of currents of change within the historical profession.

Pierre Trépanier, one of the few Quebec historians of the past twenty years to have viewed Rumilly as a historian worthy of respect, remarked, with some justice, that *Histoire de la province de Québec* was the first large-scale study of post-Confederation Quebec history. Indeed, until the emergence of the revisionists in the 1970s, most Quebec historical writing concentrated on either the French régime or the years immediately after the Conquest. Rumilly's focus on modern Quebec did not lead him, however, to ground his work in modern historical techniques. Though Trépanier described Rumilly's multi-volume history as 'a scientific work,' based on 'sources which were solid, copious and varied,' Rumilly was in fact averse to using footnotes, thus making it difficult to know precisely what documents he consulted. Trépanier also pointed to Rumilly's use of interviews with public figures of note. However, it is impossible to pass judgment on the reliability of this evidence, since Rumilly conveniently promised anonymity to his confidants. Jean Blain was probably fairly close to the mark when he observed that 'Rumilly turned his nose up at the idea of history as a scientific discipline.'[14]

By and large, Rumilly's works emphasized individuals, in particular religious and lay heroes who had provided direction for Quebec society. This biographical orientation was evident not only in his book-length treatments of such figures as Louis-Joseph Papineau, Honoré Mercier, and Maurice Duplessis, but also in his large-scale history of Quebec, roughly half of whose volumes were organized around the lives of great leaders such as George-Étienne Cartier, who was featured in the first volume. To a certain degree, these works read like chronicles of great men, but along the way Rumilly also managed to indicate his own perspective on Quebec society. In this regard, the Martinique-born Rumilly reflected his strong sympathies for the nationalism of Charles Maurras's Action française movement, which he had absorbed during his early life, spent in France. Rumilly, as one might expect from his infatuation with Maurras, was ill-disposed towards democracy, which, he believed, had allowed French society to fall under the control of the godless forces of the left. In 1928, following the papal condemnation of Action française, Rumilly emigrated to Quebec, which he imagined to be a 'pure' version of the now-debased France that he was happy to escape.

Rumilly's historical writing presented Quebec as the homeland of a French-Canadian 'race' under siege from both the anglophone majority in Canada and, more generally, the forces of modernity evident throughout the Western world. In the first volume of *Histoire de la province de Québec*, he professed his admiration for 'the men who [had been] sent by Providence to lead [the French-Canadian] people to fulfill their destiny.'[15] Accordingly, the subsequent volumes sang the praises of the great men who had tried to protect French-speaking Quebecers from their enemies. Rumilly was particularly well inclined towards Henri Bourassa, whom he compared to Charles Maurras, the historian's hero from his days in France. Though Bourassa never quite attained the level of Maurras, 'the creator of a new humanism,' the two men were still united by the 'breadth of their visions and their selflessness. Bourassa wanted to see French Canadians become a proud people who might command the respect of the Anglo-Saxons.'[16] In the end, however, even the efforts of the great nationalist leaders could never quite bring about the liberation of Quebec from the forces of darkness. Writing about Quebec in the aftermath of the provincial election of 1939, which had seen the defeat of Maurice Duplessis, one of Rumilly's heroes, the historian wrote: 'Quebec had been blackmailed [by the dominion government] and had voted out of fear ... We have to realize that we form the minority and will have to submit to the will of the majority. Neither Mercier nor Bourassa was entirely able to overcome this reality ... Poor, beloved province of Quebec, deceived by the politicians, exploited by the financiers .... Poor, beloved province of Quebec, I believe that I would probably love you less if you did not appear, from time to time, so vulnerable and so pitiful.'[17]

Rumilly concentrated on the challenges to the survival of a people whose way of life had been built on 'two pillars: the French culture and the Catholic faith.'[18] Starting from this premise, he judged the history of Quebec as a largely doomed effort to maintain the society established in the St Lawrence valley in the seventeenth century. No matter how hopeless the dream, however, Rumilly was sympathetic to the struggle for the survival of this purer form of French culture, and such feelings also led him, in the aftermath of the Second World War, to aid in the rescue of Nazi collaborators from France who were seeking a safe haven in Canada. Rumilly viewed Vichy, much as he had viewed Quebec on his arrival in Canada, as offering an opportunity to recreate an older, purer France that had been lost. Accordingly, when the war was over Rumilly formed part of a group of Quebecers who assisted such people as Jacques Dugé, comte de Bernonville, who had been the right-hand man of Klaus Barbie, better known as the 'butcher of Lyons' for his actions in occupied France during the war. From Rumilly's perspective, Bernonville was an honourable man who was being unfairly hounded by ruthless Communists.[19]

While Groulx apparently saw eye to eye with Rumilly on a number of matters, including the need to rescue Bernonville, the Université de Montréal professor had little respect for Rumilly as a historian.[20] Commenting on Rumilly's biography of Papineau, Groulx remarked that it was 'pleasantly written, but not very enlightening.'[21] He was similarly dismissive of Rumilly's treatment of Henri Bourassa, noting that it was a work which described the evolution of Bourassa's thinking 'without explaining very much.'[22] In fact, Groulx thought so little of Rumilly that he marginalized the latter in his memoirs, not even allotting him the brief biographical sketch accorded to almost anyone with whom he had had dealings. Even though Groulx may have had more in common with Rumilly than Maheux on a wide array of political and social issues, he held both of his contemporaries in equally low esteem in terms of the writing of history, viewing both as little more than amateurs.

III

Given the nature of Maheux and Rumilly's scholarship, if that is the right word, one can perhaps understand Carl Berger's conclusion that 'the main lines of French-Canadian historical writing [were] remote from some of the chief developments in English-Canadian historiography in the inter-war years.' For Berger, most Quebec historians were preoccupied with mythologizing their national experience, leaving to their English-Canadian counterparts, such as Donald Creighton and Harold Innis, the task of looking beyond 'the personal history of heroes and great figures ... [to reveal] the sordid economic motivation behind activities once glorified as feats of adventurous explorations.'[23] In fact, however, the work of Lionel Groulx, Quebec's one full-time professional historian throughout this period, indicated more contact with developments in the larger discipline than Berger's dismissive comments would suggest.

The broad outlines of Groulx's view of the past did not change during this period. He still characterized Quebecers as a people who had largely been left to struggle for their survival under both the French and the English regimes. Typical of Groulx's approach was his 1942 speech on the one-hundredth anniversary of Louis-Hippolyte LaFontaine's accession, along with Robert Baldwin, to the rank of co–prime minister. From Groulx's perspective, LaFontaine had embodied the indomitable will of Quebecers to fight on in spite of all odds. In the few short years since the imposition of the Union of the Canadas on French speakers, LaFontaine had managed to gain a certain equality for his people. This achievement, contrary to what others such as Chapais and Maheux might have claimed, was not a gift from a 'generous empire,' but rather a product of the hard work 'of our fathers.'[24]

Groulx remained convinced that historians needed to construct a view of the past that would encourage Quebecers to continue their struggle for survival as a people. Nevertheless, there were some subtle but significant changes in his approach, which reflected his interest in developments in the discipline on both sides of the Atlantic, as well as his ongoing commitment to archival research. His ability to alter his view of Quebec's past was particularly evident in his recasting in 1930 of *La naissance d'une race*, a volume of his lectures at the Université de Montréal which had first appeared in 1919.[25]

Serge Gagnon, with characteristic exaggeration, identified the first edition of *La naissance* as representative of the primitive state of Quebec historical writing at the end of the First World War. He arrived at this conclusion through a selective reading of the 1919 text, which allowed him to assert that Groulx had portrayed a New France largely devoid of conflict. In particular, Gagnon claimed that Groulx had 'hushed up the quarrels between the church and the state. This priest-historian's colony [was] a unanimous, [conflict-free] society where the civil power [lived] in harmony with the clergy.'[26] It is difficult, however, to square Gagnon's assertion with Groulx's lengthy discussion of church-state conflict. Referring to the early bishops in the colony, Groulx asked: 'Didn't they have to struggle against the gallicanism which sought to have the state dominate the church? During the reign of Louis XIV there were regulations regarding religious processions and the distribution of holy bread; one even had to receive special permission to recruit two new sisters to serve as nurses in the hospital in Quebec City.'[27]

Gagnon was closer to the mark in criticizing Groulx for the way in which the author of *La naissance* had insisted that the French Canadian people had long constituted a homogeneous 'race' blessed with both a providential mission and an Arcadian existence seemingly detached from material concerns. Curiously, however, Gagnon had nothing to say about the second edition (1930) of *La naissance d'une race*, in which claims such as these were either purged or drastically altered. In the preface to the new edition, Groulx was particularly eager to respond to critics who had been bothered by his use of the term 'race' both in the title and throughout the text. He noted: 'Numerous critics have taken me to task for the inappropriate use of the term "RACE" when applied to the French-Canadian people. These critics have been quick to refer to the work of ethnologists on this question. Let me make myself clear. I never meant to suggest that French Canadians constituted a race in an anthropological sense.'[28]

Throughout the 1930 edition Groulx consistently altered passages from the original version which had suggested that Quebecers formed a race, defined along genetic lines, with qualities that set them apart from ordinary people. For instance, in the first edition he had referred to the early French immigrants to New France as having constituted 'a superior race,' while in the second they were merely 'a group of people with some superior qualities.'[29] In line with this change, Groulx purged a phrase from the 1919 text pertaining to the 'powerful hereditary traits' which had moulded the first French-speaking settlers.[30] Moreover, while he had referred to these colonists in 1919 as having constituted 'a homogeneous group with many admirable qualities, ... who had been chosen due to their deeply held faith,' he now saw them as merely a group of 'very honourable people.'[31]

Despite these changes, Quebec historians have continued to condemn *La naissance d'une race* because of Groulx's use of the word 'race.'[32] Such criticisms were based, to a certain degree, on an anachronistic use of the term, with critics writing after 1945 assuming that it had the same connotations in the interwar period that it would take on later. In a similar caution against anachronism, Yves Gingras has defended Frère Marie-Victorin's use of the same term, noting that the botanist employed it only to 'make reference to a community, a nation, or a people, and not to advance any racist theory.'[33]

On a different level, Groulx took some responsibility for the way in which his historical work would be read by producing a large body of material during the 1920s and 1930s, most of which had nothing to do with history and in which he advanced a point of view that was highly intolerant, to say the least. Curiously, at the same time that he was apparently editing out references to racial superiority from *La naissance d'une race*, he was, according to Esther Delisle in *The Traitor and the Jew*, commenting on the racial inferiority of Jews. Without making any apologies for Groulx's hate-mongering, it is worth noting that Groulx frequently came across as less intolerant in his historical writings, which he saw as destined for consumption by a highly educated audience, than he did in his more popular writings and lectures, which were designed to mobilize the masses. Groulx was not being disingenuous when he commented in 1961 that he distinguished 'between those who write history and those who teach it.' While the former had a responsibility to be 'objective,' the latter needed to foster a sense of patriotism among Quebecers.[34]

Consistent with Groulx's softening of his initial view of the first Canadiens as a racially superior people with a providential mandate, he more generally marginalized the role of religious factors in the establishment of New France, in the process paying more attention to material concerns. The 1930 edition of *La naissance d'une race* contained references to numerous works published since 1919, which provided the larger economic context in which settlement had occurred. Moreover, Groulx inserted new passages to recognize the impact of such economic factors. He observed, for instance, in 1930 that 'the French penetration to the heart of the continent was based as much upon missionary zeal as it was inspired by the search for commercial gain.'[35]

Quite aside from his recasting of *La naissance d'une race*, Groulx also displayed greater openness to the role of economic factors in his reconsideration of the place of Dollard des Ormeaux in the history of New France. During the 1910s, Groulx, along with other nationalist leaders, had developed a cult around Dollard for the way in which he and a small band of followers had given their lives in 1660 to fight against the Iroquois at the battle of Long-Sault. In the nationalist rendition of this story, Dollard and his colleagues knowingly embarked on a suicidal mission to dissuade the Natives from attacking the nearby, fledgling evangelical colony of Ville-Marie, later known as Montreal. In 1919 Groulx argued that Dollard had been driven to act in such a heroic manner by 'mysterious and supernatural forces.'[36] The history professor called on Quebecers to emulate Dollard and dedicate themselves to the defence of the nation, and he linked himself to Dollard's cause by sponsoring pilgrimages to the site of the battle of Long-Sault and by encouraging the building of monuments in honour of Dollard both at Long-Sault and in Montreal. Moreover, Groulx occasionally used the names of Dollard's comrades from Long-Sault when looking for pseudonyms for articles, usually dealing with contemporary affairs. Consequently, it is little wonder that some commentators have defined Groulx's work as a historian through his championing of the cause of Dollard in the late 1910s. Carl Berger, for instance, remarked that Dollard stood 'at the centre of Groulx's vision of the past.'[37]

Berger failed, however, to consider the way in which Groulx had, by the 1930s, altered his view of the Dollard affair, just as he had revised *La naissance d'une race*. The spark that led to Groulx's recasting of Dollard's story was an article by E.R. Adair, a historian at McGill University, who argued that Dollard had been neither very heroic nor very successful. In Adair's rendition, Dollard had not set out to sacrifice his life for the sake of the nation, but rather had hoped to ambush Iroquois who were diverting the fur trade from Montreal. As for the suicidal nature of the mission, Adair dwelled on the way in which the young Frenchman's own incompetence as a soldier had led to his death. The McGill professor was not even willing to concede that Dollard had deterred further attacks against the French colony. Rather, he found that Dollard's bungling had encouraged further Iroquois attacks 'either in revenge for those losses [at Long-Sault] or [because they were] emboldened by their victory over Dollard ... As a saviour of his country, Adam Dollard, Sieur des Ormeaux, must be relegated to the museum of historical myths.'[38]

There were numerous reactions to Adair's claims, all of which focused on the nature of the historical evidence in question.[39] Quite aside from the issues under debate, the grounds for historical discussion had evolved considerably from the late 1910s, when Dollard's actions could be justified largely on the basis of religious faith. Groulx responded in two articles published originally in Le Devoir.[40] He argued that Dollard's place in history could be established through observation of 'a basic principle of historical scholarship.' While Adair had based his case on witnesses who were in the colony at the time of Dollard's exploits, Groulx preferred the testimony of witnesses who had arrived in Montreal shortly after the Battle of Long-Sault and who had been in a position to consider 'a variety of valuable sources' so as to 'play one off against another.'[41] Needless to say, such a selection of evidence could be self-serving, but Groulx, no less than Adair, was playing the game according to the modern rules of historical scholarship.

Groulx used this evidence to paint a picture similar to the one he had presented in 1919. He persisted in believing that Dollard and his friends had set out with full knowledge that they were unlikely to return – this in spite of the fact that there had long been considerable evidence indicating that Dollard's party had had no such suicidal intent. Groulx also continued to believe that Dollard had saved the colony through his actions, and in this regard he was supported by less nationalistic historians such as Gustave Lanctot.[42] More significant, however, were the ways in which Groulx had transformed Dollard by the 1930s. The hero of Long-Sault was no longer depicted solely as a mystical figure; rather he was now someone whose actions needed to be understood in the context of the 'intense commercial rivalry [for furs] which was one of the root causes for Iroquois hostility towards the French.'[43] Years later Groulx regretted that he had not placed even greater emphasis on the 'fur hypothesis' that he had raised.[44]

Groulx's newfound interest in economic interpretations was similarly evident in other works that he produced between the wars. For instance, in a volume published on the four-hundredth anniversary of Jacques

Cartier's first voyage to North America, Groulx concentrated first on 'the economic requirements of Europe in the Middle Ages,' only later turning to 'moral or spiritual concerns.'[45] Even more important in the long term was Groulx's 1931 lecture, 'La déchéance de notre classe paysanne,' which, as we shall see, had a considerable effect on the work of Maurice Séguin and his colleagues at the Université de Montréal in the 1940s and 1950s. In this lecture Groulx linked the proletarianization of Quebecers to the decline in the province's agricultural economy. Groulx placed responsibility for this decline with the Conquest. On one level, he blamed the British rulers for assisting English-speaking merchants involved with the staple trades, to the exclusion of supporting Quebec agriculture, which had been left 'to its own devices for far too long; it had become a marginal activity, which lacked the means for its own renewal.'[46] English culpability also extended to the conquerors' monopolization of new lands and subversion of the seigneurial system. Quebec became 'a land in which agricultural activity could not expand,' leaving little choice but a move to factories either at home or in New England.[47]

During this period, Groulx became a firm believer in the central role of economic and social factors, and in line with this more secular approach to the past he reassessed the influence of the church in Quebec history. As we have seen, Groulx pushed religious motivations a bit to the side in both his revision of *La naissance d'une race* and his volume celebrating the voyages of Jacques Cartier. Perhaps even more significant, however, was his reinterpretation of the role of the clergy in the Rebellions of 1837–8.

Up to 1926, when he published a series of articles in *Action française*, Groulx had subscribed to the authorized version of the rebellions, which found that, because of clerical condemnation of Papineau's movement, only a small number of Quebecers had participated.[48] By 1926, however, Groulx had begun to change his tune, still insisting that the people and the clergy had been on the same side, but now reinterpreting their respective roles in the affair. He was now far less categorical about the unwillingness of Quebecers to take up arms against constituted authority, though he suggested that fear of reprisals for not participating in the rebellion was often what had pushed people to rise up. 'Contemporary accounts point to the role of charivaris in intimidating lukewarm supporters of the rebellions. Those who were hesitant had to endure visits in the middle of the night from bands of masked men, carrying torches and rifles and ready to mete out a beating.'[49] If a Quebecer succumbed to these pressures, however, he did not do so, according to Groulx's new interpretation, in open defiance of the clergy. Groulx now argued that there had never really been a direct proscription against rebellious activity prior to the start of the uprising, that numerous priests had been sympathetic to the Patriote cause, and that there had been general reluctance on the part of curés to speak out against the rebels, lest they alienate their flock.

Groulx took his reinterpretation a bit further in 1936 in several new essays related to the risings. In one of these pieces, he tried to rehabilitate Papineau, long an object of clerical scorn. While Groulx did not try to hide the fact that Papineau had made some explicitly anti-clerical speeches, he generally forgave the Patriote leader, who had been denied a sufficiently rigorous Catholic education in his youth. Moreover, he found evidence in Papineau's life of a passably good Catholic lurking just beneath the surface. Groulx believed that Papineau had long suffered from nothing more than some intellectual doubts about Catholicism and that there was evidence that such doubts had dissipated over the course of the politician's life.[50] To support his case, Groulx even produced evidence that Papineau had had 'excellent relations with his bishop ... and with at least one of the curés [near his home of] Montebello.'[51]

The final element in Groulx's new conceptualization of the rebellions came with his assertion that Quebecers who participated had done so not so much out of fear of reprisals, as he had contended in 1926, but in response to a deteriorating economic and social situation. In a telling statement about his changing view of the past, Groulx now insisted that it was necessary to consider 'une histoire intégrale' so as to view 'the past in all of its complexity. We need to take into account economic, social and cultural factors.' Of these causes, however, Groulx was certain that the most significant was 'a fundamental economic problem.'[52]

In making such remarks, the Montreal professor was simply reflecting the concerns of historians on both sides of the Atlantic between the wars. For instance, when Groulx spoke of the need for 'une histoire intégrale,' one could hear echoes of the Annales approach, which received institutional status in 1929, when Marc Bloch and Lucien Febvre launched their journal *Annales d'histoire économique et sociale* following nearly a decade of close collaboration.[53] Groulx was well aware of the work of the two Frenchmen who sought to challenge the *école méthodique* of Langlois and Seignobos, whose narrow interest in political events was discussed above, in the previous chapter.[54] Moreover, to the extent that Groulx had begun to give a certain primacy to economic factors, his work also bore the mark of American historians such as Charles Beard, who were busily advancing an economic interpretation of their country's past.

By the 1930s, as he was responding to the widespread trend throughout the historical profession to move beyond simplistic explanations for human behaviour, Groulx also seemed increasingly aware of the tentative nature of any historical interpretation. In terms of the saga of Dollard, Groulx remarked that he was prepared to alter any element of the story 'the moment that someone [came] up with irrefutable evidence to alter our current view of the affair.'[55] In a similar fashion, he closed his preface to the new edition of *La naissance* with the observation that 'only those who do not understand the craft of history would dare speak about definitively understanding the past.'[56] In his memoirs, Groulx characterized the period during which he revised *La naissance* as one in which he had experienced 'the self-doubt of the historian who knows that it is impossible to recreate the past exactly as it existed ... I have often thought of History as a sort of museum with moveable walls which became harder to reach the more that one tried to touch them. Sometimes I imagined a palace whose windows grew larger the more one tried to look inside. These windows let in filtered light that only revealed obscure corners and impenetrable passageways.'[57]

Groulx's expressions of self-doubt were reflected in his reservations about the Annalistes, Bloch and Febvre, whom he found to have been too self-confident about the possibility of understanding the past as it really was. During a trip to Paris in 1931 he raised the question about the Annalistes with the historian Georges Goyau, who expressed doubts about their scientific pretensions. Groulx came away from this meeting more convinced than ever that history was 'a very imprecise science.'[58] If Groulx's scepticism put him at odds with the Annalistes, it also drew him closer to the American progressive historians of the period. As Peter Novick has observed, historians such as Beard and Carl Becker were prepared to 'break with the quest for certitude' and to 'accept the contingent nature of knowledge.'[59] In this as in other contexts, Groulx appears to have been a historian in the mainstream of developments in the profession.

IV

Through much of the 1920s and 1930s Abbé Groulx was for all intents and purposes the only full-time professional historian devoted to the history of French-speaking Quebec, a situation that he did everything he could to transform. Beginning in the 1930s and continuing into the next decade, he devoted considerable energy to building the infrastructure, both within and outside the university, for the study and teaching of Quebec history on a 'scientific' basis. At the Université de Montréal he first directed these efforts at grooming his possible successor so that whoever might replace him would be spared 'the task of self-education for a craft which does not readily forgive improvisation.'[60]

Groulx looked initially to André Laurendeau, but Laurendeau in 1934 turned Groulx down, apparently telling the latter that his health, which had long been poor, was not up to the 'demands made of the professional historian.'[61] Next Groulx turned to Jacques Le Duc, a promising student, whom he succeeded in talking into a career in history. Le Duc was so effectively convinced by Groulx that he wrote to his maître in 1937: 'I cannot imagine anything better than succeeding you. If possible, I would like to imitate you in all regards.'[62] Unfortunately, Le Duc died in 1938, forcing Groulx to offer his succession to Wilfrid Morin, a priest who also died prematurely. Groulx's fourth candidate would prove, however, to be the professional colleague that he had long been seeking.

Groulx first came into contact with Guy Frégault in 1937, when the latter, only nineteen years old, wrote to his maître about the need for 'a Laurentian revolution.'[63] Frégault, like other young Quebecers of the late 1930s such as André Laurendeau, was deeply influenced by the French intellectual movement of personalism, which, as John Hellman has noted, is not easily defined. Hellman pointed to one philosopher who referred to personalism as an 'anti-ideology,' while another 'provided little help when he condemned even the effort to define personalism as a "philosophy."' Hellman observed that the 'most prominent personalists could do no better than to call for the affirmation of the "absolute value of the human person" ... [This] assertion was not simply an abstract affirmation of human dignity but rather a movement of defence against two antithetical threats: individualism, and its manifestation, liberal capitalism, and communalism, and its manifestation, communism. It mirrored the desperate effort of intellectuals in the early nineteen-thirties to navigate a "third way" between capitalism and communism. Thus it was a philosophical enterprise at once vague in what exactly it would like to set up and precise in what it did not want to occur.'[64]

Frégault's passionate commitment to personalism was evident in the way in which he and his close friends Gérald Payer and Jean-Marie Parent formed a Quebec cell of the segment of the French personalist movement, which had coalesced around the journal *L'Ordre nouveau*. As Frégault wrote to Payer, 'Only an efficient and coherent revolution, inspired by *L'Ordre nouveau*, can hope to give the individual his rightful place in the world.'[65] In order to gain credibility for their movement, Frégault wrote to Groulx, hoping to receive the latter's blessing for the personalist revolution, which would seek 'an unconditional respect for the dignity of man ... We will do everything we can for the total liberation of the Laurentian [that is, Quebec] people. We seek to be a totally free people in a country which is free in its own right.' It was not enough for Quebecers, as a collectivity, to be free; it was also crucial for individuals to develop to their full potential.[66]

In light of this letter, written in the spirit of youthful enthusiasm, it is difficult to argue with those who have claimed that Frégault's orientation in the late 1930s was dramatically different from that of Abbé Groulx. Christian Roy, for instance, has observed that while Groulx was concerned only with the survival of the nation as an entity, Frégault emphasized the role of the individual as well.[67] What is much more difficult to maintain, however, is that Frégault's early contact with personalism was the driving force in his historical writing from the very beginning of his career. Roy has advanced such a proposition, noting that Frégault completely overturned Groulx's conception of Quebec history, which focused on 'a rather sedentary peasantry committed to the patient occupation of the land where it had taken root.' Instead, Frégault, nourished by personalist thinking, depicted a people who embodied 'the risk-taking and independence of the fur trappers.'[68] Jean Lamarre has similarly observed that Frégault, even before he had committed himself to the life of a historian, had already developed 'a distinctive view of the place of man within his larger society and of the role of the historian in describing the past. These views placed him at odds with the conventional wisdom of the time and influenced, in a fundamental manner, all of his subsequent works.'[69]

These authors provided little more than lip service to the notion that Frégault owed a significant debt to Groulx at the outset of his career, in the process seeking to minimize the latter's impact on Frégault, arguably Quebec's first professional historian. In fact, there is considerable evidence that Frégault remained closely tied to Groulx during his infatuation with personalism and that he had already pushed aside some of his passion for a personalist conception of Quebec history by the time his first works appeared in the 1940s. It is telling, for instance, that even though Frégault was troubled by Groulx's nationalism in the late 1930s he still felt obliged to send Groulx a copy of his outline for 'the Laurentian revolution.'[70] Moreover, when Groulx did not dismiss the young man's ideas out of hand, Frégault excitedly reported to Payer that Groulx 'supports us 100%.'[71] By the start of the 1940s, however, as Frégault turned towards a career in history, his contact with a youthful kindred spirit such as Payer had all but halted, to end completely in 1946, by which time he could refer to Groulx in unambiguously positive terms and to the late 1930s with a certain 'nostalgia.'[72]

Following his pronouncement regarding 'the Laurentian revolution,' Frégault pursued his studies at the Université de Montréal, where he caught the eye of both Groulx and Groulx's old nemesis from the Semaine d'histoire of 1925, Mgr Emile Chartier, who was dean of the faculty of letters and vice-rector of the university. While Groulx wanted Frégault to pursue a career in history, Chartier hoped that the young man would study literature. Chartier would probably have prevailed had it not been for the German invasion of France, where the vice-rector had wanted to send Frégault for literary studies. Groulx took advantage of the new situation to make Frégault an offer: 'I would very much like you to succeed me. This would allow you to pursue a work that I have barely begun, having started far too late in life with too little formal training.'[73] He sent his protégé off to read such works as Seignobos and Langlois's manual on historical method while he arranged for Frégault's passage to Chicago, where he would pursue a doctorate at Loyola University.

Frégault was sent to work under the supervision of the Jesuit priest Jean Delanglez, described by Groulx as 'a true maître' who had both a passion for empirical research and appropriate Catholic sensibilities. Groulx considered having Frégault attend Harvard but decided against that option, fearing that his prized pupil would be lost 'in a crush of students.'[74] One suspects, however, that Harvard had the more serious liability of being too secular for Groulx's taste. While Delanglez could offer Frégault a taste of the professional world of historical research, the Chicago professor, being a priest, did not raise Groulx's own suspicions about the dangers lurking outside Quebec. Because he helped bridge the gap between an older Catholic order and newer approaches to history, Delanglez remained a favoured guest of Quebec's historical community, receiving invitations to lecture in both Montreal and Quebec City in the 1940s.

During his time at Chicago there is no evidence that Frégault remained in any way influenced by personalism. His letters to Groulx expressed nothing but appreciation for an introduction to the intricacies of historical research. In one such letter, the doctoral student wrote: 'Every day I am increasingly grateful that you steered me in the direction of history.'[75] Groulx could barely conceal his excitement about the prospect of the return of a disciple with appropriate professional credentials. Though there had been some vague talk during the 1930s about the establishment of a formally constituted history department at the Université de Montréal, Groulx had not discussed the prospect as likely until Frégault fell into his clutches.[76] Accordingly, in 1941 he wrote to his protégé: 'Start thinking about your role as a professor ... A number of us have been talking of late about the establishment of an Institut d'histoire. This rather small institute would serve as the first step in convincing both the political leaders and the university administrators to establish in Montreal an even larger institution dedicated to the History of Canada.'[77] Frégault responded enthusiastically, looking forward to the day when history might be taught at the university level so as to spread an understanding of the technical side of the discipline as well as its role in nourishing nationalistic sentiment. He was silent as to history's contribution to the liberation of the individual.[78]

Frégault returned to Montreal in 1942, having completed his doctoral dissertation in less than two years. He found, however, that the Institut d'histoire had not yet been established, thus leaving him at loose ends. Nevertheless, Frégault remained philosophical, writing to Groulx that he would wait for his chance 'to provide a national service through history.'[79] During 1942, Groulx arranged for Frégault to work at the provincial archives in Quebec City so that he might 'improve his technical skills and learn what technique alone cannot provide, an appreciation of the scientific dimensions of historical research.'[80] Groulx also ceded to Frégault the teaching of the *cours publics* that had been his since 1915. In 1943 Frégault was able to give up the archival post when he was accorded a more regular position within the university, providing 'the first course in historical methodology ever given in a Quebec university,' and in 1944 he was made a full-fledged university professor, albeit with responsibilities for literature until the establishment of the Institut d'histoire in 1946.[81]

Throughout these early years back in Quebec, Frégault showed no reluctance in expressing his allegiance to Groulx's conception of history. In 1942 he wrote to Chartier that he had been thoroughly seduced by 'the grandeur of the programme envisaged by the old maître.' Frégault wanted to 'stand on the shoulders of giants [such as Groulx] so that he might see as far as possible.'[82] Two years later, Frégault wrote to his patron: 'My goal is to channel my energies to build upon your work.'[83] In 1945, on the thirtieth anniversary of the start of Groulx's career as a university professor, Frégault characterized his benefactor's historical writings as 'grandiose, thought out with great courage and supported by the scientific approach.'[84]

In spite of these affirmations of loyalty, however, recent works on Quebec historiography have stressed the marginal significance of Groulx to Frégault, pointing instead to the personalist imprint on the latter's early works. While Jean Lamarre has admitted to 'the influence of Groulx and of traditional historical writing' on Frégault, he has insisted that 'other influences were much more important.' Lamarre emphasized 'the influence of personalism,' which had allowed Frégault to move away from 'Groulx's emphasis upon the providential and heroic dimensions of New France' so as to present Quebec before the Conquest 'in much more human terms.' In support of this claim, Lamarre quoted from a 1943 essay in which Frégault had argued that the 'Canadiens of the French regime "had other things to think about than acting as if they were supermen; they were normal human beings, who sought to live full lives much like ordinary people throughout the world."'[85]

Frégault's alleged interest in human beings instead of mythical characters was belied, however, by his first major work, his biography of Pierre Le Moyne d'Iberville, which had begun as a doctoral dissertation before its publication in 1944. The title of the work, *Iberville le conquérant*, in presenting Frégault's subject as a conqueror, hardly conjures up notions of an ordinary man. Frégault asserted at several points that his Iberville was more than 'a wild animal who charged headlong into battle against enemy positions; rather he was a wily leader who understood the importance of strategy.'[86] From Lamarre's point of view, it was the multidimensional character of Frégault's Iberville that distinguished the author as the 'personalist' historian, who had escaped from the clutches of Groulx's more heroic view of the Quebec past.

Iberville le conquérant, however, was largely a narrow account of the military triumphs of the Canadian-born Iberville against English interests across North America, without any concern for such factors as Iberville's own vested economic interest in expanding the French sphere of influence.[87] In fact, Frégault referred in passing to the fact that Iberville had been 'a brilliant businessman' only on the third to the last page of the book. By failing to transcend the heroic mould, Frégault did not entirely depart from Groulx's initial depiction of the actions of Dollard. Moreover, by bemoaning the way in which the French ultimately abandoned the Canadiens, Frégault was echoing Groulx's heroic view of the

Canadiens as a people at the mercy of a short-sighted French imperial policy that was too devoted to earning profits and too little concerned with the best interests of the settlers in the St Lawrence valley.[88]

Frégault's ongoing debt to Groulx was similarly evident in his second work, *La civilisation de la Nouvelle-France,* written entirely after his return from Chicago. While Frégault was somewhat more inclined than his maître to describe the Canadiens as a people willing both to live in the colony's cities and to uproot themselves from their farms, he was not prepared to take these points too far, concluding that the Canadiens' rootlessness was already in decline by the early eighteenth century. Accordingly, much like Groulx, Frégault could remark: 'The foundations of New France were established by anonymous workers who plugged away day after day on their land ... Our nation is rooted in the land and our ties of blood.'[89] On the basis of such passages, Pierre Tousignant concluded that 'in one of his first works, *La civilisation de la Nouvelle-France,* Frégault depicted Canadien society much as Groulx had presented it in *La naissance d'une race.'*[90]

Frégault returned from Chicago largely as Groulx would have wanted him. The young professor maintained much of his mentor's view of Quebec's past but could advance it with a firm understanding of the intricacies of historical research. While Frégault would depart quite markedly from his maître in later years, there was little evidence of the mark of personalism when he began to publish, which might help to explain his reluctance to have one of his early personalist-inspired essays from the 1930s reprinted some years later. He responded to the editor in question: 'I was nineteen years old when I wrote that piece; it is hardly representative of a long publishing career that began in earnest when I was twenty-five.'[91]

Groulx was sufficiently pleased with Frégault's orientation that the two spent the second half of the 1940s developing the infrastructure that might encourage Quebecers to study their past in an appropriately professional manner. As early as 1943 the two were busily working on a proposal for a history department at the Université de Montréal, which was finally accepted by the faculté des lettres in December 1946.[92] The Institut d'histoire began to operate in the following November, to 'encourage both the teaching of history and the carrying out of historical research on a scientific basis ... We will introduce the student to history and to certain allied disciplines, along the way introducing him to methodological questions.'[93]

From its inception, however, the Institut was also identified with the defence of national interests. Reflecting this perspective, Frégault agreed to head the department in part out of fear that if he did not do so 'a foreigner might take control.'[94] He viewed the Université de Montréal during this period as an institution that favoured French-born over Canadian professors. Accordingly, once in charge of the Institut d'histoire, he quickly moved to assemble 'a homogeneous group of historians.'[95] He wanted to hire men like himself, young, well-trained Quebecers, who had been similarly influenced by Groulx. In November 1946, a month before the Institut had obtained official approval, Frégault offered a position to Maurice Séguin, who was still Groulx's doctoral student, working on a thesis dealing with the economic implications of the Conquest. Séguin had come to Frégault's attention via an article that he had written for *Action nationale*, of which Frégault was director. On the basis of a single meeting, Frégault promised Séguin a post if he finished his thesis by the end of the 1946–7 academic year, in time for the opening of the Institut in the fall of 1947. Séguin did not make this deadline, but he did finish in the fall of 1947 and joined the staff part-time in 1948, before receiving a full-time position in 1950 following Groulx's retirement.

Frégault did not have much to go on when he made his offer to Séguin, except that the newcomer's background had been much like his own. The two were both born in 1918, and while Séguin had spent his first few years in Saskatchewan, his family moved to Montreal in 1922, settling in the working-class district of Saint-Vincent-de-Paul, not far from the Hochelaga district, where Frégault grew up. Both studied at the prestigious Collège Jean-de-Brébeuf, before moving on to the Université de Montréal.[96] From this point on, however, their paths diverged quite considerably. Groulx had quickly sized up Frégault's prospects as a historian and was instrumental in sending him off to Chicago. By contrast, Séguin took only a single course in history as an undergraduate and had to seek out Groulx when he got the idea of pursuing a doctorate on the role of French speakers in Quebec's economy during the century following the Conquest – a topic inspired by Groulx's 1931 essay, 'La déchéance de la classe paysanne,' discussed above.

Elements of Séguin's thesis bore the unmistakable mark of Groulx's essay.[97] Séguin, much like his supervisor, spent considerable time discussing obstacles, such as poor agricultural techniques and lack of access to land, that had hindered agricultural development after the Conquest and had contributed to the movement of French speakers off the land. Much more than Frégault, however, he was prepared to contest Groulx's conceptualization of Quebec history, claiming that his maître had viewed matters too narrowly. He insisted that the problems faced by Canadien farmers were not simply technical but had been exacerbated by inadequate markets. Taking not very subtle aim at his supervisor's work, Séguin noted: 'Previous works on the subject have focused upon the ease or difficulty of acquiring land, the sophistication or primitive nature of farming techniques. Rarely has anyone considered the question of markets. However, this issue warrants more than the odd paragraph that it has received in studies focused upon territorial expansion or agricultural techniques.' Séguin continually returned to the manner in which farming practices had been constrained by 'a weak market,' which reinforced a certain 'peasant mentality' and held the Quebec farmer back from trying to 'improve his standard of living.'[98]

Séguin placed himself even more squarely in opposition to his mentor by insisting on the need to consider the problems of agriculture in the context of the larger economy. 'The roots of the crisis cannot be found in the agricultural sector. To understand the abandonment of our farms, one has to look beyond questions pertinent to the accessibility and productivity of the land ... It is about time that we looked at the obstacles to our participation in commerce and industry.'[99] Séguin posited a certain 'normal' route that all economies passed through, whereby a predominantly agricultural population diversified into 'a variety of trades and professions.'[100] There was already evidence of a certain 'balance among farmers, manufacturers, merchants [and] professionals' prior to the Conquest, when 'the Canadiens figured among the most important businessmen in North America.'[101] Following 'the British Occupation,' however, all routes to commercial or industrial success were closed to the Canadiens, leaving them with little choice but to abandon the land to take jobs in factories run by English speakers, which reinforced 'their enslavement at the hands of the British.'[102]

To Séguin, this economic inferiority was an inevitable legacy of being conquered and was not something that could be overcome simply through hard work and determination, as Groulx had often asserted. Rather, from Séguin's perspective, the only hope for French speakers lay in a major restructuring of the economic relations between the majority and the minority in Quebec. Such a transformation, however, would have required the seizing of political power by francophones, another prospect that Séguin did not find very likely in light of the willingness of his people to work within the system. In this context, the young doctoral student was critical of Groulx's 'political romanticism,' which had led him to lionize men such as Louis-Hippolyte LaFontaine. As we have seen, Groulx went out of his way in 1942 to celebrate the centenary of LaFontaine's accession to political power – evidence to Groulx of the possibility of equality for French speakers if they only struggled hard enough. To Séguin, by contrast, 'Responsible government was little more than a political tool to cement the ties between the metropolis and the colony ... In politics, there could be no equality between the Canadiens, lacking any external assistance, and the British of North America who were bolstered by the most powerful empire in the world. The Canadiens' political subordination guaranteed their continued economic subordination.'[103]

Groulx was sufficiently hurt by Séguin's pointed criticism that he later justified his view of the role of LaFontaine in his *Mémoires*. He recalled: 'The young historians did not see matters as I did. With the flick of a wrist, they were prepared to topple men such as Louis-Hippolyte LaFontaine from their pedestals ... They claimed that the phony hero of 1842 only gave legitimacy to the myth that there might be collaboration between the two races on the basis of perfect equality.' Groulx argued that if historians considered LaFontaine in terms of the times in which he had lived, they would realize that he had achieved 'all that he could. What more could he have done? The young historians would be hard pressed to answer that question.' To Groulx, LaFontaine's achievement had given 'a second wind' to a defeated people and had led to an outpouring of nationalistic literature, including Garneau's *Histoire du Canada*. Even in economic terms, LaFontaine's decision to try to play the British game was better than the alternative of isolation 'in the ghetto of Lower Canada.'[104] Séguin, of course, did not share Groulx's article of faith. The young historian was openly in favour of Quebec's independence in the early 1940s, while Groulx was ambiguous on the issue. In fact, Séguin claimed in his thesis that had Quebecers been independent in the early nineteenth century they might have been free to 'industrialize in a manner that would have been least disruptive to their society.'[105]

Because of the political implications of Séguin's thesis, much has been made of the ways in which he not only departed from his mentor but improved on him. Jean Blain, for instance, in his preface to the published version of Séguin's thesis, pointed out how the doctoral student had broken with those such as Groulx whose views of Quebec's past were based on 'a narrow conception of nationalism, in which material concerns were ignored and the hand of God played a central role.'[106] Séguin contributed to the mythology by bragging that no one had objected to his theories at the defence of his thesis because the jury, composed of the collège classique professor Jean-Pierre Houle, along with Frégault and Groulx, did not understand the implications of his arguments.[107] Of course, there is another possibility – namely, that no one doubted the value of the more conventional parts of the thesis, which concentrated on the internal workings of Quebec agriculture. These sections, supported by considerable evidence, did not depart all that much from Groulx's point of view. However, Séguin's wide-ranging speculations about the impact of the Conquest, which amounted to little more than unsubstantiated assertions, may not have given rise to much discussion precisely because they were grounded in so little research. In any event, if no one understood what Séguin was arguing, then why did Houle and Séguin end up in a heated discussion during the defence over the role of LaFontaine?[108]

Unless one ignores the evolution of Groulx's writing during the interwar period, it is difficult to see how Séguin 'improved' on his supervisor in terms of observing the conventions of professional historical writing. Both Groulx and Séguin had strongly held views, and both tried, up to a point, to support their arguments with appropriate evidence. Moreover, there is little reason to overstate the extent to which Séguin broke from his maître in questions of interpretation. Though much has been made of Séguin's pessimistic interpretation of Quebec history, which became a cornerstone of the work of the historians who succeeded Groulx at the Université de Montréal, his thesis closed with an optimistic note that would have been worthy of Groulx. Observing that the population of Quebec had remained overwhelmingly French-speaking in spite of the devastation caused by 'British Occupation,' Séguin wondered whether the economic liberation of the Canadiens might not come about someday. He concluded: 'The Canadiens have reason to hold out hope.'[109] Curiously, Jean Lamarre, who insisted on the extent of Séguin's break with Groulx, made no reference to the significance of this closing remark, while Jean Blain conveniently dismissed it as an exception.[110]

Séguin may have parted company with Groulx in certain regards, but he never lost respect for his maître. Accordingly, he could not bring himself to publish his dissertation until 1970, three years after Groulx's death. Commenting in 1966 on his ties to Groulx, Séguin remarked: 'I could never enter into a public debate with the man who introduced me to history, who gave me the taste for history, and who was responsible for my career at the Université de Montréal.'[111] Groulx was not sufficiently bothered by Séguin's dissertation to make any effort to block his integration into the new history department; in fact, Groulx's retirement was prompted by his desire to make room for Séguin.[112]

If Frégault and Séguin proved to be Groulx's closest allies in establishing a truly professional history department, Michel Brunet, while less instrumental in getting the Institut off the ground, shared their strong links to the maître. The three young historians were born within seventeen months of one another, but, unlike his two future colleagues, Brunet displayed none of their youthful rebelliousness, perhaps because he alone hailed from a relatively well-to-do family. Both Frégault and Brunet first made contact with Groulx as teenagers, but while the former did so to try out some new ideas, the latter simply wanted to be in the same room with someone whom he had admired for a number of years. Brunet's sycophancy was evident in the way in which he fondly recalled having read aloud from Groulx's works 'in the privacy of my room with only my cat as an audience.'[113] When Brunet finally summoned up enough nerve to ask Groulx for a meeting, he wrote: 'I can only hope that this long cherished dream will soon become a reality. I hope that we might be able to meet, even though I have no right to take up your time. I am merely a disciple, a follower who would like to live up to your ideal but who despairs that he is not up to the task.'[114]

In the short term, Brunet was an enthusiastic supporter of Groulx's nationalist program. In fact, in a talk that he gave in 1936, Brunet echoed some of Groulx's sentiments when he referred to the enslavement of Quebecers at the hands of 'the English, the Americans, and the Jews.'[115] It would be another decade, however, before he would commit himself to advancing the nationalist cause, as had Groulx, through the vehicle of history. Throughout the greater part of the 1940s Brunet was a primary school teacher by day and a student at the Université de Montréal by night. He was nearing the completion of his master's degree in late 1946 when the university announced that it would be setting up a history department in the following academic year. Brunet proceeded to ask the dean of the faculté des lettres if a job might be available in the new department. Not surprisingly, the dean responded: '"My dear friend, you don't have a doctorate", to which Brunet replied: "Give me the means to secure a Ph.D. and I will return with one in hand!"'[116]

As improbable as it might seem, this conversation led to Brunet's gaining a Rockefeller Foundation grant to pursue doctoral studies at Clark University in Massachusetts beginning in the fall of 1947, just as the history department was opening its doors. Much like Frégault and other Quebecers of the time, Brunet went to the United States to secure his doctorate. When, in the spring of 1949, he finished his dissertation on mid-nineteenth-century Massachusetts politics, he was immediately hired to teach American history at the Université de Montréal in the following academic year. In communicating the good news to Brunet, Frégault noted that he was pleased to welcome another 'compatriot' to the staff.[117]

In greeting Brunet in such a manner, Frégault was restating his interest, first expressed in 1945, in assembling 'a homogeneous group of historians.'[118] Even though Brunet, unlike Frégault and Séguin, had had relatively little contact with Groulx prior to joining the department in the fall of 1949, he shared his colleagues' considerable respect for the views of the maître. If Brunet distinguished himself from his new colleagues, it was only in terms of the uncritical way in which he had absorbed some of Groulx's ideas.[119] By the end of the 1940s, Frégault had flirted with personalism and Séguin had begun to reconsider the maître's view of the Conquest. By contrast, Brunet had not yet shown any particular capacity for independent thinking. In spite of these differences, however, there was much that united the three original lay members of the department. The three were roughly the same age, had similar professional training, and retained close ties with Groulx. Frégault had every reason to believe that his department had begun as he had hoped it might.

V

At roughly the time when Groulx was creating a permanent structure for the study of Quebec history within the university, he was also trying to set up yet another institution with many of the same goals outside the Université de Montréal. Groulx announced his plans for the Institut d'histoire de l'Amérique française (hereafter IHAF) at a banquet held by the Société St-Jean-Baptiste de Montréal on 24 June 1946, on the occasion of both the national holiday of French-speaking Quebecers and the thirtieth anniversary of the permanent establishment of Groulx's university position.[120] From the very start, Groulx viewed the Institut as both a vehicle to advance certain nationalist aims and a research centre faithful to a conception of history as a science. He wanted to bolster 'the role of history in the life of the nation.' He recognized, however, that the historian was 'the servant of the truth,' and towards that end he wanted to assemble 'a team of researchers and authors who would busy themselves with the study of the history of the French-speaking people of America.'[121]

Groulx had long been committed to history in both its scientific and more popular guises, and he remained true to these twin goals in setting up the IHAF. In an interview published in *Le Devoir* in October 1946 Groulx was asked if he thought that this venture would strengthen 'the fraternal ties among the French of North America.' He responded: 'Yes and no. The historian cannot place his craft at the disposal of a cause, no matter how noble ... But even though historians should never take a pragmatic view of their work ... they cannot help but influence events by the way in which they describe the past. Yes, I do believe that the Institut d'histoire will provide important services to the larger French community.'[122]

In the course of the interview, Groulx described the IHAF as a centre for the training of professional historians, the housing of archives, and the publication of members' works. It was also designed to encourage the participation of amateur historians from 'all parts of French-speaking America' who would be organized into 'sections.'[123] Groulx imagined that these 'sections,' or regional historical societies, would communicate with the more professional historians at the Institut's offices in Montreal so as to allow the writing of local history 'with respect for the rules of historical methodology.'[124] One of his early efforts in this regard was the founding of a section in New England, which would assemble Franco-Americans interested in their past. Recognizing the diverse interests of the people whom Groulx hoped to bring together via the Institut, Adolphe Robert wrote from Manchester, New Hampshire: that 'Some people will find the collaboration of professionals such as you and amateurs like myself a bit odd.'[125]

The hybrid nature of the IHAF was similarly reflected in the backgrounds of the men, hand-picked by Groulx, who formed its initial board of directors, which held its first meeting at the priest's home on 13 December 1946, three days after the establishment of the history department had received final approval from the Université de Montréal.[126] Groulx, not surprisingly, was made president of the institute, and his protégés Frégault and Séguin vice-president and secretary-treasurer, respectively.[127] As for the rest of the directors, Groulx tried to create a certain balance between lay and clerical members, with each group holding roughly half of the seats. He also sought out men who had some link with historical writing, though none was a professional in the sense that either Frégault or Séguin was. Groulx wrote to Léo-Paul Desrosiers, head of the Montreal municipal library and author of works of popular history, asking him to serve, so that the board might be filled with 'real historians ... I know that I am asking much of someone who is already overburdened, but you have to understand that we do not have an overabundance of serious historians in our midst. The Institut will not be respected unless genuine historians figure among its leaders.'[128]

The remaining members of the board were much like Desrosiers – men with a link to history, but without proper professional training. Gérard Filteau was a school inspector who had written several volumes of popular history, while Antoine Roy was the provincial archivist. The five remaining directors, Antoine Bernard, Thomas Charland, Conrad Morin, Léon Pouliot, and Gordon Rothney, were history professors at the university level, though none had a PhD in history. In addition to their amateur status, they were united also by their insistence on the need for Quebecers to remain vigilant against the dangers posed by the English-speaking conquerors. Bernard was pleased to support 'a movement which is now needed more than ever to aid in the French resistance to assimilation in North America.'[129] The only English-speaking member, Gordon Rothney, a professor of history at Sir George Williams College, had been a sympathetic translator of Groulx's *Pourquoi nous sommes divisés*, written during the Second World War to counter the antithetical views of Arthur Maheux. Rothney is quoted as having remarked: 'Don't you think it would be a waste of time to translate Abbé Maheux? He doesn't tell us English anything we don't know and one can hardly take his proposals seriously. But Groulx lets us have it straight from the shoulder.'[130]

Groulx claimed that he had no choice but to select these men whom he identified as 'real historians,' even though they lacked professional credentials. As he put it a few years later: 'At the time we had a number of excellent amateur historians, but very few highly trained ones.'[131] In at least one case, however, Groulx failed to consider an unambiguously professional historian, whose only liability would seem to have been his political orientation. As we saw in the previous chapter, Gustave Lanctot was possibly the first francophone to have earned a PhD for a topic dealing with the history of Quebec. By 1925 he had already distinguished himself as a student of the work of Garneau, and in recognition of his talents Groulx had invited him to be both an organizer of and a participant in the Semaine d'histoire that autumn. In the years that followed, there was continuing evidence of cooperation between the two men. Groulx supported Lanctot's candidacy for membership in the Royal Society of Canada in 1926, while in 1934 Lanctot asked Groulx to prepare an essay for a volume that the former was editing for the Carnegie Series on Canadian-American Relations.[132]

Lanctot's status within the professional historical community was further enhanced by his appointment in 1937 as dominion archivist, but this was not sufficient for Groulx to consider him as someone who might add prestige to the IHAF. Lanctot's exclusion can be explained only in terms of his growing estrangement from Groulx, particularly during the Second World War, when Lanctot developed a point of view that did not differ appreciably from that of Abbé Maheux. Much like Maheux, Lanctot came to see Groulx as a historian whose work merely reflected personal prejudices and stood in the way of 'national unity' in Canada's hour of need.[133] Lanctot and Maheux corresponded frequently during the war, mostly to commiserate about Groulx, described by the dominion archivist in one such letter as having distinguished himself through 'the distortion of our history.'[134] In a letter to another correspondent written during the war, Lanctot referred to Groulx as someone 'whose talent was equal only to his prejudices.'[135]

Whatever glimmer of mutual respect might have remained between Lanctot and Groulx evaporated in the fall of 1946, just as Groulx was assembling his team to launch the IHAF. In September Lanctot stoked the fires by publishing an article in the journal *Action universitaire*, which was almost identical to one he had presented to the Royal Society of Canada in 1945, concerning the 'history of our historical writing.' In this article he managed to avoid even mentioning Groulx's name, while referring to every other conceivable historian. At the same time, he discussed 'the racist school of thought' – a not very veiled reference to Groulx and his followers, who were making themselves noticed at the time by their 'xenophobia' and their failure to consider the 'economic concerns' of Quebecers.[136] Lanctot made it clear that he was attacking not only Groulx but also Frégault when he wrote to a confidant shortly after the publication of the article, referring to the young professor as the priest's 'spiritual son,' who was so pretentious that he would not even deign to greet his colleagues when he passed them in the corridor.[137] Groulx recognized Lanctot's attack as one that was directed not against him personally, but rather against 'a school of thought.'[138]

Under these circumstances, it is little wonder that Groulx did not consider Lanctot, in spite of his professional credentials, for the IHAF board, which, as as result, had a certain ideological homogeneity. Groulx, of course, saw no contradiction in dealing only with men who passed his political litmus test at the same time as he was trying to build a research institute dedicated to unearthing the 'truth' about the past. Untroubled by this tension, inherent in the affairs of the Institut from its founding, Groulx turned his attention in 1947 to the establishment of a professional historical journal under the aegis of the IHAF.

The *Revue d'histoire de l'Amérique française* (hereafter *RHAF*), much like the Institut itself, was committed simultaneously to both scientific rigour and national pride. Groulx envisioned a 'genuine historical journal, a specialized journal with original studies, well researched and written according to the rules of the craft. The journal has to be sufficiently prestigious so that its criticism of historical writing will be taken seriously.'[139] Since its founding in 1920 the *Canadian Historical Review* (hereafter *CHR*) had alienated Quebecers by its refusal to publish articles in French, a policy that would not change until the 1960s. Lanctot, perhaps betraying his close ties with the English-Canadian establishment, was one of the few French speakers to write for the *CHR* during this period.[140] As for the *Bulletin des recherches historiques*, the major French-language journal interested in historical questions, while it had provided 'incalculable services' since its creation in 1895, Groulx did not consider it sufficiently 'scientific' to 'represent our contribution to a field of high culture.'[141]

Groulx viewed the publication of a truly scientific journal as a means of showing French speakers' ability to play the historical game at the same level as English speakers. In this regard, there was no distinction between the nationalistic and the scientific aims of the *RHAF* – a point reinforced by Andrée Fortin, who found that Groulx's journal shared with others established in Quebec in the immediate aftermath of the war 'the objective of using scientific means to establish the specificity of our distinct society.'[142] Accordingly, Groulx wrote to a correspondent from Vienna who was interested in the journal, 'You will notice in the *Revue* that we are very conscientious to indicate, in each of our articles, the sources or references; we do not mind publishing numerous notes for a single article. We are labouring here in Canada in the shadow of American and English-Canadian historians. Accordingly, it is crucial that we show our own ability to live up to the standards of our discipline and its methods.' To another European correspondent, he observed, 'We are a young people which finds itself living as a minority in North America. We have to do all that we can to earn our respect.'[143]

Since Groulx had decided that the scientific rigour of the journal would serve to advance the standing of Quebecers in the world of letters, the first volumes of the *RHAF* were filled with discussions of methodological questions. Groulx noted in an introduction to the first issue: 'During the first year or two, specialists will write about historical methodology in order to educate our students and researchers. We are hoping in the process to instill proper ideas about historical research, to make better known the rules of this serious discipline.' There followed an article by one of the Institut's founding directors, Thomas Charland, dealing with historical method. Charland concluded by defining history as 'the story of human experience, based upon the hard headed analysis of the documentary evidence that has survived.'[144] Groulx's commitment to the journal's scientific vocation was similarly reflected in an exchange with Conrad Morin, another of the original directors, who congratulated Groulx for having rejected an article submitted for the first issue: 'This is the approach to take if we want a serious, scientific journal.' The rejected item 'was *not scientific*: it was not an original piece of work, based upon the examination of the sources, but rather a simplified version of the works of others ... This article has no place in serious historical writing; it was not scientific (that is to say it does not say anything new), and it provided no precise references to sources.'[145]

Groulx and his colleagues tried mightily to present the journal as a vehicle 'to express ideas, and not to serve the interests of a small group with narrowly defined concerns,' but it is difficult to ignore the fact that the *RHAF* was effectively closed to those such as Lanctot who did not toe the proper line.[146] Groulx had founded the journal to 'show to the intellectual world the existence of our team of historians,' and he was not about to provide a podium for members of another team who might present Quebecers in what he might have perceived as a less than favourable light.[147]

In fact, the only way that someone of Lanctot's ilk entered the pages of the *RHAF* was via the review section. In the first volume, Groulx reviewed a book by Lanctot dealing with Jacques Cartier. As we saw above, Groulx in the 1930s had published a work on the same subject, in which he pointed to both the material and the religious factors leading Cartier to North America. What troubled Groulx about Lanctot's interpretation was the almost complete absence of attention to 'evangelical motives.'[148] The review was written in a professional style, so much so that it was praised by Conrad Morin for having been constructed in a 'solid and scientific manner ... Such a review does honour both to our journal and to history as a scientific endeavour.'[149] Nevertheless, it is hard to imagine that Lanctot could have received a fair hearing in the *RHAF*, or in the affairs of the Institut more generally. Those who held Lanctot's point of view had to look elsewhere to advance both a scientific approach to history and a different perspective on Quebec's past.

VI

While Abbé Groulx was establishing his two 'Instituts' in Montreal – one within and one outside the university – yet another Institut d'histoire was being established in Quebec City at the Université Laval. As we saw above, there was always a certain parallel teaching of history at the two French-language universities, though the slants given to the subject differed. Accordingly, it is hardly surprising that at the same time as Groulx was looking for a successor to help him start up a truly professional history department at the Université de Montréal, Abbé Maheux was moving in the same direction at Laval. The prospect of founding such a department had been discussed as early as 1937, but action was delayed by the deaths of Mgr Camille Roy, rector and dean of the faculté des lettres, and Abbé Georges Savard, dean of the faculté des arts.[150] Final approval for the Institut d'histoire et de géographie came in November 1946, within weeks of that for the history department in Montréal. Even more significantly, this approval was secured shortly after Groulx's announcement in October that the IHAF was ready to begin operations. As one Laval administrator observed, 'The establishment in Montreal of an Institut [d'histoire] de l'Amérique française threatens to concentrate all historical work in that city; such an eventuality would have an unfortunate impact upon historical research.'[151] To reinforce the sense that Groulx and his allies were the enemy, when Laval's Institut d'histoire held its first formal meeting in early 1947, one of the first acts of the director, Abbé Maheux, was to place 'before the members a list of the names of the persons who constitute the IHAF.'[152]

From its inception, Laval's history department had a very different orientation from Montreal's. While the rationale for creation of the Montreal department was primarily, if not exclusively, put in scientific terms, at Laval the administration was eager to stress 'the importance of teaching history from a Catholic perspective.'[153] Moreover, given Maheux's role as the primary promoter and then first director of the department, there was a decided emphasis on ties with English Canada and a parallel marginalizing of links with France. Maheux resisted the integration of the Institut into the faculté des lettres, even if that faculty had been created in 1937 to provide a more 'modern' education than had been provided by the faculté des arts, set up at the founding of the university in 1852. At the Université de Montréal, there had been no opposition to integrating history into the more 'scientific' faculty, but at Laval Maheux demurred, seeing an unnecessary aping of the university system in France. In his mind, retaining history within the arts faculty would show respect for the dominant model across North America. Just as his historical works stressed the need for francophones to accommodate themselves to the English-run world in which they lived, so too did he seek a department that recognized 'our various ties to Anglo-Saxon North America'; such links demanded 'a certain measure of conformity.'[154]

In spite of Maheux's pleas, the Institut d'histoire was in the end situated within the faculté des lettres, but this did not end his efforts to steer history at Laval in a 'Canadian' direction.[155] Maheux demanded, for instance, that students in his department take 'English courses designed especially for them. They also ought to read English books with some regularity ... We suggest that they should find jobs in an English milieu during the summer, so that they might eventually be able to read, speak and write English fluently. The knowledge of English is indispensable.'[156] Moreover, Maheux valued links with the University of Toronto as a means of staffing the new department. Even before the establishment of the Institut d'histoire, Maheux had lobbied for the training of further professors of Canadian history by sending them to Toronto, where Maheux had taught for a term in 1942. He had come back impressed with both the university's resources and its 'distinctively Canadian point of view.'[157] Once his department was functioning, Maheux actively promoted an exchange of professors with the University of Toronto so as to 'make French Canada better known in an English-speaking province.'[158]

By cultivating close links with English Canada, Maheux was simply following a long-standing university tradition, which had also been evident in the writings of his predecessors Ferland and Chapais, to promote cordial relations between Canada's two linguistic communities. Going back to the Conquest, because English rule had been based in Quebec City, the city's francophone elite, lay and clerical alike, had understood the importance of cooperating with English speakers. Focusing more directly on the university, Jean Hamelin has pointed to the way in which this collaborative spirit 'influenced the way in which the humanities and the social sciences were taught, encouraged exchanges with English-speaking institutions, dictated the political positions of a number of Laval professors, and formed the basis for the heated debates between historians at the two French-language universities as to how to interpret the French-Canadian past and, by association, how to imagine its future.'[159]

Ironically, however, the first full-time member of the Laval history department proved, at least by the early 1950s, to be much closer to Groulx's view of the past than to Maheux's. Marcel Trudel was roughly the same age as Brunet, Frégault, and Séguin, but, unlike his Montreal contemporaries, he had no background in history when he was selected in 1945 to teach Canadian history at Laval in anticipation of creation of the university's history department. Rather, he had secured a doctorate from Laval in literature after completing a dissertation on the influence of Voltaire in Quebec from the time of the Conquest to the end of the nineteenth century.

From reading Trudel's memoirs, one might get the impression that the doctoral student was out to shock clerical authorities by chronicling the way in which their fiefdom had been infiltrated by heretical ideas. Writing in the 1980s, Trudel saw himself as having been a kindred spirit with Jean-Charles Harvey, who had been censured by church leaders in the 1930s for his overly liberal writings.[160] In fact, however, Trudel's thesis, which was published in 1945, must have been warmly received by Quebec's clerics. While Trudel showed that Voltaire's influence had been omnipresent, he was quick to point out that this influence had 'largely been negative. Voltaire, more than the arrival of the English, threatened the well being of the Catholic church in Canada; Voltaire distracted our first newspapers from adequately defending our interests, encouraged the Patriotes [in 1837] to stand against the Church, and led Garneau, the historian, astray.'[161] Trudel argued in an article based on the conclusion to his thesis, 'We are basically a religious people, but how many times between 1760 and 1900 was our elite duped by its adherence to the ideas of Voltaire!' That Quebec society had survived these rude shocks was the result only of 'the peasantry which provided the elite with a constant model of how sincere and devout Christians should behave.'[162]

Given his limited background in history, Trudel, on being hired at Laval, was sent off to Harvard to learn the historical trade through a program of reading. He had hoped to secure this training in France, but conditions immediately following the war did not permit it, and so he went to the United States, as had Frégault and Brunet.[163] In 1947, however, Trudel's stay in Boston was cut short when he was called back to Quebec City for the opening of the Institut d'histoire in the autumn. Within weeks of his return, he was sought out by Groulx, who did not seem unduly troubled by the fact that Trudel, in his thesis, had been more critical of Quebecers' attraction to bad ideas than to the impact of the Conquest. Just as Groulx had respected Chapais because of his professional competence, which more than compensated for political differences, so too did Groulx think highly of Trudel, whom he sized up as 'an historian who knew his trade' and for whom he soon found a place on the board of the IHAF.[164]

Trudel jumped at the chance of working with Groulx. In his first letter to his 'ancien maître,' he recalled how he had been a student at the seminary in Trois-Rivières, where Groulx's works had constituted 'the heart and soul of the teaching of Canadian history.' Now that Trudel was a professional historian, he hoped to work with Groulx's Institut d'histoire de l'Amérique française.[165] For a few years, Trudel managed to balance this enthusiasm for Groulx's more professional approach to history with a certain tolerance for the amateurism of his own superior at Laval, Abbé Maheux. To a certain degree, this tolerance was encouraged by Trudel's general acceptance of much of Maheux's view of the past. In 1948 the young professor wrote to Maheux, who was on one of his regular visits to Toronto: 'If your friends from Toronto should come here to take my summer course in history, I don't think they would notice much difference between my point of view and yours.' Reflecting Maheux's view that the Conquest had been a blessing, Trudel observed in another letter to his director: 'The French Canadians were able to play a larger part in the government following the Conquest than had been the case under French rule. Moreover, the English liberated them from compulsory military service.'[166]

By the end of the decade, however, Trudel's tolerance for both the politics and the personality of his superior had completely evaporated, and he became an enthusiastic member of the camp of young Montreal historians with close ties to Groulx. Trudel became disenchanted with Maheux's benign view of the Conquest in part because of several bad experiences with the English-Canadian academic establishment. In 1949 he complained to Groulx about having failed to secure a grant from the National Research Council to defray the costs for the publication of a book: 'I presented my manuscript, but in spite of my complaints I was refused French-language evaluators. Now, these English-minded readers have demanded that I alter certain of my conclusions which I thought had been well founded ... In addition, I have been trying as of late to have French recognized as a legitimate language by the CHR, but I have been having no greater success on this front. It is such a pleasure to deal with the RHAF.'[167]

In addition to his heightened sense of nationalism, Trudel was also increasingly alienated from Maheux because of the latter's insistence on being treated with the respect that one owes to an employer. Trudel, reflecting the attitude of the autonomous researcher, bristled at Maheux's petty attempts to control him. Ultimately, Maheux put his cards on the table when he wrote, 'As long as I am the archivist and the director [of the history department], I am going to exercise the authority at my disposal, and you will have no choice but to do as you are told.'[168]

Maheux's behaviour simply cemented Trudel's relationship with Groulx, who supported his young protégé by finding ways for him to speak out against his superior at Laval with a minimum of inconvenience. On one occasion Groulx timed the publication of a statement by Trudel to coincide with Maheux's absence from the country.[169] On another, after Trudel had made a speech on the development of the historical profession in Quebec that made no reference to the role of Maheux, Trudel entrusted its publication to Groulx, with the request that his maître take his 'delicate situation' into acccount.[170] The speech in question not only implicitly marginalized Maheux but explicitly lionized Groulx, who was depicted as the champion of the scientific approach to history. Referring to the *RHAF*, Trudel commented: 'Abbé Groulx has refused to put his journal at the disposal of any nationalist group and has insisted upon maintaining the journal's scientific reputation ... Chanoîne Groulx has sacrificed everything in order to marshall all of his energies to promote the scientific approach to history.'[171]

Trudel's falling out with Maheux and the strengthening of his ties with Groulx also facilitated a close relationship with the young Montreal historians in general, and Guy Frégault in particular. In the preface to his first historical monograph, published in 1949, Trudel praised Frégault to the hilt:

I have tried to employ in this study all of the methods of modern scholarship, knowing full well that there are those who view the writing of history as an art, akin to the writing of drama ... It seems strange that a historian should have to apologize for providing appropriate footnotes and a proper bibliography: history in French Canada is still dominated by literary types who look down upon serious researchers who observe scientific methods. While the former are preoccupied with finding the right words, the latter rely on their sources to discover the historical truth. I have chosen the scientific path so that I might follow in the footsteps that have been left so brilliantly by my learned colleague, Guy Frégault.[172]

Frégault sympathized with Trudel's predicament at Laval, providing the latter with another shoulder on which he could cry. In one letter written in October 1950 Trudel complained about the way in which Maheux had been talking disparagingly of the Montreal historians in his presence and had argued against the publication of French articles in the *Canadian Historical Review*. Trudel appeared to be at his wits' end when he noted that he was no longer prepared to suffer in silence: 'I have recently been involved in a particularly nasty exchange of letters with my director.'[173]

Sensing his friend's desperation, Frégault responded the following day. He advised Trudel not to worry about Maheux. 'I have the impression that M. Maheux is for all intents and purposes dead and that no one takes him seriously. He is only temporarily alive, and when he dies this will be no more than legal confirmation of the *de facto* situation. In short, he really cannot do you any harm.' Even though Frégault saw Maheux as harmless, he suggested that the best thing for his friend might be moving from Laval to Montréal: 'What conditions would induce you to come here?'[174] Trudel did not accept Frégault's offer and remained at Laval for another fifteen years, in the process giving shape to the Laval approach to Quebec's past, which will be discussed in chapter 4. In the final analysis, Trudel found that such practical concerns as holding on to his seniority, a good salary, and a relatively light teaching load, and even the potential loss of both an office in the library and possession of 'the keys to the archives of the Séminaire,' outweighed the attraction of escaping the grip of Maheux.[175] Given that Trudel would be at odds with the Montreal historians within a few years, his decision turned out to have been a wise one.

In the short term, Trudel was firmly in Groulx's camp, which in the late 1940s included the young Montreal historians as well. One would never come to this conclusion, however, from reading Trudel's memoirs, published in the late 1980s, which reinvented the historian's youth in various regards. Even though Trudel and Groulx had been extremely close, Trudel complained about 'the spell-binding oratory of Groulx,' which had stood in the way of the emergence of 'a new style of history freed of its nationalist message.'[176] To complete his reinvention of his early years as a professor, Trudel also became inexplicably well disposed to Maheux, who was presented simply as 'the real founder' of Laval's history department; 'he was the organizer of the department, and he did an excellent job in that regard.'[177] By claiming a certain kinship with Maheux and by maintaining a certain distance from Groulx, the Trudel of the 1980s placed himself in the mainstream of Quebec historical writing, which, as we saw above, was busily marginalizing Groulx's 'scientific' legacy. This does not really change the fact that during the late 1940s Groulx's sphere of influence among the young, professionally oriented historians extended beyond Montreal to the allegedly hostile waters of Quebec City.

VII

The tentative arrival of scientific history in Quebec during the first quarter of the twentieth century was marked, as we saw in the previous chapter, by the publication in 1913 of the fifth edition of François-Xavier Garneau's *Histoire du Canada* and the first 'professional' historical conference, the Semaine d'histoire of 1925. Hector Garneau's version of his grandfather's magnum opus received considerable criticism for its inclusion of passages that offended Catholic sensibilities but was generally praised for its use of the techniques of 'la méthode scientifique.' The Semaine d'histoire was also designed to present Quebecers with a modern approach to the historical discipline at a time when formally constituted history departments and a professional historical association were still decades away. The state of the historical profession at the end of the Second World War was similarly reflected in the appearance of another new version of Garneau's great work and in the holding of a second Semaine d'histoire. In fact, on this occasion the two events were linked to one another, as both were designed to commemorate the centenary in 1945 of the publication of the first volume of the original version of *Histoire du Canada*.

Between 1913 and 1929 Hector Garneau seemed generally unperturbed by the critics who argued that he had done his grandfather a disservice by presenting François-Xavier's somewhat liberal views of church-state relations, which dated from the 1840s but which the historian had recanted by the time of his death in 1866. Hector responded that since there were various versions of his grandfather's work on the market, readers were free to decide for themselves which was was closest to François-Xavier's 'real' view of affairs.[178] Hector remained loyal to the 'liberal' views of his grandfather, publishing two further editions of *Histoire du Canada* – the sixth in 1920 and the seventh in 1928 – neither of which differed in any significant fashion from the 1913 version.

Hector indicated his intention to produce a dramatically different version only in 1929, following publication of a critique by Abbé Napoléon Morissette, a historian at the Séminaire de Québec. Morissette shifted the grounds for debate by complaining not only about Hector's slandering of Bishop Laval but also about his transformation of his grandfather's work from one that had been 'accessible to a general readership' into 'a scholarly work which was up to the standards of the specialists, but which did not meet the needs of the large numbers of those who enjoy reading about the history of Canada.'[179] Morissette's concerns were echoed a few years later by the director of several schools in the Quebec City area, who looked forward to an edition 'designed not merely for a general public, but more particularly for the students in the colleges and the convents.'[180] The provincial archivist, Pierre-Georges Roy, suggested to Hector that this greater accessibility might be achieved by relegating the notes to 'a separate volume which would follow Garneau's *Histoire*.'[181]

Hector quickly responded to Morissette, indicating that he intended to produce a new edition, which would revert to a version of François-Xavier's text less hostile to Catholic sentiments and less likely to lead 'to controversies.' He also showed himself to be sensitive to criticism regarding the inaccessibility of his scholarly edition to a larger public. Accordingly, he set out to publish an edition pruned of notes and appendices, 'designed for the general public and for the students in the convents and colleges.'[182] In 1934, in a further letter to Morissette, Hector described the new edition that he hoped would appear in the autumn of 1935. He envisioned a version shorn of notes and appendices but 'abundantly illustrated' so as to appeal 'to all of our schools, to our youth, and to the public at large.'[183]

Hector's predictions regarding the timing of the appearance of the eighth edition of the *Histoire* were off the mark by nearly a decade because of his failing eyesight, which, according to Pierre Savard, made writing 'more and more painful.'[184] The edition that finally did appear in 1944 was based upon one that his own father had published in 1882 and which had been relatively inoffensive to Catholic sensibilities. Hector purged from the eighth edition both the introduction by the French historian Gabriel Hanotaux, which had been specially prepared for the 1913 edition, and Francois-Xavier's 'Discours préliminaire' (Introductory Remarks), which had been included in all previous versions. Hanotaux's introduction had long been a subject for criticism because it seemed to play down the positive contributions of France to the development of its colony in the St Lawrence valley. The 'Discours préliminaire' had been found troublesome in clerico-nationalist quarters for the way in which it explicitly linked Garneau to certain French historians of his time, such as Michelet. More significant, the 1944 edition saw the purging of most of the references to clerical meddling in state affairs, with even the title of one chapter changed from 'Luttes de l'état et de l'église' (Struggles between Church and State) to the inoffensive 'De Mézy à Frontenac.' More generally, Hector noted in a new introduction that he had hoped to present his grandfather as 'a respectable historian who was both a Catholic and a patriot.'[185] Finally, as Hector had promised since the late 1920s, there were also some significant changes in the form of the new edition. The notes and the appendices of 1913 gave way to 'brief references' inserted into the text and 'an up-to-date bibliography' at the end of each chapter.[186]

Hector's new edition provoked considerable controversy, but little of it was directed against his decision to return to a version of his grandfather's text less hostile to the clergy than that of 1913. Gustave Lanctot, who was hardly an advocate of clerical nationalism, had long contended that there was something odd about Hector's having returned to the original version, which even François-Xavier had rejected by the time of his death. Rather, the appearance of the eighth edition of *Histoire du Canada* provided an opportunity for the individuals discussed in this chapter to reflect on the 'scientific' methods that were increasingly influencing Quebec historical writing by 1945.

One response came from amateur historians such as Léo-Paul Desrosiers who were prepared to associate themselves with Groulx's Institut d'histoire de l'Amérique française but who were less than totally committed to a mode of historical writing that left the majority of the population out in the cold. Desrosiers praised the new edition of *Histoire du Canada* because 'M. Hector Garneau has pruned all of the scientific trappings' so as to make it more accessible 'to the general public' and to extend its appeal beyond 'a small number of scholars ... [François-Xavier Garneau] wrote his great work for all of us and not for a particular class.' Desrosiers's reaction was echoed by Bertrand Lombard, who was pleased that 'the scientific trappings had been removed from the bottom of the pages' so that the text might be 'more accessible thanks to a format that would not put anyone off.'[187]

Frégault, of course, had a different perspective. While Desrosiers unreservedly hailed the appearance of a version that might inspire the larger population, Frégault had mixed feelings, noting that in many regards he preferred the 1913 edition 'because of the precise references to sources and the various appendices' which made it 'an invaluable research tool.' Nevertheless, he recognized that the 1944 version stood to have a larger circulation because of the changes that Hector had made. Moreover, he observed that 'the scientifically inclined critic has the consolation that the substance of the information from the notes that have been removed can now be found in the text.' Frégault cautiously endorsed Hector's eighth edition because it advanced 'the interests of both history and the nation.'[188] By trying to reconcile a scientific approach to history with an interpretation of Quebec's past that was unambiguously nationalistic, Frégault reflected the perspective of the young lay historians who coalesced around Groulx during the 1940s.

Garneau wrote to Frégault, thanking him for his kind words. Hector clearly felt comfortable with the young laymen such as Frégault who reflected his own scientific approach without denying the nationalistic function of historical writing. Accordingly, Garneau was delighted to have gained the approval of someone who represented 'the new French-Canadian approach to the past which is based upon the latest methods and which reflects modern scientific developments.' Garneau looked forward to the work of Frégault and his generation, which would contribute much to 'our race.'[189]

A third perspective on Hector's work came from Gustave Lanctot, who had long advocated a scientific approach to the past, but with little enthusiasm for the use of history as a nationalist vehicle. Given his 'scientific' credentials, Lanctot echoed some of Frégault's complaints by observing that the new edition was 'for the scholar and the specialist a clumsy and unfortunate effort. It is an almost inextricable tangle of the narrative of the grandfather with the insertions of the grandson: the text is complicated by the brackets, parentheses, and references, with the result that the reading of it becomes very difficult, and the reader is never quite sure who has written the lines he is perusing ... This constitutes, in the final analysis, a deformation of a work of high quality which deserved to be edited just as it had come from the mind and the pen of François-Xavier Garneau.'[190] Lanctot had been arguing since the 1920s that the value of Garneau's work resided entirely in his commitment to a scientific approach to the past, not in its role in rallying the masses. Accordingly, while Frégault could find something of value in the popular appeal of the new volume, the archivist could find relatively little to applaud.[191]

For his part, Groulx was particularly bothered by Lanctot's article in the journal *Action universitaire*, which described François-Xavier Garneau as a man 'whose work was remarkable for both its political impartiality and its care for proper documentation.'[192] Groulx correctly read these remarks as a denial of Garneau's nationalist credentials and wrote to the editor of the journal complaining about 'the nasty archivist ... who sets us apart from Garneau' by ignoring 'the nationalistic goals' of his work. If Groulx had been interested only in history as propaganda, he might have ended here; instead he showed his more scientific persona by going on to admit that 'a university-based journal has to be open to a wide diversity of opinions.'[193] Groulx indicated the same tolerance of opposing views, albeit with a certain amount of annoyance, when he set about organizing the second Semaine d'histoire, to coincide with the centenary in 1945 of the publication of the first edition of Garneau's *Histoire*.

In the autumn of 1944 the Société historique de Montréal, which had been responsible for the first Semaine d'histoire, authorized Groulx to organize another one for the following spring, but while the first had had no particular thematic focus, the second was to be dedicated to the work of Garneau.[194] Groulx assembled a group of speakers who represented all the factions of Quebec's historical community discussed in this chapter. Léo-Paul Desrosiers and Guy Frégault were there to represent the amateurs and professionals, respectively, who would soon help set up the Institut d'histoire de l'Amérique française. Groulx also invited Hector Garneau, who declined, and even Lanctot and Abbé Maheux, two men with whom he had strained relations, to say the least.[195] While Groulx's professional conscience drove him to invite Lanctot and Maheux, his political instincts made it difficult for him to be overly enthusiastic about their presence. Lanctot later complained to Maheux about Groulx's behaviour at the Semaine d'histoire, noting that their host had barely greeted him. The dominion archivist complained, 'Not only did I receive no greeting, but during my talk, he kept showing his disapproval, mumbling under his breath, shaking his head, shrugging his shoulders, at one point even resting his head in his hands.'[196]

Groulx's bad manners aside, the conference reflected certain ways in which historical practices had changed in Quebec since the first Semaine d'histoire twenty years earlier. One is particularly struck, for instance, by the presence of highly trained professionals who emerged only in the 1940s. Accordingly, the 1945 conference was treated to a talk by Guy Frégault, which predictably emphasized Garneau's commitment to 'la méthode scientifique' – still a model for historians in the 1940s. He concluded: 'Without proper analysis, we are doomed to poverty; without careful criticism, we are lost in the dark.'[197]

The professionals who were not so close to Groulx stressed the importance of exploring the everyday lives of ordinary Quebecers. Reflecting the influence of the Annales approach to history, which had had relatively little impact at the Université de Montréal but would soon leave its mark at Laval, Lanctot observed that Garneau 'never really talked about the lives of the people that he loved so much. We know very little about the social or material history of the people he discussed.'[198] Luc Lacourcière, who had just begun what was to become a long career at Laval dedicated to the study of Quebec folk culture, urged researchers to explore 'the great mysterious forces from the past that cannot be understood by looking at the politicians, the soldiers, the heroes, and groups of powerful men. We need to look at the intimate details of the lives of ordinary families.' One can only wonder how Groulx reacted when

Lacourcière called for an exploration of such matters as regional variations in the speech of Quebecers. The folklorist was respectful of the orthodox view of the time when he referred to Quebecers as 'a homogeneous people.' Nevertheless, while Groulx had written about 'linguistic uniformity' among his people, the young Laval professor believed that careful research would unearth 'some fascinating regional variations. We will find a great variety of concepts and images.'[199]

In striking contrast with the promoters of scientific rigour, however, other speakers were less troubled about documentation. Leading the way was Thomas Charland, whose presentation considered the stories that had circulated as to how Garneau had become a historian. Disposing of those authors who had not presented Garneau in a sufficiently nationalistic light, Charland opted for one account, which he admitted might have been fabricated by its author, Abbé Henri-Raymond Casgrain. This did not bother Charland, who observed: 'I would be inclined to forgive the abbé, if it turns out that he invented this story ... When one looks at the larger picture, it is possible to say that this story was true, I mean psychologically true. There may be no documentary evidence to support the story, but it seems plausible in light of Garneau's later life.'[200]

Charland was also the author of the first article published in the inaugural issue of the *Revue d'histoire de l'Amérique française* in 1947. He was asked by Groulx to discuss historical method. Seemingly disowning what he had said at the Semaine d'histoire two years earlier, Charland began his article by observing: 'I am going to deal with history as a subject with a clearly scientific basis.' Particularly curious in light of his earlier performance was his insistence on concrete evidence as the basis for all historical writing: 'Without evidence, there is no history.'[201]

In the context of the Semaine d'histoire of 1945, which assembled speakers with a wide range of backgrounds to present their views to a general public, Charland played free and loose with the facts. Even Groulx's presentation on the centenary of Garneau's great work was little more than an appeal for Quebecers to remain loyal to 'their Latin and Catholic spirit.'[202] By contrast, Groulx advanced a scientific view of history, albeit with a nationalistic tinge, in the pages of the *RHAF*, which was aimed at a more 'professional' audience. By the late 1940s, there were still members of Quebec's historical community who were prepared, under particular circumstances, to marginalize the professional approach to the discipline. Nevertheless, few were prepared to deny the scientific basis for historical research.

VIII

By the late 1940s the historical profession in Quebec was firmly installed in the two French-language universities and had an existence outside the university through the Institut d'histoire de l'Amérique française. The individual most responsible for this situation was Lionel Groulx, who, through both his own work and the institutions that he either established or influenced, reflected a view of the discipline that would have been shared by most historians of the time. Groulx's abundant writing and lecturing for a popular audience might encourage his depiction as a primitive historian, but the record described here tells a different story. Largely under Groulx's tutelage, the Quebec historical community took on the same professional trappings enjoyed by historians across the Western world and by other disciplines within the province.

It would be misleading, however, to characterize Quebec's historical writing in the immediate aftermath of the Second World War as intrinsically 'better' than it had been a quarter-century earlier. In his introduction to the published proceedings of the second Semaine d'histoire, Jean-Jacques Lefebvre observed that the 1945 meeting had shown 'the obvious progress which has been made in our province in terms of the technical aspects of history.'[203] It would be foolish to deny the improvement in the technical aspects of historical writing between 1925 and 1945. Nevertheless, in the 1940s, as in the 1920s, most of Quebec's historians, like their counterparts elsewhere, continued to struggle with balancing their search for the truth with their interest in presenting a particular point of view. Though historians are often tempted to emphasize the steady improvement over time in the quality of historical writing, it seems more reasonable to speak of changes in style and perspective.[204] Quebec historiography in the late 1940s was different from what it had been twenty years earlier, but this is not to say that it was intrinsically 'better.'

3

The Maître and His Successors:
The Montreal Approach

I

The 1950s and 1960s saw a growing rift develop between the Quebec historians who began their careers at the Université de Montréal, such as Guy Frégault, Maurice Séguin, and Michel Brunet, and those who started at the Université Laval, such as Marcel Trudel, Fernand Ouellet, and Jean Hamelin.[1] These two groups shared a common professional training and the belief that their job was to explain why Quebecers, in the immediate aftermath of the Second World War, were both economically and politically weaker than English speakers. While the Montrealers, following in Groulx's footsteps, believed that Quebecers had never entirely recovered from the Conquest, those at Laval, following in a line that stretched back to Thomas Chapais and Arthur Maheux, tended to see Quebecers as largely responsible for their own problems.

With their interest in questions of power, both economic and political, these historians collectively reflected larger changes in postwar Quebec. While Groulx had not been entirely uninterested in economic questions, he was concerned primarily with the survival of Quebecers as a cultural group. He saw the past as one of constant, and sometimes successful, struggle, which had allowed the survival of a people defined more by its language, religion, and culture than by its access to positions of power and influence. On the eve of the war, such positions were far beyond the reach of most francophones, who remained predominantly rural and relatively poor. English-speaking Montrealers held the keys to economic and political power, with the result that the leaders of francophone Quebec, Groulx included, tended to think in limited, but realistic terms, often looking to the Catholic church and its allied institutions, such as the caisses populaires and the Catholic trade unions, to better the lot of their people. To be sure, there were francophone businessmen, but few made it very high up the corporate ladder, a situation mirrored in Ottawa, where French-speaking cabinet ministers tended to be assigned portfolios that had relatively little to do with the economy. This distance from material success encouraged leaders to focus Quebecers' attention upon what seemed possible – namely, cultural survival.

During and immediately after the war, however, social and economic circumstances led Quebecers to reassess both their access to positions of power and their attitudes towards the past. Due to the large-scale migration to the cities, the 1941 census was the first to indicate that French speakers were a predominantly urban people, and by 1961 nearly three-quarters of all francophones were living in cities, most notably Montreal, where they came into contact, albeit at some distance, with English speakers who were enjoying the fruits of the emerging consumer culture.[2] This exposure led francophones to question the basis for their economic inferiority, a process further encouraged by the improvement in their economic circumstances during the postwar economic boom. While the incomes of the linguistic majority continued to lag well behind those of the minority, they improved just the same and gave Quebecers a taste for the vast array of consumer goods that seemed ever so close with the introduction of television.

Quebecers' relative prosperity also led them to look at their provincial government in an entirely new fashion. Long before the start of the Quiet Revolution, the Duplessis governments of the 1950s put large amounts of money into the educational system so that French speakers, who had the means to stay in school much longer than had previously been the case, might be able to secure a larger piece of the growing economic pie. In the process, the power of the Catholic church was thrown into question, in no small part because of its inability to provide sufficient personnel to deliver services such as education that now fell under the increasing control of the state. Moreover, the growth of the Quebec state led to direct conflict with the federal government, which was trying to build a welfare state of its own, with headquarters in Ottawa. The growing conflict between the federal and Quebec governments led Quebecers to question their role in a federation in which they felt they wielded relatively little power and which threatened the expansion of the one government they could really hope to control – the one in Quebec City.

In light of how Quebecers were questioning most aspects of their society, it is hardly surprising that the universities became a hotbed of debate. The principal players tended to be members of a new generation of highly trained professionals who were coming to replace their somewhat amateurish predecessors, such as Lionel Groulx. These new professors gladly accepted the role of 'experts' who might help plot the way for French speakers to share in the fruits of the post-1945 world. It would be a mistake, however, to ignore the ongoing links between these relatively young professionals and their predecessors, such as Groulx, who, as we shall see, changed his views about the past in the years following his retirement from the Université de Montréal in 1949. While Groulx may have remained convinced that material success was neither attainable nor desirable for his people, he shared some of the materialistic perspective of his younger colleagues that was permeating the society more generally.

By and large, the universities saw the emergence of two very different views as to how Quebecers might secure a larger piece of the pie. On the one hand, there were those such as the historians at the Université de Montréal who argued that Quebecers had long been excluded from positions of wealth and power by the legacies of the Conquest, one of which was the Canadian federation. Accordingly, their message suggested the need for greater political autonomy for Quebec, within Confederation if possible, but outside if need be. On the other hand, a completely different prescription was offered by the Laval historians and their allies, such as the Laval economist Albert Faucher and Pierre Elliott Trudeau, who by the early 1960s was a law professor in Montreal. While these men operated on the assumption that Quebecers needed greater economic and political power, they argued that the major obstacles to that end had long been internally generated. They were fond of pointing the finger in particular at Catholicism for having impeded the material progress of Quebecers. Accordingly, Quebec did not need greater autonomy within the federation; rather it needed to put its own house in order so as to provide its citizens with such services as a secular education that were appropriate to the postwar world.

These two points of view, though united by a common materialistic orientation, had very different constitutional implications. While the Montreal perspective suggested, at the very least, that Quebec required some sort of special status, the Laval interpretation implied that Quebecers should work within the federal system as it was then constituted. These political considerations have no doubt helped earn the Montreal historians a much better press among French-language commentators over the past thirty years than their counterparts at Laval. Most accounts of the careers of Frégault, Séguin, and Brunet have pointed to the manner in which these historians broke away from the grips of Abbé Groulx so as to provide an updated, neo-nationalistic interpretation of the Quebec situation. Jean Lamarre took this point the furthest in his book-length treatment of the Montrealers. As Lamarre observed: 'It would be difficult to imagine a more radical break' than that of Frégault and his colleagues from their maître. Once free of Groulx's pernicious influence, the Montreal historians were then able to develop an 'objective' account of the past that might lead Quebecers to see the political light: 'Neo-nationalism, which provided the justification for the reforms that constituted the Quiet Revolution and which was taken to its logical conclusion by the separatist movement, owed its birth to the works and the ideas of the three [Montreal] historians ... Thanks to the pioneering efforts of the Montreal school, a growing portion of the Quebec population now understands that a nation cannot be satisfied merely with certain linguistic and cultural advances.'[3]

Lamarre criticized the historians at Laval for their 'lack of objectivity,' a point also driven home by Serge Gagnon. In various essays Gagnon has attacked the Laval school, in general, and Fernand Ouellet, in particular, for a 'present-minded bias.'[4] As for the Montreal historians, however, Gagnon had little criticism. In a similar fashion, Léon Dion, in his reflections on the role of Quebec intellectuals during the 1950s, had nothing but praise for the Montreal group, which provided the basis for all subsequent historical writing. When it came to the Laval historians, however, Dion lumped them together with other 'anti-nationalists,' none of whom had provided 'any serious analysis of French-Canadian society.'[5]

Over the past thirty years some francophone commentators have expressed reservations regarding the approach of Montreal's historians. In particular, the revisionists, who came to dominate Quebec's historical profession by the 1970s, were eager to place some distance between themselves and the Montrealers. Paul-André Linteau, who will figure prominently in the discussion of revisionist historiography in chapter 5, was eager to describe the situation at the Université de Montréal, where he had been a student. 'Contrary to the impression that one might have from the outside, Michel Brunet and Maurice Séguin had hardly any influence over the students who arrived at the university after 1965.' However, while Linteau was unwilling to be associated too closely with the historians in Montreal, he was no more interested in embracing the point of view of those at Laval.[6]

If one wanted to find individuals expressing both enthusiastic praise for the Laval historians and criticism for the Montrealers, it would be necessary to turn to English-language authors such as Ramsay Cook and

Michael Behiels, both of whom have been outspoken critics of Quebecers' demands for 'special status.' In an article published in 1967, Cook characterized Trudel and his colleagues as 'meticulous,' 'imaginative,' and committed to the 'use of new techniques' so as 'to understand the past in its own terms.' By contrast, the Montrealers were mired in the belief that history was 'a weapon in the contemporary struggle for survival.'[7] More recently, Behiels has sympathized with the Laval historians, whose works provided an 'objective and realistic assessment of the evolution and development of French-Canadian society'; by contrast, the Montrealers were guilty of practising a 'functionalist conception of history,' whereby 'their discipline [served] as a nationalist vehicle.'[8]

I have no particular interest, either in this chapter, dedicated to the Montreal historians, or the following one, on the historians at Laval, in campaigning for one 'school' or the other. Rather, I hope to move away from the perspective of previous commentators, who have tended to imbue their 'side' with objectivity in order to make political points. Neither group had a monopoly on objectivity. Rather, both were united with Groulx, in particular, and the profession, more generally, in trying to balance pursuit for the 'truth,' based on conscientious research and an understanding of the historical practices of the time, with the advancement of a particular political program.

As we shall see in this chapter, the Montreal historians had enough in common with Groulx to allow the maître to remain on relatively good terms with his disciples up to the start of the 1960s. This was facilitated in part by Groulx's own continued evolution as a historian, which did not end with his retirement from the university. While it is convenient to focus on Groulx as a figure from an earlier stage in Quebec's development who was now abandoned by men committed to the 'new' Quebec, which would flower with the Quiet Revolution, the real situation was much more complicated. Despite the more materialistic orientation of Groulx's successors in Montreal, there was also much that linked them to their maître. Accordingly, much of the story that follows concerns the painfully slow break between two generations of historians. The slowness of this divorce provides a further reflection of the way in which historical writing is as much the story of continuity as it is the saga of steady 'progress.'

II

Because of the general assumption that the only historical work of significance being done in Montreal during the 1950s and 1960s was taking place at the Université de Montréal, relatively little attention has been paid to the activities of Abbé Groulx as a historian from his retirement in 1949 to his death in 1967. Groulx disappears from most accounts following the establishment of the history department at his university and the creation of the Institut d'histoire de l'Amérique française (IHAF). Carl Berger, for instance, did not mention Groulx again following the emergence of Brunet, Frégault, and Séguin.[9] Jean Lamarre referred to the priest-historian only in terms of his very last works, published in the late 1950s and early 1960s and not entirely representative of Groulx's role in Quebec's historical community following his retirement.[10] More specifically, Lamarre managed to ignore Groulx's effort in the late 1940s and early 1950s to produce a comprehensive history of Quebec from colonial times to the mid-1940s.

In 1949, having given up his teaching responsibilities, Groulx took on the task of presenting roughly one hundred fifteen-minute radio broadcasts tracing the history of French Canada from its beginnings. Sponsored by the Société St-Jean-Baptiste de Montréal, these addresses were subsequently made suitable for publication and appeared, starting in 1950, as *Histoire du Canada français*, with two volumes treating the period up to the Conquest and another two, the period from 1760. Groulx showed himself in this work to be much like the historian that we saw in the previous chapter: painfully aware of the difficulties of finding ultimate answers regarding the past and open to revising his own views in light of the work of others. *Histoire du Canada français* went through four editions in Groulx's lifetime, and though he made few changes from one edition to the next, he did add a preface to the final edition, of 1960, in which he observed that 'a work of history can never be definitive. There is always room for improvement.'[11]

Most notably in his treatment of New France, Groulx continued revising his conception of the past. Just as he had pushed race and religion somewhat to the side and had given material concerns a more central place in the revised edition of *La naissance d'une race*, he now moved in the same direction in the first two volumes of *Histoire du Canada français*. Religious factors became so marginal that they were not even mentioned in the first fifty pages. Groulx stressed instead the emergence in New France of what he described in several places as 'a small, but well balanced society,' in which a number of groups made notable contributions.[12] While Groulx had had little sympathy for anyone other than the habitant even in the revised version of *La naissance*, he now abandoned 'this false impression of a society consisting entirely of the peasantry ...

We can never forget that the peasants of the St Lawrence valley were never very distant from the far-flung lands of the [French] empire, which provided numerous opportunities for merchants, manufacturers, explorers and soldiers.'[13] Though Groulx at times returned to his earlier view that the fur trappers were little more than 'a sickness, or a canker' because of the way in which they drained the St Lawrence valley of potential settlers, elsewhere he gave the less sedentary elements of New France their due, praising them for their 'enterprising spirit.'[14] He concluded: 'The habitant and the coureur de bois were two unique social types, each of which displayed great vitality. It was almost as if they constituted two races which complemented one another.'[15]

Once Groulx was willing to countenance various types of Canadiens, he provided early Quebec society with the same sort of diversity that might have been found in the British colonies to the south. Moreover, in moral terms he presented a rather normal society, in which the residents were not all saints. Groulx noted that 'it would be ridiculous to transform Canada in its early years into the Garden of Eden before the fall.'[16] In line with a more human, less heroic New France, Groulx even dispensed with the exploits of Dollard des Ormeaux, referring to the battle of Long-Sault only in passing, without even mentioning the name of the man around whom he had earlier tried to develop a cult.[17]

By rethinking Quebec society prior to the Conquest, Groulx was himself reflecting contemporary changes in Quebec. As French speakers came to play an increasingly central role in the economy, historians – Groulx's young disciples included – began to depict a past in which devout farmers were joined by merchants and fur trappers, among others. The Montreal historians looked more directly at individuals in the midst of the rough and tumble of economic activity who were neither saintly nor heroic.

For Guy Frégault, this shift was evident in two biographies which signalled a significant departure from his earlier writings – in particular, his life of the Canadian-born Pierre Le Moyne d'Iberville. As we saw in the previous chapter, Frégault's Iberville, in the mould of Groulx's Dollard, was a larger-than-life figure, who had little to do with the nuts and bolts of economic activity. By contrast, the Canadiens described by Frégault in his biography of the French colonial administrator François Bigot were in the mainstream of economic activity. While Bigot may have wanted to treat the Canadiens as if they constituted 'a peasant society,' in fact they belonged to 'a nation of merchants.'[18] Frégault pursued this same theme in his biography of the Canadian-born Pierre de Rigaud de Vaudreuil in his capacity as governor of Louisiana, an assignment that just preceded Vaudreuil's appointment as what turned out to be the last governor of New France. From Frégault's perspective, Vaudreuil was well-suited to the job of developing the economy of Louisiana because he had hailed from 'a country of small-scale merchants.'[19]

While Frégault's biographies provided implicit support for Groulx's increasingly materialistic approach to New France, more explicit approval came from Marcel Trudel, another young historian. Trudel admitted that he first opened *Histoire du Canada français* 'with a certain reluctance. I had always thought of Canon Groulx as someone who was best suited to writing very flowery prose, but I was forced to change my mind upon reading this book. This history of French Canada is not a simple description; nor is it an exercise in hero-worship ... He is very careful to present his ideas in an understated way; there is no reason why anyone would attack this work for ideological reasons.' Trudel described Groulx as the maître of those who were practicing 'the new history,' which was marked by a commitment to careful archival research and avoidance of unsubstantiated claims. Though *Histoire du Canada français* lacked the careful citation of sources that was evident in Frégault's biographies, Trudel noted that the priest had wanted to publish 'his history with all of the technical trappings of the modern scientific approach, but circumstances forced him to publish exactly what he had said in the radio broadcasts.' Nevertheless, Groulx's text did contain numerous references to the works of others, even if such references did not come in the form of either footnotes or bibliographies. As Trudel put it, 'The author was careful to take into account the works of others, even those with whom he did not agree.'[20]

Groulx's treatment of New France was well received by his young successors, and Groulx reciprocated this respect in the early 1950s. There is no evidence that the priest was troubled by the way in which the new professors were calling into question the heroic qualities of some of the great men of New France, nor should this come as much of a surprise, given Groulx's own tendency to play down the role of some of the traditional heroes of New France in his *Histoire du Canada français*.

Groulx's restraint in this regard is particularly evident when contrasted with the reservations expressed by Léo-Paul Desrosiers, whom we saw in the previous chapter as one of the non-professional founders of the IHAF. Desrosiers was particularly critical of Frégault's treatment of the late-seventeenth-century governorship of Frontenac. In a collection of original documents that he edited along with Brunet and Trudel, Frégault described Frontenac's tenure as 'an unfortunate fiasco.'[21]

Desrosiers took exception to this characterization, preferring to see Frontenac as 'the saviour of New France.'[22] Groulx, by contrast, had little cause to complain about Frégault's depiction of Frontenac, as he himself had commented on 'the misdeeds of the governor and the spirit of patronage and trickery that [Frontenac] had encouraged in the colony.'[23]

This mutual respect between Groulx and his successors began to evaporate with the appearance in 1952 of the volumes of *Histoire du Canada français* on the period following the Conquest. It is ironic that Groulx should be remembered by numerous commentators in both French and English Canada as someone who flirted with separation, since he always maintained that Quebecers had been able to achieve much under British rule. While his view of New France had changed quite markedly over the years, his general perspective on the post-1760 period was still much the same as it had been almost a half-century earlier. In 1905, in the manual that he prepared for his students at the collège classique in Valleyfield, he had described the Canadiens of 1760 as a people who appeared 'destined for slavery much like the Irish and the Poles' but who had become in less than a century 'one of the most progressive and independent people in the world.'[24] In 1952, he was still characterizing the era of British rule as one of 'steady improvement in our political situation.'[25]

Such political questions dominated Groulx's treatment of the post-Conquest period in *Histoire du Canada français*. While his pre-1760 volumes had dealt with a wide array of issues, Groulx insisted on 'the dominant role of political concerns' in the final two. Though he was aware of the dangers of assigning 'an exaggerated importance to political affairs,' he still insisted that political events determined the ability of a conquered people to maintain its place in the economy.[26] As we shall see, Groulx did not share the view of his successors, who were in the process of inverting this formula so as to view economic factors as shaping political life.

As for the political events leading up to Confederation, Groulx had little to say in 1952 that he had not said in his earliest lectures at the Université de Montréal. In those lectures he had argued against the notion, popularized by historians such as Chapais and later Maheux, that the British had given Quebecers the ability to advance politically. While he never doubted the fact that progress had been the dominant motif of Quebec's political life, it had been achieved through British respect for the strength of Quebecers, either collectively or individually. The numerical superiority of French speakers had made the Quebec Act necessary, and the heroic efforts of Lafontaine and Cartier had brought about first responsible government and later a relatively autonomous French state within Confederation.

Until writing *Histoire du Canada français*, Groulx had published little about the period after 1867, but when he did turn to the modern era his optimism still shone through. He embraced the notion, first advanced earlier in the century by Henri Bourassa, that Canada had been created as 'a federation of nationalities and religions.' Instead of dwelling on the apparent unwillingness of English Canadians up to the 1950s to promote a bicultural country, Groulx insisted, as had Bourassa, that article 133 of the British North America Act, which called for equality of the two languages only in several limited contexts, defended such equality 'in each and every domain.'[27] Groulx also indicated his debt to Bourassa by hailing the Statute of Westminster, which formally granted Canada its independence from Great Britain in 1931. In the aftermath of the Second World War, however, this celebration of independence from Britain seemed somehow misplaced, since, as Groulx readily admitted, the major constitutional problem facing Quebecers was the concentration of power in the hands of the central government. Despite this federal offensive, Groulx, typically, refused to give in to a 'spirit of resigned pessimism.'[28]

While Groulx's post-Conquest narrative was largely political, he did occasionally refer to the sort of social and economic issues that had dominated the earlier volumes. Even in this context, however, Groulx presented a picture that differed from the one he had crafted for the period before 1760. While he had insisted on abandoning 'this false impression of a society [New France] consisting entirely of the peasantry,' Groulx now claimed that the Conquest had had little effect on a people 'made up of peasant landowners' for whom life went on as usual.[29] Moreover, while he had previously played down religion, he now gave it pride of place. For instance, in describing French Canada in 1791 he turned first to religious matters and only subsequently to economic ones.

Just as Groulx went out of his way to accentuate the positive in post-1760 political developments, so too did he dwell on aspects of social and economic history that could be cast in a positive light. He had no difficulty in finding something encouraging to report about the growing power of Catholicism. He was able to be optimistic even regarding the lives of the farmers, if only in contrast with the French-speaking business class, which had been decimated in the aftermath of the Conquest. Even there he pointed to the continued presence of the exceptional French speaker in the highest levels of the economy.[30] In the late nineteenth century, there were still 'some French-Canadian businessmen who were beginning to occupy important positions in the grocery trade, real estate, transport companies, banks, and even industrial firms.'[31]

While he was critical from time to time of British policies towards Canada that would have affected all businessmen, Groulx was reluctant to blame English speakers for Quebecers' economic weakness. Describing the situation at the middle of the nineteenth century, he recognized that there had been injustices committed by the conquerors. Nevertheless, the primary problem was that the Canadiens constituted 'a people who were trapped in the narrow confines of a peasant economy,' unable to prepare themselves 'for the complicated and costly enterprises connected with both commerce and industry.'[32] As to whether there was a link between this concentration of francophones in the agricultural sector and the advent of new political masters in 1760, Groulx was silent. He refused to recognize that structural problems stemming from the Conquest might have blocked the upward mobility of Quebecers. To have done so, however, would have been out of character for Groulx, who depicted the post-Conquest period in a manner that would give his compatriots hope for the future.

If Groulx was reluctant to focus on the economic problems stemming from the Conquest, he had no hesitation in criticizing the invasion of American capital, which he described as 'the most pernicious invasion in the history of modern capitalism.' The Americans had moved in to develop the province's natural resources and by means of 'their business practices' had taken control of existing firms. The result was 'a Conquest which was perhaps even more disastrous than the first' because of rapid urbanization of the population. From Groulx's perspective, the British invasion had allowed a few French speakers to succeed in the business world, while most of the population continued to live its Arcadian existence in rural Quebec. The American invasion, by contrast, resulted in 'a complete and alarming destabilization of society,' in which local businessmen were chased away and rural Quebec was destroyed by the ravages of urbanization.[33]

The move to the city particularly troubled Groulx, since it threatened the survival of a society that had distinguished itself by 'its spiritual values and its devotion to the development of the best qualities of the individual.' Accordingly, the early twentieth century saw greater changes 'in the social sphere than in the material or economic domain.'[34] By viewing the situation in this manner, Groulx was able to remain hopeful to the very end. Had he seen the issue as one of francophones needing to recapture the sectors of the economy now controlled by Americans, the situation might well have seemed hopeless. Since the issue was a 'moral' one, however, it sufficed that some French speakers were still trying to inject a certain morality into the economy through the establishment of cooperatives and other forms of small-scale enterprise. Groulx was heartened by the fact that 'today, more than in the past, our people are interested in having their own businesses; rather than having a large salary, they are seeking to be the owners of small-scale firms.' Such behaviour gave the lie to the doomsday scenarios of the 'pessimists' and indicated that 'there is no reason to give up all hope.'[35]

Groulx's description of the post-Conquest period sits oddly with that which he presented for the French régime. Gone was a more materialistic interpretation, which recognized the existence of several classes, to be replaced by a much narrower celebration of French-Canadian political successes, which had allowed the survival of a devoutly Catholic people. Groulx's view of the period after 1760 sits oddly even with his earlier writings on post-Conquest Quebec. As late as 1931, in his essay 'La déchéance de notre classe paysanne,' discussed in the previous chapter, Groulx had recognized that urbanization had not begun with the arrival of American capital in the twentieth century, as he would later argue in *Histoire du Canada français*. Rather, in 1931 Groulx discovered the roots of urbanization in the mid-nineteenth century, when the British, not the Americans, were the dominant economic force. Accordingly, he linked the abandonment of the land to 'the pitiful state of our agriculture,' caused by 'the economic policies of the political system put in place in 1760.'[36] Groulx made no effort to qualify his critique of British rule and did not conclude with any uplifting prediction of improvement for Quebecers in the foreseeable future.

Groulx backtracked when it came to the post-Conquest history of Quebec, in part at least in reaction to the view of the past beginning to be developed by his successors at the Université de Montréal in the late 1940s and early 1950s. As we saw above, Maurice Séguin picked up on Groulx's interpretation, as it stood in 1931, in a dissertation presented in 1947. Subsequently, Séguin passed along his bleak view of post-1760 Quebec to his two young colleagues in the history department at the Université de Montréal. Michel Brunet, by his own admission, was quickly drawn to Séguin's thesis in the late 1940s.[37] Frégault was seduced by Séguin's ideas particularly during a seminar that the three young professors directed during the 1951–2 academic year.[38] At roughly the same time that Groulx was preparing the post-Conquest volumes of *Histoire du Canada français*, Frégault was thinking through ideas, which were communicated publicly for the first time in the Gray Lectures, which he presented at the University of Toronto in the fall of 1952.[39]

Frégault was especially eager, in these lectures, to point to the folly of Quebecers, a people who had lived for nearly two hundred years with the illusion that they had the power to determine their own fate. 'The French Canadians style themselves stronger than they are. This great illusion stems from a particular historical interpretation. Any historical explanation of the present situation of French Canada in regard to English Canada must begin with a consideration of the fundamental fact in the history of this country: the British Conquest.' In the aftermath of this Conquest, French Canadians had fallen back on their farms 'not because they liked it, [but] because they had to,' given the monopolization of economic power by English speakers. As time went on, however, Quebecers began to see this rural existence as a fate that providence had reserved for them. In fact, this was little more than a myth that had helped them 'adjust themselves culturally to a situation that they dared not try to understand. They simply extolled some values that allowed them not to lose face completely.' If French speakers had survived as a group it was through sheer luck, not because of their collective strength, as Groulx would have had it. Quebecers had survived as a people, but Frégault saw the victory as a hollow one. While Groulx could not contain his optimism about the future, Frégault sourly concluded that francophones had little to show for the two centuries following the Conquest: 'Here we are with our four million people and our illusions.'[40]

At roughly the time when Groulx was backtracking on his view of the Conquest as a cataclysmic event, his young followers were arguing quite pointedly that the powerlessness of Quebecers in the postwar era could still be linked to the advent of British rule in the eighteenth century. Frégault and his colleagues were beginning to distance themselves from their maître, and they responded with silence to the final volumes of Groulx's great synthesis so as to avoid publicly criticizing him. But while the leading French-speaking historians were keeping a discrete silence, Groulx was receiving high marks from one English-language critic who had never been overly enthusiastic about his work. Mason Wade admitted that he had found 'much to quarrel with' in the last volumes of *Histoire du Canada français*, yet he was pleased by Groulx's 'frequent and favourable citations of Lower and Scott, and his references to Innis, Burt,

Creighton, McInnis, Beer, Shortt and the standard English sources, which were neglected in his earlier studies of the period ... It is encouraging that ... [Groulx] now finds allies and sympathetic understanding among his historical brethren on the other side of the ethnic fence.' Wade was so enthusiastic about Groulx's reaching out to the other side that he saw it as an element in forging closer ties between French and English Canadians. 'With the merging of the two streams of Canadian historiography, better understanding between French and English should be achieved, and history may become a force for national union in the future, rather than a divisive force, as too often in the past. This reviewer is confident that many English-speaking historians, regardless of their own views, will wish to join Canon Groulx's disciples in hailing this culmination of a life's work given to history.'[41]

Wade's comments point to one of the more striking aspects of the post-Conquest volumes of *Histoire du Canada français* – Groulx's heavy reliance on English-language sources, including not only English-Canadian historians but also American authors such as Walter Lippmann and George Kennan. This familiarity with authors writing in the 'other' language flies in the face of the often-repeated criticism that Groulx had not been well versed in the literature published in English. Frégault commented in the 1970s: 'Groulx had only a superficial familiarity with English-Canadian authors ... If Lionel Groulx had known the English-Canadian literature as well as he knew the literature from France, if he had known English-Canadian society as well as he knew the political movements of the right in France, he would have developed a more realistic view of the past.'[42] More recently, Jean Lamarre has commented on the way in which Groulx was virtually unaware of the 'the new directions that historical writing was taking in English Canada in the 1930s.'[43]

While both Groulx and his successors were familiar with the writings of English-Canadian historians, by the start of the 1950s they were under the sway of different forces in the other 'solitude.' The Montreal school was greatly influenced by Donald Creighton and Harold Innis, who had insisted, mostly in works published prior to 1939, on the way in which Canadian history had been shaped by the country's economic ties first with France and later with England. In the hands of the Montrealers, this emphasis on the links with the imperial power became a crucial element in viewing the Conquest, and its severing of ties to Paris, a cataclysmic event that had permanently deformed Quebec society. Accordingly, Brunet wrote to Creighton, 'Thanks to your works, it is now possible for French-Canadian historians to see in a clear fashion the disastrous consequences of the Conquest for our people.'[44]

By the early 1950s, however, both Creighton and Innis had moved beyond the economic underpinnings of political activity. Creighton's marginalizing of economic factors was particularly evident in his biography of John A. Macdonald, the first volume of which appeared in 1952, the same year as the first post-Conquest volume of *Histoire du Canada français*, and had some of the same characteristics as Groulx's last major work. Groulx was reacting against his successors' tendency to reduce the history of French Canada to a saga of futility in the face of daunting, impersonal economic forces. Creighton, like many other historians in the Cold War era, looked to biography as a means of accentuating the ability of the individual to make a difference in the political system. In the process, historians such as Creighton hoped to challenge the growing influence of communism.[45] Both Creighton and Groulx were reflecting the same move away from economic determinism and towards a celebration of Western civilization that was evident in American historical writing of the time. As Peter Novick has noted, the relativism of the interwar years was pushed aside as 'part of an effort to rearm the West spiritually for the battle with the totalitarians.'[46]

While Groulx travelled some of the same route followed by Creighton, he was more influenced by Arthur Lower, whose *Colony to Nation*, which first appeared in 1946, was regularly cited in the post-Conquest sections of *Histoire du Canada français*. In the immediate aftermath of the war, Lower shared Creighton's retreat from an earlier emphasis on economic factors, which was now replaced by a largely political narrative, focusing on Canada's march to independence. Just as Groulx had celebrated the constitutional gains that culminated with the Statute of Westminster, Lower thought that there was 'good ground for holding December 11, 1931 as Canada's Independence Day, for on that day she became a sovereign state.'[47]

In addition to stressing constitutional development, Lower also pointed to 'the basic Canadian antithesis' – the clash of values that divided francophones and anglophones from one another. Lower contrasted the spiritual, anti-materialistic values of the former as incompatible with those of the latter, who 'appeared to have just one idea about life – improve on nature and put the proceeds in their pockets; this they called progress.'[48] Creighton had also pointed to francophones' apparent lack of interest in entering the mainstream of economic life, but while this seemed a negative attribute to Creighton, it was meant as a compliment coming from Lower. As Carl Berger has written, 'Where Creighton celebrated the achievements of the dynamic North American commercial class, Lower shared the point of view of French Canada as he saw it.' Berger remarked: 'Lower's portrait of French Canada was sympathetic, romantic, and sentimental. He seemed unaware of the possibility that the allegedly anti-commercial, anti-business spirit of that society might have been accentuated by the Conquest itself.'[49] Of course, Groulx was similarly unwilling to perceive the Conquest as an economic disaster, and Groulx and Lower also shared a general revulsion at the growth in the power of the American corporation over the first half of the twentieth century.

The Groulx who emerged from the post-Conquest volumes of *Histoire du Canada français* had more than a little in common with Lower, and less and less in common with his disciples. Moreover, thanks to his view of the period after 1760, Groulx developed a sympathetic following even among the Quebec historians who refused to view the Conquest as an unmitigated disaster. By the late 1950s, Groulx had patched up his shaky relationship with Gustave Lanctot, and in the early 1960s Fernand Ouellet, a vocal opponent of Groulx's successors at the Université de Montréal, had no difficulty in discussing Groulx's career in positive terms: 'It would be grossly unfair to refuse to recognize the scientific dimensions of this work of substance. To the extent that the author has constructed a work based upon sound methodology, his ideological predispositions have been pushed to the side. *Histoire du Canada [français]*, even though it is still a nationalist history, reflects [Groulx's scientific] orientation towards the end of his career.'[50]

Ouellet turned out to be right in viewing *Histoire du Canada français* as having marked the end of Groulx's career as a professional historian. The maître wrote several further books before his death in 1967, but none of them indicated continued interest either in archival research or in keeping up with the most recent literature in his field. Rather, as we shall see, his last works were designed primarily to refute those of his successors who were finding greater and greater favour with the general public. While Groulx had long set the agenda for historical debate in Quebec, by the mid-1950s the mantle had passed to younger historians such as Frégault. Over the last years of his life Groulx could do little more than object to a view of the past that he could not embrace.

III

By the mid-1950s two of Groulx's successors were beginning to publish works that were openly at odds with the maître's rather positive view of the post-Conquest era. While Maurice Séguin continued to communicate his bleak perspective only via his lectures at the Université de Montréal, Guy Frégault and Michel Brunet deeply wounded Groulx by advancing their views in written form. Frégault had already insisted on the traumatic nature of the Conquest in the Gray Lectures in Toronto in 1952, but he developed this perspective more fully in two works that appeared in 1954 and 1955. In the first of these publications – a small, but still much-used, pamphlet prepared for the Canadian Historical Association – Frégault simply and clearly laid out his view of the cataclysmic effect of the Conquest. Without denying the shortcomings of French rule, he insisted that the role of the mother country had been far from 'superfluous.'[51] Rather, a commercial elite had emerged prior to 1760 that was crushed with the arrival of a new imperial power. This group had provided direction for the colony, and with its passing the larger society was left in disarray.

Frégault criticized other historians, presumably including Groulx, for underestimating the contrast between the sophistication of the colony prior to the Conquest and the disastrous situation that followed. Accordingly, Groulx's successor insisted that 'the old-time Canadian society was something more than a rustic community. It had all the elements which made up the society of a normal colony.'[52] The Groulx of the 1950s could accept Frégault's conception of New France as a normal North American colony. What he could not agree with, however, was the notion that the Conquest had left nothing but rubble in its wake – a point that Séguin drove home forcefully in his lectures, appropriately entitled 'Les normes' ('The norms'), which he presented from the early 1950s in his course on French-Canadian civilization. Much like Frégault, Séguin dwelled on the normal path that societies followed unless faced by catastrophes such as the Conquest.[53]

Frégault amplified the points made in the 1954 pamphlet in his more substantial *La Guerre de la Conquête*. Once again, he stressed the normalcy of Quebec's past, at least until the departure of the French. Up to 1760, 'the perspectives in French America [were] similar to those in British America ... Here were societies that had lived through, and were living through, the same collective experiences. They were colonial societies and they had the same attitudes towards their respective mother countries. They belonged to the same age and cherished the same basic aspirations ... Basically that means that they were all Americans, ... and nothing is more like an American than another American.'[54] This state of normalcy was, of course, destroyed by the arrival of the British, which permanently altered the lives of all Quebecers: 'It was the direct result of the Conquest that had disrupted their society, destroyed their political structure, and so thoroughly sapped their inner resources.' Other historians such as Groulx might have had illusions regarding the prospects for the Canadiens following the Conquest, but Frégault could see only one consequence – namely, that they had been 'broken' as a people.[55]

If Frégault were willing to break openly with Groulx, then Groulx was willing to do the same in return. Accordingly, he harshly reviewed *La Guerre de la Conquête* in the *Revue d'histoire de l'Amérique française*.[56] One has the impression that he did this with some reluctance, since he remarked that he had stepped in to fill the void when another reviewer had failed him. Nevertheless, Groulx took the task seriously, pointing to the limitations of Frégault's work. He criticized its weak organization and the author's tendency to present too much documentation. He reserved his most severe criticism, however, for Frégault's conclusions regarding the long-term implications of the Conquest, which sounded to the priest much like 'a funeral oration.' Groulx did not want to minimize the significance of the Conquest, but he wondered if Frégault had not gone overboard in characterizing the Canadiens after 1760 as 'if they had been dispossessed or made into outlaws.'[57] Groulx argued that the subsequent growth of both the political power of the Canadiens and the influence of the Catholic church suggested that the Conquest had not been as disastrous as Frégault contended.

Groulx's review also reflected the state of the relationship between the maître and his first disciple. Frégault clearly hurt Groulx by claiming that all previous historians had glossed over the impact of the Conquest. Liberally citing his own work, as well as that of Arthur Lower, Groulx reminded anyone who might have forgotten that he had long argued against the view of the Conquest as having been a providential event. However, even though Groulx was exasperated with Frégault, he was also eager to finish with some kind words, much as an annoyed father might try to sugar-coat a lecture to a bad child. He was confident that Frégault, 'who was still young,' had 'the wherewithal to survive the difficulties that he was encountering.' Frégault had better days ahead of him, thanks to the way in which he had been allowed 'to work under conditions that no previous French-Canadian historian had known.'[58] Of course, those conditions – doctoral studies in the United States and the security of a university position – had been arranged by Groulx.

Groulx knew what he was doing when he tried to soften his critique, because he had already seen the extent to which Frégault needed his approval. In 1949 Groulx reviewed Frégault's biography of Bigot kindly, following which the young historian wrote to his mentor: '[The review] was a great honour to me; who would not have felt honoured? In particular, it was satisfying to me because it seemed to indicate that I had achieved a goal I had long aspired to attain. The praise was doubly satisfying because it came from you ... When I first came to the faculté des lettres in 1938 I was the most miserable creature in Lower Canada ... Ultimately, I learned that if I wanted to go far, I needed to follow your example and stand on my own two feet.'[59]

By the mid-1950s Frégault had shown a certain independence, having developed an interpretation that differed from Groulx's. Nevertheless, he still needed his maître's approval when times were tough. Only days before the appearance of Groulx's review of *La Guerre de la Conquête*, Frégault wrote complaining about the way in which others had treated his work. After listing critiques, he concluded grimly: 'These drops of rain which have been falling on me seem to be taking on the proportions of a real flood.'[60] When Groulx wrote back a few days later, following the appearance of his review, he comforted Frégault: 'I am still convinced, having followed your progress since the start of your career, that you will construct, in history, a body of work of the highest calibre.'[61]

Even when Groulx's successors began to break with him, the split came with a reluctance on both sides that belies Jean Lamarre's depiction of a clean break.[62] This hesistancy was evident not only in the case of Guy Frégault, but also in that of Michel Brunet, who by 1954 had also gone public with a view of the past that put him at odds with Groulx. The relations between Brunet and Groulx began to sour following a speech by the former dealing with 'the three illusions that have dominated French-Canadian thought.' As we have seen, in 1952 Frégault insisted in his Gray Lectures that Quebecers had managed ever since the Conquest to develop an unrealistic view of the past in order to shield themselves from facing up to their precarious status.[63] Two years later Brunet similarly attacked the illusions that French speakers had developed – a theme to which he would return throughout his career.

In this case, Brunet identified 'agriculturalism,' 'anti-imperialism,' and 'Canadianism' as illusions that had to be discarded.[64] The first, derived by Brunet from Séguin's thesis, blinded Quebecers from recognizing that their agricultural past had been foisted on them by the conquerors. 'Incapable of continuing the commercial and industrial traditions of the founders of the French empire in North America, [the Canadiens] convinced themselves that they were an agricultural people. Obliged to take refuge on the land, they concluded – or rather their conquerors concluded for them – that they had an agricultural mission to fulfill.'[65]

The second and third illusions struck more directly at the political notions that Groulx had advanced in his *Histoire du Canada français*. While Groulx believed that the anti-imperial sentiments of Quebecers had played a role in the dismantling of the British empire and the creation of the Commonwealth, Brunet argued that an exaggerated assessment of their own influence had blinded his people from recognizing Canada's ongoing ties to Britain, which had been evident in the Second World War. As for Quebecers' place within Canada, while Groulx argued that francophones had achieved much since 1867, Brunet, once more, was sceptical. He viewed his people's 'Canadianism' as preventing them from seeing federal incursions into provincial jurisdictions, which Groulx conveniently ignored.

Faced again with a public attack from one of his successors, Groulx was annoyed but unwilling to make a clean break. He wrote to Brunet: 'I have had much difficulty in defending you and those of your school in the face of criticism from our friends ... People are annoyed with the way in which you seem to want to start [the struggle for our survival] from square one. From your point of view, it was as if our history since 1760 was nothing more than one big mistake, or, to employ harsher words, it was as if we had followed a tradition of incredible stupidity. All that I have been able to say in your defence is that you form part of a generation which has gone too far against the one that preceded it.'[66]

Brunet was unprepared to turn his back entirely on Groulx, even if he was openly challenging some of the 'illusions' of his maître. In his collection of essays published in 1954 as *Canadians et Canadiens* Brunet returned to the subject of illusions, pointedly condemning all earlier historiography as flawed by the illusion that a conquered people could live more than a marginal existence. It is telling that Brunet linked Groulx together with Chapais as if there were nothing to distinguish the one from the other.[67] Despite his criticism of Groulx, however, Brunet, much like Frégault, hoped that he might receive a sign of approval from the master. Waiting for some reaction to his new book, Brunet wrote to Groulx: 'I am waiting for your response with the uneasiness of a disciple who admires his "maître" but who has no choice but to go his own way in certain regards ... Still, I know that we are working for the same cause.'[68]

Brunet's papers contain no response from Groulx regarding *Canadians et Canadiens*. Nevertheless, they do include a telling letter, written in 1957, which indicated that the maître continued to feel some affection for his successors. Groulx made it clear that he was annoyed with Brunet's pessimism, which originated with Séguin, the prophet of 'a deep-seated and all-encompassing pessimism.' Groulx was incapable of being so negative, because of his belief in the possibility of people improving their lot. 'I will tell you in all honesty, dear Michel, that I have managed to keep going throughout my life, which has not always been easy, because of my faith in the spiritual values of our people.' Groulx paternalistically closed, 'I can only wish you the same faith.' In the following year, Groulx sent Brunet a stinging criticism of his *La présence anglaise et les Canadiens*, which continued to advance the view of 'the Conquest as an irreparable catastrophe.' Groulx rejected Brunet's defeatism, which denied the progress that Quebecers had already made and which would simply encourage them to resign themselves to an inferior status within Canada. Groulx minced no words in his criticism of Brunet's approach and yet indicated continued concern for the younger historian when he asked that Brunet not unduly upset his wife by showing her the critique.[69]

Relations between Groulx and those who succeeded him remained civil, if strained, throughout the late 1950s. The younger historians wrote little in that period that added much to the conception of Quebec history that they had already advanced. While they were implicitly, though never explicitly, criticizing the underlying assumptions of their master's work, they continued to cooperate with him in running the Institut d'histoire de l'Amérique française. Moreover, Groulx's last two historical works were published in a series that Frégault and Marcel Trudel were editing for the Montreal publisher Fides. In spite of this collaboration, however, Groulx wrote the first volume in direct response to the point of view of his successors.

Notre grande aventure was not so much a monograph as a collection of essays and documents on New France. It was the product of considerable archival research – certainly more than one could find in the essays that Brunet was writing at the time, which were little more than polemics. In light of this attention to sources, it is ironic that Groulx should have distanced himself in this work from an exclusive concern with 'historical objectivity,' while Brunet, the indifferent researcher, was claiming to belong to a generation committed to a view of the past 'impartial, comprehensive, and free of ideology.'[70] The two historians were staking out positions that would differentiate the one from the other. To the extent that Brunet and his colleagues were claiming the 'objective' high ground, Groulx found himself with little choice but to take on the mantle of 'subjectivity' whether it fitted or not.

Groulx also sought to distance himself from his former disciples on a more substantive level by emphasizing the heroic qualities of the men who had played a central role in the affairs of New France. In the pre-Conquest volumes of *Histoire du Canada français*, published in the early 1950s, he had all but abandoned any lingering interest in such heroism so as to emphasize the material concerns of the founders of the colony. Now, however, he purposefully marginalized the role of 'economic and social forces' and paid respect 'to the mysterious forces that came from a higher power.'[71] Referring to the French 'commercial and military posts,' which he had discussed in *Histoire du Canada français*, Groulx now transformed them into 'centres for the advancement of civilization.'[72] He felt that 'young French Canadians were searching for heroes,' but that the historians at the Université de Montréal were not providing such role models, given their pessimism as to what the Canadiens had achieved.[73] As Groulx observed in his memoirs, 'Most of the younger historians refuse to take the French empire which was established in North America very seriously. They see nothing more than a short-lived enterprise, a fantasy of a few idealists, really nothing more than a dream.'[74]

Groulx departed even further from the increasingly materialistic history that he had been writing over the previous three decades in his final monograph, *Le Canada français missionaire*, which appeared in 1962. Subtitled 'une autre grande aventure' (another great adventure), this work seemed to Groulx an extension of the previous one. While *Notre grande aventure* had emphasized the 'civilizing' work of laymen, the subsequent volume turned to the missionary activities of Quebecers, not only in Canada during the French regime, but also around the world over the two centuries following the Conquest. By pointing to what Quebecers had achieved on the international stage, Groulx was contradicting the Montreal historians, who saw nothing but darkness after 1760. Groulx was thinking precisely of them when he remarked on the launching of the book: 'I will probably be criticized for having written an overly optimistic history through rose-coloured glasses.'[75]

Neither of Groulx's last works was a great success, either critically or commercially. While amateur historians such as Léo-Paul Desrosiers embraced them, the professionals who had succeeded the priest at the Université de Montréal were discreetly silent, to avoid breaking completely with their maître. This silence bothered Groulx. He noted in regard to *Notre grande aventure*: 'The "official" critics, those who distinguish between works of importance and those of no significance, were completely silent.'[76] Groulx cogently explained the failure of these works by their appearance 'at the wrong time.'[77] Just as Quebecers were simultaneously becoming more secular, more successful materially, and more sceptical regarding their political prospects, here was someone trying to convince them of their heroic, largely anti-materialistic heritage. As Guy Frégault put it: 'No one really wanted to argue about whether New France had given rise to the heroes discussed in *Notre grande aventure*. Rather, Quebecers were simply ready to move on to consider different matters.'[78]

Writing after the maître's death, Frégault explained the failure of Groulx's last books in greater detail, stressing the way in which his mentor had lost touch with developments in postwar Quebec and giving the impression that works such as *Le Canada français missionaire* were typical of Groulx's entire career.[79] Frégault, hoping to establish the scientific virtues of his own generation, conveniently forgot that these books were unrepresentative of Groulx's writing over the previous three decades. Frégault argued that 'there was no room for professional dialogue between those who had been fifty years old in 1930 and those who were thirty years old in 1950.' On the one hand, there was Groulx, the octogenarian, who had inspired Quebecers but who lacked the skills of the modern historian, and on the other hand, there were the Young Turks at the Université de Montréal, who viewed history 'as a discipline built upon scientific methods.'[80]

If Frégault had only unflattering recollections of Groulx's career as a historian, these were no doubt encouraged by the fact that the maître, by the 1960s, was finally prepared to come out openly and bitterly against his successors. In the late 1950s, as Frégault and his colleagues were going their own way, Groulx grumbled about them in private to his closest friends. For instance, he confided to François-Albert Angers that there was 'a seemingly unbridgeable gap which separates us from subsequent generations ... I don't think that I ever denied the catastrophic nature of 1760. I think I know that it did much harm to our development. But I have believed that this damage could be fixed. I have always thought that our history, both before and after our great defeat, was marked by a certain grandeur. I always tried to use this history as much as possible to give our people a sense of pride and to prevent them from being overwhelmed by a sense of defeatism.'[81]

In a similar fashion Groulx privately supported Léo-Paul Desrosiers's public attack on 'the young historians' in the journal *Notre temps*. Desrosiers said nothing that Groulx had not said privately regarding the cynicism and materialism of the younger historians. While claiming to support their right to say what they wished about the past, Desrosiers cautioned them against writing in an unpatriotic manner. He encouraged them 'to produce the best possible works which respected the rules of historical science.' However, they needed 'to be very careful when it came to dealing with their own history and their own leaders.' Moreover, Desrosiers counselled them against cavalierly dismissing the work of previous generations. He reminded Frégault and his colleagues that '[their] predecessors had not had at their disposal the masses of documents that are available today.' While admitting that 'a certain reaction' against previous interpretations was understandable, Desrosiers failed to appreciate 'the conviction that in each and every case one could get closer to the truth simply by saying the opposite of what our older historians have said.'[82]

Groulx welcomed Desrosiers's article and wrote to his friend: 'You have said things that it would be very difficult for me to write, given that I have been the professor, the maître, of at least three of the historians. I wouldn't want to take on the guise of an old schoolmaster armed with a rod. Much like you, I deplore their perverse delight in being paradoxical, their tendency to contradict whatever older historians had written ... Much like you, I fear that the way in which they work – which has nothing to do with the scientific method – invalidates their findings.' In spite of his strong feelings, however, Groulx felt that he could not clash too openly with these men, who were also his colleagues in the *Revue d'histoire de l'Amérique française*. Nevertheless, even with reasonably cordial relations, Groulx complained about the difficulties of reconciling 'two schools of thought which clash so violently with one another.'[83]

Despite the tensions, both sides remained relatively discreet regarding their differences until 1961, when Michel Brunet attacked the way in which Quebec's history was being taught, provoked by a speech by François-Albert Angers.[84] Angers insisted that teachers at all levels should encourage 'enthusiastic admiration for the French-Canadian nation,' leading Brunet to fear that history might be transformed into 'a morality play that could be placed at the service of Catholicism, of the clergy, of the "race," or of the established powers more generally.' In light of what he saw as the widespread belief that 'history has been written once and for all and that we only need to transmit it,' Brunet wondered why Quebecers needed serious research into their past. Pointing the finger fairly clearly at individuals such as Groulx, he attacked those who used their 'powerful positions to advance the point of view that history is a science in which conclusions, once arrived at, never change ... These same persons have no problem with encouraging research into the mysteries of nature and science, but they would never see history as a science in the same sense. They sincerely seem to believe that there is nothing left to learn in history, especially in our national history, that we know everything that can be known, and that we should be content to repeat the findings of previous generations of historians.'[85]

Groulx carefully chose the annual meeting of the Institut d'histoire de l'Amérique française (IHAF), roughly three weeks after Brunet's speech, to deliver his response. As he put it in his memoirs, he was 'at the end of his rope' when he finally went public with his own frustrations.[86] 'I believe that I have always respected the right of my former students, my successors, to study history as they see fit.' But he could no longer remain aloof when Brunet presented himself – and, by extension, his generation – as the first that was interested in finding the 'truth' without concern for the political implications of any historical interpretation. Groulx agreed with Brunet that history should not become a form of 'patriotic propaganda.' He was bothered, however, by his successor's pretension that everything written previously could be dismissed because it lacked 'impartiality or scientific reason.' Groulx bristled at Brunet's suggestion that earlier practitioners had been unaware of 'scientific' history and that the younger ones had no political program of their own: 'The historian needs to be modest; he must remember that every generation of historians believes that it is reinventing historical writing. The historian can rest assured that there will always be someone, either after his career is over or even in his own time, who will tell him that he has badly distorted the past ... I feel the need to tell the younger generation that it can do better than pull down the work of its predecessors; perhaps it would be better to try to improve upon what they have done.'[87]

In the aftermath of this speech, relations between Groulx and Brunet all but ended. Their correspondence, which had continued for a quarter century, came to a close, and Brunet stopped contributing to both *Action nationale* and the *Revue d'histoire de l'Amérique française* (*RHAF*), two journals over which Groulx had considerable influence, until after the maître's death. While there is no evidence that Groulx was personally responsible for Brunet's being blacklisted, at the very least this indicated that the priest's friends were coming to his rescue. The maître's allies provided more tangible proof of their ongoing support by publishing attacks against Brunet in various journals, including the two that closed their doors to Groulx's nemesis.[88] *Le Devoir*, on the day following the publication of Groulx's speech, ran an editorial by Gérard Filion that characterized intellectuals such as Brunet as adolescents for their dismissive attitude towards their predecessors.[89] Ten days later, the same newspaper ran a two-part commentary by Jean Genest which asked, 'Qu'est-ce que le "brunetisme"?' (What Is Brunetism?). Given Brunet's insistence that his generation was the first to practise truly scientific history, Genest quite appropriately examined Brunet's writings only to find 'a popularizer' who seemed ill-equipped for a profession that demanded 'integrity and respect for the truth.'[90]

It is not very difficult to understand the bitter reaction of Groulx and his friends to Brunet's speech, which came in the immediate aftermath of the 1960 election victory of Quebec's Liberal party. The new premier, Jean Lesage, and his colleagues, seemed intent on instituting a program inspired substantially by the view of the past that the Montreal historians had been communicating for nearly a decade. To the extent that the new régime sought to transform Quebec into a more secular society, with an interventionist state that might undo the ongoing legacy of the Conquest, Groulx, Angers, and Desrosiers may justifiably have concluded that their enemies were now in positions of power. This situation no doubt encouraged them to fight Brunet with the tools that remained in their hands. On a more personal level, Groulx must have been annoyed at being publicly criticized by Brunet, of all people, for having failed to change his views over time. Such criticism must have hurt Groulx, whose career had displayed a remarkable capacity for growth, particularly when it came from a historian who was fond of brash talk but who rarely set foot in the archives and whose own work had changed little over time.

As Quebec entered the era of the Quiet Revolution, Groulx found himself increasingly isolated from the men who had succeeded him. Not only had he fallen out with Brunet, but his relationship with Guy Frégault had cooled. In 1959 Frégault left the Université de Montréal, fed up with the limited funds available to the history department, which he had directed since its establishment. On Frégault's departure for the University of

Ottawa, Groulx wrote to him in a manner that indicated that their relationship was strained: 'In spite of whatever you might think, I have
always followed your career with the greatest interest and have often
admired the way in which your historical work has evolved.'[91] Frégault's
stay in Ottawa was short-lived, as he was named Quebec's first deputy
minister of cultural affairs under the Liberals. Groulx learned of this
appointment only days after his speech against Brunet.[92] With Frégault's
passage to the civil service, Groulx's correspondence with his protégé
effectively came to a halt.[93]

Groulx spent his last years in isolation from the community of scholars
that he had helped form. Only a few months after his public debate with
Brunet, he asked Léo-Paul Desrosiers to succeed him, on his death, as
director of the *RHAF*. Fearing that the journal might fall 'into the wrong
hands,' he wanted to settle the succession, even though he recognized
that it was not really in his power.[94] Groulx had held the directorship of
the journal by dint of being president of the Institut. The internal regulations of the IHAF did not specify how a future director might be selected,
but there was no evidence that it was within Groulx's mandate to make
such a decision. The legality of his unilateral action became a moot point
when Desrosiers declined the offer so as to devote more time to journalis-
tic interests. Reflecting Groulx's siege mentality following the Liberals'
accession in Quebec City, Desrosiers remarked: 'I have recently been
paying more attention to my career as a journalist than had previously
been the case ... The symptoms that we currently observe are very serious. The attack against religion, although it is rather indirect as of now,
has the potential of becoming large and all-encompassing ... Today we
see the beginnings of a movement, but soon it will be impossible to
stop it.'[95]

Groulx wanted to resolve the succession partly in order to encourage
continued support for the journal from individuals outside the ranks of
the professional historians. Ever since 1956 the financing of the activities
of the IHAF, including the *Revue*, had been the responsibility of the
Fondation Lionel-Groulx, formed with an initial fund of $10,000 and the
goal of amassing a principal of $100,000. In 1957 Groulx ceded to the
Fondation his house on Bloomfield Avenue in Outremont, which had
been given to him in 1939 so that he might have a permanent base from
which to work, and in 1966 he willed to it all of his belongings and
royalties. From its inception the directors of the Fondation had tended to
be professionals – in particular, doctors, lawyers, and notaries – with
more than a passing interest in nationalist causes. The initial president of

the board was Maxime Raymond, a lawyer who had led the Bloc populaire canadien, an anti-conscription party formed during the Second World War.[96] Groulx counted on the financial assistance of the loyal supporters associated with the Fondation, and he feared that control of the journal by such untrustworthy characters as Brunet and Frégault might dry up contributions.[97]

In the last years of his life, Groulx and his friends came to view the Fondation as a tool to block the takeover of the *RHAF* – clearly the maître's prized possession – by his enemies.[98] In 1966 Groulx, along with Rosario Bilodeau, by then his assistant at the *RHAF*, proposed that the future president of the Institut be chosen by simple vote of the board, which was increasingly under the sway of the professional historians. At the same time, Groulx and Bilodeau wanted the Fondation to have 'a role equal to that of the board of directors of the Institut' in the choice of Groulx's successor as editor.[99]

This proposal met with little enthusiasm from the professionals, and the matter remained unresolved. In March 1967, another, but no more successful, proposal was presented to the Institut by Bilodeau and another Groulx loyalist, Lucien Campeau. This scheme called for a formal merger of the Fondation and the IHAF so that members of the Fondation, 'who have long been supporting the Institut with their money and their influence ... might be able to serve on the board of directors' of a new Institut Lionel-Groulx. While the report insisted on there being a majority of professional historians on the board, as well as a historian as president, clearly the idea was to give the Fondation more direct control over the journal.[100]

Groulx wrote a memo just before his death in May in which he proposed that the Fondation should continue to support the Institut only under certain conditions. While he claimed that he had no interest in limiting 'the freedom' of the IHAF, he was insistent that it remain 'independent of the Université de Montréal,' where his enemies reigned. As for the *Revue*, Groulx wanted it to remain much as it had been since 1947. He feared that the younger historians might turn it into 'a French version of the *Canadian Historical Review* which deals with a wide array of historical issues.' If the Institut were not prepared to accept these conditions, Groulx was willing to have the Fondation transfer its assets to support 'a charitable organization dedicated to encouraging the young to commit themselves to the defence of our nation, and which might use the house at 261 Bloomfield for its offices.'[101]

Nothing came of these proposals prior to Groulx's death, but collectively they reflected the maître's isolation from the professional historical community. Earlier in his career Groulx had shown himself a reasonably conscientious researcher, able to alter his views in line with larger developments in the profession. Over the last years of his life, however, he backtracked in the face of what he saw as the treachery of his former students and the more general transformation of Quebec society. In the process Groulx was supported by men who had never particularly appreciated the more scientific side of his career. His final years provided considerable fuel for those who sought to characterize him as having long been a primitive historian; the record, of course, was much more complicated.

IV

By the time of Groulx's death, his successors at the Université de Montréal had already seen their most productive years as historians. Frégault never returned from the Quebec civil service to resume his career as a full-time historian prior to his death in 1977.[102] Brunet, though he lived until 1985, produced little historical work of substance after the publication, in 1969, of *Les Canadiens après la Conquête*, his 'only work of synthesis.'[103] In spite of his outspoken condemnation of Groulx, who had produced numerous volumes based on considerable research, Brunet managed but a single book-length monograph in a career that spanned nearly four decades. His other efforts were little more than collections of loosely connected essays, leading Fernand Ouellet to remark that this was 'his first real book.'[104] Brunet had been working on it for nearly twenty years and, according to Jean Lamarre, finished it only after Ouellet produced his *Histoire économique et sociale* in 1966.[105] When it finally did appear three years later, *Les Canadiens après la Conquête* suffered by comparison. As we shall see in the next chapter, Ouellet was employing new tools of the trade, while Brunet was still reinforcing the cataclysmic view of the Conquest that Maurice Séguin had developed more than twenty years earlier.

Brunet seemed painfully aware of the disadvantageous comparisons that would be made between his book and Ouellet's. As he noted in his preface to *Les Canadiens après la Conquête*, 'Columns of figures and fancy charts might be useful to finish off a work of history. However, they cannot take the place of the historian who seeks to understand all aspects of a people's experience.'[106] Despite his claims to the contrary, however, Brunet did not study 'all aspects' of the situation of Quebecers between

1759 and 1775 – an era that extended from 'the Canadian revolution to the American one.' Rather, he generally focused on the treachery of the political elite, both French- and English-speaking. He reserved particular venom, however, for the post-Conquest leaders of francophone Quebec, who were overly dependent on the goodwill of the conquerors and too little interested in their own people.[107] While Brunet did a significant amount of research concerning the political leaders of the time, his efforts were frequently compromised by his exaggerated conclusions, such as his suggestion that the Canadiens who had cooperated with the British were 'collaborators,' thus invoking comparisons with Nazi collaborators in Second World War France.[108]

Brunet's unwillingness to accept any of Ouellet's methodological innovations and his insistence on defending the ideas of Séguin made the text seem badly outdated. So too did his considerable reliance on A.L. Burt's *The Old Province of Quebec*, a narrowly cast political narrative that had appeared in 1933 and which Brunet credited, without explanation, with having 'cleared the way for a new historical perspective upon these crucial years in the history of Canada.'[109] However, if Brunet's sources were sometimes dated on political issues, they were largely non-existent beyond that realm. While he claimed to have shown that 'the unfortunate French-Canadian businessmen' had been 'victims of the arrival of a new empire,' there was little evidence to support the assertion.[110] Rather, he offered the banal claim that 'the least scrupulous businessmen usually come away with the largest profits.'[111]

Such unfounded assertions were scattered throughout Brunet's text. Nevertheless, his conclusion, called 'a tentative assessment,' was curiously modest. Having shown no reluctance to overstate his points, Brunet was now unwilling to push his conclusions too far until completing a second volume, which would carry his narrative up to 1800.[112] As we have seen above, however, this was to be Brunet's only 'real book.' Since the second volume never appeared, Brunet's career as a serious researcher began and ended with a work that was narrowly conceived, frequently outdated, and often marred by unfounded claims.[113] None the less, Jean Lamarre still placed Brunet among the leading scholars of his time because he had sought 'to uncover new historical insights.'[114] Brunet published relatively little, and what he did produce was not of a particularly high quality. Accordingly, there is good reason to view him as representative of a generation that did not quite live up to either the expectations of Groulx or the assessments of commentators such as Lamarre.

Following Groulx's death, the maître's errant disciples wrote little that had much influence on the way in which Quebec historians viewed the past. Rather, by the late 1960s Quebec historiography was coming under the sway of a new generation with a perspective quite different from that of the two generations that had dominated the field at the Université de Montréal since the 1910s. At roughly the time that Groulx died, the revisionist historians – referred to above and discussed below at length in chapter 5 – were beginning to characterize Quebec's past as 'normal.' In the process, the revisionists denied the central role of the Conquest that had long been a staple of historical writing emanating from Montreal. Moreover, these younger professionals, such as Paul-André Linteau and René Durocher, were making their presence known in the affairs of both the journal and the historical association that Groulx had founded. Accordingly, Frégault, Séguin, and Brunet were left with only a very narrow 'window of opportunity' to leave their mark on the profession.

After Groulx's death, control of the *RHAF* passed to his assistant, Rosario Bilodeau, who, over the next five years, tried to stay true to the maître's insistence that the journal remain apolitical and open to various points of view. Perhaps anticipating that people such as Frégault might want to politicize the journal, Bilodeau staked out his own, and presumably Groulx's, view of the *RHAF*, one month before the maître's death. In a review of the first twenty years of the journal, Bilodeau noted that 'as early as its second year in operation there were those who wanted to know why the journal had not been more active in advancing nationalist causes.' Groulx had rejected such criticisms, and now Bilodeau did the same, arguing that the *RHAF* was 'a meeting place for people of various perspectives as long as they were prepared to write about the past on the basis of objectivity and honesty, and with a certain literary flair.'[115]

It is impossible to know what Frégault and his colleagues might have had in mind for the journal, because Bilodeau passed the mantle on to an entirely new generation in 1972. Groulx's immediate successors did just slightly better in the Institut itself, exercising only fleeting control. As we saw above, during Groulx's day the director of the journal was also president of the IHAF, but this arrangement ended in 1968, when Frégault acceded to the presidency, while Bilodeau remained in charge of the *RHAF*. On the return of the provincial Liberals to power in 1970, Frégault left the Institut to return to his old post as deputy minister of cultural affairs. Séguin, secretary-treasurer of the Institut since its inception, also stepped aside in 1970, and Brunet, who followed Frégault as president, held that post only until 1972. When Brunet resigned from the board of directors in 1974, it marked the end of his generation's influence over the Institut.

In the early 1970s the passing from the scene of Bilodeau, Frégault, Séguin, and Brunet coincided with the rise of an even younger genera-tion, made up of historians such as Linteau, born approximately when the Institut and the *RHAF* were being established. Recognizing the need to find a place for these young historians, Groulx's niece and long-time assistant, Juliette Rémillard, who had stayed on to manage the day-to-day affairs of the Institut, informed Frégault that there was a crisis brewing:

I have the impression, and we give the impression, that the Institut is moribund ... There are rumours that if we do not change the way in which we operate, that a new association of historians will be formed ... The young historians, who have already provided invaluable services to the Institut, have now become university professors ... We have to find room for two or three of them on the board of directors. They have some good ideas, even if they get carried away at times. We have to give them the opportunity to express themselves; otherwise they will become discouraged. Now is the time, more than ever, that we have to take advantage of their good will or they will form an organization of their own. There is so much work that remains to be done.[116]

The rise of these newcomers was evident in the management of both the journal and the Institut. In 1970 an editorial board, made up of such historians as René Durocher, Paul-André Linteau, and Pierre Savard, was established to assist Bilodeau in presenting a journal more professional in its orientation and open 'to younger authors.' The professionalization of the journal was evident, for instance, when the editors encouraged the submission of 'research notes and review essays, the latter dealing with the nature of recent historical writing on a specific issue.'[117] Once installed on the board, the Young Turks pushed for greater control, and Bilodeau resigned in 1972.[118] Savard soon assumed the editorship of the *RHAF*, and, to mark the passing of the torch, the first issue following Bilodeau's resignation included an assessment of the journal over its first twenty-five years. This analysis, by Linteau and Fernand Harvey, noted the way in which the journal had, up until the mid-1960s, been preoccupied with studies of the pre-Conquest period, which were just as likely to have been written by priests as by well-trained lay historians. Groulx and his colleagues, according to Harvey and Linteau, were interested primarily in portraying New France as 'a lost paradise' in order to advance their perspective on the providential mission of Quebecers. By the late 1960s, however, with Groulx's passing, there was a radical shift. Professionals began to dominate the journal, and with their arrival there was 'the shift from imposing value judgements to presenting serious explanations.' Attention now moved to more modern aspects of Quebec history, and the earlier preoccupation with 'the future of the nation' gave way to scientific analysis of 'problems and social conflicts in terms of the class structure of society.'[119]

This analysis by Harvey and Linteau served the interests of the emerging generation by unfairly running down those generations that had preceded it. The young historians portrayed the journal, and by extension Quebec historical writing, during the era of Groulx's influence as more primitive than the evidence would allow. While they focused on the journal's preoccupation with New France, they failed to comment on the way in which the *RHAF*, in its first issues, had tried to communicate the principles of 'scientific history' to a largely untrained audience. Moreover, Harvey and Linteau managed to minimize, more than was appropriate, the influence of the Montreal historians over the discipline. At one point, in trying to explain why there had been no 'radical tradition of historical writing in Quebec,' they concentrated on the general absence of historians from the intellectual ferment of the 1950s that had paved the way for the Quiet Revolution.[120] While one can question the extent to which the Montrealers transformed their discipline, it is difficult to ignore their role in the redefinition of Quebecers' self-image in the postwar period.[121]

Much like the journal, the affairs of the Institut in the late 1960s and early 1970s also provided evidence of the rise of the new generation and the rapid disappearance of Groulx's immediate successors. In response to the sorts of fears expressed by Juliette Rémillard, the board of the Institut was transformed with the addition of a number of relatively young professionals such as Linteau and Jean-Pierre Wallot. These newcomers altered the composition of a board that had long balanced the interests of laymen and clerics, and of professional historians and their more amateur counterparts.[122]

This new generation soon made its presence known with the adoption in 1970 of a revised set of regulations to govern the affairs of the IHAF. In particular, Groulx's original regulations were amended so as to reduce, if not eliminate, the role of the amateur historian. In 1947 there were no particular specifications as to the sort of person who could join the Institut. Moreover, there was explicit reference to the 'membres-correspondants' – isolated amateur historians whom Groulx wanted to involve in the activities of the IHAF. If there were at least three such amateurs residing in an outlying area, they could form a 'section,' which would be aided by the Institut to produce regional historical studies. By 1970, however, the Institut's regulations no longer made reference to either the 'membres-correspondants' or the 'sections.' Membership, more generally, was reserved for 'researchers, authors and professors' who thought of themselves as historians.[123] To guarantee the marginalization of amateurs, Jean-Pierre Wallot called in 1972 for closer scrutiny of requests from prospective members and 'the transformation of the Institut into a real professional association for its members.'[124] In line with this change, the new leaders scrapped the long-standing policy of organizing the annual meeting around a number of unconnected lectures. Now there would be a series of sessions looking at particular problems, so that scholarly debate might reign.[125]

In the short term at least, these changes did little to strengthen the Institut. Juliette Rémillard wrote to Brunet in early 1971 about the danger of marginalizing the amateurs who had supported the IHAF from the start: 'I am concerned that we are acting in a manner that will alienate a large number of people ... The problem is both delicate and complex.'[126] Only a few months later the IHAF attracted just thirty people to its annual meeting, thus reflecting the limited professional clientele then in existence.[127] Over the next twenty-five years the ranks of Quebec's professional historians would grow, while the revisionists would develop an entirely new perspective on Quebec's past. The long-term direction for historical writing was set not by Groulx's immediate successors, but rather by historians who had had little, if any, contact with the maître.

V

While this chapter has focused on the so-called École de Montréal, it has also considered the role of Abbé Groulx over the last two decades of his life, as well as that of a new generation coming of age in the late 1960s and early 1970s. Much of the literature that has elevated Frégault, Séguin, and Brunet to the ranks of cultural icons has failed to place them in a larger context. Accordingly, there has been a tendency to consider Groulx as a spent force by the late 1940s, so as to magnify the innovations of the young Montrealers. In fact, however, Groulx wrote his most 'modern' work in the early 1950s and maintained cordial relations with his successors as long as he could because he sympathized with their professional ambitions. By the end of his career, Groulx, like many of his generation, felt betrayed by the direction that Quebec society was taking in the 1960s and struck out against his former colleagues in his last books. While some have dwelled upon these works both to emphasize the primitive nature of Groulx's writings and to exaggerate the contribution of Frégault and his colleagues, the exercise is strained.

The Montreal historians did develop a new way of viewing the impact of the Conquest on Quebec society, and there is no reason to minimize their role in the articulation of a new self-image for Quebecers. No longer willing to accept Groulx's belief that Quebec's history could be interpreted as one of successful resistance to the implications of the Conquest, Frégault and his colleagues argued that mere survival had been a dubious legacy and that Quebecers needed new political strategies to become a 'normal' people once again. At the very least, this historical interpretation helped legitimize the reforms embodied in the Quiet Revolution.

In spite of the significance of the Montreal historians' new way of looking at the past, their contributions to the discipline have frequently been overstated. Jean Lamarre has described Maurice Séguin's work as 'a model of unity and coherence'; of course, he published but one significant work – his doctoral dissertation, which finally appeared in the 1970s.[128] As for Michel Brunet, most of his works were collections of essays. Even Guy Frégault's output, while impressive early in his career, tailed off with his departure for the civil service. Moreover, the limited body of work that these historians produced was not always based on exhaustive archival research. Groulx was a much more diligent researcher than either Séguin or Brunet. Frégault followed in the maître's footsteps in this regard, but only early on. Not only did the Montreal historians produce few works of significance, but they also played a relatively minor role in directing the fortunes of the journal and association that Groulx had established. Placing these historians in a broader context only serves to diminish their significance, for it was an even younger group that finally transformed the structures that Groulx had put in place.

Despite their limitations, the Montreal historians have maintained a relatively good press over the past thirty years, in no small part because they were Groulx's immediate successors. To the extent that Groulx has been seen as a primitive historian, Frégault, Séguin, and Brunet, professionally trained and with a new way of looking at the past, have served as symbols of the new Quebec which was emerging in the postwar period and flowered with the Quiet Revolution. Some commentators have argued that their approach was dramatically innovative, but such exaggerated assessments can be maintained only by assuming that early-twentieth-century Quebec had been passed over by larger changes within the historical profession. In fact, as we have seen, a number of Quebec historians, Groulx included, had embraced new methods long before the Montrealers emerged. The Montreal historians did make a difference in terms of the way in which they conceptualized the past. Nevertheless, we should keep their influence in perspective, so as to avoid giving them undeserved credit either for methodological innovation or for scientific objectivity.

4

Maybe It Was Our Fault:
The Laval Approach

I

In the aftermath of the Second World War, Quebecers were no longer prepared to accept the bromides of nationalist leaders such as Abbé Groulx who insisted that there was something to celebrate about the long struggle for mere survival. French speakers wanted to share in the considerable economic prosperity that followed the war, and this demand led to general reconsideration of the way in which they perceived both themselves and the world around them. One way of coming to grips with, and rebelling against, their 'inferiority' was to blame it on others – most notably, the English speakers who had conquered Quebec in the eighteenth century and whose descendants still dominated the scene. This view of the world was communicated quite effectively by the Montreal historians.

Another way of approaching economic and political weakness was to view it as something for which Quebecers themselves had some responsibility. This viewpoint was advanced after 1945 by such historians as Marcel Trudel, Jean Hamelin, and Fernand Ouellet, all of whom began their careers at the Université Laval. By placing some, if not most, of the responsibility on the shoulders of francophones, the postwar historians at Laval showed themselves uninterested in vilifying the British conquerors and their successors. In this regard, they were following in the footsteps of Thomas Chapais and Arthur Maheux, who, as we saw above, used their positions as historians at the Quebec City campus of Laval to advance a view of the past in which the British emerged more as liberators than as conquerors. More specifically, Groulx's contemporaries at Laval perceived the British Conquest as a providential act, which had permitted the survival of a Catholic people which, had it remained under French rule, would have been subjected to the anti-clericalism of the French Revolution. Instead, Catholicism flourished under British rule, thus providing a bulwark against assimilation into the sea of North Americans who spoke English and professed various forms of Protestantism. While Chapais and Maheux may have parted company with Groulx in terms of how the Conquest should have been interpreted, they shared the maître's emphasis on the cultural survival of Quebecers.

This preoccupation with survival per se was replaced after the war by a desire for economic and social equality. At the Université de Montréal, where there had been a long tradition of seeing the Conquest as a pivotal and cataclysmic event, Frégault and his colleagues shifted from Groulx's concern about the negative cultural implications of British rule to explore the economic and political plight of French speakers that followed in the wake of the defeat of 1760. Meanwhile, at Laval, where the British had always had a much easier time of it, the postwar historians turned from praising the positive cultural ramifications of the Conquest to blaming Quebecers for their own economic and political weaknesses.

While Marcel Trudel and his colleagues followed in a tradition of historical writing at Laval going back to the early twentieth century, they also formed part of a larger movement of post-1945 intellectuals unwilling to blame the economic and political weakness of francophones solely on the presence of English speakers. Michael Behiels has described these intellectuals as liberals who were interested more in the betterment of the individual than in the defence of the collectivity. Accordingly, they were bothered by 'the all-pervasive influence of clericalism ... and the persistence of an outmoded nationalism which advocated the preservation of a rural and elitist society and neglected the development of the individual and the pursuit of social equality.'[1] Behiels sometimes went overboard in singing the praises of these liberals while condemning their more nationalistic contemporaries. Nevertheless, he did put his finger on a significant intellectual movement, which had a profound impact upon historical writing in Quebec.

The movement's best-known figure was Pierre Elliott Trudeau, who, in an important essay written in 1956, observed that Quebecers were relatively powerless because their leaders had created institutions ill-suited to the demands of the modern world. Without completely denying the legacy of the Conquest, Trudeau complained that the 'system of security' devised to protect Quebecers from their conquerors had become 'over-developed. As a result [French speakers] overvalued all those things that set them apart from others, and showed hostility to all changes (even progress) coming from without.' Ultimately, French Canadians were the architects of their own difficulties by having rejected everything associated with the conquerors, including democratic values and materialism.[2] By opposing democratic values, francophones had readily accepted 'political ideas imbued with authoritarianism,' while in the realm of economics they had focused on the virtues of small business and co-operatives, to the exclusion of competing in the mainstream.[3]

While Trudeau was at the time an outsider to the academic establishment, his point of view was reinforced by a number of Laval professors in the social sciences. In the early 1940s, while Arthur Maheux was lobbying for a history department at Laval, some major changes were taking place in the university's School of Social Sciences, created in 1938 under Père Georges-Henri Lévesque, who wanted to incorporate Catholic values into practical disciplines. Père Lévesque hoped that if Laval established the social sciences with a Catholic face, it would provide needed services and give the church the means for perpetuating its place in society.[4] During the 1940s the School was upgraded into a Faculty of Social Sciences with an increased budget, new departments, and more professors. These men, much like the Quebec historians of the time, had to leave home for graduate training. While they might have preferred Europe, they chose North American universities because of the war.[5]

In 1943 alone, three young, highly trained professors – Jean-Charles Falardeau, Albert Faucher, and Maurice Lamontagne – were hired by Laval's new Faculty of Social Sciences. Falardeau had just returned from graduate training in sociology at the University of Chicago, where he worked with Everett Hughes, best known in Quebec for his book *French Canada in Transition*. Hughes examined the way in which urbanization was transforming Quebec society but without giving benefits to French speakers, who had an outmoded way of looking at the world. From Hughes's perspective, the problem with Quebecers was their tendency to participate in the economy on the basis of 'strongly held familial' values.[6] A French Canadian was content to remain in a dead-end job because he felt that he 'owed it to his family to stay where he was safe.'[7] Even in business, francophones preferred to deal with their own and to avoid becoming indebted to lenders outside the family. Anticipating Trudeau's critique more than a decade later, Hughes argued that French Canadians failed to 'seek new solutions for their economic problems.' Instead, they depended on 'a set of traditional rural and town institutions ... to consolidate their position in smaller and older forms of enterprise.'[8]

Hughes left his mark on the sociology department at Laval. He helped design a long-term research program for the department during the 1942–3 academic year, which he spent in Quebec City. Moreover, he influenced Falardeau, who examined the way in which the structure of Quebec society had discouraged individual initiative. Falardeau pointed particularly to the power of the Catholic church, which had made the Quebecer, as far back as the French régime, 'much less an active and enterprising citizen than a submissive and faithful parishioner.'[9] In the postwar period Falardeau found Quebecers still overly reluctant to 'express [their] opposition to the ideas or actions of a priest.'[10] If French speakers were second-class economic citizens, it was due more to their own failings than to the Conquest.

In addition to gaining Falardeau, Laval's Faculty of Social Sciences became home to two economists in 1943. Albert Faucher took his graduate studies at the University of Toronto, while Maurice Lamontagne did the same at Harvard. Together they advanced a more self-critical view of Quebec's past in their 1953 study of the history of industrial development in the province. In this article Faucher and Lamontagne argued that 'Quebec's industrialization had nothing specific to do with, and was not fundamentally influenced by, its cultural environment ... Rather, it was a mere regional manifestation of the overall economic evolution of the North American continent.'[11] While the timing of Quebec's industrial development had been governed by the province's resource base, the economists turned to other, less materialistic causes to explain why 'industrialization had not been a realization of the main ethnic group of the province.'[12] The Montreal historians would have explained this situation as a natural outgrowth of the Conquest, which had placed English speakers in positions of control. The Laval economists, however, made not a single reference to 1760. Rather, they wondered 'whether social institutions [had] been able to go ahead or keep abreast of [industrial] change.'[13] While they did not think that Quebecers were incapable of taking control of the economy, they doubted that the province's institutions were up to providing the services needed to put francophones in positions of leadership. Economic inferiority was the product of internal, not external forces.

Lamontagne made this point even more explicitly in *Le fédéralisme canadien*, his 1954 defence of an increasingly centralized federation. While the Montreal historians were putting their view of the Conquest at the disposal of Quebec politicians eager to resist inroads into provincial jurisdictions, Lamontagne wanted to set the record straight to justify such incursions. He mocked those who believed that French speakers should isolate themselves from all 'outside' influences. From Lamontagne's perspective, this fear of outsiders had extended even to the federal government, which was perceived as just another foreign body 'responsible for the various problems weighing upon the province of Quebec.'[14] Lamontagne argued that Quebecers had become incapable of imagining that they bore any responsibility for the challenges to their survival as a people. The Laval economist, who was about ready to leave the university for a career in Ottawa – first as a federal bureaucrat and later as a cabinet minister – counselled Quebecers to transform their institutions, instead of carping about the evils of outsiders, and urged them to play a central role in both the economy and the more interventionist federal state. If they failed to secure positions of economic or political influence, they had only themselves to blame.

This self-critical approach gradually took hold among the historians who were hired at Laval during the 1940s and 1950s. As we saw in chapter 2, when Marcel Trudel was hired as Laval's first professionally trained Quebec historian, his views were closer to those of Groulx and the Montreal historians than to those of his superior, Abbé Maheux. By the 1950s, however, Trudel had become much more critical of Quebec society. He was joined in that decade by Fernand Ouellet and Jean Hamelin, who held very similar views. Accordingly, by the end of the decade one could identify a Laval approach to Quebec history, which was consistent with the orientation of earlier Laval historians such as Chapais as well as contemporary social scientists such as Falardeau, Faucher, and Lamontagne.

II

In his glowing tribute to the work of the Montreal historians, Jean Lamarre, not surprisingly, was critical of those historians who had plied their trade at Laval. Among his criticisms, Lamarre observed that Trudel and his colleagues had not been united by 'a common hypothesis concerning the overall direction of their society ... This is what distinguished the Montreal school from the Quebec school.'[15] As we shall see, Lamarre was selling the Laval historians short by refusing to view their self-critical perspective as 'a common hypothesis.' Nevertheless, there was some justice in his comments, if only vis-à-vis the early 1950s. At that time, the Montreal history department had a clear ideological focus, thanks to the way in which Groulx had assembled a group of men with a particular nationalist program and the scientific credentials to give that perspective credibility. By contrast, the Laval history department, in its early years at least, presented no clear profile, either methodologically or in its interpretation of Quebec's past.

The first director of the Laval department, Abbé Arthur Maheux, compensated for his lack of professional credentials by his strongly held view that French speakers were responsible for their own shortcomings. In 1958, for instance, Maheux wrote: 'In spite of [the French Canadian]'s insistence on his business efficiency my own experience is that he is incredibly inefficient and lazy ... I have met very few who have any real knowledge of the world outside Quebec and they are suspect by their compatriots.' French Canadians, along with the South African Boers and the Irish, constituted 'the world's most neurotic minority.'[16]

In selecting Marcel Trudel to be Laval's first 'professional' historian, Maheux chose someone who did not share his rather casual attitude towards historical research and who, by the early 1950s, was also hostile towards Maheux's critical view of Quebec society. As we have seen above, Trudel had just received his doctorate in literature when he was sent off to Harvard in 1945 for training as a historian in anticipation of the opening of Laval's history department. He returned to Quebec City to take up his professorial duties in 1947 and bristled under Maheux's control of the department before taking charge himself in 1954.

While he served under Maheux, Trudel developed close ties with the Montrealers, to whom he confided his displeasure with his chair's view of history. While Trudel did not entirely share Groulx's perspective, he did appreciate the maître's efforts to promote a more scientific approach to history. Trudel had sufficient respect for Groulx that he invited the latter to speak at Laval, even if this required setting up a meeting 'outside the walls of the university,' where Groulx was persona non grata because of his conflicts with Maheux.[17] Groulx thought sufficiently highly of the young Laval professor to appoint him to the board of directors of the Institut d'histoire de l'Amérique française in 1948.

Trudel similarly developed a close friendship with the younger historians at Montreal, which was strengthened by their shared sense that Quebec was under siege from a federal government eager to make inroads into provincial jurisdictions. For instance, in 1953, in the aftermath of the report of the Massey Commission on cultural affairs in Canada, Trudel wrote to Frégault about the real intention behind Ottawa's claim that it wanted to encourage Canada's bicultural character. Trudel saw this as part of a devious plot to lead Quebec academics to think 'of themselves less as French Canadians and more as members of a larger bicultural country. This campaign has resulted in some disastrous consequences. We now see some of our university professors publishing in English instead of French, and generally mocking everything about the province of Quebec.'[18] Given their common view of the dangers facing Quebecers, Trudel and the Montrealers were also on the same wavelength when it came to interpreting the past. Accordingly, while Frégault was beginning to lay out his view of the disastrous consequences of the Conquest, Trudel was writing that British civil rule had brought a cataclysmic change, 'which undermined the entire society and resulted in the suppression of the French language.'[19]

By the early 1950s Trudel and the Montrealers found themselves cooperating on a number of projects. For instance, in response to Trudel's complaints about the unilingual policies of the *Canadian Historical Review* (*CHR*), Frégault suggested a common front of the young francophone historians at the next meeting of the Canadian Historical Association (CHA). 'Wouldn't it be possible for us to make a direct attack against the position of Maheux regarding the use of French in the *Review*? Our position would be seconded by my colleague Brunet ... We would also have the support of Séguin.'[20] (It was curious that Frégault should have chosen to protest before the CHA about CHR policy, since the journal was, and still is, published by the University of Toronto Press, not by the CHA.) Trudel responded enthusiastically, since he had been engaged in a debate with the CHR over the publication of a review that he had submitted in French, but which the journal insisted on publishing in English. Trudel saw this as a matter of principle: 'In Canada, a French Canadian should never be forced to translate his work into English.'[21]

Frégault also suggested to Trudel that the young francophone historians publish a collection of documents on the history of Quebec. Denied access to original documents, students were producing not 'serious works, but merely whimsical pieces of homework.' To facilitate the preparation of such a volume, which would include short essays laying out the context for each document, Frégault proposed a division of labour: he would be responsible for the French régime, Trudel for the period from the Conquest to Confederation, and Brunet for the modern era. Nevertheless, Frégault wanted the three historians to participate collectively in all parts of the volume. 'We would present our work so that no one could ever ask: "Pourquoi sommes-nous divisés?" (Why are we divided?)' – a mocking reference to Maheux, Trudel's nemesis, who had published a volume with the same title to condemn Quebec's reservations regarding participation in the Second World War.[22]

Trudel enthusiastically agreed to participate in this joint venture, which resulted in the appearance of *Histoire du Canada par les textes* in 1952. In the process, Trudel developed close ties with Michel Brunet, with whom he began to correspond about the deficiencies of Laval's social science professors, who were already arguing, as would Trudel a few years later, that Quebec's problems had been substantially self-inflicted. In 1954, for instance, Brunet wrote to Trudel that he doubted 'the intellectual honesty of the social scientists at Laval.'[23] A few days later Trudel responded in the same spirit, dismissing the Laval professors as defenders of an out-moded perspective on Quebec society.[24] Trudel's outlook in the early 1950s was clearly closer to that of the Montreal historians than to that of such Laval historians as Fernand Ouellet. Though he had been Trudel's student, Ouellet was already beginning to express a critical view of Quebec society, a perspective that Trudel would come to appreciate within a few years.[25]

Trudel was, for all intents and purposes, a member of the 'École de Montréal' during the early 1950s, virtually indistinguishable from Brunet and Frégault in the eyes of Groulx's friend Léo-Paul Desrosiers, who was discomfited by their tendency, in their *Histoire du Canada par les textes*, to question the purity of the motives of some of the leaders of New France.[26] Desrosiers would have come to a very different conclusion regarding the relationship between Trudel and the Montrealers, however, had he looked at the revised, 1963 edition of *Histoire du Canada par les textes*. While the original version had, at Frégault's request, said nothing regarding authorship of the sections, the new edition dispensed with the illusion of collective responsibility. Now, Frégault was credited with the section on New France, which remained unchanged from the 1952 original – a fact that can be explained by the historian's duties in the early 1960s as Quebec's deputy minister of cultural affairs. Brunet's section, dealing with the period since 1854, contained new documents, most pertaining to the post-1945 era and focused on federal efforts to intrude on Quebec's jurisdictions. Brunet was advancing the perspective of the Montreal historians, who constantly emphasized the way in which Quebecers had long been at the mercy of external forces.

Trudel, however, added documents pertinent to the period from the
Conquest to the mid-nineteenth century, several of which suggested that
the consequences of the Conquest had not been entirely negative. For
instance, he included two new documents designed to deflect attention
from the early-nineteenth-century governorship of James Craig. While
the Montreal historians might have seen Craig's francophobic behaviour
as evidence of the evils of British rule, Trudel commented on the way in
which British authorities tended to disavow their governor's actions.[27] In
his foreword to a document dealing with Lord Gosford's 1835 'diplomatic mission' to resolve the constitutional problems in Lower Canada,
Trudel cautioned against the tendency of some historians to condemn
'imperial policies' without serious analysis.[28] Finally, he suggested that
the Conquest had not been entirely cataclysmic when he spoke kindly of
the role of Philemon Wright in opening up the Ottawa valley to settlement.[29] Trudel's positive depiction of an English speaker contrasts sharply
with the Montrealers' view of the linguistic minority as having constituted a problem.

Trudel also distinguished himself from the Montrealers in the 1963
version of *Histoire du Canada par les textes* by looking at certain problems
that were deeply rooted in French-Canadian society, and for which British rule could not easily be blamed. More specifically, Trudel added
documents that stressed the growing role of the Catholic church in the
social and economic lives of francophones in the late eighteenth and
early nineteenth centuries. As he put it, 'During the French regime, the
Church played its normal role, staying clear of any involvement with
either agriculture or the settlement of new lands; in the middle of the
nineteenth century, however, it went beyond the spiritual sphere to help
French Canadians deal with their social problems ... It was at precisely
this moment that the Canadian church began to promote the concept of
"agriculturalisme" [the idea that French Canadians were destined to be
an agricultural people].'[30]

By using the term 'agriculturalisme,' Trudel was taking dead aim at
Brunet, who had used it on several occasions over the previous decade.
The Montreal historian, however, meant it as an unrealistic rejection of
the materialistic world, foisted on French speakers by leaders, such as the
clergy, who had had little choice but to cooperate with the British rulers.
From Brunet's perspective, Quebecers' problems had been externally
imposed, while for Trudel, who made no reference to the impact of the
Conquest, clerical domination had developed without assistance from
the British. By suggesting that Quebecers' problems were of their own

making, Trudel was now on the same wavelength as his counterparts in other disciplines at Laval, sharing their profound impatience with the ongoing role of the clergy, an impatience that ultimately resulted in Trudel's departure from the province in 1965. In the meantime, however, his doubts about the propriety of clerical influence became a recurring theme in his writings.

Trudel first advanced a somewhat critical view of the clergy in a 1952 study of the immediate impact of the Conquest in the Trois-Rivières region. In this work he pointed to 'the reprehensible conduct' of two priests whose behaviour indicated 'a lack of discipline and a weak character.' The issues involved were relatively minor ones – laziness in one case and unwillingness to respect figures of authority in the other – and even Trudel referred to the discussion as 'a digression.'[31] Nevertheless, his willingness to focus on clerical improprieties foreshadowed the break that was coming with the Montreal historians. While Frégault and his colleagues had tried to make the early history of Quebec appear more secular, nothing in their work was openly critical of the clergy. They reserved their criticism for the British, who had forced the clergy to occupy a leadership role after the destruction of the lay elite from the French régime. By focusing on negative aspects of the role of the clergy without making any reference to British responsibility, Trudel was opening the door for an interpretation that was both anti-clerical and self-critical.

After 1952 the gap between Trudel and his Montreal counterparts steadily widened. While Frégault and Brunet were becoming increasingly explicit about the cataclysmic effect of the Conquest, the Laval professor was exploring problems emanating from within. In 1955 he returned to clerical improprieties in his study of the nineteenth-century renegade priest Charles Chiniquy, whose clerical career was characterized by an unwillingness to play by the rules and who was ultimately chased from the Catholic church, ending his life as a Protestant.[32] Next, Trudel published his two-volume L'église canadienne sous le régime militaire, in which he returned to the years immediately following the Conquest. While his study of the Trois-Rivières church during the same period had made only passing reference to the improprieties of two troublesome priests, Trudel now emphasized internal weaknesses and paid little attention to externally induced problems. For instance, an entire chapter dealt with 'the personal problems of the parish priests.' In introducing this chapter, he recognized that he was dealing with 'a touchy issue ... If I have decided to deal with this matter, it is not out of any malicious spirit. It is not the role of the historian to dwell upon the mistakes of the past with the sole purpose of titillating a certain section of the population; nevertheless, he ought to tell the entire truth about the past, when it is relevant to making sense of an era. This is why I have decided to look into the private lives of the clergy.'[33]

Trudel's depiction of the post-Conquest church led Brunet to break with his friend. The Montreal historian's bitterly negative review of *L'église canadienne* concentrated on Trudel's treatment of James Murray, the first governor of Quebec following the Conquest, and Mgr Briand, the leader of the Catholic church at the time. Brunet complained that Murray had been depicted as 'someone who was unpredictable and who enjoyed ruling in an arbitrary fashion.'[34] Brunet speculated, perhaps correctly, that this portrayal was designed to allow Trudel to distance himself from Abbé Maheux, who had written sympathetically about Murray. Brunet complained, however, that by focusing on Murray, the individual, Trudel had lost sight of the major structural change that had taken place in 1760. Similarly, Brunet could not understand Trudel's critique of Briand's willingness to work with the new rulers. More concerned with placing the blame firmly on the shoulders of the conquerors, the Montreal historian had little interest in blaming one of the conquered. 'It is about time that we make it clear, once and for all, that the Conquest and the permanent occupation of Canada led inevitably to the enslavement of the Canadiens and the destruction of all of their institutions.'[35]

Brunet concluded oddly that Trudel's work lacked 'a clear point of view.'[36] Perhaps he meant that Trudel's emerging interpretation differed from his own, but in any event the Laval professor would soon elaborate on his view of Quebec's history as having been marked as much by internal difficulties as by externally imposed constraints. Trudel did this by shifting his attention, which had heretofore been directed to the period following the Conquest, to the French régime. In the same year as Brunet's review appeared, Trudel depicted New France as an economic disaster, in which only the fur trade had generated any profits. Because of its own weaknesses, not the evil designs of the British, when the Seven Years' War came, 'New France quickly collapsed.'[37] Trudel returned to the same argument in a 1961 lecture: 'Our weakness goes back for three centuries. As a French colony, we lagged desperately behind the fantastic development of the American colonies ... [This] was a colony that, according to the first hand account of one intendant, could not provide a living for a single printer. Conquered by the British and ceded by France, the people of the colony remained illiterate for many years. Frozen in time, [we were] antagonistic to anything in the nature of progress.'[38]

By the early 1960s little was left of Trudel's ties to the Montreal historians. His correspondence with Frégault and Brunet had all but ended by the mid-1950s, and, as we have seen, his ongoing participation in the *Histoire du Canada par les textes* project only increased his isolation from his old friends.[39] This distancing was paralleled by his increasing alienation from Quebec society more generally – the result in part of his rather distasteful experience with the new Quebec state that was emerging in the 1960s. Convinced that Quebecers had been the architects of their own difficulties, Trudel would have been troubled philosophically by the construction of a state designed to undo the alleged wrongs suffered since the Conquest. Philosophical qualms aside, however, he agreed to serve as an original member of the Conseil des Arts du Québec, established in 1961 to advise the new Ministry of Cultural Affairs, whose deputy minister was Guy Frégault, with whom Trudel had not had cordial relations for some time.

Frégault saw the Conseil des Arts as a potential competitor for the minister's ear and sought its destruction, which ultimately came about in 1971, during Trudel's presidency.[40] In his memoirs, Frégault made it clear that there was little room for dissenting views in the new Quebec that he was helping to build. Real Quebecers shared Frégault's belief that French speakers constituted 'a people whose history had been shaped by a great humiliation.' Those who operated from such a premise wanted Quebec to have exclusive control over cultural matters, while those who were open to some cooperation with the federal government, such as the majority of the members of the Conseil des Arts, including Trudel and the Laval sociologist Jean-Charles Falardeau, were 'Canadians first, and only Québécois thereafter.' While Trudel and Frégault had joined forces in the early 1950s to protest against potential federal incursions in cultural affairs following the report of the Massey Commission, they now found themselves in direct conflict.[41]

If Trudel was disturbed in the early 1960s by zealots such as Frégault, who seemed too eager to get even for ancient wrongs, he was equally concerned by what he saw as a certain intolerance left over from the period prior to the Quiet Revolution. Since the early 1950s Trudel, through his historical writings, had had some harsh words regarding the role of the church. He had not gone public with his concerns about the role of the church in modern Quebec, but this situation changed in 1963 when he became president of the Quebec City chapter of the Mouvement laïque de langue française (MLF). This organization was lobbying for a more tolerant Quebec society, open not only to practising Catholics but also to 'the minority which consisted of both non-Catholics and non-believers.' In education, the MLF did not wish to 'to run the brothers and sisters out of the schools; we seek only to develop a system that more accurately reflects our pluralistic society.' Trudel's call for tolerance made little impression on clerical authorities, who reminded the public that Trudel was the same person who, in his guise as a historian, had given publicity to Chiniquy, the renegade priest, and had provided evidence of clerical ownership of slaves.[42]

As a result of his actions on behalf of the MLF, Trudel came into conflict with his dean, a layman 'well known for his kowtowing to clerical authorities,' who apparently did the church's bidding by removing Trudel as chair of the history department in 1964. This indignity was followed by denial to the historian of both a promotion and an increase in salary.[43] After this experience Trudel found little to keep him in Quebec, and he began to look for a job outside the province. In the end, he had to decide between Carleton University and the University of Ottawa, finally opting for the former, since the latter was still dominated by the clergy. Frégault had not seem bothered by this clerical presence when he left the Université de Montréal for the University of Ottawa in 1959, but Trudel looked at the matter very differently. While Frégault had always pushed for a more secular view of Quebec history, he had never spoken harshly of the clergy; this, of course, was not true of Marcel Trudel. Accordingly, the Laval professor set out in 1965 for Carleton, where he remained for only one year before moving on to the University of Ottawa, just recently secularized.[44]

From relatively early in his career Trudel had been bothered by the frequently negative influence of the Catholic church on Quebec society. His early criticisms of the church led, over time, to a more general critique of Quebec society and, ultimately, to the conclusion that the Conquest had been a blessing of sorts. As he noted in a radio interview recorded in 1995, 'French-Canadian authors have completely ignored the advantages brought about by the Conquest ... It provided us with new commercial possibilities ... It led to the introduction of the printing press which did not exist during the French regime. We were able to enjoy newspapers and a form of criminal justice which was much better than that which we had had under French rule.'[45]

Trudel's self-critical approach was his lasting contribution to the writing of Quebec history, even if he himself was reluctant to see his work as having been marked by anything more than a search for the truth. In a 1981 interview, Trudel insisted that when he turned in the 1950s to the history of New France, he did so 'without any particular ideology. I have never been interested in interpretation, or the development of some grand point of view.' While the Montrealers were attributing 'all of our misfortunes to the Conquest, I was trying to find out exactly what happened, without any preconceived idea, free of any spirit of nationalism. This has been my policy throughout my career: to be completely neutral in the face of competing ideologies.'[46] In spite of such claims of objectivity, Trudel did have a distinctive vision of the past that eventually distanced him from both Groulx and the maître's Montreal disciples. Moreover, he advanced that point of view not only through his writing but also through his decade-long direction of Laval's history department.

III

Just as Trudel denied that his writing had been marked by any ideological predisposition, so too did he refuse to see any common orientation in the department that he had assembled at Laval between 1954 and 1964. In his memoirs he noted, 'There was a Montreal school; and so people tended to speak of a Quebec school. But there really was no Quebec approach, if one means by that a certain way of thinking, a certain common methodology, that united a well-defined group of historians. To be sure, there was a Quebec school in the sense that we had a particular way of approaching the past; we tried to make sure that our findings were based upon what could be found in the documents; we were open to any interpretation and to all approaches.'[47] Trudel's claims notwithstanding, the Laval historians were in fact united by much more than an openness towards just 'any interpretation.'

On taking over the direction of Laval's Institut d'histoire et de géographie from Abbé Maheux, Trudel was the only full-time Laval professor teaching courses relevant to Quebec history, assisted by members of the Faculty of Social Sciences, such as Jean-Charles Falardeau and Albert Faucher, who, as we saw above, shared Trudel's doubts about the the assumptions of the Montreal historians.[48] Trudel was also linked to Falardeau and Faucher by the fact that they, like their counterparts in Montreal, had left Quebec for other parts of North America for their graduate training. However, by the early 1950s, as conditions in Europe began to return to normal, the Laval history department developed close ties with the profession in France. As Trudel wrote in the early 1960s, his department had been 'established upon the French model of the Institut, [and] it developed with the ongoing support of professors who were either from France or had been trained there.'[49]

Laval's French connection stood in sharp contrast with the situation at the Université de Montréal, where Frégault, the first chair of the history department, made no great secret of his francophobia. After the establishment of his department, Frégault made it clear that he did not want a curriculum that would give 'a central place to the history of France.' Given his concern with the effects of the Conquest, he wanted students to pay more attention to the history of England, which 'has played a greater role in our political and economic history than ... France.'[50] In the years to follow, Frégault became more insistent on the cataclysmic dimensions of the Conquest and referred to France in his writings only in order to emphasize its negative role in Canadian history, stressing, for instance, the way in which France had abandoned the Canadiens in the 1750s and suggesting that the French might have deported the Acadians had the British not done the job.[51] This francophobia also extended to the way in which Frégault carried out his administrative duties. Even though he kept the department's links with France to a minimum, he complained fairly regularly about the way in which the French were favoured over Quebecers within the university.[52] On leaving for the University of Ottawa in 1959, he remarked that he was happy to escape from the influence of the French-educated dean, Arthur Sidéleau, whom Frégault categorized as an unrepentant francophile.[53]

Brunet shared Frégault's negative view of France, mocking those such as Maurice Lamontagne who believed that Quebecers had much to gain from closer ties with Paris. Lamontagne, a professor of economics at Laval from 1943 to 1954, whose views regarding the appropriateness of a strong federal government were discussed above, was taken to task by Brunet for suggesting in Le fédéralisme canadien that Quebecers needed to forge 'strong cultural links to France.' This indicated to Brunet Lamontagne's willingness to have Quebecers placed under the tutelage of others: 'We could be ruled from Ottawa and taught from Paris.'[54]

By contrast, there was not the slightest hint of francophobia in the Laval history department. Even before Trudel succeeded Maheux as chair, ties with France were given high priority. In his memoirs, Trudel described the way in which Laval's curriculum had been shaped to give appropriate attention to the role of France. Unlike Frégault, who proposed concentrating on England, Trudel asked: 'How can we hope to make sense of the French regime, for instance, without a sound understanding of the history of France, the country from which we came, as well as the history of England and of Europe more generally?' Moreover, while Frégault wanted to limit the influence of French professors in Montreal, Trudel was actively recruiting from France such historians as André Latreille, Robert Mandrou, and Roland Mousnier, who not only ensured that Laval students would be well versed in French history but also provided a conduit for those who wished to pursue graduate studies in France. Trudel noted: 'These links with French professors provided our students with easy access to French universities ... These students had a privileged status; they had ties to these professors that the students from France could not even imagine.'[55]

Between the establishment of the Laval history department in 1947 and Trudel's departure in 1965, four men were hired to teach Quebec history at the university, each of whom began his education at Laval before going on to France for further training.[56] The first to follow this path was Claude Galarneau, who has described himself as the 'the first history student in a [French-language] university in Quebec ... I had always wanted to study history, but this was not possible at the moment that I was thinking about going to university. I could have gone to McGill or Toronto, but this was out of the question for someone from Quebec City. Then in March 1947, I learned that an Institut d'histoire et de géographie was opening at the Université Laval in the following September.' Galarneau soon found himself face to face with instructors who had been imported from France, 'since we did not have professors trained for the job at hand.'[57]

The young student's exposure to these French professors led him to abandon the 'the very strong current of francophobia' in postwar Quebec.[58] Galarneau was influenced particularly by André Latreille, who was visiting from Lyon, and when he decided to continue his education, he followed his French maître. From 1950 to 1953 Galarneau studied at Lyon and Paris, before returning to take up a teaching post at Laval. A decade later Galarneau's itinerary would be replicated by Pierre Savard, who would follow Latreille to Lyon before returning to teach at Laval.[59] Fernand Ouellet has suggested that Latreille was the perfect choice to begin the links between Laval and France because of his impeccable views on religious questions. Latreille wrote several works on the role of religion in French society, and when, in 1961, he edited a collection of essays on Quebec, he described the province as 'a place from which the spirit of French culture and Catholicism might spread.'[60] As Ouellet put it, 'The Laval history department was open to the outside world, but not to all outside worlds, because Quebec society in 1950 was still dominated by the clergy.'[61]

Ouellet had been a classmate of Galarneau's, but while the latter set off for graduate studies in Europe, the former found employment in the provincial archives in Quebec City. Ouellet finally made it to France when his employer sent him to Paris in 1953 to take part in the 'stage international d'archives,' a course to train aspiring archivists. During his stay, Ouellet came into contact with some of the leading French historians, who lectured the archivists on the use of documents. As Ouellet recollected, however, 'There was one historian, [Ernest] Labrousse, who influenced me profoundly and who gave a class at the time. I already knew of Labrousse's work, but the talk that he gave profoundly influenced me.'[62] On his return from France, Ouellet went back to the archives before taking up a position teaching economic history in Laval's Faculty of Commerce, where he remained from 1955 to 1965.[63] Because he had openly admitted that he was a non-believer, Laval's clerical administrators denied Ouellet a regular post in the history department. In fact, the commerce faculty was able to employ him only because of its then somewhat autonomous status vis-à-vis the church-run university.[64] Ouellet ultimately had enough of being marginalized, and when the opportunity presented itself, he left Laval for Carleton, never again to hold a university position in Quebec.[65]

Jean Hamelin, the last of the Quebec historians from the Trudel era, followed Ouellet's itinerary, earning his first degree from Laval, before going off to France in 1954. Unlike Ouellet, however, Hamelin went to Europe to pursue his doctoral studies at the centre of the French historical profession – the new sixth section of the École pratique des Hautes Études, or EPHE, in Paris (discussed in greater detail below), where he studied with Labrousse. Hamelin returned to Quebec in 1957 to take up a post in the Laval history department, where he remained for the rest of his career.

Thus by the late 1950s Trudel had been joined by a group of Quebec historians who were united by a French connection, and this link was given concrete form in 1963, when the Laval history department hosted a conference for scholars from France and Quebec. Quite appropriately, the organizer was Claude Galarneau, the first Quebecer after the war to study history in France. Perhaps reflecting a bit of the colonial mentality that Brunet had condemned, Galarneau closed the conference with the remark that it had shown 'our French maîtres that French historical methods are being used in the most recent works of our Canadian historians.'[66] Writing about the gathering some years later, Alfred Dubuc saw it as confirmation of the 'the close cooperation among [an] important group of historians from Quebec and the Annales school.'[67]

While the 1963 conference was an important event, Dubuc missed some of its significance by failing to look more closely at the participants. While he claimed that it had shown off the wares of Quebec historians, in fact all of the Quebecers presenting papers were from Laval; the Montreal historians were conspicuous by their absence. While Dubuc claimed that the French participants represented the Annales approach, in fact it was difficult to find any historian in postwar France who was untouched by the Annales school. Accordingly, to call someone an adept of the Annaliste approach was not saying very much. The situation had been very different, however, in 1929, when Marc Bloch and Lucien Febvre established the journal *Annales d'histoire économique et sociale* (hence the name Annales for the movement as a whole) as part of their rejection of the narrowly conceived political history that had long dominated French historiography.[68] The Annalistes hoped to deal with a wider array of issues by considering a broader range of sources and incorporating the methods of other disciplines. Bloch and Febvre were interested in examining both the material conditions of people's lives and the way in which groups of people perceived the world – their *mentalité collective*.

While Bloch was murdered by the Germans during the Second World War, Febvre lived to see the movement, which had been born in opposition to the status quo, become the establishment after the war. Over the next twenty years its influence was symbolized by the journal, renamed *Annales. Économies, Sociétés, Civilisations* in 1946 to indicate the breadth of its concerns, and by the establishment in 1947 of the sixth section of the EPHE, where the Annaliste emphasis on 'histoire totale' held sway. With institutionalization of the Annales approach, however, some particular tendencies became privileged, while others remained at the margins. Accordingly, even if the Annaliste credo called for an understanding of societies in all their complexities, there were profound differences of opinion as to how this goal should be achieved.

These differences left Ernest Labrousse, who had a considerable influence on the careers of Ouellet and Hamelin, in a rather ambiguous position, at the margins of the Annales movement. Guy Bourdé and Hervé Martin noted that Labrousse 'did not really belong to the Annales school; he was too influenced by Marx ... ; nevertheless, he did work with the disciples of Bloch and Febvre.' This ambiguity was further reflected in Labrousse's holding teaching positions at both the Sorbonne, whose historians did not tend to be well disposed to the Annales approach, and at the heart of the movement, the sixth section of the EPHE.[69]

In more substantive terms, Labrousse reflected the interests of the founders of the Annales movement in seeking to understand the economic conditions faced by ordinary people, particularly in eighteenth-century France. In the 1930s and 1940s he became an important figure in the French historical profession with the publication of a number of studies in which he employed quantitative methods to trace the movement of prices and incomes. His careful use of data extending over a long period of time became a defining characteristic of the Annales approach. Labrousse also left his mark by the way in which he distinguished between long-term trends and ones of a much shorter duration – what he called 'conjonctures.' This concept was to prove so important to the Annalistes that when Fernand Braudel, who succeeded Febvre as leader of the movement, edited a volume in honour of Labrousse, he entitled it *Conjoncture économique*. Braudel remarked in his introduction to the volume that Labrousse 'was responsible for making the term "conjoncture" part of the historical vocabulary ... He has given the concept a new meaning, and in the process he has created a way of looking at the past that has influenced all ... contemporary French historians.'[70]

While Labrousse offered much to the Annalistes, he also studied the past in a manner that set him apart from the mainstream of the movement as embodied by Braudel in the post-1945 era. While Braudel pushed individual events, particularly political ones, to the side in order to focus on underlying geographical, social, and economic forces, Labrousse, true to his Marxist instincts, was interested in how these underlying factors moulded political action. Lynn Hunt has observed that the Annales paradigm, in its emphasis on long-term continuities, did not prove particularly 'amenable to the investigation of major periods of upheaval such as revolutions.'[71] Labrousse, however, had little difficulty in concentrating on revolutions and during the 1940s made his mark by linking such risings with social and economic circumstances.[72] Moreover, he looked at the way in which these risings had been influenced by what he called 'the psychology of revolution.'[73] This interest in psychological factors, which had been a part of the original program of Bloch and Febvre, was marginalized by Braudel and his contemporaries, who felt that they could not 'get a purchase on mentalities as easily as they could on the economic and social structure.'[74] Because he was exploring how various factors, including psychological ones, moulded political behaviour, Labrousse was a relatively marginal figure within Annalisme.

Labrousse was probably the French historian with the greatest influence on the postwar Laval historians, but his marginality suggests that claims regarding the Quebec connection to the Annalistes have to be qualified. In fact, the two French scholars who joined Labrousse as participants at the 1963 conference at Laval were similarly peripheral. Alphonse Dupront was outside the mainstream because he was both a professor at the Sorbonne and a student of 'la psychologie collective.' The final French participant, Robert Mandrou, had close links with the Laval history department, since he taught there from time to time. Mandrou was perhaps somewhat closer to the centre of the French profession, since he was attached to the EPHE. However, like both Labrousse and Dupront he was also interested in questions of 'mentalité,' and this orientation, which placed him at odds with Braudel, contributed to Mandrou's resigning his position with the journal *Annales* in 1962.[75]

The French professors who taught at Laval from time to time were also at the margins of the Annales movement. In addition to Mandrou, there was also Roland Mousnier, described by Peter Burke as yet another outsider: 'Mousnier published his articles in the *Revue historique*, not in *Annales*. He was professor at the Sorbonne, not the Hautes Études. He was persona non grata to Braudel. If the Annales circle is a club, Mousnier is certainly not a member.'[76] Though Mousnier did not share Labrousse's Marxism, the two collaborated on a volume dealing with the eighteenth century, which examined France while dealing more broadly with Western civilization. There was little about Mousnier and Labrousse's *Le XVIII siècle* that bore the imprint of the Annales school; as the subtitle suggested this was a study of 'an intellectual, technical and political revolution.'[77]

Laval's history department, under Marcel Trudel's direction, cultivated ties with a very specific group of French historians who did not embody the preoccupation of Annalistes such as Braudel, who had little interest in either political events of psychological factors. Labrousse was clearly the most significant of these historians because of his impact on both Hamelin and Ouellet. Curiously, however, those who have analysed Quebec historiography have tended to distort the debt of the Laval historians to their French colleagues. Jean Lamarre, for instance, discussed the way in which Labrousse had encouraged Hamelin and Ouellet to consider 'social and economic questions, to the exclusion of political ones.'[78] Lamarre ignored Labrousse's fascination with political issues, in the process distorting the orientation of the Laval historians, who, as we shall see in the following section, were intensely interested in such matters, though they did not share the political perspective of the Montrealers. Serge Gagnon similarly cast the French connection in simplistic terms, noting only the impact of an Annales approach that, by the 1950s and early 1960s, was embodied by Fernand Braudel. Of course, as we have seen, Braudel held relatively little sway over the Laval historians, who were interested in more than 'socio-material history.'[79]

IV

While Marcel Trudel encouraged the cultivation of his department's ties with France, it was his colleagues, Fernand Ouellet and Jean Hamelin, whose work most explicitly reflected the French influence. On a somewhat technical level, Ouellet and Hamelin were encouraged by their French mentors to break down the boundaries between disciplines, to look for tools outside the traditional range of historical methods, and to consider the influence of social, economic, and psychological forces on political behaviour. However, the historians' openness to French influence also reflected their sense that Quebecers did not possess all the solutions for their problems. There may have been some justice in Brunet's observation that Laval academics such as Lamontagne demonstrated a colonial mentality by looking to France for answers. Nevertheless, this search for outside assistance, to put it in a somewhat different light, also reflected a self-critical disposition, which, as we have seen, was evident in Trudel's writings and occupied a central place in the works of Ouellet and Hamelin.

Ouellet's doubts about Quebecers' ability to solve their own problems were evident from the start of his career. After graduation from Laval in 1950, Ouellet immediately went to work in the provincial archives, where, thanks to his access to the papers of the family of Louis-Joseph Papineau, he soon became interested in the connection between the affairs of the Papineau family and the circumstances surrounding the Rebellions of 1837–8. In fact, almost all of Ouellet's research-based publications in the late 1950s and early 1960s dealt with that family, with the not-very-hidden aim of bringing Papineau down to size. While both Groulx and his successors in Montreal were, by the 1950s, viewing the Rebellions as a glorious, if ill-conceived, effort to throw off British oppression, Ouellet viewed the situation very differently.[80] By portraying Papineau as the ineffectual head of a dysfunctional family, he wanted to show the folly of

Quebecers in thinking that here was a man capable of leading them to the promised land by getting rid of the British conquerors. Ouellet believed that the Quebecers of the 1950s were repeating the mistakes of the 1830s by focusing on externally induced problems instead of tending to their own house, which, from his perspective, was badly in need of repair.

As he looked at the frequently troubled relationship between Papineau and his wife, Julie Bruneau, and between Julie and their children, Ouellet seemed preoccupied at times with washing the family's dirty linen in public. He made a considerable part of their correspondence available to a larger audience through the archives' published reports, and in his brief introductions to these collections Ouellet made his own perspective on the family very clear.[81] In one case, he referred to Papineau as personally responsible for having provoked 'a crisis of conscience among the Canadiens of the nineteenth century,' while in another he dwelled on the mental instability of Julie Bruneau, whom he introduced as *'the mournful madame Papineau.'*[82]

At other times, however, Ouellet tried to use the Papineau family as a route to understanding the collective mentality of a class instrumental in the outbreak of 'the revolution of 1837–8.'[83] Ouellet's use of the term 'revolution' instead of 'rebellion' clearly placed him in the camp of Labrousse, who, as we have seen, had developed a general model for the outbreak of revolutions based on the French experiences of 1789, 1830, and 1848. While Labrousse paid close attention to the influence of prices and incomes, as would Ouellet in the 1960s, the French historian also drew attention to the role of class conflict, pointing, at least in terms of the first two revolutions, to the conflict between a landed aristocracy and a rising bourgeoisie: 'This was a clash, not only between members of two classes, but of two ways of life, one based upon the land and the other based upon industrial production ... ; here was a conflict between a conservative aristocracy and a risk-taking bourgeoisie, between the old world and the new.'[84]

Ouellet similarly examined the conflict between 'conservative' and 'modern' forces in Quebec in his writings of the late 1950s. He characterized Papineau as representative of the doctors, notaries, and lawyers – the French-speaking political leaders, 'reared in the same milieu as the peasantry.'[85] It was important for Ouellet to link the peasantry and the professionals, because he was convinced that both groups were unable to cope with changing economic circumstances of the late eighteenth and early nineteenth centuries.

He pointed to the self-imposed difficulties of the peasantry, for instance, in a 1956 study of the role of auctions in Quebec peasant communities at the time of the Conquest. Echoing the French historians who were trying to transcend disciplinary boundaries, Ouellet borrowed freely from ethnology and sociology to represent the auctions as widespread events in which the habitants spent money that they could ill afford for goods that they did not really need. 'Habitants frequently ruined themselves financially by acquiring useless articles; they acted as they did solely to impress their neighbours. *The auction* suggested a conception of wealth that was far from that of the rational economic man.'[86] Ouellet was particularly struck by the absence of grain from the auctioned estate of Ignace Adam, who had died in March 1760. Even though spring had been approaching, Adam had left himself no resources to acquire seed, which signified to Ouellet that 'the peasants were selling their goods without the least concern about what would remain for the next season.' From all of this the historian concluded that any difficulties experienced by the habitant were entirely the result of his 'mentality.'[87]

In much the same fashion, Ouellet depicted the 'Canadian bourgeoisie' – Papineau's class – as incapable of adjusting 'to modern urban life.' Here was a class whose 'revolution' (Labrousse's expression) was doomed because of its inability to find a place 'in an economic world based upon competition and individual initiative.'[88] On the other side of the barricades were the winners in the revolution of 1837–8 – Quebec's counterparts to Labrousse's 'risk-taking bourgeoisie.' Ouellet described the rising, and the largely English-speaking and Protestant merchant class of the 1830s, as having been well served 'by an ideology grounded in a long-term economic strategy.'[89]

Had Ouellet simply employed Papineau as the representative of a class incapable of confronting new economic circumstances, then he would have been reasonably loyal to Labrousse's model. While the French historian was not fond of focusing on individuals, he was deeply interested in the 'mentalité collective' of classes. However, while Labrousse was convinced that class behaviour had an economic underpinning, Ouellet, driven by his need to present the leaders of French-speaking Quebec in the worst possible light, felt obliged to document the psychological problems of the Papineaus. He did not do this to point to behaviour that had an economic basis, as Labrousse might have done. Rather he frequently concentrated on the Papineaus' difficulties strictly to demean the 'Canadian bourgeoisie,' which had led Quebecers astray.

Ouellet's preoccupation with the Papineaus' emotional problems first became clear in a 1958 article which offered a 'psychological portrait' of Julie Bruneau-Papineau. Ouellet had no evident training in psychology and did not, if we judge by the sources that he provided, have a profound knowledge of the relevant literature. Nevertheless, he felt free to make extravagant claims based on relatively little evidence. From his perspective, the wife of the Patriote leader was 'easily excitable. Day-to-day problems, even when they were rather minor ... caused her much anguish, fear, and grief.'[90] Even the repeated cases of illness and death among her children were insufficient to Ouellet to justify Julie's behaviour. He was convinced, for instance, that he had found evidence of mental instability in her reaction to the death of a four-year-old daughter in 1830. 'Objectively, this was a difficult experience, but Papineau's wife had taken it in a manner that made it difficult for her to recover.'[91] If Julie was not building what Ouellet saw as a rather minor event – the death of a child – into a major calamity, then she was busily inventing 'imaginary difficulties.' At times, she even manifested physical problems that Ouellet diagnosed as psychosomatic.[92]

Ouellet clearly had little sympathy for his subject, who, he claimed, used her mental and physical infirmities as tools to 'seduce and control her household.' She had clear ideas as to how the lives of both her husband and her children should proceed, and if matters did not work out exactly as she had hoped then she was prone to feigning illness to try to get her way. Ouellet portrayed her as constantly frustrated because Papineau did not satisfy her 'need for social status' and because her children never managed to live up to her expectations.[93]

Ouellet was not interested merely, however, in the mental instability of this particular woman. Rather, he viewed her as representative of women who had long tried to dominate Quebec society since the seventeenth century. Ouellet argued that the patriarchal family imported from France had been undone by the fur trade, with the result that women came to assume 'the direction of the family' – a state of affairs still in existence in the early nineteenth century, even if the fur trade had ended. Women made the important decisions in the family so that 'the husband played a secondary role to maternal authority.' Unfortunately, the wives, such as Julie, were not up to the challenges before them and were frequently overwhelmed by their responsibilities. Unable to cope with a changing order, 'the woman came to depend upon her family and to strike out against everything outside the family circle.' Children who emerged from this inward-looking family were incapable of functioning in a liberal society, which valued individual achievement.[94]

In this article-length study, Ouellet argued far beyond his evidence as he tried to explain all of the problems of early nineteenth-century Quebec society by making generalizations based on the life of one woman. He went on to develop this argument even further in a book-length version that he attempted to publish in 1961. *Julie Papineau: un cas de mélancolie et d'éducation janséniste* never appeared because of legal wrangling that tied it up in the courts for nearly a decade.[95] Roughly half of the book was simply a reprinting of what he had already published on the subject. Most of the remainder was new material pertaining to the Papineau children, with the author seeking to reinforce his portrait of the dysfunctional Québécois family.

While Ouellet commented on the difficulties of most of the children, forced as they were to contend with the influence of Julie, he reserved his harshest treatment for the Papineau daughters, in the process reinforcing the points that he had made in his published article regarding their mother.[96] Even before attempting to publish *Julie Papineau*, Ouellet had already given some hint of his perspective on at least one of the daughters in a public talk in which he characterized Azélie Papineau as 'authoritarian, strict, hard to please, [and] aggressive.' Much like her mother, Azélie 'complicated the lives of all those around her.'[97]

In focusing on the Papineau daughters, Ouellet tried to amass more evidence of a certain pathology within Quebec society, as unstable and yet domineering women had been allowed to exert considerable influence. In his book manuscript dealing with Julie Papineau, he made sweeping statements that touched even on Julie's mother, Marie-Anne Robitaille, whom he described in a magazine article as 'pessimistic, authoritarian, devout [and] superstitious.'[98] While Ouellet had published parts of his assessment of the role of women in Quebec society in a number of journals, it was only in his book-length treatment of Julie Papineau that he brought all of the pieces together.[99] Accordingly, this manuscript constituted a sustained attack against the pernicious role of the Quebec family, undermined as it had been by the role of women.[100] In the context of Ouellet's larger body of work, this manuscript was designed to provide further evidence that the problems besetting Quebec society had been internally generated, not externally imposed.

As Ouellet developed his portrait of the Papineau family through the 1950s, he knew that at least one other Quebec historian was also interested in many of the same people. In 1956 Lionel Groulx had presented a paper about Lactance Papineau, but touching also on the other sons. Not surprisingly, the two historians agreed on very little. Ouellet was generally well disposed towards Amédée, in part because of his conversion from Catholicism, towards which the Laval historian had little sympathy.[101] Groulx, in contrast, found the new Presbyterian to have been 'mentally unstable.' While Ouellet saw in Gustave the negative influence of Julie, Groulx saw a man who was both 'precocious and distinguished' and whose life provided no evidence of mental instability.[102]

The two historians differed most profoundly, however, over Lactance, whom Ouellet, predictably, saw as having suffered from the influence of his mother.[103] By contrast, in Groulx's hands, Lactance became a very sympathetic character, a man with some mental difficulties, who did his best to overcome them. If Lactance could not cope with a changing world, the problem was attributable not to his upbringing, but rather to the very factors responsible for change in Quebec society. This was a classic example of the tendency of Ouellet, and the Laval historians more generally, to focus on internally induced problems, while Groulx, as well as his successors at Montreal, always saw the difficulties as having originated externally. Accordingly, to Groulx, Lactance was the victim of 'the problems of his times,' which included the collapse of the seigneurial regime and the arrival of large numbers of immigrants, mostly from Ireland. He belonged to a generation that had seen 'the collapse of a social structure that had held fast over such a long time, as if it were an armour made of steel.'[104] With the demise of that world it was hardly surprising to Groulx if some young men, such as Lactance, found themselves incapable of coping.

In his lifetime, Groulx never published anything about the Papineau daughters. However, a lengthy portion of his memoirs, which was written in 1955 but appeared only after his death, touched on Azélie Papineau-Bourassa.[105] While Ouellet used Azélie to help explain the depravity of Quebec in the time of Papineau, Groulx was concerned with her impact on one of her children, Henri Bourassa. More specifically, Groulx wanted to understand why Bourassa had inexplicably abandoned nationalist causes during a period that stretched from the early 1920s to the start of the Second World War. In Groulx's hands Bourassa emerged as pathetic; here was a man who had turned his back on nationalism in order to be true to Catholicism. Groulx, of course, who had managed to combine Catholicism with nationalism without any great difficulty, could not understand Bourassa's problem in rational terms. Accordingly, he described Bourassa as the victim of 'a hereditary weakness.' Both Azélie and one of her daughters, Adine, had suffered from what Groulx described as 'the illness of religious doubt.'[106] Azélie's 'doubt' had led her to compensate by going to church even when it put her life at risk; and in the case of Henri Bourassa compensation took the form of abandoning, for a time, his faith in nationalism.

Ouellet and Groulx were united by their conviction that women such as Azélie Papineau-Bourassa had the power to undermine the effectiveness of the natural leaders of Quebec society, the men. Nevertheless, there were some crucial differences in their approaches to Azélie. While Ouellet noted her personality defects, Groulx never spoke of more than a crisis of faith.[107] In fact, the latter was careful to note that he had found no evidence of 'any mental defect'; rather, Azélie simply had 'a strange disposition.'[108] As for Henri Bourassa, his own crisis of faith came to an end with his return to the nationalist fold on the outbreak of war in 1939. Accordingly, Groulx managed to end his account of the Bourassas in his memoirs on a positive note.

Because Groulx had been generally well disposed towards the Bourassa family, he was seen by the surviving members as someone who might defend their good name against a less sympathetic historian such as Ouellet. When they became aware that the Laval historian was busily sorting through the family papers that had been deposited in the provincial archives, they turned to Groulx for help, providing him with 'seventeen volumes of the correspondence of the Papineau family.'[109] Ultimately, however, the family wanted more than Groulx's sympathy in light of the impending publication of Ouellet's book focusing on the life of Julie Papineau. Accordingly, in May 1961 three of Henri Bourassa's daughters filed suit against Ouellet and his publisher, Les Presses de l'Université Laval (PUL), to block the appearance of his book.[110]

According to Anne Bourassa, who took the leading role in the family's case against Ouellet, she first became aware of the historian's interest in her family in the autumn of 1960, when she read an account of a talk that the historian had given on the mental instability of Azélie Papineau, Anne's grandmother.[111] In the following spring, while in Quebec City, she met with Ouellet, who indicated that he was only weeks away from publishing an even fuller account of the family's difficulties. Early in May 1961 Ouellet allowed Bourassa to examine his manuscript, which was already being printed. Not surprisingly, she responded negatively to the historian's depiction of two of the Papineau daughters, Ezilda and Azélie, and more generally to his discussion of 'some very painful details of an extremely personal nature. These details have nothing to do with history; and they are going to result inevitably in great harm' to the family.[112] She asked Ouellet to edit out certain offensive passages, but when this was not done and publication seemed imminent, she and her sisters felt that they had no choice but to sue both the author and PUL. Though no injuction against publication was ever issued, Ouellet's publisher was so concerned about its legal position that it immediately made sure that the copies of the book that had already been printed were removed from circulation, eventually shredding them.[113]

The lawsuit, which began in late May 1961 and lasted for nearly a decade, dealt with two issues. First, the Bourassas questioned Ouellet's right to publish passages from the Papineau-Bourassa papers that had been left with the provincial archives twenty years earlier, claiming that there had been restrictions on their use which Ouellet had managed to circumvent as an employee of the archives. When Judge Frédéric Dorion finally rendered his decision in January 1970, he categorically rejected this part of the Bourassas' claim, noting that the documents had been 'a gift to the province with no strings attached.'[114]

This part of Dorion's decision might appear to have been a victory for Ouellet, but, if so, it was a rather hollow one. It seems that while the lawsuit was before the courts, the Bourassa family removed some of the documents that were at the centre of the controversy. Operating on the assumption that the documents still belonged to the family, Anne Bourassa was able to act in good conscience when, in 1968, she 'signed an agreement with the [Quebec] Department of Cultural Affairs which authorized her to withdraw some of the Papineau-Bourassa collection from the Archives.' Nevertheless, when Judge Dorion ruled, two years later, that the documents in question had in fact been gifts to the archives, Blair Neatby, Ouellet's colleague at Carleton, argued in a memorandum to members of the Canadian Historical Association that the 'Archives should regain possession immediately.' Sensing that the Bourassa family had removed the documents to prevent further exposés such as Ouellet's, Neatby closely linked the reconstruction of the Papineau-Bourassa collection with the freedom of the historian to explain the past as he or she saw fit.[115]

The question of the historian's freedom of speech was even more central to the second aspect of the Bourassas' lawsuit, which focused directly on how Ouellet had interpreted his evidence. The Bourassas contended that Ouellet's work was defamatory and, if published, would result in 'serious and irreparable damage to their reputations and their peace of mind.' They were outraged that Ouellet had decided to probe 'the most sordid details of the lives of the members of the Papineau-Bourassa family.' In particular, the Bourassa sisters pointed to the way in which he had depicted women in the Papineau family, arguing that Ouellet's highly negative treatment, if published, would cause 'serious and irreparable harm to their reputations and their feelings.'[116] As compensation, they demanded damages of only $600, but they wanted a ban on publication and a withdrawal from bookstores of any copies already distributed.[117]

The lawsuit was a significant event for the Quebec historical profession precisely because it constituted a public challenge to the right of the historian to interpret the past as he or she saw fit, on the basis of available documentation. Ouellet contended that he was 'a historian and his work [was] a work of history based on the accuracy of the facts.' He was a professional who had 'an inalienable right to consult the appropriate documents in the exercise of his profession so as to arrive at judgments on both people and periods from the past.'[118] This position was supported by the witnesses who appeared on his behalf.[119] In particular, Jean Hamelin pointed to the way in which Ouellet had striven for objectivity, even if his conclusions might have been troubling for some. Ouellet's objectivity was contested by the Bourassas' 'expert' witness, François-Albert Angers, an economist and longtime ally of Abbé Groulx, who dismissed the book as 'extremely disagreeable.' He claimed that Ouellet had not presented appropriate evidence to support his assertions. Accordingly, the book was not 'sufficiently objective to constitute a work of history ...'[120]

Notable by their absence throughout most of this affair were Ouellet's counterparts at the Université de Montréal, who might well have sympathized with him, since they were, in their own way, engaged in the process of making history more 'scientific.' In fact, at roughly the same time as the Bourassa sisters were filing suit against Ouellet, the Montrealers were parting company with Groulx over historians' responsibility to work with a certain scientific rigour.[121] Nevertheless, it would appear that the only evidence of their support for Ouellet came in the form of a letter sent by Michel Brunet to Blair Neatby, who was actively championing Ouellet's cause within the Candian Historical Association. Brunet wrote that 'the freedom of all researchers in the social sciences is at risk here. The future of our disciplines would be in danger if Professor Ouellet were to lose this case.'[122]

The apparent lack of interest on the part of the Montreal historians was also reflected in the failure of the Institut d'histoire de l'Amérique française (IHAF) to lift a finger on Ouellet's behalf. One might have understood the position of the IHAF while it was under the control of Groulx and somewhat in conflict with the 'scientific' pretensions of the younger historians both at Laval and at the Université de Montréal. Groulx died, however, in 1967, and over the late 1960s and into the early 1970s, the Institut was under the control of Frégault and Brunet who, if we judge from the minutes and correspondence of the IHAF, did nothing to help Ouellet. At the same time that the Canadian Historical Association (CHA) was receiving contributions from numerous individuals interested in helping it to defray Ouellet's legal expenses, the IHAF appears to have been inactive.[123] The Institut was apparently prepared to ignore Ouellet's plight, and the potential dangers of this lawsuit to all historians, simply because the Laval historian had a view of the past that clashed with that of most of its members.[124]

The CHA consistently supported Ouellet between 1966 and 1973.[125] The matter first came to the attention of most members in May 1968 by means of an open letter from Blair Neatby to the president. Neatby pointed to the implications for all historians if Ouellet were to be found guilty of damaging the reputation of living people by discussing the lives of their ancestors. '[The Bourassas] do not deny the facts, but they deny the historian's right to refer to these facts and his right to draw conclusions from them. Canadian historical writing will be emasculated if the courts can decide what facts are historical and what deductions from these facts are permissible.' Since the issues were relevant to all Canadian historians, Neatby asked the CHA to help cover Ouellet's legal costs, which it agreed to do up to and following the rendering of Dorion's judgment in January 1970.[126]

While the judge upheld Ouellet's right to employ the documents in the Papineau-Bourassa collection, he went a long way towards accepting the Bourassas' argument regarding the defamatory nature of Ouellet's work. Dorion did not grant an injuction against publication, but he did rule that Ouellet's actions had caused the Bourassas suffering, for which the historian was ordered to pay $400. Needless to say, it was not the award itself that Ouellet and his defenders in the CHA found so troubling. Rather, they were bothered by the notion that a historian could be dragged before the courts and fined, no matter how lightly, for making well-documented remarks about people no longer living. However, Ouellet probably could not have expected any other judgment from someone of Dorion's background. The historian was highly critical of the church's role in Quebec society, while Dorion had long been involved in defending that role. As a young man in the 1910s he was active in Catholic youth organizations, and in the 1960s he was defending Quebec's Catholic schools against the forces of secularization. Moreover, while Ouellet was highly critical of nationalism, Dorion had been active in nationalist politics, particularly during the 1940s, when he served as an independent, anti-conscriptionist member of Parliament.[127]

In light of the implications of Dorion's ruling, the CHA continued to pursue the Ouellet case, financing appeals first to the Court of Queen's Bench and then to the Supreme Court of Canada. In both instances, the justices ruled that the amount demanded by the Bourassas had been too small to permit an appeal.[128] The CHA failed to have the Dorion judgment overturned but in both cases was prepared to argue forcefully for the rights of the historian.

Even when the appeal route came to an end late in 1970, the CHA carried on, this time to convince the Presses de l'Université Laval that it had a moral, if not legal, obligation to distribute Ouellet's work, since Dorion's decision had not forbidden publication. The publisher feared being dragged before the courts yet again, but the CHA was still trying to change the minds of the PUL's directors as late as the association's annual meeting in the summer of 1972, when a resolution was passed urging the press to do the right thing.[129] In a memorandum designed to bring members up to date on the affair, Blair Neatby eloquently observed: 'It is no exaggeration to say that if the book is not distributed it will have been suppressed. It would mean that the great-grandchildren of Julie Papineau have prevented the publication of facts which have not been questioned and conclusions which have not been challenged. A publishing firm should not deliberately publish libelous material but nor should it refuse to publish merely because of the threat of a libel suit.' Neatby noted that after Dorion's judgment Fides had put out the second volume of Groulx's memoirs, which, as we saw above, dealt at some length with the mental instability of the Papineau family. 'If Fides could publish this material, a university press, with its commitment to scholarship, should not hesitate.'[130] This appeal fell on deaf ears; neither PUL nor any other publisher was willing to tangle with the Bourassas, and the book was effectively killed.[131]

The Bourassas' victory extended even beyond the effective suppression of Ouellet's book on Julie Papineau. The lawsuit apparently forced Ouellet to tone down his published comments regarding the Papineau family. One is struck, for instance, by the contrast between his *Papineau: A*

Divided Soul, a pamphlet that appeared approximately when the Bourassas began their legal action, and his piece on Papineau in the *Dictionary of Canadian Biography (DCB)*, published in 1972. In the first case, though he made no extravagant comments regarding mental instability among the women in the family, Ouellet did refer to Papineau as 'unstable ... if not neurotic' and the children as 'timid, uneasy, highly strung and unfit to mix well outside the family circle.' By contrast, in his *DCB* biography he paid relatively little attention to family matters.[132] As for Ouellet's idea of producing a full-scale biography of Papineau, hinted at in some of his correspondence dealing with the lawsuit, it never saw the light of day, presumably to avoid further entanglements with the Bourassas.[133]

Ouellet's book-length treatment of Julie Papineau would not be well thought of were it to be published in the 1990s. His insistence that women were responsible for Quebec's problems would not be taken seriously in light of both changing views regarding the role of women and studies published since 1961 on the place of women in Quebec history.[134] Moreover, Ouellet would be taken to task both for his depend-ence on a single source of information – the Papineau family papers – and for his lack of familiarity with the psychological literature relevant to his assessment of Julie Papineau and her children.

Late-twentieth-century standards of scholarship are not really relevant, however, to understanding why Quebec historians have generally shied away from this unprecedented episode in the history of their profession. Over the long period during which Ouellet's book was tied up in the courts, neither the Montreal historians, as a group, nor the IHAF, as an association, showed the least interest in taking up his cause. The histori-ans of the day had little reason to complain about either Ouellet's view of women or the nature of his archival research. In the first matter, the Laval historian was simply reflecting the values of the time, while in the second he compared favourably with the Montrealers whose work was not always based on careful documentation. One is left with the impression that Ouellet had to fend for himself because of his unacceptable views regarding the responsibility of Quebecers for their own problems.

In the quarter-century since Judge Dorion rendered his decision, the Ouellet case has largely disappeared from view in published accounts regarding Quebec's historical profession.[135] For instance, Serge Gagnon, in his collection of essays on twentieth-century Quebec historiography, criticized Ouellet endlessly for the nature of the work that he produced in the 1960s and 1970s. However, Gagnon's only reference to Ouellet's legal difficulties was a comment in passing that the latter had had a book 'removed from circulation by court order.'[136] In fact, there never was a court order of any kind prohibiting the book's publication, though the Bourassas had sought one. More troublesome, however, than his failure to get his facts right was Gagnon's unwillingness to explain the circumstances of the Ouellet case. Of course, if Gagnon had done so, he might have been forced to show some sympathy for Ouellet – a gesture of support that the profession has been little inclined to extend to someone who looked at Quebec society in starkly negative terms.

V

The debt of the Laval historians to their French maîtres such as Labrousse was not adequately reflected in Ouellet's writings during the 1950s. While his work on the Papineaus mirrored Labrousse's interest in both revolutions and the *mentalité collective* of social classes, he had done little up to 1960 to reflect Labrousse's painstaking analysis of quantitative data to explain why revolutions occurred when they did. During the 1960s, both Ouellet and his colleague Jean Hamelin would ground their studies in the sort of data that so interested Labrousse. In the process, however, they would continue to reflect the predisposition of the Laval historians, more generally, to view their society as fundamentally flawed, controlled as it was by classes ill-equipped to respond to a changing world.

By Ouellet's own admission, his interest in trying to develop a more complete picture of Quebec's economic and social history began with Jean Hamelin's return from France. In an interview recorded in 1981 he recalled that he 'became much more ambitious in 1957 upon the return of Jean Hamelin from France where he had studied with Labrousse and had been influenced by the Annales school ... Jean Hamelin came to see me and said, "We need to produce an economic and social history of [French] Canada from the beginning to the present." ... This is how dreams are formed.'[137] While Ouellet and Hamelin did not complete their ambitious project, they did manage to leave their mark on a period extending from New France to the end of the nineteenth century.

The first link in their chain came with the publication in 1960 of Hamelin's dissertation as *Économie et société en Nouvelle-France*. This work was roughly the same length as Ouellet's ill-fated manuscript on Julie Bruneau-Papineau. Moreover, the two works were finished at about the same time and were slated for publication in the same series. In substance, however, Hamelin's book was far superior to Ouellet's. While the latter was trying to come to conclusions about an entire society on the basis of relatively few personal letters, Hamelin set off to do the same through analysis of data on a vast array of social and economic factors. Accordingly, his work began with a discussion of the methodological problems with which he had to contend and the candid admission that 'compiling statistics is no simple matter.'[138]

Hamelin's analysis led him to a conclusion that contrasted starkly with the one then being promoted by the Montreal historians. While Frégault had been trying to depict New France as a viable colony destroyed by the Conquest, Hamelin found that on the arrival of the English 'New France was no more than a shadow of the commercial colony imagined by Champlain in 1618.'[139] Moreover, while Groulx's successors were interested in the way in which the Conquest had led to the demise of 'a powerful French-Canadian bourgeoisie,' Hamelin doubted that such a class had ever existed. He described New France as a colony plagued by a chronic shortage of both capital and skilled labour. Accordingly, opportunities for profits were limited, and those that did exist were monopolized by the French, who took the profits back home. If there were few prominent French-speaking businessmen in the aftermath of the Conquest, this was 'a consequence of the French regime, and not ... the result of the Conquest.'[140]

Hamelin, much like Ouellet, absolved the English of responsibility for the economic difficulties of Quebecers. Moreover, the two Laval historians were united in the early 1960s by the habit of making sweeping, and generally negative, generalizations regarding Quebec society that were not justified by the evidence at hand. In *Économie et société*, Hamelin diligently worked his way through a considerable amount of data to show that relatively few of the immigrants from France had arrived in the St Lawrence valley with useful skills. He was not content, however, to deal only with the immigrants' imported skills but also wanted to know why their descendants had not developed skills of their own. While he might have argued, as he did from time to time, that there were too few opportunities to warrant the training of a significant number of habitants, Hamelin went on to discuss how 'an ethnic characteristic' stood in the way of transforming habitants into craftsmen. 'The immigrants from France ... were accustomed to seasonal work which alternated with periods of unemployment. Accordingly, is it so surprising if their descendants exhibited an aversion to hard and conscientious work? ... The fundamental characteristic of the outlook of the Canadien was his disinclination to settle down and ply a trade in the face of the attractions of the frontier.'[141]

For both Hamelin and Ouellet, Quebecers had been largely responsible for their own fate – a view that they continued to pursue as they started to think about writing an economic and social history of Quebec from the Conquest to the end of the nineteenth century. This work, had it ever been published, would have constituted a sequel to Hamelin's *Économie et société*. Nevertheless, the article – 'La crise agricole' – in which they announced their grandiose plans helped shape Quebec historical writing for several decades by launching a debate as to whether there had been an agricultural crisis in early-nineteenth-century Quebec.[142] Ouellet and Hamelin insisted that French speakers' outmoded agricultural techniques had resulted in a succession of poor harvests, which made them easy prey for a demagogue such as Papineau, who sought to mobilize a hungry population against the British in order to satisfy his own visions of grandeur.

Ouellet and Hamelin's discussion of 'the agricultural crisis' bore several characteristics of the Laval approach to Quebec's past. The French influence was evident in their use, à la Labrousse, of both economic data that stretched over a long period and the concept of 'la conjoncture.' Moreover, their ties to France were reflected in the fact that the article was published not only in Canada, but also in the journal *Études rurales*, which emanated from the Annaliste stronghold, the École pratique des Hautes Études.[143]

The Laval approach was also evident at the interpretive level, as Ouellet and Hamelin were eager to contest Maurice Séguin's characterization of the early nineteenth century as a period marked by British oppression. While the Montrealer insisted that the conquerors had relegated Quebecers to an impoverished existence on the land, the Laval historians held French speakers responsible for their own fate. They claimed that in the late eighteenth century, under the influence of strong British demand for their crops, francophone farmers had overworked their lands to such a degree that the soils in the St Lawrence valley had lost much of their fertility by the early years of the new century. They reached this conclusion on the basis of such indices as declining exports, which might have reflected a variety of factors, including increased internal demand. Nevertheless, Hamelin and Ouellet, eager to depict Quebecers in the worst possible light, found, on the basis of relatively little evidence, a self-induced crisis, grounded in 'the attachment to routine that had been evident for generations' among French speakers.[144] They agreed with Donald Creighton, who had described early-nineteenth-century Quebec as 'a decadent feudal society' in which the farmers had been encouraged to pursue 'an outdated form of agriculture' by leaders, such as Papineau, fearful of the more dynamic English-speaking population.[145]

While Hamelin and Ouellet continued to publish works marked by the Laval approach, they never produced the sweeping, collaborative study promised in 'La crise agricole.' Nevertheless, they contributed to the production of two studies that together covered the period from 1760 to 1896 – Ouellet's *Histoire économique et sociale du Québec, 1760–1850*, which appeared in 1966, and Jean Hamelin and Yves Roby's *Histoire économique du Québec, 1851–1896*, which came out in 1971.[146] Ouellet's substantial work, easily the most significant publication of the Laval historians, was the logical outgrowth of his collaboration with Hamelin going back to the late 1950s. Once again, there was the French connection, on this occasion given concrete form in the preface by Robert Mandrou, who praised the author both for his concern with the 'close relations between economic factors and collective mentalities' and for his refutation of earlier historians, including both Groulx and his successors, who had continued 'the process of idealization of the French régime.' Mandrou indicated his clear understanding of the political implications of Ouellet's work when he noted that it was essential reading for anyone who wanted to make sense of the Quebec of the 1960s.[147]

Moreover, Ouellet's magnum opus shared with the previous works of the Laval historians the sometimes awkward mingling of quantitative data and unsubstantiated assertions. There were almost two books here, one characterized by the careful assembling of statistical series on a wide array of issues. True to his French maîtres, Ouellet set out to study the 'tonnage of internal and external traffic, the details of the principal articles of import and export, the range of foreign markets, the numerous data on changes in price levels, the agricultural price curves, [and] a multitude of figures on demographic evolution.'[148] On the basis of these data, he proposed nothing less than a complete rethinking of the way in which Quebec history had heretofore been conceived.

While nearly all Quebec historians, stretching back to Garneau, had viewed the Conquest as the great watershed in Quebec's past, Ouellet saw some basic shifts in both long- and short-term developments in the early nineteenth century. He indicated his debt to the Annalistes in this regard by incorporating the terms 'structure' and 'conjoncture' into the subtitle of his work. From Ouellet's point of view, in the years immediately after the Conquest, the structure of the economy remained unchanged. By the early nineteenth century, however, with the decline of the fur trade and the growing British demand for new staple goods –

most notably grain and timber – the economy had been transformed. While Quebecers seemed to respond, as he and Hamelin had indicated earlier, by putting new land into production, farmers never really abandoned their primitive agricultural practices. Accordingly, the short-term situation – the 'conjoncture' – deteriorated, first with a decline in production, and after the end of the Napoleonic wars in 1815 with a rapid fall in prices. Farmers found themselves in the grips of an agricultural crisis, which extended well into the century and, from Ouellet's perspective, played a crucial role in the outbreak of rebellion in 1837. While many of Ouellet's conclusions would be contested in the years to follow, the basis for debate among Quebec historians had been permanently altered by his presentation of large amounts of data designed to shift the focus away from the Conquest.[149]

Ouellet attempted to present a well-documented argument that would compare favourably with the impressionistic accounts of others such as Brunet. In the end, however, his tendency to make rash assertions, unsupported by evidence, constituted a second book within his *Histoire économique et sociale* and showed him to have more in common with the Montreal historians than he was prepared to admit. From his earliest work on the Papineaus, Ouellet had shown a fascination with psychological issues, and this preoccupation, which he had also secured from his French maîtres, was still evident in 1966, when he tried to blame francophone Quebecers for their early-nineteenth-century economic malaise. From his perspective, French speakers had chosen to remove themselves from the economic mainstream, preferring to complain about imagined wrongs inflicted by the conquerors instead of doing what was necessary to better themselves. Ouellet's criticism was directed towards both the farmers and the emerging elite of professional men, such as Papineau, who had hailed from the same rural society. Ouellet expanded on themes that he had developed in the 1950s when he criticized 'the French-Canadian farmer for lavish spending and unproductive investments [which] constituted a characteristic of his mentality and a lasting element in his culture.'[150] In contrast with his scrupulous use of data in other contexts, Ouellet provided no evidence to substantiate such assertions.

As for the doctors, notaries, and lawyers who made up the political leadership of French-speaking Quebec, they constituted a class that sought escape from 'all of the uncertainties of the beginning of the nineteenth century.'[151] In order to show their contempt for the rising and largely English-speaking business elite, Papineau and his colleagues used the parliamentary system to advance their nationalistic views, playing to the insecurities of the rural masses instead of tending to the concrete problems at hand. Ouellet saw the impulse to withdraw from the emerging capitalist order as so complete that the few French-speaking businessmen of substance were treated by their compatriots as if they were foreigners. Consequently, French-Canadian society suffered from a lack of leadership in the economic domain.[152] Once again, however, Ouellet had relatively little evidence to support his assertions, preferring to assume that the members of the liberal professions were hostile to capitalism without examining the economic program that they had developed in the Lower Canadian assembly.

Given both the innovative and the polemical features of Ouellet's study, it is hardly surprising that his work has given rise to a significant body of criticism, which, in its own right, says much about the state of Quebec historical writing over the past thirty years. As one might have expected, Ouellet was taken to task by Michel Brunet, who failed to distinguish among the different aspects of the Laval historian's work. There was some justice in Brunet's remark that Ouellet had been overly seduced by the 'pseudo-science that holds that each people has a specific psychological makeup,' but he was unwilling to give his nemesis any credit for his innovative marshalling of data. The Montrealer complained that Ouellet seemed to believe that 'quantitative history is able to take the place of a careful analysis of the various forces which shape the behaviour of people in any society.'[153] Brunet seemed incapable of distinguishing between Ouellet's efforts to establish the 'conjoncture,' supported by quantitative data, and his more speculative remarks regarding the *mentalité collective*.

If Ouellet was judged harshly by the Montreal historians, he did much better with the old guard of Quebec's historical community. Abbé Groulx, in a brief note in the *Revue d'histoire de l'Amérique française*, recommended *Histoire économique et sociale* to the journal's readers.[154] Given Groulx's declining health, the task of reviewing Ouellet was left to the maître's loyal ally Léo-Paul Desrosiers, who provided a reasonably warm reception, giving the author full marks for his statistical analysis, which 'increases our understanding of the past; it expands our horizons; it is full of new ideas.' Yet Desrosiers was bothered, as presumably was Groulx, by Ouellet's failure to appreciate 'the almost complete destruction in 1760 of the French population of Canada.' Nevertheless, 'this work is worthy of praise. Questions will undoubtedly be raised about many of [Ouellet's] views and conclusions. These questions should not prevent us from recognizing the breadth, the vast dimensions of this work.'[155]

Writing more than a quarter-century after the publication of Ouellet's book, Jean Lamarre suggested that Groulx's warm reception was linked to the latter's interest in putting his former disciples, the Montreal historians, in their place.[156] While Groulx and Desrosiers might have taken some satisfaction in Ouellet's battles with Brunet, it seems unfair to both Groulx and Ouellet to assume that the latter's efforts could be judged kindly only for political reasons. However, Lamarre, in his not-very-subtle effort to promote the Montrealers as initiators of modern historical techniques in Quebec, found it convenient to marginalize both Groulx and Ouellet in one shot, ignoring the innovative features of the Laval historian's work, which Desrosiers appeared genuinely to appreciate.

Histoire économique et sociale also came in for rather severe treatment from Serge Gagnon, who returned to it on numerous occasions in his volume on twentieth-century Quebec historical writing.[157] While Gagnon quite appropriately commented on the combination of careful analysis and rash assertion, he seemed to find something unique or, worse, sinister in Ouellet's work. 'The experienced reader of history will immediately notice that Fernand Ouellet's narrative contained certain peculiarities of style rarely found in contemporary work. Elementary semantic analysis shows how ideology has discreetly slipped in behind a screen of words, turns of phrases, and circumlocutions unusual in modern writing.' It is hard to understand, however, how Ouellet's study was 'unusual,' since he shared with such contemporaries of the 1960s as Groulx and Frégault the inclination to combine careful research with a clear ideological position. Moreover, given the lack of subtlety that marked Ouellet's work when it came to questions of *mentalité*, it is odd that Gagnon should have seen him as having written in a manner 'that concealed a subjective thrust.'[158]

Lamarre and Gagnon represent only two of the many French-language commentators who have found fault with Ouellet, frequently on the basis of a curious reading of his text.[159] Ouellet's work deserved criticism, but among his co-linguists he rarely received a fair hearing. He tended, however, to be very well received among English-speaking historians, a situation that only encouraged his most vitriolic opponents to characterize him as a *vendu* (a francophone who had sold out to anglophones), particularly since many of the English-language reviewers were as uncritically positive as the French ones were unfairly critical.[160] Ramsay Cook, for instance, could find no fault with Ouellet, whose work indicated 'a deep concern for careful documentation, a willingness to use new techniques of analysis ... , and an obvious desire to understand the past in its own terms.' Just as Brunet failed to appreciate Ouellet's methodological sophistication, Cook seemed oblivious to the value judgments that leapt off the pages of *Histoire économique et sociale*.[161] Allan Greer was so seduced by Ouellet's use of quantitative data that he could not understand why some Quebec historians had 'suggested that Ouellet's thesis [was] in some sense anti–French Canadian. Far from considering French Canadians inferior, he attempt[ed] to explain their collective difficulties in terms of specific institutional and ideological problems linked to a particular historical situation.' Greer could reach such a conclusion, however, only by ignoring Ouellet's groundless attacks on the social and economic behaviour of Quebecers.[162]

VI

The three central figures in the early decades of Laval's history deparment – Trudel, Hamelin, and Ouellet – continued to promote their self-critical view of the Quebec past well into the 1970s and 1980s, long after the Montreal historians had died, moved on to other concerns, or ceased to produce works of any significance. Jean Hamelin, for instance – the only one of the three who remained at Laval after the mid-1960s – showed his loyalty to a point of view that he had first advanced in the late 1950s when, in 1971, he, along with Yves Roby, published *Histoire économique du Québec, 1851–1896*. As the title suggests, this study was both the logical sequel to Ouellet's *Histoire économique et sociale* and the completion of the series on Quebec's economic and social history that Hamelin and Ouellet had projected a decade earlier.[163] While Hamelin and Roby, in true Laval fashion, discussed the 'conjonctures' of this period, they spent even more time pointing to the shortcomings of French speakers that guaranteed their second-class status in late-ninteteenth-century Quebec. Accordingly, Hamelin and Roby closed their volume with the assertion that francophones' relatively low incomes attested to 'a time-lag between economic changes and social ones, between social changes and changes in mentality. There was considerable evidence of an inability to respond to new situations.' This viewpoint did not differ greatly from that evident in Ouellet's writings from the 1950s on.[164]

During the 1970s and 1980s Hamelin continued to produce research of significance, frequently in areas that he had not previously discussed, such as the history of labour. He moved in yet another new direction by writing, with Nicole Gagnon, a two-volume history of Catholicism in twentieth-century Quebec. In this work, published in the early 1980s, Hamelin still maintained his conviction that French speakers were fundamentally different from their English-speaking neighbours for reasons that transcended rational economic analysis. In one telling passage, Hamelin and Gagnon noted the existence at the start of the twentieth century of a 'French-Canadian culture' that distinguished itself in a variety of ways: 'The French Canadian has faith in people, he seeks to live in harmony with nature, he focuses on the here and now, he attaches great importance to the family and to his closest friends. He distinguishes himself from the English speaker, who is less outgoing and who wants to leave his mark on nature in the name of progress. While the French speaker thinks only in the short term and is overly concerned about the feelings of others, the English speaker is the rational economic man.'[165]

Much like Jean Hamelin, Marcel Trudel also remained loyal to a point of view that he had long held. During the two decades following his departure from Laval in 1965, Trudel published a number of studies of New France. He completed a multi-volume history of the French regime to the mid-seventeenth century, the last part of which appeared only in 1983, a year after his retirement from the University of Ottawa.[166] However, the clearest statement of Trudel's unwavering view of the pre-Conquest period came with his publication in 1968 of *Introduction to New France*, which amounted to 'a summary of what I have taught my students for more than fifteen years.' Though Trudel characteristically refused to see this work as offering any 'definitive answers to the problems posed by New France,' it contained all the elements long central for the author, and for his former colleagues at Laval.[167] For instance, in discussing the impact of the Conquest, Trudel was categorical in rejecting the stance of the Montreal historians. For him, 'the disappearance of the French-Canadian businessmen upon the arrival of the English merchant class was probably not due to the Conquest, but to the loss of their traditional area of exploitation in 1783. There was also a decline in the beaver trade, and these men refused to adapt to the new economic structure.'[168]

Finally, there is Fernand Ouellet, who has belligerently maintained the perspective on Quebec's past that he developed in the 1950s. In 1976 he published a second major monograph, designed to reinforce the points in his *Histoire économique et sociale*. When *Le Bas Canada* appeared in an

English adaptation in 1980, Ouellet proudly announced that the 'interpretive approach conceived for *Histoire économique* has proven valid in the light of further research ... and is reaffirmed in the present work.'[169] More recently, Ouellet has restated French speakers' responsibility for their own shortcomings in several critiques of the revisionist historians of the 1970s and 1980s, who are the main players in the next chapter. While the revisionists insisted that Quebec had been constantly on the road to modernity during the nineteenth and twentieth centuries, Ouellet read the historical record differently, insisting instead that 'the notion of backwardness ... usefully illuminates the profile of French-speaking Quebecers.'[170]

While all three of the Laval historians were still publishing significant pieces as late as the 1980s, they never really deviated from their view of the Quebec past outlined in the 1950s. This perspective conceived when Quebecers had relatively little political power in Ottawa and relatively little economic power in their own province, saw French speakers as largely responsible for their own problems. This point of view, however, held out little attraction to young francophones, who, in the aftermath of the Quiet Revolution, were searching for the roots of Quebec's modernity, not the basis for its backwardness. While, as we shall see in the next chapter, the historians of the 1970s and 1980s were not always enthusiastic about the approach of the Montreal historians, there was almost no support for the Laval perspective. Accordingly, while it is almost impossible to find any francophone with a kind word for the Laval historians, despite their longevity, methodological innovations, and frequently painstaking research, there are still those willing to portray the Montrealers as having played the central role 'in the modernization of Quebec historical writing.'[171] This claim is curious, given that the historians in Montreal produced a small body of work based on relatively limited archival research; rather the reservoir of sympathy for them reflects the greater acceptability of a view of the past that placed responsibility for any weaknesses with others.

5

Searching for a Normal Quebec: Revisionism and Beyond

I

The previous chapters have considered both what divided and what united Quebec's historians from Garneau, writing in the immediate aftermath of the Rebellions of 1837–8, to Ouellet, writing in the wake of the Quiet Revolution. These historians differed from one another both in the techniques that they employed and in the conclusions that they reached. For all these differences, however, most were responsive to larger trends in their profession and genuinely sought objectivity, even if that quest was doomed to failure because of the inherently subjective nature of all historical writing. Even more significantly, up to the 1960s these historians were united by their focus on the distinctiveness of Quebec society. In particular, they tended to concentrate on the ways in which French-speaking Quebecers had long differed from the English speakers with whom they shared the North American continent.

Up to the Second World War, historians as diverse as Garneau, Groulx, and Chapais all pointed to the distinctive characteristics of Quebecers that had allowed cultural survival – *la survivance*. Then, in the aftermath of the war and the growing interest of Quebec's new elite in challenging the long-standing status of francophones as second-class economic citizens, the basis for analysis changed. No longer were historians interested in exploring how cultural survival had been achieved; rather, they wanted to know why economic inferiority had been perpetuated. In this regard, the Montreal and Laval historians were united with one another and with their predecessors going back to the mid-nineteenth century, since they all began with the assumption that Quebecers had long differed from their neighbours. For Frégault and his colleagues, this difference was the legacy of the Conquest, while to Ouellet and his friends the issue was unwillingness to face up to the challenges of economic change. For both schools of thought, Quebecers constituted – to borrow an expression from the Meech Lake Accord – a distinct society.

Beginning in the 1960s, however, historians abandoned this preoccupation with Quebecers' distinctiveness so as to concentrate instead on the ways in which their society had long been normal. Henceforth, most would explore the past in order to indicate how Quebec's experience had been scarcely distinguishable from that of other Western societies. In charting this normal past, the historians of the past thirty years have emphasized the role of material forces, in the process marginalizing such long-standing mainstays of Quebec historiography as the role of Catholicism or the antipathy of English-speaking conquerors – aspects of the past that somehow placed Quebecers outside the mainstream of the larger Western experience. The historians who began to emerge in the 1960s preferred to focus instead on such forces as immigration, urbanization, and secularization, which had shaped the experience of much of the Western world over the four centuries since the start of European occupation of the St Lawrence valley. As Gérard Bouchard has put it, historians now wanted to show that Quebec was 'in the mainstream of developments both in North America and across the western world. From this perspective, Quebec was as industrial, as capitalistic, as liberal, as developed, in short as modern as other societies.'[1]

Because the historians who began to become prominent in the 1960s rejected the discourse of difference that had dominated Quebec's historical writing for over a century, they have been identified throughout this volume as 'revisionists.' Of course all historical writing is revisionist, because it tends to qualify what came before it, but such an observation obscures more than it explains. From time to time, a group of historians will redefine fundamentally the way in which a national history is conceptualized. The revisionists found themselves in precisely such a position in the wake of the social and political transformation during, and immediately following, the Quiet Revolution. With the election of the Liberal government of Jean Lesage in 1960, Quebecers voted to reject many aspects of the more 'traditional' society associated with the Union Nationale regime of Maurice Duplessis. While it would be inaccurate to represent Quebec as suddenly having become 'modern' with the rise of Lesage, the new government both responded to and encouraged some fundamental changes.

In fairly short order, Quebec took on the appearance of a normal,

late-twentieth-century society, with the building of the modern interventionist state, which left its mark in many ways. For instance, through
the expansion of such agencies as Hydro-Québec, French speakers
were steadily integrated into the mainstream of the economy, and the
centuries-old wage gap between francophones and anglophones was
eliminated by the 1970s. The more general orientation of some Quebecers
towards business was reflected in the growth of the École des hautes
études commerciales, the business school of the Université de Montréal,
which became the largest such institution in Canada. The Catholic church
fell into decline, in no small part because the state assumed many of its
functions, such as the running of the province's education system. Finally, the state made its presence felt through legislation designed to
respond to the increasing ethnic diversity of the province's population.
More specifically, the 1970s saw language legislation that sought to integrate newcomers into the French-speaking majority. This was a far cry
from the situation in the early twentieth century, when Catholic institutions, such as the caisses populaires, had been created to keep 'outsiders'
at a distance. Now, however, most Quebecers wanted to integrate newcomers into the mainstream in order to create a normal Western society.[2]

The reforms of the Quiet Revolution, introduced by Quebecers who
had been demanding fundamental changes since the 1940s, aided in the
emergence of a new generation of Quebecers who quickly moved up the
ladder in both the public and the private sectors. These young Quebecers,
of course, shared much with 'baby boomers' across the Western world
who had had the good fortune of joining the labour force just as employment opportunities were expanding. Nevertheless, François Ricard has
called attention to the way in which this generation in Quebec differed
from its counterpart in places such as the United States and English
Canada. Quebec had a rather strong remnant of a more traditional society while the new generation began to emerge. As Ricard has written,
'There is no point in going back to the old clichés that held that Quebec
before the Quiet Revolution constituted a society that was entirely cut off
from the larger world and generally opposed to change. At the same
time, however, we have to face up to the fact that this was a society that
distinguished itself by a certain slowness, by a certain reluctance to
embrace those changes ... that signalled the arrival of modernity.'[3] Because of the continued presence of an old guard, Quebec's new leaders
were convinced that they were engaged in 'a radical break' with the
past.[4] More specifically, the people who came to dominate institutions
such as the universities saw themselves as belonging to the first genera-

tion of Quebecers with the tools to resolve problems in a rational way, 'free of passion and value judgments.'[5]

Because it was intent on dispelling any lingering notions that Quebec might have been different, the new generation of the 1960s and 1970s projected the image of a normal society whenever it had the opportunity. In the political arena, for instance, sovereignists have long linked their project with the normal evolution of Quebec towards the logical status for a modern people. Lucien Bouchard put it quite nicely when he observed that 'Quebec requires the normal tool box of a normal state.'[6] In a similar fashion, discussing 'the "normalization" of Quebec literature,' François Ricard has observed that since the 1970s there has been 'a weakening of the distinctive characteristics of Quebec literature and a growing tendency for it to resemble the literature of other industrial nations.'[7] Finally, revisionist historians have reinforced the notion that Quebec today constitutes a normal society by looking at its long process of modernizing, much like that of other western societies. The discourse of difference that had long dominated historical writing ceased to make any sense with Quebecers wielding considerable power in both the private and the public sectors.

This fundamental shift in the orientation of Quebec's historians came about in two stages. Some of the assumptions of the older historiography were thrown into question during the 1960s by historians such as Jean-Pierre Wallot and Louise Dechêne, who were a bit too old to qualify as 'baby boomers,' but whose professional training in the 1960s made them susceptible to the new ideas that were in the air. The more sweeping change came, however, with the generation born in the 1940s, which attended university in the 1960s and acceded to new jobs in the expanding universities of the late 1960s and early 1970s. These were the revisionists, whose ranks included Serge Courville, Paul-André Linteau, Jean-Claude Robert, Jacques Rouillard, and Normand Séguin, to name only a few.[8] As we shall see, some of these historians were influenced by the Annales school, while others were Marxists or enthusiasts of the quantitative methods being refined in the United States. All of them, however, accepted the premise that there were certain paths that all societies followed and that material factors were responsible for social change. As Jocelyn Létourneau has observed, they shared 'the underlying assumption that all individuals are rational beings'; and since history was populated by rational beings, there was little reason why developments in Quebec should have differed much from those evident elsewhere in the Western world.[9]

The revisionist interpretation remains the dominant approach as the twentieth century draws to a close. Nevertheless, some historians have criticized it over the past decade for its preoccupation with the alleged normalcy of Quebec's past and its frequent failure to consider ways in which Quebec's experience was distinctive. In the final sections of this chapter, we shall see how this critique has grown out of a certain malaise among some Quebecers about the state of their society in the wake of the Quiet Revolution. By producing works that reflected both the society in which they lived and the profession to which they belonged, the revisionists and their critics were linked both to one another and to twentieth-century historians stretching back to Groulx.

II

Certain aspects of the revisionist paradigm received their first public airing through the work of two historians with pronounced links to the Montreal and Laval schools of historical writing. As we saw above, the two French-language universities had long been home to historians with different perspectives. In the 1960s, however, these differences began to fade because of the way in which Jean-Pierre Wallot and Louise Dechêne chose to interpret these seemingly irreconcilable approaches; and while their interpretations of Quebec history differed, their publications displayed a growing emphasis on the normalcy of the Quebec past, which would become much more pronounced in the next generation of historians. They constituted a transitional stage between the postwar historians, such as Frégault and Ouellet, and the revisionists, such as Linteau and Robert.

Wallot and Dechêne were both born in the early 1930s, and though they followed different career paths, they both played crucial roles in adapting the message of the postwar historians to the circumstances of the Quiet Revolution. Wallot, who began his studies at the Université de Montréal in the 1950s, was nearly two decades younger than the trio that had dominated the teaching of Quebec history there since the late 1940s and strongly influenced much of his writing. Much like Séguin, his supervisor, for whom he had considerable affection, Wallot was preoccupied with the relationship between the conquered and the conquerors in the early nineteenth century.[10] He never entirely abandoned the notion that the central drama in Quebec's history was 'the all encompassing clash between two nations, two races, two societies.'[11]

While Séguin was content to dwell on the way in which this conflict inevitably led to the marginalization of French speakers, Wallot came to see things differently as he equipped himself with the tools of the social sciences during the late 1960s. One is struck, for instance, in examining Wallot's collection of essays, *Un Québec qui bougeait*, by the way in which his early works were marked by both a narrow political orientation and an emphasis on the powerlessness of francophones. In contrast, by the late 1960s and early 1970s, Wallot was employing, with the help of the economist Gilles Paquet, the methods of the new economic history, which was then taking on importance in the United States. Equipped with economic theories and large amounts of data, Paquet and Wallot depicted Quebecers as rational, and relatively successful, economic beings. In their conclusion to a 1973 work, they showed an ongoing debt to Séguin by making reference to the presence of 'two distinctive communities ... within a restricted territory.' At the same time, however, they distanced themselves from Séguin by noting the considerable evidence 'of the general modernization of both the economy and the society of Lower Canada.'[12]

By the late 1960s Wallot was arguing on several fronts that French-speaking Quebecers had constituted, in many respects, a normal society. Francophones may have been removed from positions of power and influence, but they were essentially rational economic beings, much like their English-speaking neighbours. He conveyed this impression in part by offering an alternative to the depiction of early-nineteenth-century Quebec that Fernand Ouellet had been advancing since the late 1950s. While Ouellet had insisted on the responsibility of Quebecers for an agricultural crisis in the early nineteenth century, Wallot, mostly in works written with Paquet, argued that there had been not a crisis per se, but rather a rational response to changes in the market for agricultural goods. Paquet and Wallot had no difficulty in collecting 'evidence of the responsiveness of the habitants to changing market conditions. There was considerable proof to indicate that they were out to maximize their profits ... We have observed habitants who behaved *normally*.'[13] Here was an early example of a hallmark of revisionist writing – the depiction of the Quebecer as a profit-maximizing business person, an appropriate motif for a people that was by the early 1970s making great gains in the business world.

Wallot was also involved in modernizing the image of French speakers by re-examining the role of Catholicism. If Quebecers were to be seen as serious players in the economy, it was useful to dismiss notions that they had been impeded by their subservience to the Catholic church. Once again referring to the early nineteenth century, Wallot observed that 'the

Catholic church was *not* a strong, prosperous, and triumphant institution at the head of a quasi-theocratic society ... [Quebecers'] moral outlook and social manners were no better than normal in a society of farmers and labourers of some affluence and little education in a time of economic restructuring and economic change.'[14]

By depicting the early-nineteenth-century Quebecer as a rational economic person with only a weak connection to Catholicism, Wallot was distancing himself from his predecessors while almost embracing the revisionist view of the Quebecer as normal. In the final analysis, however, Wallot was a transitional figure who could neither entirely break with the postwar historians nor totally identify with the revisionists. As we have seen, he never completely abandoned his insistence on the conflict between francophones and anglophones as the fundamental source of tension within Quebec society. This position tied him to his predecessors while placing him at odds with the revisionists, who, as we shall see, were preoccupied with the role of social class. Moreover, he never entirely escaped from using his writing as a means of justifying the demands of nationalists. His work had an explicitly political dimension that was part of an older style of historical writing, but which stood at odds with the coldly rational analyses of the revisionists, who were unwilling to engage in explicit political commentary.

III

While Jean-Pierre Wallot and Louise Dechêne both helped advance parts of what would become the revisionist interpretation, they differed from one another in the paths of their careers, their relationships with their predecessors, and their perspectives on Quebec's past. While Wallot and Dechêne were roughly the same age, the former was much younger than his mentors at the Université de Montréal, while Dechêne was not all that much younger than the historians she encountered at Laval. She was approximately the same age as Jean Hamelin and only slightly younger than Ouellet, who directed her studies until she went on to pursue her PhD in France. Nevertheless, Dechêne really did belong to a different intellectual generation than either Hamelin or Ouellet, in the sense that she did not even begin her studies until the early 1960s. As she said in an interview: 'I did not come to the profession by the regular route. I took up my studies in earnest only after my marriage and the birth of my children.'[15]

Under Ouellet's influence, Dechêne wrote an MA thesis, completed in

1964, on the early-nineteenth-century business career of the lumber baron William Price. This rather narrowly cast study gave little indication of the contribution that Dechêne would make to the writing of the history of New France and to the historical profession.[16] In fact, after finishing her master's degree, Dechêne had every reason to believe that her studies were at an end.[17] Much like Ouellet more than a decade earlier, however, she soon found herself in Paris, first to carry out research in connection with the reconstruction of the fortress at Louisbourg and later to collect documents for the Quebec archives; and just as Ouellet had been transformed by his encounter with historians such as Labrousse, Dechêne was won over by the brand of the Annales approach shaped by Fernand Braudel.

As we saw in the previous chapter, the Laval historians, and Ouellet in particular, were especially influenced by the wing of the Annales school represented by Robert Mandrou, whose interest in *mentalités* dovetailed with the Laval historians' preoccupation with the distinctiveness of Quebecers. Up to the 1960s, however, Quebec historians had indicated little interest in what was by then the dominant approach among Annalistes. Fernand Braudel had long been examining the way in which material factors shaped the everyday lives of people in a manner that did not greatly change over time. Unlike Mandrou, Braudel's perspective had 'little to say about attitudes, values or mentalités' and left little room for human agency.[18] As he noted in 1980, 'The individual has very little freedom to influence the course of his life; that is my conclusion following my long career as an historian.'[19] In light of such a statement, it is hardly surprising that the Braudelian approach has been criticized for its 'insistence upon economic determinism' and its marginalizing of 'the role of the individual to make a difference in history, to be an active player, conscious of the alternatives before him.'[20]

This type of criticism, made with the benefit of hindsight, had little impact on the young French researchers who followed Braudel's lead during the 1950s and 1960s. There was something attractive about his model, which suggested that there were certain 'scientific' tools that might be applied to all societies. In the aftermath of the Second World War, this comforting tribute to the power of science over the irrationality of humanity contributed not only to the development of quantitative methods among historians but to the growth of the social sciences more generally.[21] In France, Braudel's perspective inspired a new generation of historians to produce a series of monographs dealing with particular regions of France, all of which owed a considerable debt to Braudel's earlier work on the Mediterranean world. These studies, produced by such prominent young French historians as Pierre Goubert and Emmanuel Le Roy Ladurie, writing about the Beauvais and Languedoc regions, respectively, have been praised for the quality of their research and yet criticized, as was Braudel himself, for neglecting questions of 'mentalité.'[22]

During her stay in France from 1964 to 1968, Louise Dechêne absorbed the sort of view of the past that had inspired her French counterparts such as Goubert. On arrival in Paris, Dechêne, reflecting her Laval training, was well aware of developments in France, more than would have been the case for Wallot at a comparable stage in his career. She even had a certain familiarity with Robert Mandrou, who had spent some time at Laval and who encouraged Dechêne to sit in on his seminar and later to pursue doctoral studies. There is more than a little irony in Mandrou's role here, since his perspective on the past was one that Dechêne subsequently rejected. As her views evolved, she came to have little sympathy for the emphasis on 'mentalités' that had marked the work of both Mandrou and Ouellet. Instead, she became keen to pursue a doctorate inspired by the work of her French peers, who were interested in 'the social history of the ancien régime ... I discovered, through contact with the social historians, that there were various ways to understand the past very precisely ... by using sources which had not yet been employed. Among these sources were notarial records which constitute an invaluable source for understanding everyday life.'[23]

Dechêne left France in 1968 to take up a teaching position in Canada, and in 1973 she completed her dissertation, under Mandrou's supervision, which subsequently appeared as *Habitants et marchands de Montréal au XVII siècle*, perhaps the most lavishly praised monograph on the history of Quebec published since the Quiet Revolution.[24] Mandrou's role here did not prevent Dechêne from bringing Braudel's perspective to Quebec. 'I adopted a now widely accepted structural approach, with an emphasis on economic activities.'[25] In adopting such a method, Dechêne challenged much of the conventional wisdom on New France, which had depicted the habitant as an indifferent farmer, at best, little interested in establishing his family on the land, influenced as he was by the attractions of the fur trade, exploration, or military expeditions. There was little to choose between Groulx's emphasis on the habitant's 'independent spirit,' Frégault's reference to his 'insubordination and independence of character,' and Jean Hamelin's criticism of his 'adventurous temperament.'[26] Unwilling to accept these clichés, based on the off-hand comments of colonial officials, Dechêne examined a wealth of documents, most notably notarial records, which touched on the experiences of the habitants and allowed her to discover the 'seriousness of purpose of these peasants concerned with the security of their families.'[27]

Dechêne emphasized the manner in which the habitants lived in relatively self-contained communities, in which they produced mostly for their own survival, essentially cut off from the international trade that interested the merchants of Montreal, who were dealing largely in furs. These merchants, much like the habitants, had also been the focus of a considerable literature, particularly in the 1950s, when the Montreal historians emphasized their prowess, while the Laval historians barely recognized their existence.[28] Dechêne had little time for either interpretation, referring to the 'debate around the bourgeoisie of New France [as] a non-issue.' Rather, she depicted the merchants, much like their farming cousins, as level-headed businessmen, not building up incredible fortunes but 'seeking respectability and profits.'[29]

Dechêne's study was consciously modelled after those of 'the French historians of the 1960s [who] placed a heavy emphasis on structures and continuities and great faith in numbers.'[30] Less obvious, but just as significant for subsequent developments, her view of the past formed a crucial element in the emergence of the revisionist paradigm. Dechêne noted, in the preface to the English translation of her work, that her book examined settlers whose way of life reflected 'the normal pattern of European and colonial history.'[31] Writing about a later period, Wallot was also keen to depict Quebecers as normal. However, while Wallot never entirely stopped making explicit political commentary – a habit secured from his mentors – Dechêne stayed clear of such editorializing, thus placing herself more squarely in the revisionist camp. She was so successful in this regard that few commentators have made any reference to the political implications of the point of view that she developed in the late 1960s and early 1970s.[32] Dechêne always cultivated the persona of the value-free social scientist, and yet by emphasizing the habitants' 'seriousness of purpose' she was stripping away the underlying assumptions of the discourse of 'difference' that had long dominated Quebec historical writing. From her perspective, the habitants were simply ordinary people seeking the same security as peasants elsewhere in the world.

Dechêne's work, even though it dealt primarily with the seventeenth century, also challenged the significance of the Conquest by presenting the merchants as neither unusually successful (and hence doomed to destruction by the arrival of the English) nor unusually incompetent (and thus providing evidence that the English had been needed to develop Quebec's economic potential). The Conquest had long been a crucial element in Quebec historical writing, precisely because it pointed to the distinctiveness of French speakers as either victims or economic bumblers. Wallot reflected an older tradition in his continued preoccupation with the Conquest, while Dechêne was in tune with the changing self-image of Quebecers who, in the context of the Quiet Revolution, were interested in stressing their abilities rather than their disabilities. Accordingly, there was little reason to dwell any longer on the significance of the arrival of the conquerors. Instead, Quebecers, embodied in this case by Dechêne's merchants, were normal players, whose fate had been moulded by larger economic structures. The Conquest was neither 'good' (and thus justifying the presence of English speakers) nor 'evil' (and thus justifying the conquerors' removal). Rather, the fate of Quebecers had been shaped by the same economic forces evident elsewhere in the Western world. Accordingly, as Dechêne put it, if one had a student interested in studying Quebec history, 'there would be no reason to have him view 1760 as a watershed.'[33]

IV

Louise Dechêne clearly had a much greater influence on historical writing in Quebec than did Jean-Pierre Wallot. While Wallot never entirely shook off the influence of his mentors, Dechêne brought Fernand Braudel to Quebec; and while Wallot wrote a number of intriguing but not always easily digestible articles, Dechêne published what was effectively the first 'revisionist' monograph, on the basis of sources not previously employed to any great extent.[34] She received the Governor General's Award and the Canadian Historical Association's Garneau medal for the best book in Canadian history published in the 1970s. On the twentieth anniversary of the publication of *Habitants et marchands* there was a conference organized to consider the impact of Dechêne's masterpiece.[35] While Wallot has remained a respected figure, his work has received no such adulation.

Despite these differences, however, Wallot and Dechêne were both transitional figures, who suggested ways in which Quebec's past was normal, but who were easily distinguishable from the younger historians who pushed the revisionist paradigm much further than had either of them. Paul-André Linteau, one of the most influential of these historians, has described his generation as one made up of individuals 'who were born in the middle of the 1940s [and] who went to university during the second half of the 1960s.' Linteau and his peers, such as Jean-Claude Robert, Jacques Rouillard, and Normand Séguin, had been strongly marked 'by the Quiet Revolution's ideology of modernizing Quebec society' and were little interested either in dwelling any longer on the Conquest, as was Wallot, or in qualifying the entrepreneurial credentials of Quebecers, as was Dechêne.[36]

The author of *Habitants et marchands* rescued the habitant from the simplistic clichés that had long passed for historical analysis. She viewed habitants as normal peasants in the European mould who were preoccupied with their limited milieu, but not necessarily aware of larger market forces. However, by playing down their market orientation, Dechêne presented peasants who were not normal enough for the revisionist historians of New France who, in the 1970s and 1980s, were intent on placing Quebecers in the mainstream of modern capitalist society. In touting the works that had moved beyond Dechêne's, Béatrice Craig remarked in 1990 that 'recent French-language historical writing has either rejected the idea of the peasant economy, or has proposed ways of going beyond it.'[37] As market forces intruded on the life of the habitant, historians found not Dechêne's relatively undifferentiated peasantry, but rather evidence of 'social stratification in the ranks of the peasants.'[38] Class distinctions would prove a recurring theme in revisionist historiography.

By and large, however, the historians of Linteau's generation were not interested in revising the work of predecessors such as Wallot and Dechêne, who had been concerned with pre-industrial Quebec. Rather, they moved on to entirely new questions relevant to a modern industrial society. As Linteau observed: 'Coming of age in a Quebec where everyone was talking about modernization, living in an urban-industrial society, it was natural that we would want to understand the roots of contemporary Quebec. The historical writing of the time, focusing upon New France and the early years of British rule, was not responding to our concerns. Accordingly, we set off to explore the various factors that led to the emergence of an industrial, capitalist society in Quebec by the middle of the nineteenth century.'[39]

This new preoccupation with the more modern aspects of Quebec social and economic history was evident when, in 1967, René Durocher introduced a new course at the Université de Montréal on twentieth-century Quebec.[40] Previous historians, including Groulx, had touched on the twentieth century, but generally in the context of the history of

'Canada français' – a term that had no precise territorial basis. Since courses on French Canada paid attention not only to francophone Quebecers, but also to groups such as the Acadians and the Franco-Ontarians, there was a tendency to focus on the sad plight of a linguistic minority. By the late 1960s, however, in the midst of the construction of the modern Quebec state, historians had begun to turn to the territory of Quebec, where French speakers constituted a majority and where one could witness the unfolding of developments such as urbanization, industrialization, secularization, and immigration that were as relevant to Quebec as to any other part of the Western world. Instead of French Canadians being victims, Quebecers became central players in the major developments of the twentieth century. As Jocelyn Létourneau has put it, the French Canadian, 'conquered, humiliated, and demoralized,' gave way in the historical record to the Québécois, 'successful, entrepreneurial, and ambitious.'[41]

While Durocher's course hinted at what the revisionists had in mind, the precise contours of their view of Quebec gradually emerged in print through the 1970s and 1980s. At first, they made their perspective known through articles in the professional journal of Quebec historians, the *Revue d'histoire de l'Amérique française (RHAF)*. As we saw in chapter 3, the Montreal historians had barely replaced Abbé Groulx in the management of both the Institut d'histoire de l'Amérique française (IHAF) and its journal, the *RHAF*, when Linteau and his generation emerged. By the early 1970s the revisionists had become influential members of both the board of the Institut and the new management of the journal. In both capacities, they helped marginalize the remaining amateur influences left over from Groulx's day. In the Institut this meant eliminating the special role of local historical societies and making annual meetings into genuine professional conferences; for the journal, eliminating articles that were not up to scientific standards.[42]

As the *RHAF* became more academic, it also came to reflect the revisionists' interest in modern Quebec. In 1972 Linteau and his colleague Fernand Harvey, in an analysis of the first twenty-five years of the journal, hailed the way in which its long-standing preoccupation with New France was starting to be replaced with a focus on the late nineteenth and the twentieth centuries. Not surprisingly, articles on religious issues were giving way to ones dealing with the economy. The journal had begun to move away from describing 'a paradise lost' to dealing with questions relevant to 'the current situation.'[43] This general trend became even more pronounced as Harvey and Linteau's generation firmly established itself in the province's universities. While only 14 per cent of the articles published in the *RHAF* prior to 1972 pertained to the post-Confederation era, nearly half of those over the next twenty years dealt with the period since 1867.[44]

Over the 1970s and 1980s a number of journals, including *Recherches sociographiques* and *Cahiers de géographie du Québec*, published the work of the new generation of Quebec historians, whose research frequently transcended disciplinary lines, influenced as it was by larger developments in the social sciences. However, it was particularly in the *RHAF* that the revisionists began to describe a modern Quebec, which was profoundly urban, whose French-speaking majority was little influenced by Catholicism and profoundly instilled with the spirit of capitalism, and which was divided more frequently by class divisions than by ethnic ones. The journal's role in spreading the revisionist perspective was evident in the 1970s as it published numerous articles and 'research notes' by historians such as Linteau, Jean-Claude Robert, and Normand Séguin, who had completed, or were near completing, their doctorates, but were not yet ready to produce full-length monographs.

These historians concentrated on the nineteenth and early twentieth centuries to show a Quebec divided along class lines, so much so that religious or ethnic distinctions, long central in Quebec historical writing, largely disappeared. Francophones were rescued from the margins of the economy and recognized as participants in sectors that historians had heretofore ignored in their concentration on the largest commercial, financial, and industrial firms, run by English speakers. The revisionists looked instead to land developers and owners of medium-sized businesses to find significant participation by French speakers who may have lacked capital, but not entrepreneurial verve.[45] These modest business people may have been squeezed out by larger firms, which were increasingly dominating economies across the Western world, but this marginalization had nothing to do with the ethnic or religious identity of French speakers. As Linteau wrote in an influential research note: 'It was not the French Canadians who were marginalized; rather it was the medium-sized business people more generally, in whose ranks there just happened to be a large number of French speakers.'[46]

Here was a Quebec in which francophones were firmly committed to the precepts of capitalism. Accordingly, it made little sense for the revisionists to depict Catholicism as a force that had sidelined Quebecers in the economy. Rather, the church at times facilitated economic development. This point was forcefully made by Normand Séguin in a research note on the start of large-scale settlement in the Saguenay region during the late nineteenth century.[47] Previous authors had looked to such regions to find evidence of a Catholic clergy intent on developing a stable agricultural population, isolated from the larger world. However, Séguin discovered a church willing to work closely with lumber companies to establish a population that might combine subsistence farming with seasonal employment in the lumber camps. Séguin depicted a church shaped by capitalism, which was stretching into even the most remote regions of the province; in the process he rejected the long-standing view of the church as an institution capable of keeping Quebecers at a distance from the forces of modernity.

These early contributions of the revisionists to the RHAF suggested a Quebec shaped by such forces as industrialization and urbanization during the nineteenth and twentieth centuries. These forces tended to divide Quebecers by class, and only incidentally by ethnic or linguistic identities. Moreover, Catholicism, from this perspective, was simply another institution responding to industrialization and incapable of shielding the population from the influences of modernity.

As their research progressed, the revisionists continued to develop their perspective through monographs published during the 1970s and 1980s. Both Linteau and Séguin, for instance, produced books that presented the Montreal industrial suburb of Maisonneuve, on the one hand, and the Saguenay parish of Notre-Dame d'Hébertville, on the other, as normal communities where material forces determined social relationships.[48] The depiction of Quebec as a society in the Western mainstream was similarly advanced by René Hardy in his study of Quebec's involvement in the Papal army of the late 1860s. Hardy showed that support for the Zouaves did not come spontaneously from the population, but rather had been cultivated by the clergy.[49] Just as Normand Séguin had found the clergy as a slightly sinister force, because of its manipulation of the population of the Saguenay region, so too did Hardy, this time in collaboration with Serge Gagnon, refer to the church as an institution prepared to use all the means at its disposal 'to condition the population, to establish social control.'[50] From this vantage point, Catholicism ceased to be somehow part of Quebec culture, to be seen instead as an ideology imposed on the people.

This declericalization of Quebec's history was also evident in such works as Jean-Paul Bernard's study of the Rouges, a mid-nineteenth-century political party with a liberal and anti-clerical program.[51] Bernard's claim that Quebecers had supported such a party in relatively large numbers was designed to indicate the weakness of clerical influence, but it also drew attention to the affinity of Quebecers to liberalism, an ideology long seen as alien to their past.[52] A similar point of view was also developed by Jacques Rouillard in several books on the history of trade unions in Quebec. Rouillard was eager to show that Quebec workers were as likely both to form trade unions and to go on strike as their counterparts outside the province, who were allegedly more materialistic because they did not have to bear the burden of Catholicism. Rouillard attached little importance to the church's involvement in the establishment of some of Quebec's unions, noting only that it 'coloured' the nature of the union movement, which was moulded more fundamentally by 'the way in which Quebec belonged to the North American continent.'[53]

This emphasis on the North American nature of Quebec society was also evident in Serge Courville's *Entre ville et campagne*, one of the few French-language monographs of the 1970s and 1980s to deal directly with the seigneurial lands of Quebec after the French regime. However, even if Courville was examining a part of Quebec that was predominantly rural, his work was profoundly revisionist in its marginalization of the role of agriculture. Instead, he concentrated on the activities, largely urban in nature, carried out in the numerous villages that emerged over the first half of the nineteenth century. In order to counter notions that rural Quebec, and by extension Quebecers, had been less than dynamic, Courville painted a picture of frenetic activity: 'There was a jumble of stores, shops and machinery of all kinds. There were warehouses, mills, workshops and small factories which were thrown together so as to create the impression of constant movement, an impression very different from that which has normally been presented in the past.'[54] This activity gave the lie to those who might have seen Quebec's farmers as not very productive and its businessmen as not very enterprising. In the final analysis, these villages indicated that the development of rural Quebec was 'similar to that of other lands, such as New England, where the market economy was well established.'[55]

Given Courville's urban orientation, it is hardly surprising that he, like his fellow revisionists, paid considerable attention to the way in which Quebecers had been differentiated from one another on the basis of their 'belonging to particular social [classes].'[56] Yet he minimized ethnic distinctions, even characterizing the village as a place where people of all types of backgrounds were welcome. 'There are very few villages that did not benefit from the arrival of newcomers, who brought with them new ideas, new businesses, and new services ... In the towns where there was a significant immigrant element, these newcomers developed relationships which benefited everyone, English-speakers and French-speakers alike.'[57] Quebec's openness to people of various backgrounds reinforced the impression that this was 'a normal society ... shaped by the forces of modernity.'[58]

V

By the late 1970s the revisionists had moved beyond tentative articles and had begun to prepare monographs on specific aspects of the modern Quebec which they had discovered. However, long before they began to publish their findings, they had already come to see themselves as a coherent group with a particular perspective on Quebec's past. Linteau, for instance, looked back with great fondness to an early meeting of his future colleagues at a conference in the late 1960s when they were still undergraduates. These contacts continued 'for the minority among us which decided to go on to graduate school.'[59] By the end of the decade, the revisionists were able to pursue their goals as university professors thanks to the 'incredible expansion of the Quebec university system ... There was a great demand for professors so that many of us were able to find good jobs relatively easily while we were still quite young,' sometimes at one of the older universities, but more commonly at branches of the Université du Québec, established in 1968. Linteau correctly viewed his as an incredibly lucky generation, many of whose members had taken up teaching positions while still in their early twenties.[60]

Building on the ties that they had already established, the revisionists frequently worked collaboratively in the 1970s and 1980s. This situation was in part a reflection of the integration of Quebec historical writing into the mainstream of social science research, which saw teams of scholars handling large amounts of data.[61] An early example was the Groupe de recherche sur la société montréalaise au 19e siècle (Research Group on Montreal Society in the Nineteenth Century), which in the early 1970s brought together such young scholars as Linteau and Robert.[62] Similarly, the 1980s saw Courville, Robert, and Normand Séguin form a team to study economic developments in the St Lawrence valley in the mid-nineteenth century.

In an early statement in the journal *Interface*, the three colleagues indicated that they wanted to show that 'the French-speaking population of Quebec' had not been 'poor, agricultural, devout and with little interest in the modern world.'[63] They then developed these ideas further in their *Atlas historique du Québec: le pays laurentien*, which examined the transformation of agricultural, industrial, and commercial activity in an area populated largely by French speakers.

True to the revisionists' penchant for minimizing differences between French- and English-speaking Quebecers, Courville, Robert, and Séguin rarely distinguished between the roles of the two groups within the economy of the St Lawrence valley. In the process, they managed to attribute to francophones the economic vitality of the region as a whole. For instance, in their *Interface* article, they included anglophones in their calculation of the number of merchants, so as to maximize the extent of commercial activity, which they attributed to the modernity of 'the French-speaking population.'[64] By contrast, in the same article they removed English speakers from their calculations concerning emigration from Quebec; by separating the two groups, they were able to lower the volume of emigration, in the process suggesting that French speakers who left Quebec were not fleeing an unproductive economy.

In their *Atlas historique du Québec*, Courville, Robert, and Séguin distinguished between English and French speakers in economic activity only in the context of census records, which, they argued, were unfair to the linguistic majority.[65] There may have been other comparisons – for instance, between francophone and anglophone farmers – that would have been less flattering to the former, but these were not included. Nor, for that matter, was there any comparison between the St Lawrence valley and other regions, such as the Eastern Townships, where English speakers were in the majority at mid-century. In their contribution to the *Historical Atlas of Canada*, Courville, Robert, and Séguin admitted that 'the two [linguistic] groups produced different agricultural systems; the townships, whose production was more oriented to a market economy, forged ahead in output.'[66] One might have reasonably expected similar differences between French and English speakers within the St Lawrence valley, but Courville and his co-authors largely ignored such distinctions so as to use this region as a proxy for French speakers. Accordingly, when they wrote about 'the socio-economic *progress* of the last century,' they were really touting the modernity of francophone Quebecers.[67]

The portrait of Quebec provided by the threesome was also at the heart of the most significant collaborative effort among the revisionists, the one that brought Linteau, Robert, and René Durocher together to produce a two-volume synthesis of Quebec history since the mid-nineteenth century.[68] *Histoire du Québec contemporain* reflected their common vision of modern Quebec. As Durocher put it, the project 'was thought out collectively. The plan was discussed at length, was allowed to mature, and was continually refined ... This was a real collaborative effort, based on very intense intellectual cooperation.' Durocher claimed that the project had been discussed for ten years prior to the publication of their first volume in 1979, and the second volume did not appear until 1986. The three historians pursued a common goal, which had grown out of the way in which they had 'been shaped in a very profound and intense manner by the years of the Quiet Revolution.'[69] Inspired by the changes of the 1960s, they worked to produce a synthesis that would explain 'how modern Quebec was brought into existence, in the process making our own times more understandable ... Contemporary Quebec has roots that extend far into the past.'[70]

Linteau, Durocher, and Robert could not have prepared their work, however, without the studies of their revisionist colleagues. Accordingly, their synthesis also brought together the efforts of historians such as Bernard, Courville, Rouillard, and Normand Séguin, whose names showed up regularly in bibliographical references. This work of synthesis reflects the times in which it was written and, because of its clear point of view, stands as the best statement of the historical vision of the generation that grew up in the midst of the Quiet Revolution and was fixated on the problems of an urban-industrial society. While this generation produced a history of Quebec since 1867, no such synthesis of the pre-industrial era has yet been attempted.

The revisionists' preoccupation with larger economic forces was evident in the organization of the two volumes of *Histoire du Québec contemporain*. Each of its five sections dealt with an era defined largely in economic terms. For instance, 1896 formed a watershed between eras because it saw the close of 'three decades of slow growth,' which was followed by 'a period of rapid expansion.'[71] Moreover, within each section the authors examined first the structure of the economy, turning subsequently to social issues via discussion of the classes in Quebec society; they dealt with political and cultural issues last so as to reinforce the socioeconomic nature of the revisionist agenda.

In handling these socioeconomic questions, Linteau and his colleagues gave pride of place to urban issues, and one reviewer wondered whether the book was 'an outgrowth of their understanding of the urban world.'[72] For instance, in the section on the period from 1867 to 1896, considerably more space went to urban issues than to rural ones, even though, as the authors admitted, 'Quebec society was made up largely of rural inhabitants.'[73] It was crucial to these revisionist historians, however, to dispute the way in which 'Quebec [had] long been characterized as a society which was largely rural and relatively homogeneous, and in which the family was the central institution.'[74] Like their colleagues whose work formed the basis for this synthesis, they looked instead at the growth of Quebec's cities, where the unequal power of classes was most evident. Along the way, they drew attention to the role of French speakers as key players in the economy and played down the impact of the Catholic church, which they depicted as only one institution among many vying for control over the Quebec people. Even if the church sought 'to assert a leading role in society,' it was unable to overcome the 'social and ideological changes linked to the development of capitalism.'[75] Accordingly, Linteau and his colleagues were quite explicit in inserting Quebecers into the mainstream of liberal thinking in the late nineteenth century, arguing that 'businessmen and political leaders, even those who identified with ultramontanism, were liberals when it came to economic questions.'[76]

Having marginalized Catholicism, or religion more generally, Linteau, Durocher, and Robert were equally dismissive of ethnicity. Accordingly, they introduced their first volume with a lengthy statement of purpose that defined revisionist historical writing:

The Quebec that we are studying here is defined in territorial, rather than ethnic, terms. We are interested in phenomena which were experienced by the men and women who inhabited this territory. We have consistently used the word 'Québécois' in a very precise sense. It pertains to all residents of Quebec including those whose ancestors came from the northwest thousands of years ago, those who came from France in the time of Jean Talon, those who came from Scotland in the late eighteenth century or from Ireland during the Great Famine, those Jews seeking refuge from the pogroms of Eastern Europe, and those emigrating from a southern Italy which had little to offer them.[77]

By unambiguously defining their subject matter as all those who lived in Quebec, independent of their countries of origin, they conveyed to the minorities, including those whose mother tongue was neither French nor English, a certain acceptance as real Quebecers that they had never had before, in the process making Quebec into a normal, pluralistic society divided principally along class lines.

VI

The revisionists' view of the past was most obviously shaped by the Quiet Revolution. Over a relatively short period, Quebecers built a modern, interventionist state, rejected much of their Catholic heritage, took over direction of both the public and the private sectors, and embraced the idea of integrating immigrants into their midst. This redefinition of the identity of the Quebecer went hand in hand with the revisionists' view of Quebec's past. As Jean-Paul Bernard has remarked, the revisionists sought evidence of a history with relatively little trace of Catholicism in order to uncover 'the type of past that seemed consistent with the present.'[78] In a similar fashion, the revisionists' emphasis on class, to the exclusion of ethnic conflict, reflected French-speaking Quebecers' unwillingness to continue to see themselves as members of an ethnic group that lived primarily, but not exclusively, in Quebec. Instead, francophones came to see themselves as residents of a multi-ethnic territory, governed by the newly empowered Quebec state. In line with this new self-image, historians reconceptualized the past. As Linteau put it, 'The focus of our attention shifted from an ethnic group to the population of a territory. In the process, we needed to pay attention to a variety of questions including the structure of the economy, the role of the various classes, and the emergence of a cosmopolitan, urban world.'[79]

It would be an oversimplification, however, to see the work of the revisionists exclusively as a reflection of changes in Quebec. Going back to the days of Groulx, historical writing in Quebec, like historical writing more generally, reflected both local circumstances and larger developments in the discipline, and revisionist writing was no different. Linteau's generation responded also to influences within the profession, most strikingly in the United States. Prior to the late 1960s most professional historians in Quebec had had to leave the province to secure further training. While the generation of Frégault and Trudel had been forced to go south because of the Second World War, under normal circumstances most Quebec historians of note from Groulx through to Dechêne had gone to France.

Thanks to the reforms of the Quiet Revolution, which facilitated the expansion of the province's French-language universities, it was now possible for historians to stay at home. Revisionists such as Jean-Claude Robert and Gérard Bouchard, who went to France, constituted the exception by the 1970s, and so French approaches had less influence than previously. Linteau observed that he and his peers had been shaped less by the Annalistes, largely preoccupied with pre-industrial societies, than by American historians, who were using the techniques of the social sciences to deal with such 'modern' phenomena as urbanization and class conflict.[80] There was something fitting about this American identification, since, as we saw above, much revisionist writing was designed to show Quebecers as a normal North American people who had made the break with traditional European society.

The revisionists seemed to have absorbed in particular the view of some American social scientists who believed that they were carrying out value-free research. Most of the historians considered in this volume, from Groulx through to Ouellet, believed that they were, on some level, seeking the 'truth.' They were sufficiently aware of the polemical nature of historical writing, however, that they tended to be explicit about their social and political preoccupations. The revisionists, by contrast, were circumspect about supporting any political position. Similarly, they were careful not to appear overly strident in their description of the lot of certain groups in Quebec harmed by urbanization and industrialization. In the case of workers, for instance, Linteau, Durocher, and Robert pointed to the fact that 'the urban world was characterized by social inequalities ... which deepened during the second half of the [nineteenth] century.'[81] There was something very clinical about their approach; there was certainly little evidence of the sort of strident Marxism that was visible in the historical profession in the 1960s and 1970s, but made relatively little headway among Quebec historians.[82]

By adopting American notions of social science research, the revisionists placed themselves in the tradition of historians such as David Landes and Charles Tilly, who in 1971 took a clear stance on the objectivity question by arguing that 'some history is more objective and less biased, better documented and more cogently argued. Most of us would call that better history.'[83] The revisionists seemed sympathetic to the notion, as presented by Landes and Tilly, that history should be 'problem oriented [and based on the assumption] that there are uniformities of human behaviour that transcend time and place and can be studied as such.' Needless to say, this search for universal patterns that might assimilate Quebec into larger schemes of Western development appealed to the revisionists, who found early statements of their own point of view discussed by Landes and Tilly. The two Americans praised 'the research of French historians of Quebec that now enables us to scrutinize and revise those sociological explanations of contemporary French Canada that find their deus ex machina in an alleged French Canadian backwardness.'[84]

Many of the early studies in the 1960s employing the social science approach, such as Stephan Thernstrom's quantitative analysis of social mobility in one American city, had rather conservative political implications, seeming to point to the existence of some upward mobility, thus 'backing up the old American dream of success.'[85] Much like Thernstrom, Quebec historians such as Linteau and Robert chronicled the well-being of the American dream in Quebec by focusing on the successes, however limited, of French-speaking businessmen. The social science approach did take a radical turn among some American historians, who by the late 1960s and the 1970s were looking to the experiences of 'ordinary people' in order to legitimize the challenge to the U.S. political system coming from such groups as Blacks, workers, and women. As Peter Novick has said, Landes and Tilly's approach was contested by 'a diverse collection of those who repudiated the idea of discovering "what really was" in favor of private visions or political purpose.'[86]

Some historians, Novick included, bemoaned this emphasis on the history of certain groups such as workers and women, whose experiences transcended national boundaries. These critics recognized the challenge to the long-standing preoccupation of historians with national history that would result if attention shifted to the groups that constituted the nation. In the English-Canadian context, the clearest expression of such dismay came from Michael Bliss, who regretted the 'privatization' of the historical record with the switch from national history to such 'non-national connections as region, ethnicity, class, family and gender.'[87] In Quebec, however, relatively few commentators have complained over the past twenty years about the decline of national history, even though Quebec historical writing has been greatly influenced by interest in the experiences of the working class and of women. There has been none of the hand wringing found in the rest of Canada, because of the relative ease with which the recent work on the history of both workers and women could be integrated into the revisionist portrayal of Quebec's national history as one marked largely by normalcy.

In working-class history, for instance, English-Canadian historians and their Quebec counterparts have approached the topic in different ways.[88] Over the past twenty years, a number of English-Canadian historians such as Bryan Palmer and Greg Kealey have been analysing the everyday experiences of workers in order to arrive at a far-reaching critique of modern Western society, in the process offering little that could be incorporated into the more traditional preoccupation with the national experience. Influenced by such Marxist historians as E.P. Thompson, Palmer and Kealey were fairly explicit in linking their interest in all dimensions of working-class life with a larger political agenda. As Palmer put it, 'The sympathies, engagement and commitment of [our] group are generally to the subjects [we] study, rather than to the profession.'[89]

By contrast, Palmer and Kealey's contemporaries in Quebec, historians such as Jacques Rouillard, showed little interest either in advancing the interests of the contemporary working class or in raising the sorts of theoretical questions that were being raised in English Canada and across the historical discipline more generally. Instead, as we saw above, Rouillard was concerned primarily with documenting the integration of Quebec's workers into a 'normal' trade union movement, which had not been warped by its affiliation with the Catholic church. Because he looked at what made Quebec normal, instead of what made workers' experiences unique, his perspective was easily integrated into the new national history being constructed by the revisionists. Though Joanne Burgess has suggested that Quebec's labour historians were interested in 'understand[ing] Quebec's unique labour past,' historians such as Rouillard were denying the existence of a distinctive experience.[90]

This emphasis on normalcy has also been evident in the last two decades of writing on the history of women in Quebec. Prior to the 1970s, there were very few women in a position to leave their mark on the Quebec historical profession – hardly surprising, given the obstacles that women had long faced in Quebec's educational system. In the absence of women historians, to the extent that women were mentioned at all in historical writing up to the 1970s, it was rarely in a very flattering manner. Groulx tended to place women on a pedestal, viewing them either as members of religious orders or as mothers, but in either case limiting their role to the provision of moral direction. For Groulx's successors at the Université de Montréal, women became even more marginal, as Frégault and his colleagues charted the fortunes of Quebecers, invariably men, in the world of business.[91] Women became more central in Fernand Ouellet's view of the Quebec past, but he tended to depict them as having prevented French-speaking men from getting ahead.

Since the 1970s, in Quebec as elsewhere in the Western world, women have become significant within the historical profession, and there has been an explosion of historical writing on women. From the start, however, women's historians in Quebec, much like their counterparts studying the history of workers, concentrated on what made the experience of women in Quebec like that of women elsewhere, in the process providing considerable support for the revisionist perspective. As Denyse Baillargeon has observed, women's historians in Quebec 'have focused on the ways in which the experiences of Quebec women were much like those of women across the Western world.'[92]

This approach was evident, for instance, in the introduction to the first collection of essays published in Quebec dealing with women's history. Writing in 1977, Marie Lavigne and Yolande Pinard noted that their anthology was designed to demystify the role of women in Quebec history, pushing to the side the notion that Quebec was somehow 'backward' when it came to women's issues. The effort at demystification was evident in their insistence that Quebec women, much like their counterparts across the Western world, had entered the labour force in large numbers in the nineteenth century.

In the same spirit of demystification, Lavigne and Pinard addressed the issue of why women in Quebec had received the vote in provincial elections long after their counterparts in the other Canadian provinces. They were concerned that emphasis on the role of such institutions as the Catholic church in delaying the enfranchisement of women might be seen as evidence that Quebec had been somehow out of step with developments elsewhere. Accordingly, Lavigne and Pinard insisted that 'the fact that women gained the right to vote in 1940 requires a serious analysis of the hypothesis that there had already been a strong women's movement which had allowed feminist concerns to prevail.' They were also reluctant to view Quebec men in an overly negative fashion, even if Quebec history would appear to provide considerable evidence of hostility on the part of most Quebec men towards women's concerns. Fearful of tarring all Quebecers as overly traditional, Lavigne and Pinard called on researchers to explore sources that would provide evidence of a more 'progressive' Quebec.[93]

Since 1977 there has been continued support for this paradigm, which tended to normalize the experience of Quebec women. In particular, a significant amount of literature has appeared on the links between women and Catholicism. As Baillargeon has observed, women's historians in Quebec have been eager to push aside 'the stereotypical view of French-speaking Catholic women who passively submitted to the authority of the clergy.'[94] Those who entered religious communities were no longer viewed, as had long been the case, as religious enthusiasts trying to satisfy their maternal instincts. Rather, women's historians now seemed to view nuns as hard-headed individuals, many of whom took orders to pursue a profession such as nursing or to administer large institutions such as convents. Accordingly, when Lavigne and Pinard produced a second edition of their anthology in 1982, they could refer to the work of such historians as Marta Danylewycz, which had looked at the 'history of nuns and their religious communities in the context of the emergence of a feminist consciousness in Quebec ... These studies indicated that a certain number of women had behaved in a manner that could be described as feminist and had shown the ability to resist the power of men.'[95]

The relative powerlessness of the leaders of French-speaking Quebec to shape the lives of women was similarly evident in Andrée Lévesque's study of marginal women in interwar Quebec. Lévesque began *Making and Breaking the Rules* with the comment that 'there is theory and then there is real life.'[96] As in much of what has been written about the history of Quebec women since the 1970s, the 'theory' was the point of view communicated repeatedly by the leaders of Quebec society, lay and clerical alike, who insisted that women occupied a special nurturing role. Had women actually listened to this discourse between 1919 and 1939, their status might have been different from that of women elsewhere. By pointing to women who broke the law, who sought the means to avoid motherhood, or who earned a living through prostitution, Lévesque provided further evidence of the normalcy of the Quebec experience.

The last two decades' most significant historical studies of Quebec women have gone out of their way to deny the distinctiveness of the Quebec experience. The one major exception, the only synthesis produced on the subject – *L'histoire des femmes au Québec depuis quatre siècles* – appeared in 1982, and a second edition a decade later. In both editions, the four authors – the Clio Collective – concentrated on the victimization of women by the leaders of Quebec society. The authors, Micheline Dumont, Michèle Jean, Marie Lavigne, and Jennifer Stoddart, frequently pointed to the role of the Catholic church. Accordingly, when they looked at the role of nuns, they did not see women trying to turn life in religious communities to their own advantage. Rather, they found that this was a 'strategy [that] proved disadvantageous for women ... The activities undertaken by religious communities reinforced the popular belief that women could play a role in society only if they were involved in a life of devotion or in charitable work.'[97]

By the time the Clio Collective produced a largely unchanged second edition of its work in 1992, it appeared even more out of step with the dominant direction in Quebec women's history. Its perspective can be understood by considering the role of the senior member of the team, Micheline Dumont, who, born in 1935, was of an earlier generation than the revisionists. Dumont produced what was probably the first history of women in Quebec from the French régime to the present – a short study written in 1968 for the Royal Commission on the Status of Women. She observed: 'The special cultural conditions prevailing in New France – French in language and Catholic in religion – have tended to reinforce the differences and to place Quebec women in a historical situation appreci-ably different from that of other Canadian women.'[98] Dumont was still concerned with the problems faced by Quebec women when, nearly twenty years later, she pointed to the 'totalitarian hold of the Quebec church prior to the 1960s.'[99]

This perspective, which emphasized the distinctiveness of Quebec, was in line with historical writing up to the 1970s, but it seemed out of step with the research-based monographs being produced by a younger generation that wanted to view Quebec women as normal. In a sense, then, the writing of Quebec women's history reflected the same shift from a preoccupation with difference to an emphasis on normalcy that was part and parcel of the rise of revisionism.

Not surprisingly, women's historians in English Canada have felt little need to look at questions of normalcy. Rather, their literature has been marked by the passage from early insistence on inserting women into the historical narrative to growing interest, over the past decade or so, with new perspectives on the issue. They have broadened their horizons by considering the ways in which all social relations were shaped, to one degree or another, by 'gender,' a term that began to show up repeat-edly in their work. At the same time, they have analysed the ways in which women were divided by such factors as class, race, and sexual orientation.

The more recent preoccupations of women's historians in English Canada were evident in the way in which the standard text, *Canadian Women: A History*, evolved between its first edition of 1988 and the second, of 1994. While *L'histoire des femmes* remained unchanged, *Canadian Women* turned to consideration 'of the differences among women deriving from differing experiences of race, class, ethnicity, religion, bodily condition and sexual orientation.'[100] These same trends in English Canada were also evident in an anthology, published in 1992, entitled *Gender Conflicts*. As the title suggests, the authors moved beyond the works of the first generation of women's historians who 'felt compelled to emphasize the contributions of women in the past. In the process, however, their work at times neglected the class bias and xenophobic views and practices of some of the women they studied.' To correct this situation, the newer women's historians employed the theoretical concepts in the larger international literature and committed themselves to producing studies that would support 'a socialist, feminist and anti-racist politic.'[101]

This integration of English-Canadian women's history into international debates, and by definition away from national history, paralleled the work of historians such as Palmer and Kealey, studying English-Canadian workers. Yet the concerns of these women's historians were far removed from most works coming from Quebec, which spoke to the normalcy of the Quebec experience. The latter had little to say about the condition of women more globally, divorced as they were from the new theoretical approaches that were shaping the studies of the historians in English Canada. As Andrée Lévesque, herself a major contributor to the dominant perspective on the history of Quebec women, has observed: 'One cannot help but notice the paucity of theoretical debates [in Quebec] which so enliven the practice and development of feminist history.'[102]

Influenced as they were by the more general currents of thought in Quebec, which insisted on the normal development of Quebec society, women's historians, like their colleagues in working-class history, shied away from the larger theoretical debates raging throughout the profession.[103] Accordingly, their work did not really threaten the dominance of national history, as was the case throughout much of the historical profession across the Western world. Rather, by dwelling on the normal development of Quebec society, historians such as Jacques Rouillard and Andrée Lévesque had no difficulty in complying with the revisionist paradigm, which constituted a new version of Quebec's national history.

These works were also compatible with the revisionist approach because of the relative absence of the sort of political commitment evident among historians of both the working class and women in English Canada. In the absence of a theoretical edge, Quebec's social historians wrote with a relatively detached tone, which placed them in the mainstream of Quebec historical writing since the 1970s and set them apart from the explicitly polemical nature of most historical writing prior to the emergence of revisionism. One suspects, for instance, that Rouillard would have been in accord with Louise Dechêne, who remarked in 1994 that she had never been 'out to prove this or that theory.'[104] Similarly, Courville, Robert, and Séguin differed from previous Quebec historians, whose work had been deformed by 'preconceived notions and value judgments.'[105] Yves Gingras argued that Quebec historians since the 1960s had turned from polemical writing to scientific research so as to avoid 'being overly influenced by current social or economic concerns.'[106]

The Quebec historians who have dominated the profession since the 1970s could hardly be blamed for emphasizing the scientific rigour of their work, given the way in which the highly trained 'expert' became a much respected figure in the aftermath of the Quiet Revolution. Business people became persons worthy of respect precisely because they projected the image of the modern Quebecer who was capable of succeeding on the international stage. Similarly, in the public sector, highly trained technocrats were hailed as successors to the representatives of the Catholic church who had long managed the province's educational and social service systems. These civil servants contributed to the new image of the Quebecer by helping to provide the trappings of the modern interventionist state. In this context, the revisionist historians had every reason to see themselves as experts easily distinguishable from predecessors such as Groulx and Ouellet, whose works had been explicitly polemical, and thus deemed insufficiently scientific. The revisionists both looked for a modern past and marketed themselves as thoroughly modern in their own right.

VII

Since the emergence of the revisionist paradigm in the 1970s, there has been relatively little critical analysis of its implications. Most Quebec historians, some of the revisionist generation and others a bit younger, continue to chart Quebec's march towards modernity. This preoccupation has been reflected in the publication in the 1980s and 1990s of a flood of books with titles stressing the link between Quebec and modernity or between Quebec and liberalism, an ideology often linked to modernity because of its emphasis on the individual's liberation from the fetters of traditional societies.[107] In this context, Fernande Roy, in an overview of Quebec intellectual history, stressed the adherence of French speakers to liberal ideas. In the process, she marginalized alternative ideologies and institutions, such as the Catholic church, that might have been sceptical about liberalism. As Roy wrote, 'Liberal ideas were circulating in Quebec society in the eighteenth century, they took root over the course of the nineteenth century, and they have dominated the twentieth century.'[108]

The general acceptance of the revisionists' interpretation has also been evident in the considerable praise that these historians have received from their peers. In particular, there has been a tendency to give the revisionists high marks for their ability to describe the past without imposing value judgments. Accordingly, the reviews of *Histoire du Québec contemporain* generally lauded Linteau and his colleagues for their objectivity. Discussing the first volume, Roberto Perin called it 'a breath of fresh air' because the authors presented an analysis 'free of the slightest hint of either persecution or masochism ... The tone here is serene and detached. If Quebec achieved a certain maturity with the coming of the Quiet Revolution, the work of Linteau, Durocher and Robert is a reflection of the same maturity in Quebec historical writing.'[109] Bernard Vigod, reviewing the second volume, described the authors' treatment of the contentious issue of nationalism as 'a model of objectivity.'[110]

Most critics have taken the revisionists at their word, seeing them as experts engaged in a search for the truth. These commentators have, however, ignored the larger debates raging for several decades regarding the nature of historical writing. Some historians, such as Peter Novick, have bemoaned the demise of objectivity with the entry into the academy of groups, such as women and people of colour, that had the not-always-very-subtle intention of incorporating their groups' experience into the historical record.[111] Others, mostly from outside the discipline, have written extensively about the irrelevance of the historian's concept of objectivity in light of the inevitably artificial nature of all reconstructions of the past. In the hands of some critics, historians became indistinguishable from writers of fiction, since both produced texts capable of being read in a variety of ways.[112] In light of the host of challenges, both internal and external, facing the discipline, Joyce Appleby, Lynn Hunt, and Margaret Jacob have remarked that the only thing that is certain about the historical profession in the 1990s is that 'it rarely has been such a subject of controversy.'[113]

In spite of the growing literature on the nature of historical writing, there has been remarkably little reflection on the subject in Quebec over the past twenty years. As Jocelyn Létourneau has written, 'One can count on the fingers of one hand the number of historians in Quebec who seem interested in understanding the assumptions underlying the conceptual model that they have constructed.'[114] By and large, Quebec historians have been comfortable with the way in which they have provided an appropriately modern view of their people's past and have not overly troubled themselves about the implications or the limitations of the revisionist approach. The general mood of most Quebec historians at century's end was perhaps best captured by John Dickinson, who in 1995 complained about the uselessness of historiographical debate. 'Quebec historical writing has already lost too much time, going round and round in circles debating issues such as the impact of the Conquest upon the bourgeoisie or the nature of the agricultural crisis [in the early nineteenth century].'[115] While these debates, most of which were discussed in previous chapters, eventually did outlive their usefulness, they also encouraged historians to rethink the nature of the Quebec past. Dickinson, however, had little time for such debate or for consideration of the historian's craft. Rather, he spoke for many of his colleagues when he remarked that the historian's primary obligation was to 'fill in the gaps in our knowledge,' as if it were possible to define a single interpretation of Quebec's past that required only filling in the blanks.[116]

To the extent that there has been some criticism of the revisionist approach, the most strident attack has come, perhaps not surprisingly, from Fernand Ouellet. In a number of essays, Ouellet has questioned the revisionists' objectivity by arguing that their emphasis on the long-standing modernity of Quebecers was little more than a thinly veiled attempt to promote sovereignty. In one such piece, he discussed how the 1970s had seen the appearance of a new 'version of history ... According to this new school, Quebec was never backward. Rather, urbanization and industrialization began as early as 1850. Starting in Montreal, this process spread over the length and breadth of the province. Quebec modernized in a uniform fashion down to our own day. Seen from this perspective, eventual independence would not be a violent break with the colonial past, but the inescapable culmination of the Québécois' long march to modernity.'[117] Referring to the work of historians interested in portraying French-speaking entrepreneurs in positive terms, he claimed that they were supporting 'the principal tendencies of the Québécois independence movement.'[118]

Ouellet's simplistic reduction of revisionist writing to a form of separatist propaganda provides a further example, if one were needed, of the tendency he has shown throughout his career to take a good idea and push it to an illogical conclusion. Ouellet made a number of observations that were worth airing. For instance, in order to challenge the revisionists' emphasis on the long-standing urbanization of French speakers, Ouellet pointed out, quite appropriately, that francophones had moved to the cities later than had other Quebecers.[119] Similarly, to counter notions that Catholicism had exerted relatively little influence in Quebec society, Ouellet asked why trade unions dominated by the church had been considerably less inclined to go on strike than those free of clerical influence.[120]

Ouellet, of course, was incapable of simply raising such questions, because his primary concern was to present the internal workings of Quebec society in the bleakest possible terms. In the process, he hoped to deflect attention from externally imposed limitations, such as the bad faith of the federal government or the general hostility of English speakers, that might have provided some ammunition for the sovereignists. Accordingly, anyone who questioned his belief that Quebec's history offered 'more support for the thesis of backwardness than for that of modernization,' or who doubted that the province had long been dominated by 'a class of celibate men and women fired with spiritual fatherhood and motherhood and dominated by fear of liberalism and secularism,' was playing into the hands of the separatist enemy.[121]

There were no shades of grey here – only militant sovereignists, in this case represented by the revisionists, versus people such as Ouellet, who were unwavering defenders of the federal system. However, because he could view the revisionists only from this narrow political perspective, Ouellet was blinded to the fact that most of these historians, as we have seen, were self-consciously apolitical.[122] Moreover, his heavy-handed approach led him to underestimate the diversity of influences that had shaped their work. He drew a straight line from Maurice Séguin, through Jean-Pierre Wallot, to the generation of Linteau and his colleagues, without making the slightest reference to the impact of his former student Louise Dechêne, who had brought with her a different set of influences, largely derived from France; nor for that matter did he perceive the role of the American social scientists.[123] By ignoring the currents that had moulded revisionist writing, Ouellet was able to depict these historians as committed to a narrow nationalist agenda that seemed inextricably linked to the sovereignist movement.

Because Ouellet's has been the loudest dissenting voice amid a general chorus of praise, it has been relatively easy for the revisionists simply to dismiss what he has had to say. For instance, in a review of a collection of Ouellet's essays published in English, José Igartua concluded with the hope that English-speaking students might also be exposed to other points of view that would allow them to appreciate 'the diversity of the output of Quebec historians over the past twenty years.'[124] However, Igartua felt no obligation to address any of Ouellet's specific observations regarding such issues as urbanization and the role of the Catholic church; nor did he explain what he meant by the diversity of Quebec historical writing over the last two decades. There may have been a kernel of truth to Ouellet's criticisms, but they were so overstated as to preclude the need for a reasoned response.

In fact, Ouellet raised some legitimate questions in his essays. He was, by and large, correct in viewing historical writing of the 1970s and 1980s as committed to the depiction of a past that emphasized the modernity of Quebec, in general, and of French speakers, in particular. Moreover, he was generally correct in cautioning revisionists against overstating the extent of Quebec's modernity. While Robert, Séguin, and Courville insisted that 'the French-speaking population of Quebec' had not been made up of 'poor farmers, who were devout Catholics, with little interest in the modern world,' the fact remains that French speakers wielded considerably less power and were not as urbanized as their English-speaking counterparts throughout most of the nineteenth and twentieth centuries.[125] Moreover, a relatively high percentage of Quebecers of both sexes joined religious orders, attended mass, patronized cooperatives set up with the indispensable support of the church, and belonged to unions in which the clergy played a significant role. Until the 1940s non-francophones were denied equal treatment in these cooperatives and unions, and they received scarcely better treatment at the hands of the Catholic schools – public institutions that were less than enthusiastic about receiving 'outsiders.' While Linteau and his colleagues presented Quebec history in an inclusive fashion that gave the impression of a society tolerant towards immigrants, one has to wonder how French-speaking Quebecers who patronized these institutions could have been particularly open to newcomers.[126]

None of these comments is intended to suggest that Quebec was any more influenced by religion or intolerance than other societies; nor do they justify Ouellet's conclusion that Quebec was somehow 'backward' as if there were a single correct path for all societies to follow – a path that Quebecers, through their own fault, had somehow missed. Nor are these comments intended to support Ouellet's conclusion that the Catholic church was a monolithic force that was able to control Quebecers. Nevertheless, one wonders if there is not room for Quebec historians to consider both the ways in which their province has been normal *and* the ways in which its experience has been unique.

VIII

Fernand Ouellet has not been entirely alone among historians in expressing reservations about the revisionist paradigm, though he has certainly been the most outspoken and the easiest for revisionists to dismiss. While the revisionist interpretation remains dominant as the twentieth century comes to a close, in the past few years dissenting voices, more difficult to ignore than Ouellet's, have begun to be heard, as other historians have started to question the revisionists' preoccupation with the normalcy of Quebec's past. It is impossible to know, as I finish this volume, whether these relatively isolated voices will ultimately converge to develop a 'post-revisionist' explanation of Quebec's past in which both the 'normal' and the 'unique' would be given significant attention.[127]

However, even if these dissenters never develop a new paradigm, their very existence at century's end reflects the malaise among some Quebecers about the direction of their society. This unease has relatively little to do with the constitutional future of the province, which so preoccupied Ouellet. Rather, what is at issue here is a fundamental disenchantment with the society that emerged out of the great hopes of the Quiet Revolution.

Many of the sorts of problems that Quebec has experienced over the past twenty years have been evident throughout the West. With the end of the long economic boom that followed the Second World War and with growing competition from developing economies, unemployment rates soared. Because of limited revenues caused by weak economic growth, and the costs of looking after those pushed out of the job market, governments found themselves with growing deficits. Among people who had jobs, particularly those with relatively well-paying and secure positions, there emerged a certain disillusionment about the ability of the state to resolve problems that seemed so intractable. Such disillusionment led in turn to demands that government reduce expenditures so as to place a lid on taxes. There was little apparent concern for the well-being of those groups, such as the poor, women, and people of colour, who had never achieved the equality promised at the start of the construction of the Quebec welfare state, referred to in French as the 'état-providence,' in the 1960s. In Quebec, as elsewhere in the West, the end of the twentieth century has been marked by a growing rift between the haves and the have-nots and a certain sense that the gap was beyond the capacity of governments to close.

Deindustrialization, chronic unemployment, and widespread opposition to the role of the state have been as evident in late-twentieth-century Quebec as in other Western societies. Quebec, however, has been home to certain unique problems. Perhaps the two most striking indicators of malaise pertain to the province's youths. For every 100,000 males between 15 and 19 years of age, there were 28.7 suicides in 1987, as opposed to 8.1 in 1970. Moreover, among 15-to-19-year-old males, 40 per cent of all Canadian suicides in 1991 took place in Quebec, a province with only one-quarter of the Canadian population.[128] Paralleling the despair evident in the youth suicide rate was the propensity with which Quebec students dropped out of school. Between 1986 and 1992 the proportion of Quebecers failing to finish high school increased from 27 to 36 per cent, reaching 42 per cent among boys.[129] Since French speakers were twice as likely to drop out as other Quebecers, it was reasonable to conclude that 'the French-speaking population of Quebec has one of the highest drop-out rates in the developed world.'[130]

Despite evidence that Quebec constituted, in certain regards, a 'distinct' society, some historians still refused to see anything but normalcy. For instance, Linteau and his colleagues, in their *Histoire du Québec contemporain*, referred to 'the youths of the 1980s ... as an abandoned generation,' but only because of the high rate of unemployment that linked the young people of Quebec with their counterparts across the Western world.[131] In order to reinforce their depiction of Quebec as a normal society, these historians said nothing about the extent to which the province's youths were dropping out of school and taking their own lives at extraordinary rates. The revisionists accepted the premises of the Quiet Revolution, which saw the individual as 'rational' and the state as his or her logical extension. Phenomena such as youth suicide negatively emphasized Quebec's distinctiveness, raised questions about the nature of rational behaviour, and showed the state as powerless to devise policies that made any difference – not the sort of issues that the revisionists wanted to handle.

The revisionists' insistence on the normalcy of contemporary Quebec was consistent with their view of a past in which the province only rarely departed from the general pattern of Western social and economic development. Accordingly, the task of pointing to the distinctive aspects of the

Quebec experience has fallen, over the last decade or so, to commentators, such as Fernand Dumont, who have expressed disenchantment with some of the more troubling characteristics of Quebec society at century's end. While Dumont is a sociologist by training, he has written extensively over the last thirty years about the role of historical thinking in Quebec society.[132] Over the past few years, he has published three books, all of which touched on the current malaise in Quebec society, which he attributed somewhat to Quebecers' loss of a common identity.[133]

Without denying the difficulties faced by Quebecers prior to the Quiet Revolution, Dumont has written with considerable affection about a time in which individual French speakers felt that they belonged to a larger community based on a shared language and, even more important, a shared religion and a common view of the past. Then came the Quiet Revolution, inspired 'by the principles of technocratic rationality.' Quebecers were encouraged to forget about their past, abandon their religion, and place their fate in the hands of 'experts,' whose own personal success reflected the individualism of the late twentieth century.[134] Nearly forty years after the start of the Quiet Revolution, however, Dumont wondered if these changes had not created more problems than benefits. He chronicled the ills of Quebec society at the start of 1994: 'There are 750,000 Quebecers on social assistance, 400,000 are unemployed, 130,000 workers earn the minimum wage, one person in four is illiterate, and 40,000 youngsters drop out each year without graduating from secondary school.'[135]

What particularly troubled Dumont, however, was the incapacity of Quebecers to respond to these problems, having abandoned so much of what he called their traditional culture. He described a cultural crisis in which Quebecers found themselves cut off from their past in part because of the way in which intellectuals, historians included, had emphasized the power of 'anonymous forces' to shape the experiences of the individual.[136] Accordingly, with the passing of the high hopes of the Quiet Revolution, Quebecers found themselves with a 'collective memory that [had] been devastated.'[137] They no longer had any sense of collective struggle for their national survival and had even been encouraged to forget about their links to Catholicism. 'With the Quiet Revolution ... our elites decided that ... the only way to take charge of the future was by denying our past.' While Dumont made it clear that he was not advocating a return to the historical vision of Abbé Groulx, he did think that Quebecers had been short-changed by the revisionist emphasis on structural factors. Along the way, the population had been denied any sense of a common identity, which might have been used to confront the problems of Quebec at the end of the century.[138]

Dumont's critique of modernity, like the revisionists' uncritical acceptance, was derived from a personal perspective – in his case, that of a Catholic man, born in the 1920s, discomfited by recent developments in Quebec.[139] Consistent with this view, Dumont had no difficulty in mocking the women's movement, because the society that he longed for was one in which certain 'communal' values had been enforced, albeit by men.[140] Dumont's attitude is indicative of a more general discomfort among some Quebecers, mostly men, who were born before 1939 and who looked back with a certain fondness at the Catholic Quebec which had distinguished itself from the Protestant world that surrounded it.

Dumont's concerns have been echoed in some of the recent writings of Serge Gagnon, a historian born in the late 1930s and referred to throughout this volume as the author of several books on Quebec historiography. In these writings he generally sympathized with the revisionists and harshly criticized those such as Fernand Ouellet who dwelled on the distinctive mentality of Quebecers. Moreover, as we saw earlier in this chapter, during the 1970s Gagnon, along with René Hardy, subscribed to the revisionist perspective on Catholicism, viewing it generally as something imposed on Quebecers. In the 1980s and early 1990s this point of view was reinforced by Hardy and Jean Roy, who analysed the strategies employed 'to guarantee the greatest possible adherence to church-sanctioned behaviour.'[141] Gagnon, however, moved in a different direction, publishing a trilogy 'focused on the religion and the behaviour of the French-speaking inhabitants ... of Lower Canada.'[142] In these volumes, Gagnon was particularly interested in comparing the ways in which a religious society, Quebec of the early nineteenth century, and a secular one, contemporary Quebec, dealt with such issues as death, sexuality, and marriage. By and large, these comparisons led him to prefer the older society to the newer one. He parted company with his colleagues by expressing both his disillusionment over the state of society in contemporary Quebec and his insistence on the distinctiveness of Quebec's past.

In the volume dealing with death, for instance, Gagnon touched on suicide, noting that clerical influence had frequently been decisive in convincing nineteenth-century Quebecers not to kill themselves.[143] The clergy were concerned with the community as a whole and recognized the costs associated with a suicide. 'When a desperate father killed himself, the entire community found itself looking after the family he left behind.' Accordingly, clerical denunciation of suicide was directed not solely towards saving the person considering the act, but also, in the case noted above, towards 'protecting women and children.' By contrast, there was no force in modern Quebec to preclude suicide, given the destruction of clerical influence and the late twentieth century's preoccupation with the satisfaction of the needs of the individual. Gagnon concluded that society might be improved by the reassertion of the values of 'prudence, sobriety, and restraint' that had been instilled by Catholicism in early-nineteenth-century Quebec.[144] In a similar fashion, Gagnon preferred the nineteenth century for the way in which sexual promiscuity had been held in check and marriage had been indissoluble. In both cases, the interests of the individual were controlled so as to minimize the harm that might be done to others. 'The encouragement of self-restraint created a force of value to all in the community.'[145]

Gagnon was obviously preoccupied with contemporary concerns as he departed from revisionist orthodoxy by singing the praises of a Catholic Quebec that seemingly stood outside the mainstream of secular developments across the Western world. As he observed, 'Regardless of the period under study, history always reflects contemporary concerns. The living find themselves imposing their concerns upon the dead. I have not escaped from this presentism in the trilogy dealing with ethical and religious questions in the experience of Quebecers.'[146] Gagnon was troubled by the way in which the changes in Quebec since the Quiet Revolution had destroyed Catholicism, leaving in its wake the cult of the individual – a characteristic of most Western societies today, but one that had taken on enormous proportions in Quebec.[147] 'Having abandoned the notion of self-restraint, should we be surprised that our youths resort to mindless violence and that they give up on school, where results can be achieved only after persistent effort over the long term.' In the same spirit, he saw individualism gone wild as responsible for Quebec's being home to 'the lowest rate of marriage recorded by any population for which data are available.'[148] Gagnon recognized that he would be taken to task by the revisionist historians, who preferred to see Catholicism as 'no more than a vile sedative imposed by the ruling classes.' From the perspective of a secular society with serious problems, however, he wondered if the time had not come to abandon this negative view of Catholicism and to recognize that 'Christianity had an important meaning to those who followed it and remained faithful to it generation after generation.'[149]

Gagnon's studies of the role of religion in Quebec society were not without their problems. Much like Fernand Dumont, his longing for the good old days sometimes led him astray, as in the case of his attack on the women's movement.[150] Moreover, he has been taken to task for his use of anecdotal evidence, which did not always adequately prove his case.[151] Nevertheless, Gagnon's generally positive depiction of Quebec's Catholic past was an accurate reflection of the distance that separated some scholars born before 1939 from their younger, revisionist colleagues.

Gagnon insisted that Quebecers might have embraced Catholicism not because it had been imposed on them, but rather because it had constituted an important element of their society. This perspective has also been advanced by Louis Rousseau, yet another scholar of Gagnon's generation. Over the last twenty years Rousseau has written extensively about Quebec Catholicism, particularly in the nineteenth century. Rousseau's work has received curiously little attention from Quebec historians, in part because of his training in religious studies, not history, but also because of his tendency to see Catholicism as something other than a form of social control.[152] While the revisionists viewed the Catholic church as an institution that had been thrust on Quebecers, Rousseau insisted that it was also necessary to consider the spiritual needs of the population. He found something curious about the way in which historians had managed to study Catholicism as an institution, in the process pushing questions of religion to the side.[153]

More specifically, Rousseau has been at odds with the revisionists in a lively debate over the role of Catholicism in mid-nineteenth-century Quebec. Rousseau's opponent in this debate has been René Hardy, who insisted that Catholicism had gradually become more powerful by means of coercive measures.[154] By contrast, Rousseau found that Catholicism's resurgence had been quite rapid. He argued that the spectacular success of efforts in the 1840s to revive the Catholicism of Quebecers was not so much the work of imperious priests as it was a response to the social and political circumstances. As Rousseau observed, Quebecers were responding to the 'general perception that Quebec had reached a dead end after the events of 1837–8. This constituted the immediate context for a cultural revival which took the form of a religious awakening. [Quebecers] were responding to a shock, to the consequences of a series of events that had led to the impression that their society had run out of gas.' By turning attention away from the actions of the clergy and towards the people, Rousseau made Catholicism part of a 'new mass culture' that was being created by Quebecers, not being imposed on them.[155]

Rousseau has made much the same point regarding the central role of Catholicism by focusing on certain contemporary aspects of Quebec culture. While Gagnon was prepared to accept the revisionists' conclusion that religion was dead, Rousseau wondered how it was possible to explain, without dealing with Quebecers' spiritual values, the fact that nearly all Catholics in the province continue voluntarily to expose their children to religious training in the schools. To avoid thinking about such inexplicable behaviour among a secular people, most researchers have simply chosen to ignore such conduct, which contradicts 'our sense of the specific manner in which we have embraced modernity.'[156] While the revisionists sought to reduce human behaviour to a series of concrete responses to material circumstances, Rousseau found a more complex situation, in which Quebecers continued to value aspects of the religion of their ancestors, sometimes for spiritual reasons, which to late-twentieth-century eyes could appear only as irrational.[157]

Reservations regarding the revisionist perspective, though of a different sort, have also been recorded by a few members of the revisionist generation. Most notably, Gérard Bouchard has broken ranks with his peers by wondering if they had gone too far in emphasizing the normalcy of Quebec's past. Bouchard was in a particularly strong position to criticize revisionist writing, since his own career has been closely associated with establishing Quebec's kinship with other North American societies. For instance, in *Quelques arpents d'Amérique*, a study of the history of the Saguenay region, he noted, 'Instead of looking for the differences [between Quebec and the rest of North America], I decided to look for the similarities.'[158] Even though Bouchard was depicting Quebecers as profoundly American, he still recognized revisionist writing for what it was – namely, 'a rehabilitation of Quebec society in order to show that, by and large, it had followed a model of change that was entirely comparable to that evident across North America and the Western world.' He wondered, however, whether the revisionists' emphasis on the similarities with the larger world had not prevented them from viewing 'the specificity of the Quebec experience, of what made it different.' Bouchard saw similarities between the Quiet Revolution, which had outlived its usefulness, having achieved construction of the Quebec state, and the revisionist perspective, which could no longer provide 'the conditions for the development of new scientific insights,' having successfully chronicled the ways in which Quebec had long been normal. He was concerned that 'the paradigm of modernization had run out of steam, much like the Quiet Revolution itself, once it had achieved its initial goals.'[159]

While Bouchard shared Gagnon's unease over the legacy of both the Quiet Revolution and revisionist writing, the two historians also parted company in fundamental ways. While Gagnon had little sympathy for many of the reforms of the Quiet Revolution, Bouchard wondered only if the efforts to bring Quebec up to the standards of other societies had been achieved, thus leaving the door open to different priorities. Moreover, while Gagnon looked back with fondness to the Catholic past, Bouchard interpreted the role of Catholicism as a largely negative aspect of Quebec history that needed to be confronted. He made this point most forcefully in an essay considering the history of Quebec in the context of other 'new societies' established in the Americas. Without rejecting the revisionists' insistence that Quebec had developed much like other Western societies, he hoped that 'a recognition of the similarities might open the way to thinking more seriously about the differences.' He wanted Quebec scholars 'to engage in serious comparative research, not with an eye towards denying Quebec's distinctiveness ... but in order to acquire a clearer view of ourselves as well as others.'[160]

Bouchard pointed to both the 'normal' and the 'distinctive' characteristics of Quebecers in the North American context in his handling of the touchy issue of religion. He showed his sympathy for the revisionists' efforts to play down the distinctiveness of Quebec's Catholic heritage by pointing to the considerable evidence of religious zeal in the American experience, beginning with the arrival of the Pilgrims fleeing religious persecution in England. Bouchard was not prepared, however, to push the similarities in religion too far, insisting instead that 'the two societies had ... differed, and in some very important ways' in this regard. In particular, he pointed to the manner in which Quebec had been shaped by the domination of a single religion, as opposed to the American situation, where no single sect had prevailed. 'The absence [in the U.S. context] of a hierarchical structure prevented the sort of authoritarianism that was long evident among the Quebec clergy.' Moreover, Bouchard recognized that Quebec's Catholic heritage had restrained 'the individualism that was encouraged by the various Protestant faiths.' He argued that Americans had long had certain advantages over Quebecers when it came to succeeding in the modern world. 'It goes without saying that a population trained in the reading of the Bible, given greater responsibility and with a higher rate of literacy, will [more] readily develop a critical spirit.'[161]

Bouchard differed fundamentally from Gagnon in refusing to see the considerable power of Quebec Catholicism in positive terms – he was younger than Gagnon and belonged to a generation that was cynical about the church. By pointing out that Quebecers may have lacked certain qualities necessary for success, he also parted company with the revisionists, who would have rejected his efforts to draw attention to the distinctive aspects of Quebec's past.

Bouchard's point of view also stands apart from the criticism of Quebec historiography developed by younger historians such as Jocelyn Létourneau. If Serge Gagnon's reservations about revisionism reflected the perspective of the preceding generation, and if Bouchard was himself a 'baby boomer,' then Létourneau represented the generation that came of age a bit too late to share in the fruits of the Quiet Revolution. For those born in the 1940s, entry into university jobs was relatively easy, given the rapid expansion of the educational system in the late 1960s and early 1970s. However, the situation was not so straightforward for those born a bit later, who did not necessarily find jobs ready for the asking and who were more familiar with governmental restraint than with the building of 'l'état-providence.' Létourneau, in a highly insightful discussion of the differences between the generation of the Quiet Revolution and the one that followed, pointed to the ways in which the former was wedded to 'the discourse of modernity.' The revisionists' generation was eager to push aside traits too closely associated with a 'traditional' Catholic Quebec, in order to portray the Quebecer as 'a rational being who acted in a systematic fashion.'[162]

Létourneau argued that the revisionists tended to marginalize all aspects of behaviour that defied 'rational' explanation. In the process, they managed to ignore a whole world of 'lived experience' because they could not believe that 'there exists a reality beyond the material forces, which do not always guide people's behaviour.'[163] Létourneau here set himself apart not only from the revisionists, but also from Gagnon and Bouchard, both of whom still believed that it was possible to find rational explanations for most behaviour. For Gagnon, the nineteenth-century Quebecers' embrace of Catholicism, while it may not have been imposed by mean-spirited priests, still had little to do with religious zeal; rather it was a rational way of ensuring enforcement of certain community standards. Similarly, Bouchard argued that Catholicism made inroads in societies that lacked alternative sources of social cohesion; once again religion was something that was rationally embraced when it filled a void.[164]

Létourneau wondered if there was not room to look at the way in which Quebecers' behaviour had also been shaped by their imaginations and their 'irrational' passions. Moreover, he wondered if historians did not need to find new tools to read 'texts' so as to appreciate various levels of meaning in the documents they employed. In essence, Létourneau called for a sort of postmodernist view of Quebec's history by urging his colleagues to study 'the individual in all of his dimensions, including the existential and the spiritual.'[165] He doubted that the revisionists were capable of incorporating such concerns into their own research, as they had been creatures of the Quiet Revolution. Younger scholars, however, had little incentive either to glorify the Quiet Revolution or to retreat in horror from Quebec's more 'irrational' past. Accordingly, they were in a position to broaden research by going beyond the analysis of social and economic factors in order to understand the various forces, ranging from the economic to the spiritual, that had shaped Quebecers' past. Létourneau concluded, in a rather overstated way, that 'this orientation is largely the domain of young researchers.'[166]

Létourneau may have been right in pointing to the reasons why some younger scholars have developed alternatives to the revisionist paradigm. Nevertheless, as we have seen above, his generation has not had a monopoly in this regard. In fact, in the past few years there has been significant cooperation between these new scholars and their somewhat older colleagues in the development of new approaches to the Quebec past. For instance, one is struck by the orientation of a number of the essays on Quebec history in a recent volume edited by Létourneau, Jean-Marie Fecteau, and Gilles Breton. In the introduction to *La condition québécoise*, the editors carved out a position that set them apart from 'the technocratic point of view,' arguing that people's identities were shaped not only by their concrete social and economic circumstances, but also by more spiritual concerns. 'Quebecers have redefined their identity by distancing themselves from spiritual matters. It has come to the point that any discussion of [such] matters is ridiculed by the secular discourse ... Nevertheless, this interest in spiritual concerns has not, and cannot, disappear because it constitutes a fundamental part of the human condition.'[167]

This general perspective was supported by Louis Rousseau's contribution to the volume, which, as we saw above, called for a more serious appreciation of the role of Catholicism in modern Quebec culture.[168] While Rousseau was born prior to the Second World War, this type of interest in the values of Quebecers has also been evident, albeit in a different fashion, in the work of Jean-Marie Fecteau, another younger scholar and one of the editors of *La condition québécoise*. As Fecteau has observed, historians have become irrelevant to political debates because they have limited themselves to describing social and economic circumstances. Echoing the concerns of Rousseau, Fecteau argued that historians 'have been silent when it comes to explaining matters that do not lend themselves to easy explanation with the tools of the social sciences. Over the past twenty years, historians have been very good at describing, sometimes in great detail, the various characteristics of our society ... But history has had nothing to say about matters that cannot easily be quantified such as ... xenophobia.' Historians have shown themselves incapable of confronting such passions as envy, anger, and hate, and so they have been left with little to say about a world in which such emotions play a key role on the political stage.[169]

Fecteau has not been alone in his concern about the retreat of social scientists from political issues. The French sociologist Alain Caillé, for instance, has observed that researchers trained to explore rational behaviour have had nothing to say about such phenomena as the disintegration of Yugoslavia, marked by such irrational impulses as 'racism, hatred, and intolerance towards the "other."'[170] In a similar fashion, the Canadian historian Ian McKay complained that social scientists had tended to shy away from the discussion of 'irrational' behaviour, which they viewed as 'embarrassing outbreaks, like acne, to be remedied with the clear, refreshing, balm of empiricism and common sense.'[171] While McKay's comments were aimed at the social sciences in general, they have a particular relevance to Quebec, where the revisionist historians have worked so hard to cultivate the persona of the value-free expert and to remain above political debate. In fact, Quebec's historians have been so successful in presenting themselves as social scientists divorced from political concerns that they largely remained hidden from view during the 1995 referendum on Quebec sovereignty. While such English-Canadian historians as Michael Behiels, David Bercuson, and Michael Bliss regularly comment on contemporary affairs, one rarely hears the voice of a Quebec historian.

In light of the apolitical nature of revisionism, one can see another challenge, however modest, to its dominance – the appearance in 1992 of the

Bulletin d'histoire politique, the first new professional journal dedicated to Quebec history since the founding of the *Revue d'histoire de l'Amérique française* by Abbé Groulx in the late 1940s. *Bulletin* was founded by a team headed by Robert Comeau, a member of the revisionist generation, but one who had for some time been at odds with many of his peers. In his introduction to a volume of essays generally praising the contributions of Maurice Séguin – hardly a favourite of the revisionists – Comeau bemoaned the way in which 'Quebec historians, schooled in the precepts of "the new [social] history," have provided us with the image of a people becoming more and more modern over time.' While Séguin had tried to remind Quebecers that they were different precisely because they had been conquered, the revisionists pushed such concerns to the side in their efforts to show how the people of Quebec had managed to secure 'the benefits of the consumer society.'[172]

Comeau's impatience with the revisionists' efforts to normalize Quebec's past was shared by a number of younger colleagues who helped start up the *Bulletin*. One of these historians, Michel Sarra-Bournet, complained that revisionists, committed as they were to the 'precepts of the methods of the social sciences,' had discouraged political thinking by linking all human behaviour to social and economic circumstances.[173] He insisted that 'ideas exist with a certain independence from social and economic structures' and that historians in general, and the *Bulletin* in particular, had a responsibility to revive 'l'histoire politique,' which he defined as 'an exercise in rediscovering the nature of the human experience, taking into account the role of the individual, his institutions and his ideas.'[174]

In addition to the *Bulletin d'histoire politique*, there has appeared in the last few years a further challenge to revisionism, and to its journal, the *RHAF*, in the form of the *Cahiers d'histoire du Québec au XXe siècle*. This journal was founded in 1994 by the Centre de recherche Lionel-Groulx, an arm of the Fondation Lionel-Groulx, which, as we saw in chapter 3, had been established in the 1950s to defend Quebec historical writing from the excesses of 'scientific' historians such as Frégault. Both the past president of the centre, Jean Éthier-Blais, and the editor of the journal, Stéphane Stapinsky, have been dismissive of accusations that Groulx was 'anti-English, anti-Canadian, anti-Protestant, even anti-French.'[175] Accordingly, it should come as little surprise if the *Cahiers d'histoire* set out to provide a reading of Quebec's pre–Quiet Revolution past that differed from that of the revisionists. Stapinsky and Benoît Lacroix noted in the first issue of the journal that it had the goal of 'overcom[ing] the reluctance of Quebecers over the past few decades to face up to certain aspects of their past.'[176]

This re-reading of the past, however, was very different from that proposed by the *Bulletin d'histoire politique*. While the two journals shared scepticism about revisionism and a commitment to presenting the work of young Quebec historians, they were at odds in their political perspectives.[177] While the *Bulletin* wanted to re-establish political history in order to focus attention on the ills plaguing the postmodern world, the *Cahiers* sought to rehabilitate certain figures and movements from Quebec's past that had fallen into disrepute. Stapinsky and Lacroix asked whether Quebecers were 'sufficiently mature to pay their respect to certain of [their] benefactors, even if we are no longer willing to share, collectively, the goals that motivated them.'[178] Clearly, Abbé Groulx was not very far from their minds, and their interest in reading Groulx's record more positively was reinforced by the publication of a series of interviews with Groulx's niece Juliette Lalonde-Rémillard, who had served as the priest's assistant in his history-related activities.[179]

IX

So here we are at the end of the twentieth century, still not having fully escaped the clutches of Lionel Groulx. In the early chapters of this book, I tried to argue that it is too easy to dismiss Groulx, thereby overlooking the ways in which he was a fairly normal early-twentieth-century historian, whose work reflected both the society in which he lived and the discipline with which he identified. Similarly, it is simple enough to dismiss a journal such as *Cahiers d'histoire du Québec au XXe siècle* as little more than a tool of propaganda for reactionary nationalists. In fact, it forms part of a reaction against revisionism, albeit one that lacks much direction, including as it does such diverse critics as Serge Gagnon, Gérard Bouchard, and Jocelyn Létourneau. These historians have expressed both disillusionment with aspects of contemporary Quebec and frustration with the limitations of the revisionist view of the past. Nevertheless, their pleas for a 'post-revisionist' perspective on Quebec's history that might take into account both what was normal and what was distinctive have fallen largely on deaf ears. The revisionist interpretation remains the dominant perspective on Quebec's past – a situation that makes Quebec rather distinctive.

The revisionist school turned all previous historical writing on its head by insisting on the ways in which Quebec's past had been largely indistinguishable from that of other Western societies. Nevertheless, for all that was new about revisionism, Linteau, Robert, Rouillard, and their colleagues, much like their predecessors stretching back to Groulx, were charting a national history, albeit one in which Quebecers were constantly on the march towards modernity. This continued dedication to defining the national experience stands in stark contrast to the situation in much of the historical profession across the Western world over the past twenty-five years, roughly the period during which revisionism has reigned in Quebec. While the revisionist view of Quebec's history managed to incorporate the diverse experiences of groups such as women and workers, in places such as English Canada and the United States the emphasis on the groups that constituted the nation put the very concept of national history in doubt, thus giving rise to the complaints of such critics as Peter Novick, who proclaimed in 1988 that there had not been since the late 1960s 'any overarching interpretation which could organize American history.' Historians no longer felt the need to define the national experience, but sought rather 'to fashion accounts serviceable to particularistic constituencies.'[180] In Quebec, however, there was no comparable challenge to the idea of a national history, thus allowing the creation of the revisionist perspective.

Quebec historiography also appears somewhat distinctive at century's end because of continued widespread support for the notion that historians are engaged in a scientific endeavour, relatively free of value judgments. Parallel to the challenge to national history, in the past twenty years there has also been steady erosion in the belief that historians were capable of describing the past in an objective fashion. As historians became more closely identified with advancing the interests of specific groups, they frequently abandoned the notion that they were trying to understand the past through scientific means. As Novick wrote, 'Earlier postures of detachment gave way to more explicit avowals of commitment.'[181] Simultaneously, there were individuals from outside the profession – literary critics, in particular – who dismissed the whole concept of scientifically establishing the nature of the past.

In the midst of this intense questioning, there has been remarkably little reflection in Quebec about the way in which value judgments may have shaped the revisionists' work. Accordingly, Normand Séguin, a leading revisionist, had no difficulty in remarking in 1991, long after the scientific pretensions of the discipline had been thrown into doubt, that history constituted 'a scientific exercise' designed 'to correct mistaken impressions and to fill the gaps in our knowledge.'[182] Séguin's statement, on its own, was not very exceptional. Numerous historians across the profession would be prepared to support Séguin's article of faith, but in most contexts such a statement would have been greeted with considerable cynicism. In Quebec, however, Séguin's faith in the scientific mission of historians met with little opposition, given that it was in the mainstream of the conviction, shared by most revisionists, that they were engaged in an exercise relatively undistorted by value judgments. The relative absence of critics prepared to doubt the objective pretensions of history as a discipline was a further sign of the rather distinctive nature of historical writing in the 1990s in Quebec.

Much like their predecessors, both the revisionists and their critics reflected more general trends in the discipline as well as features of Quebec society. While the revisionists may have seemed a bit out of step in the late 1990s because of their insistence on national history and their belief in the scientific nature of their work, they came to this perspective in the first place by absorbing approaches that were popular within the historical profession during the 1960s and 1970s. In particular, they absorbed the value-free approach of some American social historians, who believed that, via scientific tools, it might be possible to come closer to understanding the past as it really was. There was something fitting about the revisionists' reliance on American methods, since their work frequently depicted Quebec as a normal American society.

If the revisionists did not eventually distance themselves from a position that had lost much of its support in the larger profession, this was because of the particular circumstances of Quebec society, which, in the aftermath of the Quiet Revolution, was modernizing as rapidly as possible. The revisionist historians, themselves products of the Quiet Revolution, devised a vision of the past that was consistent with the new identity of Quebecers as a thoroughly modern people. Given the strength of this newfound identity, it is little wonder that critics of revisionism have emerged rather slowly. Nevertheless, these critics reflected both disillusionment with Quebec society and, in the case of a historian such as Létourneau, a desire to integrate into the study of Quebec's past some of the tools now being widely used throughout the profession. Through the twentieth century, successive generations of Quebec historians have produced works that both mirrored developments within the larger profession and reflected changes within Quebec society.

Postscript

Over the past two decades or so, revisionist historians have completely transformed our understanding of Quebec's past by exploring the ways in which this society had long been on the road to modernity. Curiously, however, while the revisionists had no difficulty in discovering the roots of an urban, secular society going back to the mid-nineteenth century, if not earlier, they were incapable of perceiving the early-twentieth-century beginnings of 'modern' historical writing in Quebec. While some were prepared to see the coming of serious scholarship with the emergence of the Montreal historians after the Second World War, still others saw little but darkness until the arrival of revisionism following the Quiet Revolution. As Jean-Paul Bernard has observed, there was something paradoxical about the way in which the revisionists insisted on 'the early modernization of Quebec society' at the same time that they described 'the late modernization of Quebec historical writing.'[1]

The revisionists might have avoided this paradoxical situation had they viewed historical writing – much as they viewed Quebec society – as having steadily become more modern during the twentieth century. Had they done so, however, they would probably have fallen into the trap, fairly common among those who comment on historical writing, of providing a Whiggish view of a discipline that was constantly getting closer to the 'truth' about the past. As matters stand, the revisionists have provided a fairly celebratory view of a profession that had escaped, only relatively recently, from the grips of propagandists masquerading as historians. Had they recognized the depth of the modern currents in Quebec historical writing that stretched back to the early decades of the century, the revisionists might still have retained the celebratory tone that I have tried to avoid in this book. At the same time, however, they would have at least discovered a historical profession that took root in Quebec about the turn of the century, when such professions were emerging across the Western world.

Up to now, despite the enthusiasm of the revisionists for looking high and low for evidence of Quebec's modernity, they have indicated little interest, for instance, in viewing Lionel Groulx, the individual most responsible for the emergence of a historical profession in Quebec, as anything other than a remnant of some more traditional Quebec, which, by the early twentieth century, was well on its way to extinction. Had the revisionists been true to their general inclination to stress the deep roots of modernity in Quebec, they would have conveyed professional status to someone such as Groulx, despite his willingness at times to place his historical skills at the service of causes that we might find distasteful.

Had the revisionists read Groulx more carefully, they would have recognized that he, like his successors, was engaged in the struggle, common to historians everywhere, to find the balance between using scientific techniques to understand the past 'as it was' and employing history as a means of providing lessons relevant to a particular society. By viewing Groulx in this fashion, the revisionists might have come to the conclusion that a historical profession has existed in Quebec since early in the century. However, such an admission has not come easily to the revisionists, who formed part of a generation that perceived itself as the first to have brought truly professional standards to Quebec in the wake of the Quiet Revolution.

Though the revisionists viewed themselves as innovators who had broken with their more traditional predecessors, in nearly every other context they perceived Quebec as long having been in the mainstream of modern developments. In projecting this modern image of the Quebecer on the past, they assisted in one of the most important, if not much discussed, shifts in Quebec over the past thirty years – namely the re-invention of the self-image of the Quebecer. While the attention is often focused on the divisions among French speakers regarding Quebec's constitutional future, this book has shown how the revisionists helped unite Quebecers, regardless of their political differences, around the notion that they had long constituted a modern people.

In addition to considering the relevance of the revisionists to an understanding of contemporary Quebec, this book has more generally stressed the way in which diverse historians were tied to one another by the common experience of trying to reconcile application of scientific methods with the communication of a message pertinent to the larger society.

Though the revisionists might not have realized it, they were connected both to their counterparts across the historical profession and to their predecessors in Quebec by the need to balance their professional instincts and their sense of social responsibility. I have tried to avoid the celebratory tone of much analysis of historical writing by looking at the ties that bound together such individuals as Lionel Groulx, Guy Frégault, Fernand Ouellet, and Paul-André Linteau. As we have seen, these historians employed different techniques and came to different conclusions about the nature of Quebec's past. While all of them tried to employ the professional methods of their times, none of them could escape the pressures that led them to shape their work in response to the specific demands of the society and the times in which they lived.

Notes

Abbreviations

ANQ   Archives nationales du Québec (Quebec City)
ANQM   Archives nationales du Québec (Montreal)
ASQ   Archives du Séminaire de Québec
AUL   Archives de l'Université Laval
AUM   Archives de l'Université de Montréal
BRH   *Bulletin des recherches historiques*
CHR   *Canadian Historical Review*
CRCCF   Centre de recherche en civilisation canadienne-
        française (University of Ottawa)
CRLG   Centre de recherche Lionel-Groulx (Montreal)
HP   Canadian Historical Association, *Historical Paper*
IHAF   Institut d'histoire de l'Amérique française (Montreal)
NA   National Archives of Canada
RHAF   *Revue d'histoire de l'Amérique française*
SRC   Société Radio-Canada

Introduction

1 The resilience of Groulx's legacy was evident in the early 1990s in both the controversy over the publication of Esther Delisle's *The Traitor and the Jew* and the launching of *Cahiers d'histoire du Québec au XXe siècle*, a journal openly dedicated to a positive reading of Groulx's contribution to Quebec history.

2 Berger, *Writing*, ix–x.

3 Ibid., 319.

4 Ibid., x.

5 Ibid., ix.
6 Cited in Novick, *Noble Dream*, 13.
7 The revisionists are analysed below, in chapter 5. I have also discussed their search for a 'normal' past in my 'Revisionism and the Search for a Normal Society,' a slightly modified version of which appeared in French as 'La quête d'une société normale: critique de la réinterprétation de l'histoire du Québec,' *Bulletin d'histoire politique* 3 (1995), 9–42.
8 Serge Gagnon, *Le Québec et ses historiens*; part of this work appeared in English as *Quebec and Its Historians, 1840–1920*; see also Gagnon, *Quebec and Its Historians: The Twentieth Century*; and Jean Lamarre, *Le devenir de la nation québécoise*.
9 Lamarre, *Devenir*, 17.
10 Gagnon, *Twentieth Century*, 82.
11 Harvey and Linteau, 'L'évolution de l'historiographie,' 181.
12 White, 'The Politics of Historical Interpretation.' Also see White, *Metahistory*; and LaCapra, *History and Criticism*. The postmodernist critique of historical writing is much more complicated than the brief summary presented here. For a more detailed discussion see Rosenau, *Post-Modernism and the Social Sciences*, chap. 4. The challenges faced by the historical profession are also discussed in Appleby, Hunt, and Jacob, *Telling the Truth about History*.
13 Novick, *Noble Dream*, 2, 6.
14 Ibid., 7. One is reminded here of Sisyphus rolling the rock up the hill, but never quite getting to the top.
15 See, for instance, Haskell, 'Objectivity Is Not Neutrality'; Kloppenberg, 'Review Article: Objectivity and Historicism.'
16 Haskell, 'Objectivity Is Not Neutrality,' 139.
17 Gagnon, *Le Québec et ses historiens*, 7.
18 See, for instance, Dubuc, 'L'influence de l'école des Annales.'
19 Novick, *Noble Dream*, 13.

1: Not Quite a Profession: The Historical Community in Early-Twentieth-Century Quebec

1 Novick, *Noble Dream*, 44–6.
2 This process has been described by Novick for the United States, and by William Keylor for France. See the latter's *Academy and Community*.
3 See my *In Whose Interest?*; on Catholic trade unions, see Jacques Rouillard, *Histoire du syndicalisme québécois*.
4 Fournier, *L'entrée*, 77.

5 Ibid., 81.
6 Ibid., 49.
7 Michael Behiels, 'Father Georges-Henri Lévesque,' 323.
8 See, for instance, Raymond Duchesne, 'D'intérêt public et d'intérêt privé: l'institutionalisation de l'enseignement et de la recherche scientifiques au Québec (1920–40),' in Lamonde and Trépanier, eds, L'avènement de la modernité, 189–230; or Yves Gingras, Pour l'avancement des sciences.
9 Fournier, L'entrée, 77.
10 Claude Ryan, Le Devoir, 14 November 1967; cited in Fournier, L'entrée, 47.
11 Gingras, 'Introduction,' in Marie-Victorin, Science, culture et nation, 7–8.
12 The redefinition of Quebecers' self-image since the Quiet Revolution is discussed at length in chapter 5.
13 Delisle, The Traitor and the Jew.
14 Éthier-Blais, Le siècle de l'Abbé Groulx; Mordecai Richler, Oh Canada, Oh Quebec (Toronto, 1992). The controversy is discussed at some length, though in a rather one-sided manner, by Gary Caldwell in 'The Sins of the Abbé Groulx,' Literary Review of Canada 3 (July 1994), 17–23. An extended version of Caldwell's English text has been published in French as 'La controverse Delisle-Richler,' L'Agora, June 1994, 17–26.
15 As part of the storm over Delisle's book, a spirited panel discussion was held at the Bibliothèque nationale in Montreal in early December 1991. The only professional historian to take part was Pierre Trépanier, who vigorously defended Groulx. However, Trépanier was shortly thereafter removed from his position as director of the RHAF because of his own association with some rather intolerant views.
16 Gagnon, Le Québec et ses historiens; part of this work appeared in English as Quebec and Its Historians, 1840–1920 (hereafter 1840–1920); see also Gagnon, Quebec and Its Historians: The Twentieth Century (hereafter Twentieth Century).
17 Lamarre, Devenir, 78–9.
18 Ibid., 21.
19 Mathieu and Lacoursière, Les mémoires québécoises, 320.
20 Micheline Dumont, 'Un bon manuel,' RHAF 45 (1991), 255.
21 Other aspects of Groulx's career have been considered in such works as Gaboury, Le nationalisme de Lionel Groulx, and Trofimenkoff, Action française.
22 RHAF 15 (1961–2), 157.
23 Fournier, L'entrée, 10. A similar point has been made in Duchesne, 'D'intérêt public et d'intérêt privé.'
24 Groulx, Mes Mémoires (hereafter Mémoires), I, 260. As the reader will soon note, I have made extensive use of Groulx's memoirs, published posthu-

mously by Fides in four volumes between 1970 and 1974. There is obviously a danger in leaning too heavily on an individual's reconstruction of his own life. The limitations of these memoirs have been discussed at some length by Guy Frégault in *Lionel Groulx: tel qu'en lui-même*. Frégault, by the time that he prepared this book, had already had a falling out with Groulx. Accordingly, he tended to be critical of many of Groulx's observations. I do not intend to accept what Groulx said about himself uncritically. However, his memoirs, if used carefully, provide some useful insights into his career as a historian.

25 Groulx, *Mémoires*, I, 251.

26 Groulx, *Journal*, I , 293–4. This work is listed in the bibliography below as a 'printed source.'

27 'À l'occasion du Prix Duvernay,' *Action nationale* 40 (1952), 173.

28 Groulx, *Journal*, I, 334, 552.

29 Ibid., I, 120.

30 Ibid., I, 328–9.

31 *Action nationale* 40 (1952), 172–3.

32 Groulx, *Correspondance*, I, 542. A 'printed source.'

33 An exception to this rule is Giselle Huot, 'Le "Manuel d'histoire du Canada" de Lionel Groulx ou l'apprentissage du métier d'historien,' paper presented to IHAF, 1980. This unpublished manuscript, available at the Centre de recherche Lionel-Groulx, is largely descriptive.

34 CRLG, Groulx papers, *Manuel d'histoire du Canada préparé pour mes élèves de Valleyfield de 1905–1906* (hereafter *Manuel*), III, 130.

35 Groulx, *Manuel*, III, 65.

36 Ibid., III, 131–2.

37 Garneau, *Histoire du Canada*, 4th ed., I, 188. This fourth (1882) edition – the version on the market when Groulx became interested in history – was published by Garneau's son essentially as the historian had left it on his death in 1866. Regarding the changes made to the various editions of Garneau's *Histoire*, see Charles Bolduc, 'Métamorphoses de l'*Histoire du Canada* de François-Xavier Garneau,' in Wyczynski, ed., *François-Xavier Garneau*, 129–67.

38 Gagnon, *1840 to 1920*, 42.

39 Groulx, *Manuel*, III, 131–2.

40 Garneau, *Histoire*, 4th, II, 343; Groulx, *Manuel*, I, 46.

41 Garneau, *Histoire*, 4th, II, 396.

42 Groulx, *Manuel*, I, 49.

43 Ibid., II, 60.

44 Ibid., III, 3.

45 Ibid., III, 61.
46 Ibid., III, 71.
47 See the contrasting views of Bourassa and Tardivel in Ramsay Cook, ed., *French Canadian Nationalism* (Toronto, 1969), 147–61.
48 Groulx, *Manuel*, III, 112–3.
49 Ibid., II, 50; III, 114. Groulx's mention of 'un état français indépendant' is, as far as I can tell, his first reference, however vague, to independence. Most accounts of Groulx's flirtation with separation have dwelled on a similar comment made in 1937 that resulted in considerable controversy.
50 Groulx may have learned about García Moreno from Augustine Berthe, *García Moreno, président de l'Equator: vengeur et martyr du droit chrétien* (Trois-Rivières, n.d.). This work was probably published in the 1890s.
51 CRLG, Groulx papers, Groulx to Jean de Laplante, 24 December 1951.
52 Ferland, *Cours d'histoire du Canada*, I, v.
53 Ibid., I, iii.
54 Cited in Gagnon, *1840–1920*, 64.
55 Groulx, *Manuel*, II, 60.
56 Chapais, *Discours*, 1st series, 27.
57 Groulx, *Manuel*, I, 21, 36–7.
58 Ibid., III, 131–2.
59 Gaboury, *Nationalisme*, 109.
60 Groulx, *Mémoires*, I, 109.
61 Ibid. I, 127, 167.
62 Jean-Marie Mayer and Madeleine Rebérioux, *The Third Republic from Its Origins to the Great War, 1871–1914*, trans. J.R. Foster (Cambridge, 1984), 245, 248.
63 Rogues, 'L'image de l'Europe,' 253–4.
64 Pierre Trépanier, 'L'éducation intellectuelle et politique de Lionel Groulx (1906–9),' in Groulx, *Correspondance*, II, xxxix.
65 Bourdé and Martin, *Les écoles historiques*, 141.
66 Alice Gérard, 'A l'origine du combat des Annales: positivisme historique et système universitaire,' in Carbonnell and Livet, *Au berceau des Annales*, 79–88.
67 Langlois and Seignobos, *Introduction to the Study of History*, 303.
68 Gérard, 'A l'origine du combat,' 86, 84.
69 Keylor, *Academy and Community*, 157.
70 Ibid., 144.
71 Bourdé et Martin, *Les écoles historiques*, 110.
72 Christian Amalvi, 'Fustel de Coulanges,' in Lucian Boia, ed., *Great Historians of the Modern Age* (New York, 1991), 240.

73 Jean Capot de Quissac, 'L'Action française à l'assaut de la Sorbonne historienne,' in Carbonnell and Livet, eds., *Au berceau des Annales*, 154. There were those who resented this appropriation of Fustel by Maurras's forces. While Fustel had insisted on the central role of religion in history, he had been a non-believer himself. Accordingly, while Fustel's widow had originally approved of the celebrations, apparently unaware of their political implications, she, along with a number of his students, were outraged when it became clear that the organizing committee was made up exclusively of Action française sympathizers. There were debates in the French press over the appropriateness of the event, and the Académie française, which was originally to host the celebrations, begged off. The 'bagarre' became the 'first great historiographical debate carried out in the public arena' (de Quissac, 143).

74 Rogues, 'L'image de l'Europe,' 253.

75 This point of view has been advanced in Mason Wade, *The French Canadians* (Toronto 1968), II, 867, and in Gagnon, *Twentieth Century*, 6. For a very different perspective, see Trépanier, 'L'éducation intellectuelle et politique de Lionel Groulx,' in Groulx, *Correspondance*, II, xl.

76 CRLG, Groulx papers, Notes from Cours de vacances, 26.

77 Ibid., 32–3.

78 Actually, only the first of two volumes appeared in 1913, with the other appearing after the First World War.

79 Hector Garneau, 'François-Xavier Garneau,' *Bulletin du parler français*, IX (1911), 216.

80 Mawer, 'The Return of the Catholic Past,' 461.

81 Garneau, *Histoire du Canada*, 5th, I, 94.

82 Ibid., I, 585.

83 Ibid., I, xxxix.

84 *Revue critique d'histoire et de littérature*, no. 19, 9 May 1914. For a fuller discussion of this and subsequent versions produced by Hector Garneau, see Savard, 'Les rééditions.'

85 Paul Kaeppelin in *Revue d'histoire moderne et contemporaine*. This and other favourable reviews were reproduced in *Le Canada*, 6 June 1914.

86 René du Roure, *Revue moderne* 2 (15 December 1920), 38.

87 *Le Devoir*, 27 November 1913; CRCCF, Hector Garneau papers, Bruchési to Hector Garneau, 27 September 1913. I am grateful to Pierre Savard of the University of Ottawa for giving me access to the Hector Garneau papers.

88 CRCCF, Hector Garneau papers, F. Langelier to Hector Garneau, 9 March 1914.

89 *Le Devoir*, 3 September 1913.

90 Ibid., 27 October 1913. Similar responses were published on 31 October, 8 November, and 10 November.

91 Groulx, *Mémoires*, I, 214.

92 Ibid., I, 215.

93 CRLG, Groulx papers, *Manuel d'histoire du Canada*, revisions 1913–16.

94 *Le Devoir*, 19 November 1913. Bourassa provided the italics.

95 Université Laval à Montréal, *Annuaire* (1916–17), 'Rapport des travaux de la faculté des arts, pour les années 1914–5 et 1915–6,' 235.

96 Groulx, *Mémoires*, I, 250.

97 Ibid., I, 260.

98 *Le Devoir*, 13 April 1916; cited in Groulx, *Mémoires*, I, 265.

99 Groulx, *Lendemains de conquête*, 202.

100 Groulx, *Nos luttes constitutionnelles*, 21.

101 Groulx, *Vers l'émancipation*, 8.

102 Mathieu, *Les dynamismes de la recherche au Québec* (Quebec City, 1991), vii.

103 Groulx, *Mémoires*, I, 293.

104 Ibid., I, 266–7.

105 Groulx, *La confédération canadienne*, 7.

106 Groulx, *Mémoires*, I, 379.

107 AUL, Journals of the Superior, Séminaire de Québec, VIII, 26, 12 February 1907. These journals, compiled by the superior of the seminary, include references to the affairs of the university, which were under seminary control.

108 *Annuaire de l'Université Laval* (1916–7), 251.

109 Chapais, *Cours d'histoire du Canada*, I, 3.

110 Ibid., I, 21.

111 Ibid., I, 171.

112 Ibid., V, viii.

113 Chapais, 'La critique en histoire,' in *Discours*, 3rd series, 399.

114 Chapais, 'La science et l'art dans l'histoire,' in *Discours*, 3rd series, 311.

115 Chapais, 'La science et l'art,' 305, 310. In light of these remarks it is difficult to understand the basis for Carl Berger's claim that Chapais was a 'devotee of scientific objectivity' (*Writing*, 181).

116 AUL, Journals of the Superior, Séminaire de Québec, X, 163–4, 3 April 1918.

117 Ibid., X, 233, 20 December 1918.

118 Ibid., X, 251, 28 February 1919.

119 Groulx, 'M Thomas Chapais,' 15.

120 Ibid., 12.

121 CRLG, Groulx papers, Groulx to Chapais, 25 June 1921.

122 Ibid., Chapais to Groulx, 5 July 1921.

123 AUM, History Department papers, Chapais to Emile Chartier, vice rector, 17 January 1934.

124 Serge Gagnon, 'Cours d'histoire du Canada,' in Lemire, *Dictionnaire des œuvres littéraires*, II, 299.

125 Lanctot preferred that his name be spelled without a circumflex.

126 He may well have been the first such Quebecer, but there are always dangers in asserting that someone was first at anything.

127 See, for instance, Lanctot's review of *Lendemains de conquête* in *Revue moderne* 2 (15 December 1920), 18. Lanctot also criticized Groulx in a review of the latter's *Notre maître, le passé*, in *CHR* 5 (1924), 366–8.

128 Lanctot, review of *Lendemains*, 18, 21.

129 Ibid., 18.

130 Lanctot, 'Garneau, fondateur de l'histoire scientifique en Canada,' *HP* (1925), 28.

131 Lanctot, *François-Xavier Garneau*, 154.

132 Lanctot, 'Garneau, fondateur,' 28.

133 CRLG, Groulx papers, Lanctot to Groulx, 4 and 13 January 1926.

134 Société historique de Montréal, Archives, minutes, 23 December 1925. The published proceedings inflated this figure to 10,000 (*Semaine d'histoire du Canada*, xviii).

135 Henri d'Arles, 'Une nouvelle révélation,' *Action française* (March 1926), 152.

136 Hamelin and Gagnon, *Histoire du catholicisme québécois*, I, 228–9.

137 Société historique de Montréal, Archives, minutes, 29 October 1924.

138 *Semaine d'histoire*, 112.

139 Ibid., 148.

140 CRCCF, Hector Garneau papers, Aegidus Fauteux to Hector Garneau, 24 October 1925.

141 *Semaine d'histoire*, 324, 335–6. Even if Hector Garneau did not participate in the Semaine d'histoire he was particularly interested in Chapais's discussion of his grandfather. Prior to the conference, Hector had written to Chapais urging him not to be too critical of François-Xavier's views regarding issues such as the exclusion of the Huguenots. Hector characterized such questions as open to interpretation; this, of course, was not the clergy's view of the matter. Hector subsequently attended Chapais's presentation and was pleased by the latter's point of view. CRCCF, Hector Garneau papers, Garneau to Chapais, 5 and 26 November 1925.

142 *Semaine d'histoire*, 25, 29.

143 *Le Devoir*, 26 November 1925; 'L'histoire et la vie nationale,' in Groulx, *Dix ans d'Action française*, 267–8. Groulx's speech was the only one not pub-

lished in the proceedings of the conference. *Le Devoir* printed extracts, including a preface that was not reproduced in the otherwise complete version published in *Dix ans d'Action française*. Groulx's motives for not allowing his talk to appear in the 'official' proceedings are discussed in greater detail below.

144 Groulx, *Dix ans*, 252.

145 *Action française* (October 1925).

146 *La Presse*, 13 November 1925.

147 Chartier, 'Les points de vue en histoire,' in *Semaine d'histoire*, 389–405.

148 Bruchési, 'En marge de la Bonne Entente,' *Action française* (February 1925), 121.

149 Lévesque, 'Une Semaine d'histoire,' *Action française* (December 1925), 371.

150 d'Arles, *Action française* (March 1926), 164–5.

151 Société historique de Montréal, Archives, council minutes, 4 December 1925.

152 The first two volumes of Groulx's published correspondence indicate a very close relationship between the two men, who met first in 1902. Accordingly, at the end of that year Groulx wrote to Chartier: 'I will always have the fondest memories of 1902 when we first met and when we began to work together so passionately for the survival of our nation. Each time that I think about the circumstances that brought us together, I give thanks to providence.' Groulx to Chartier, 29 December 1902, in *Correspondance*, I, 314. Whatever Groulx's motives for attacking Chartier may have been, he was called to task by administrators of the Université de Montréal, who were interested in defending one of their number. See Groulx, *Mémoires*, III, 14.

153 Bruchési, *Action française* (December 1925), 373.

154 d'Arles, *Action française* (March 1926), 153–6, 159, 169. Bruchési and d'Arles also sounded a bit like the American historians of the 1920s who had grown sceptical about the possibility of presenting the past exactly as it was. In this regard, see Novick, *Noble Dream*, chap. 6.

155 Gagnon, *1840–1920*, 6.

156 *Semaine d'histoire*, 385.

157 de Barbezieux, 'De la manière d'écrire l'histoire,' 215, 218–9.

158 Gagnon, *1840–1920*, 7.

159 Jean-Pierre Wallot, 'Préface,' in Groulx, *Lendemains de conquête*, n.p.

160 There was also considerable ambiguity among English-Canadian historians as to the proper role for their discipline. By the mid-1920s English Canadians had already established both a professional journal (the *Canadian Historical Review*, or *CHR*, in 1920) and a professional association (the Canadian Historical Association, in 1922), but the existence of such

institutions, which would not see parallels in Quebec until the 1940s, did not necessarily mean that historical writing was somehow more advanced among English Canadians. As Marlene Shore has observed about the *CHR* of the 1920s: 'Supporters of scientific methods in history existed alongside those who were sceptical about the absolute veracity of its findings, and those who had never abandoned the idea that history belonged to the realm of literature.' Shore, '"Remember the future,"' 413.

These various approaches to historical research were also evident in the early meetings of the CHA. For instance, the 1925 convention, held only a few months before the Semaine d'histoire, was treated to a presidential address in which Lawrence Burpee referred to 'stories,' to use his expression, that Canadian historians might be interested in telling. Burpee's antiquarianism stood in contrast to the more 'scientific' approach of George Wrong who insisted: 'It is the function of the historian to refrain from taking sides and to judge historical problems as if he were a citizen of some other planet.' *HP* (1925), 21.

161 Fortin, *Passage de la modernité*, 106–7.
162 Gingras, *Pour l'avancement des sciences*, 25.
163 *Semaine d'histoire*, v. This point regarding the role of early-twentieth-century Quebec journals in spreading scientific ideas among the elite has also been made in Fortin, *Passage*, 105.
164 Gingras, *Pour l'avancement des sciences*, 12, 116.

2: Nuts and Bolts: Lionel Groulx and the Trappings of a Profession

1 On this second generation, see Fournier, *L'entrée*; Dion, *Québec, 1945–2000: Tome II*; and Behiels, *Prelude*.
2 Fournier, *L'entrée*, 10.
3 Gagnon, *Twentieth Century*, 41.
4 Lamarre, *Devenir*, 20–1.
5 Blain, 'Économie et société en Nouvelle-France: le cheminement historiographique,' 16.
6 On the caisses populaires, see my *In Whose Interest?*; or Yvan Rousseau et Roger Levasseur, *Du comptoir au réseau financier* (Montreal, 1995).
7 On the Whiggish nature of much historiographical writing, see the discussion in the introduction to this volume.
8 CRLG, Groulx papers, Groulx to Tessier, 18 January 1941. Groulx made this same point in 'Une heure avec l'Abbé Groulx à propos de "37,"' in his *Notre maître, le passé*, 2nd series, 70.

9 AUL, Journal of the Superior, Séminaire de Québec, 11 February 1941.

10 Maheux, *Ton histoire est une épopée*, 28.

11 Godbout, 'Les préoccupations,' 36.

12 ASQ, Maheux papers, annotated copy of *Pourquoi nous sommes divisés*, C65, no. 5.

13 Ibid., Maheux to Séraphin Marion, 4 April 1952.

14 Trépanier, 'Histoire de la province de Québec,' in *Dictionnaire des œuvres littéraires du Québec*, III, 459; Blain, 'Les trois ou quatre derniers Rumilly,' *Action nationale*, 45 (1956), 941.

15 Rumilly, *Histoire de la province de Québec*, I, 94.

16 Ibid., XVII, 93.

17 Ibid., XXXVIII, 60.

18 Rumilly, *Quinze ans de réalisations* (Montreal, 1956), 191.

19 The fullest version of the Bernonville story can be found in Lavertu, *L'affaire Bernonville*, available in English as *The Bernonville Affair* (Montreal, 1995).

20 Groulx and Rumilly were in touch with one another as to how the former might best help Bernonville's cause. See CRLG, Groulx papers, Rumilly to Groulx, 20 April 1950.

21 Groulx, *Notre maître*, 2nd series, 165.

22 Groulx, *Mémoires*, II, 226.

23 Berger, *Writing*, 182–3.

24 Lionel Groulx, 'Vers l'indépendance politique,' in *L'indépendance du Canada*, 105.

25 *La naissance d'une race*, 1st ed. (Montreal, 1919); 2nd ed. (Montreal, 1930). The third edition, published in 1938, was generally indistinguishable from the second.

26 Gagnon, *1840–1920*, 113.

27 Groulx, *La naissance*, 1st ed., 130.

28 Ibid., 2nd ed., 10.

29 Ibid., 1st ed., 181; 2nd ed., 174.

30 Ibid., 1st ed., 73; 2nd ed., 71.

31 Ibid., 1st ed., 69; 2nd ed., 66.

32 Blain, 'Economie et société en Nouvelle-France,' 20.

33 Gingras, 'Introduction,' in Marie-Victorin, *Science, culture et nation*, 172.

34 *RHAF* 15 (1961–2), 157. This passage is cited at length in chapter 1.

35 Groulx, *La naissance*, 2nd ed., 107.

36 Groulx, 'Si Dollard revenait,' in *Dix ans d'Action française*, 92. This text was originally presented as a speech in 1919.

37 Berger, *Writing*, 182. Ramsay Cook has made the same point in his *Canada and the French Canadian Question* (Toronto, 1966), 125. Cook used the 1919 Dollard as representative of Groulx's approach.

38 Adair, 'Dollard des Ormeaux and the Fight at the Long Sault,' *CHR* 13 (1932), 137–8.

39 See, for instance, Gustave Lanctot, 'Was Dollard the Saviour of New France?,' *CHR* 13 (1932), 138–45; Emile Vaillancourt in *Montreal Gazette*, 29 March 1932, 7 April 1932.

40 Groulx's response to Adair was reprinted in a slightly expanded version as 'Le dossier de Dollard,' in *Notre maître*, 2nd series, 23–53.

41 Ibid., 29–30.

42 Lanctot, 'Was Dollard the Saviour of New France?'

43 Groulx, *Notre maître*, 2nd series, 41.

44 Groulx claimed that he had been discouraged from pursuing this hypothesis by Aegidus Fauteux, director of the Bibliothèque St-Sulpice and an organizer of the Semaine d'histoire in 1925, who had told him: 'Don't give your opponents an opportunity to attack this hypothesis.' Groulx later remarked that he had 'always regretted having listened to [his] friend Fauteux.' (Groulx, *Dollard est-il un mythe?* 36).

45 Groulx, *La découverte*, 29, 36.

46 Lionel Groulx, 'La déchéance de notre classe paysanne,' 64. In Groulx's memoirs and elsewhere, this lecture is referred to as 'La déchéance de notre classe moyenne.' The difference is not as great as one might think, since to Groulx the middle class was embodied by the farming population – what he called 'owners of small-scale farming activities' (57).

47 Ibid., 88.

48 Groulx, *Manuel*, II, 135; III, 5

49 Groulx, *Notre maître*, 2nd series, 122. The role of charivaris in the rebellions is discussed at length in Allan Greer, *Patriots and the People: The Rebellion of 1837 in Rural Lower Canada* (Toronto, 1993).

50 Groulx, *Notre maître*, 2nd series, II, 184.

51 Ibid., 192.

52 Ibid., II, 73.

53 For a concise overview of the Annales approach, see Burke, *French Historical Revolution*. Its impact on Quebec historical writing is examined at length in chapter 4.

54 Wallot, 'Groulx historiographe,' 410, fn. Guy Frégault offered the impression that Groulx was poorly informed about new trends in the field, but by the time that he made such claims he had fallen out with Groulx and had

cause to demean his former mentor. See Frégault, *Lionel Groulx: tel qu'en lui-même*, 109.

55 Groulx, *Notre maître*, 2nd series, 52.

56 Groulx, *La naissance*, 2nd ed., 12.

57 Groulx, *Mémoires*, III, 38.

58 Ibid., 117.

59 Novick, *Noble Dream*, 153.

60 Groulx, *Mémoires*, IV, 165.

61 Ibid., 166. In his recent biography of Laurendeau, Donald Horton comments at considerable length on Groulx's influence on Laurendeau but makes no reference to this offer. See Horton, *André Laurendeau: French Canadian Nationalist* (Toronto, 1992).

62 CRLG, Groulx papers, Le Duc to Groulx, 7 August 1937.

63 Ibid., Frégault to Groulx, July 1937.

64 Hellman, *Emmanuel Mounier*, 5.

65 CRCCF, Frégault papers, Frégault to Payer, n.d.

66 CRLG, Groulx papers, Frégault to Groulx, July 1937.

67 C. Roy, 'Le personnalisme,' 471.

68 Ibid., 476.

69 Lamarre, *Devenir*, 207. A similar point is made by André-J. Bélanger in his 'Guy Frégault au temps de *La Relève*,' in Savard, ed., *Guy Frégault*, 24.

70 CRCCF, Frégault papers, Frégault to Payer, 6 November 1937. Frégault expressed concern about Groulx's ties to the ideas of Charles Maurras.

71 Ibid., Frégault to Payer, n.d.

72 Ibid., 15 February 1946, 17 November 1946. The latter is the last letter in the collection.

73 CRLG, Groulx papers, Groulx to Frégault, 7 June 1940.

74 Ibid.

75 Ibid., Frégault to Groulx, 5 November 1940.

76 In 1946 Chartier wrote to Frégault, 'Should you decide someday to write a history of your history department, you will need to look back at the university calendars. You will find a reference to early efforts to establish such a department around 1936 or 1938.' CRCCF, Frégault papers, Chartier to Frégault, 23 December 1946. The *Annuaire de la faculté des lettres* (1935–6) includes a reprint of an article from *Action universitaire* of April 1935 in which it is noted that the faculty 'is thinking about expanding the place of history within the university. More attention needs to be given both to the manner in which history is taught and to the methods employed in historical research. We need to think about these matters in terms of

general history; but more specifically we should consider the establishment of an institute for research pertinent to the history of Canada' (63).

77 CRLG, Groulx papers, Groulx to Frégault, 26 March 1941.
78 Ibid., Frégault to Groulx, 1 April 1941, 27 May 1942.
79 Ibid., Frégault to Groulx, 3 July 1942.
80 Ibid., Groulx to Antoine Roy, 15 October 1942.
81 Lamarre, *Devenir*, 237.
82 AUM, History Department papers, Frégault to Chartier, 3 November 1942.
83 CRLG, Groulx papers, Frégault to Groulx, 7 August 1944.
84 CRCCF, Frégault papers, P168/42/12, n.d. The context of the text makes it obvious that this was composed on the thirtieth anniversary of Groulx's appointment in 1915.
85 Lamarre, *Devenir*, 255; the reference is to Frégault, 'Les mères de la Nouvelle-France,' in *Programme souvenir de la Société St-Jean-Baptiste de Montréal: la mère canadienne* (Montreal, 1943), 21.
86 Frégault, *Iberville*, 64.
87 On this matter, see Yves Zoltvany in *Dictionnaire des œuvres littéraires*, III, 490.
88 Frégault, *Iberville*, 412.
89 Frégault, *Civilisation*, 93.
90 Tousignant, 'Maurice Séguin, maître à penser de l'école néo-nationaliste de Montréal,' unpublished paper presented to CHA, 1980. A copy of this manuscript can be found in AUM, Brunet papers, P136/C121. Tousignant, of an earlier generation than either Lamarre or Christian Roy, was able to see the links between Frégault and Groulx. The preoccupation of the younger historians with distancing themselves from remnants of an earlier, less modern Quebec is examined in chapter 5.
91 CRCCF, Frégault papers, Frégault to P.-M. Paquin, 27 September 1968.
92 CRLG, Groulx papers, Frégault to Groulx, 13 February 1943.
93 *Annuaire de la faculté des lettres de l'Université de Montréal* (1947–8), 31.
94 Lamarre, *Devenir*, 259. Lamarre claims that this statement was found in a letter from Frégault to Chartier dated 11 January 1947, housed in the archives of the Fondation Lionel-Groulx. While I assume that this letter did in fact exist, Lamarre's reference was so poor as to make it impossible for me, working in concert with the archivist of the Centre de recherche Lionel-Groulx, to confirm its existence.
95 Frégault, 'Souvenirs d'apprentissage,' 61.
96 Jean Lamarre has also tried to give Séguin 'personalist' credentials that would have linked him even more explicitly to Frégault, but this is a bit

strained in the absence of any writings – as even Lamarre admits – from Séguin's youth. See Lamarre, *Devenir*, 89.

97 The thesis was published in 1970 as *La 'nation canadienne' et l'agriculture*. Much has been written about why Séguin took so long to publish his thesis. One recurring theory is that he did not want to publish it during Groulx's life so as not to hurt the maître's feelings. This issue is discussed in greater detail below.

98 Ibid., 71, 128–9.

99 Ibid., 253.

100 Ibid., 231.

101 Ibid., 231, 54.

102 Ibid., 257.

103 Ibid., 260–1.

104 Groulx, *Mémoires*, IV, 37–9.

105 Lamarre, *Devenir*, 132; Séguin, *La 'nation canadienne,'* 233.

106 Blain, Foreword to Séguin, *La 'nation canadienne,'* 31.

107 Lamarre, *Devenir*, 132. Lamarre was told of Séguin's boast in an interview with Jean-Pierre Wallot. Houle was also editor of the journal *Action universitaire*.

108 Lamarre, *Devenir*, 132–3.

109 Séguin, *La 'nation canadienne'*, 264.

110 Blain, Foreword to Séguin, *La 'nation canadienne,'* 31.

111 Michel Lapalme, 'Le nouveau chanoine Groulx s'appelle Séguin,' *Magazine Maclean* (April 1966), 16. Lapalme did not entirely believe this explanation, noting some years later that for Séguin 'putting pen to paper was a painful experience' (Comeau, *Maurice Séguin*, 264). Séguin's almost non-existent publishing career will be discussed in chapter 3.

112 Groulx, *Mémoires*, IV, 172.

113 Société Radio-Canada (SRC), *Écrire l'histoire au Québec*, Brunet interview, 5.

114 AUM, Brunet papers, Brunet to Groulx, 3 September 1936.

115 Lamarre, *Devenir*, 354. Brunet's preoccupation with Jews was still evident in 1949, when, following the completion of his dissertation, he visited several American universities. He kept a journal of that trip in which he never failed to record snide remarks whenever he encountered Jews. At the University of Illinois, for instance, he met a Professor Randall: 'I am pretty sure that he is a Jew. There is something Semitic about him. No foolishness. A certain uneasiness that was evident in his nervous mannerisms.' A few days later, while visiting the University of Wisconsin, Brunet commented on his dinner at the home of the historian Merle Curti: 'They were all Jews.

Always the same shyness.' The next day Brunet met the chair of the Wisconsin history department, 'yet another Jew.' AUM, Brunet papers, Journal of travels in the United States, 24 April–25 May 1949.

116 SRC, *Écrire l'histoire au Québec*, Brunet interview, 4.

117 AUM, Brunet papers, Frégault to Brunet, 12 March 1949.

118 Frégault, 'Souvenirs d'apprentissage,' 61.

119 In the following chapter, we see Brunet's uncritical acceptance of the views of Maurice Séguin.

120 In announcing the idea of the IHAF, Groulx said that he would establish it 'in our university if possible' (*Le Devoir*, 29 June 1946). It is difficult to take this claim too seriously, however, given Groulx's often difficult relationship with the university's administration. In the 1920s the university had tried to silence him by offering him a pay raise on the condition that he stop criticizing Confederation and say nothing that would outrage English Canadians. Matters had not improved by the late 1940s, as is evident from his rancorous negotiations for a pension on his retirement (Groulx, *Mémoires*, III, 14; IV, 172–81). Moreover, even before the public announcement of the IHAF, Groulx had written to one of his confidants about 'the idea of an institute based outside the university' (CRLG, IHAF papers, Père Adrien Pouliot to Groulx, 4 May 1946).

121 *Le Devoir*, 29 June 1946.

122 Ibid., 26 October 1946.

123 Ibid. Groulx indicated that the 'sections' would retain 'as much autonomy as is possible.' This model was very similar to that which had long been respected in Catholic-inspired organizations such as the caisses populaires. In contrast with large-scale bureaucratic organizations such as the corporation and the modern state, power was left, as much as possible, in the local community. It is hardly surprising that Groulx would have been sympathetic to this model; however, the decentralized model was already under attack in the caisses populaires by the time Groulx was drawing up the constitution for the IHAF. The parallel with the caisses populaires was also evident in Groulx's interest in establishing 'youth groups or student groups' (*Le Devoir*, 26 October 1946). Caisses populaires were normally established on a parish-wide basis to encourage adult participation, but there were also caisses scolaires designed to give youths a taste for saving. In the case of Groulx's 'youth groups,' the idea was to give the young an interest in history. For a fuller discussion of the organization of the caisses populaires, see my *In Whose Interest?*

124 CRLG, IHAF papers, dossier 12.9, Constitution of IHAF, 24 February 1947. Unless I am mistaken, I am the first researcher to have been given access to

the archives of the IHAF. I am deeply grateful to Jean Roy, past president of the Institut, for helping me secure this access.

125 CRLG, IHAF papers, Adolphe Robert to Groulx, 5 November 1946.

126 The board had relatively limited power during Groulx's lifetime. As Marcel Trudel remarked some years later: 'Much like the higher clergy of the time, Groulx made up his mind before consulting others' (Trudel, *Mémoires d'un autre siècle*, 186). This management style explains the absence of recorded minutes of the board of directors until after Groulx's death.

127 Séguin's selection indicated the maître's confidence in his doctoral student, whose thesis was still nearly a year away from completion.

128 CRLG, IHAF papers, Groulx to Desrosiers, 9 December 1946.

129 Ibid., Groulx papers, Bernard to Groulx, 13 November 1946.

130 Ibid., Maurice Lebel to Groulx, 29 May 1944. Rothney left Sir George Williams in the 1950s but kept up a correspondence with Groulx until the latter's death.

131 Groulx, 'Un Institut d'histoire,' *RHAF* 2 (1948–9), 475.

132 CRLG, Groulx papers, Lanctot to Groulx, 30 April 1934. This volume ultimately appeared, without an essay by Groulx, as *Les canadiens-français et leurs voisins du Sud* (Montreal, 1941). For more on the Carnegie series, see Berger, *Writing*, chap. 6. Lanctot's dealings with the larger French-speaking intellectual community during this period are discussed in Pierre Savard, 'Gustave Lanctot et la Société Royale du Canada,' *Cahiers des dix*, no. 48 (1993), 225–54.

133 During the war, Lanctot and Maheux stood apart from the historians close to Groulx by advocating compilation of a common Canadian history textbook that might be used across the country to facilitate harmony. NA, Gustave Lanctot papers, Lanctot to Charles Bilodeau, Association d'Éducation du Canada et de Terre-Neuve, comité d'étude des manuels d'histoire, 27 March 1944.

134 Ibid., Lanctot to Maheux, 18 July 1944.

135 Ibid., Lanctot to Père George Simard, 31 December 1942.

136 Lanctot, 'Évolution de notre historiographie,' 5. This article also strained relations between Groulx and Lanctot in another context which is discussed below in this chapter.

137 NA, Lanctot papers, Lanctot to Gabriel Nadeau, 24 October 1946.

138 CRLG, Groulx papers, Groulx to J.-P. Houle, 6 November 1946.

139 Groulx, 'Un Institut d'histoire,' 475.

140 In the early 1930s the editor of the *CHR*, George Brown, wrote numerous letters to both Lanctot and Groulx to try to increase francophone participation, though he showed little interest in publishing their submissions in

French. Lanctot agreed to participate, while Groulx did not. See, for instance, NA, Lanctot papers, Brown to Lanctot, 10 August 1931; CRLG, Groulx papers, Brown to Groulx, 28 July 1931.

141 Groulx, 'Un Institut d'histoire,' 475.

142 Fortin, *Passage*, 243.

143 CRLG, IHAF papers, Groulx to G. Debien, 23 July 1948; Groulx to Maurice Delafosse, 27 September 1948.

144 *RHAF* 1 (1947–8), 3, 14. Marlene Shore, writing on the seventy-fifth anniversary of the founding of the CHR, noted that from its start 'the RHAF was concerned with improving historical scholarship, and gave more prominent attention than the CHR to articles on methodology.' Shore, '"Remember the future",' 429.

145 CRLG, IHAF papers, Morin to Groulx, 17 June 1947.

146 *RHAF* 1 (1947–8), 314.

147 Groulx, 'Un Institut d'histoire,' 475.

148 *RHAF* 1 (1947–8), 293.

149 CRLG, IHAF papers, Morin to Groulx, 28 September 1947.

150 Jean Hamelin claimed that the idea for a history department at Laval came from the founders, in 1937, of the Société historique de Québec. See Hamelin, *Histoire de l'Université Laval*, 179.

151 AUL, History Department papers, 'Notes sur la fondation d'un Institut d'histoire, 16 November 1946.'

152 Ibid., Minutes, Institut d'histoire, 27 February 1947.

153 Ibid., 'Notes sur la fondation d'un Institut d'histoire.'

154 Ibid., Maheux to Cyrille Gagnon, 14 April 1944.

155 Jean Hamelin claimed that had it not been for the death of Abbé Savard the history department would have ended up in the arts faculty. Hamelin, *Histoire de l'Université Laval*, 183.

156 *Annuaire de la Faculté des lettres de l'Université Laval* (1950–1), 26.

157 AUL, Séminaire de Québec papers, Maheux to Cyrille Gagnon, univ. 319, no. 21, 1944.

158 Ibid., History Department papers, Minutes, Institut d'histoire, 19 April 1948.

159 Hamelin, *Histoire de l'Université Laval*, 206.

160 Trudel, *Mémoires d'un autre siècle*, 143.

161 Trudel, *L'influence de Voltaire*, 256.

162 Trudel, 'La littérature canadienne et la religion,' 160–1.

163 Trudel, *Mémoires d'un autre siècle*, 161.

164 CRLG, Groulx papers, Groulx to Maurice Lebel, 10 November 1947; IHAF papers, Groulx to Trudel, 31 December 1947, 18 May 1948. All of the Trudel correspondence employed here was found in the collections of his corre-

spondents. Trudel's personal papers were destroyed in 1965 when the moving van transporting his goods from Quebec to Ottawa, where he was about to take a teaching post at Carleton, caught fire. Trudel, *Mémoires d'un autre siècle*, 246.

165 CRLG, IHAF papers, Trudel to Groulx, 9 December 1947.
166 ASQ, Arthur Maheux papers, Trudel to Maheux, 14 March 1948.
167 CRLG, IHAF papers, Trudel to Groulx, 24 October 1949.
168 ASQ, Maheux papers, Maheux to Trudel, 10 October 1950.
169 CRLG, IHAF papers, Trudel to Groulx, 6 October 1950.
170 Ibid., Trudel to Groulx, 28 October 1950. This situation was also discussed by Trudel in correspondence with Frégault; CRCCF, Frégault papers, Trudel to Frégault, 29 October 1950.
171 CRLG, IHAF papers, Trudel, 'La nouvelle histoire,' speech to Club Richelieu de Québec, 25 October 1950.
172 Trudel, *Louis XIV*, x. Maheux reviewed this work rather strangely, noting: 'Does M. Trudel's book have any weaknesses? M. Trudel would be the first to admit that there were some problems. In any event, I am not going to go out of my way to find them; the reader will find the difficulties soon enough, and I would not want to stop someone from buying the book.' *Revue de l'Université Laval* 4 (February 1950), 549.
173 CRCCF, Frégault papers, Trudel to Frégault, 29 October 1950.
174 Ibid., Frégault to Trudel, 30 October 1950.
175 Ibid., Trudel to Frégault, 5 November 1950.
176 Trudel, *Mémoires d'un autre siècle*, 180, 185–6.
177 Ibid., 196.
178 Hector made this point in various letters; see CRCCF, Hector Garneau papers, Hector Garneau to Thomas Chapais, 5 November 1925; to Mgr Gauthier, archbishop of Montreal, 2 April 1928; and to Napoléon Morissette, 20 April 1929.
179 Morissette, 'En marges des nouvelles éditions,' 562. Hector Garneau was also taken to task in the 1920s in d'Arles, *Nos historiens*, and Robitaille, *Études sur Garneau*. The public debate over Hector's rendition has been discussed in Mawer, 'The Return of the Catholic Past,' and Pierre Savard, 'Les rééditions.'
180 CRCCF, Hector Garneau papers, Soeur Marie de la Présentation to Hector Garneau, 9 September 1937.
181 Ibid., P.G. Roy to Hector Garneau, 1 February 1935.
182 *Le Canada français*, 16 (April 1929), 562.
183 CRCCF, Hector Garneau papers, Hector Garneau to Morissette, 21 November 1934,
184 Savard, 'Les rééditions,' 547.

185 Garneau, *Histoire du Canada*, 8th ed., I, 16.

186 Ibid., 7.

187 *Le Devoir*, 18 March 1944; *Culture* 5 (1944), 175; 'Huitième édition,' *Le Canada français* 33 (1945), 167.

188 Frégault, 'L'Histoire du Canada de Garneau,' *Lectures* 1 (1946), 22; also printed in *Le Devoir*, 28 September 1946.

189 CRCCF, Hector Garneau papers, Hector Garneau to Guy Frégault, n.d. This was probably written in 1946, since it was sent in appreciation of Frégault's favourable review published in the same year in *Lectures*.

190 Lanctot, 'Review of Histoire du Canada, 8th ed.,' *CHR* 27 (1946), 315. The same review appeared in French as, 'Le huitième édition de Garneau,' *Revue de l'Université Laval* 1 (1947), 354–60.

191 Lanctot first made this point in his 'Garneau fondateur.' He developed the same position more fully in his biography of Garneau which appeared in both French and English in the 1920s but was reissued in French in 1946 as *Garneau: historien national*.

192 Lanctot, 'Évolution de notre historiographie,' 3.

193 CRLG, Groulx papers, Groulx to J.-P. Houle, 1 October 1946.

194 Société historique de Montréal, Archives, Council minutes, 20 September 1944.

195 There was further evidence of Maheux's distance from the historical profession as it was emerging, when he, alone of all the participants in the Semaine d'histoire, failed to provide a manuscript for publication. As for Hector Garneau's invitation, see CRCCF, Hector Garneau papers, Mgr Olivier Maurault to Garneau, 17 January 1945.

196 NA, Lanctot papers, Lanctot to Maheux, 27 April 1945.

197 *Centenaire de l'Histoire du Canada*, 373, 381.

198 Ibid., 23.

199 Ibid., 431, 435.

200 Ibid., 119–20.

201 *RHAF* 1 (1947), 6, 8.

202 *Centenaire de l'Histoire du Canada*, 53.

203 Ibid., 8.

204 The tendency of historians, especially in Quebec, to view historical writing from a Whiggish perspective is discussed in the introduction to this volume.

3: The Maître and His Successors: The Montreal Approach

1 As we shall see, these historians began their careers at either the Université

de Montréal or the Université Laval, but they did not all stay at the same institution throughout their careers. Accordingly, the terms 'Montreal school' and 'Laval school' pertain to historians who began their careers at one institution or the other.

2 Behiels, *Prelude*, 12. The flip side of this transformation was the decline of the farming population, which had constituted over 40 per cent of the population in 1941, to only 13 per cent twenty years later.

3 Lamarre, *Devenir*, 21, 14, 489.

4 Ibid., 452; Gagnon, *Twentieth Century*, 82

5 Dion, Québec, *1945–2000*: Tome II, 332. Dion's effusive praise for the Montrealers has been echoed by Jean-Paul Bernard, who credited them with playing a central role 'in the modernization of Quebec historical writing' (Review of Lamarre, *Le devenir de la nation québécoise*, *RHAF* 48 (1995), 446. The ongoing adulation for the Montreal historians has also been evident in the reissuing of several of their works in a collection brought out by the Montreal publisher Guérin in 1995: Frégault, *François Bigot*; Brunet, *À la minute de vérité* (a reissuing of Brunet's *Notre passé, le présent et nous)*; and Séguin, *Une histoire du Québec*.

6 Linteau, 'La nouvelle histoire,' 38. For another rather cool assessment of the Montreal approach, see Jean Blain, 'Économie et société: Guy Frégault et l'école de Montréal.'

7 Cook, 'French Canadian Interpretations of Canadian History,' *Journal of Canadian Studies* 2 (1967), 14–16. Cook's view on these issues has not changed over time. In 1995 he still doubted the 'validity of the Séguin-Brunet thesis as history,' while referring to Jean Hamelin as 'brilliant.' *Canada, Quebec, and the Uses of Nationalism* (Toronto, 1995), 125–6.

8 Behiels, *Prelude*, 116, 104.

9 Berger, *Writing*, 185.

10 Lamarre, *Devenir*, 460.

11 Groulx, *Histoire du Canada français*, 4th ed. (hereafter *Histoire*), I, 9.

12 Ibid., I, 42; also see 17, 210, 216, 366.

13 Ibid., I, 306.

14 Ibid., I, 160, 306.

15 Ibid., I, 112.

16 Ibid., I, 84.

17 Ibid., I, 44.

18 Frégault, *François Bigot*, II, 18.

19 Frégault, *Le Grand Marquis*, 386.

20 CRLG, IHAF papers, Trudel dossier, Trudel, 'La nouvelle histoire,' speech before Club Richelieu, 25 October 1950.

21 Brunet, Frégault, and Trudel, *Histoire du Canada par les textes* (1952), 47.
22 *Notre temps*, 21 June 1952.
23 Groulx, *Histoire*, I, 147.
24 Groulx, *Manuel*, II, 50.
25 Groulx, *Histoire*, II, 9.
26 Ibid., II, 8.
27 Ibid., II, 285–6.
28 Ibid., II, 393.
29 Ibid., I, 306; II, 39.
30 Ibid., II, 87.
31 Ibid., II, 374.
32 Ibid., II, 216.
33 Ibid., II, 374–5.
34 Ibid., II, 374.
35 Ibid., II, 377–9.
36 Groulx, 'La déchéance,' 58.
37 Regarding Brunet's rapid acceptance of Séguinisme, see Brunet, 'Guy Frégault: l'itinéraire d'un historien de *La civilisation de la Nouvelle-France* (1944) à *La Guerre de la Conquête* (1955),' in Savard, ed., *Guy Frégault*, 35. Brunet's quick acceptance paralleled the way in which he uncritically adopted Groulx's ideas in his youth, as discussed above, in chapter 2.
38 Brunet, 'Guy Frégault,' 36; Lamarre, *Devenir*, 293.
39 One has to wonder if Frégault consciously chose to break publicly with Groulx before an English audience in Toronto. As we shall see below, Frégault continued to seek Groulx's approval of his work well into the 1950s. Perhaps it was easier for him to break with his mentor at some distance from home.
40 CRCCF, Frégault papers, Gray Lectures, presented in November 1952.
41 *CHR* 34 (1953), 174–5. This must be one of the few comments from an English-language critic pointing to Groulx's work as a hopeful sign for national unity.
42 Frégault, *Lionel Groulx*, 120–1.
43 Lamarre, *Devenir*, 119.
44 AUM, Michel Brunet papers, Brunet to Creighton, 10 July 1956. This was presumably not the lesson that Creighton had expected readers to derive from his work.
45 Berger, *Writing*, 220.
46 Novick, *Noble Dream*, 282.
47 Lower, *Colony to Nation* (Toronto, 1946), 485.
48 Ibid., 159.

49 Berger, *Writing*, 127.

50 NA, Lanctot papers, Groulx to Lanctot, 8 January 1958; Ouellet, 'L'étude du dix-neuvième siècle,' 30–1.

51 Frégault, *Canadian Society*, 15.

52 Ibid., 16. As we shall see in chapter 5, the revisionist historians of the 1960s and 1970s took the concept of normality even further, seeing Quebec as having constituted a normal society both before and after the Conquest.

53 Séguin's notes for these lectures were published in their 1965 state in Comeau, ed., *Maurice Séguin*, 81–220. Some commentators, most notably Jean Lamarre, have dealt with these notes as one might treat a published work. This assumption was undoubtedly necessitated by the fact that Séguin published so little over the course of his career. While it might be argued that large numbers of students came into contact with 'Les normes,' perhaps more than actually read Frégault's books, lecture notes lack the coherence of a printed work. One cannot know exactly how the lecturer presented the material, and the lecturer was under no obligation to support his views by reference to sources. At best, Séguin's notes form an outline, while his colleagues produced finished works.

54 Frégault, *Canada: The War of the Conquest*, 65.

55 Ibid., 342–3.

56 *RHAF* 9 (1956), 579–88.

57 Ibid., 584.

58 Ibid., 587–8.

59 CRLG, Groulx papers, Frégault to Groulx, 14 March 1949.

60 Ibid., Frégault to Groulx, 1 April 1956.

61 Ibid., Groulx to Frégault, 5 April 1956.

62 Lamarre, *Devenir*, 332.

63 CRCCF, Frégault papers, Gray Lectures, presented in November 1952.

64 Brunet, 'Trois illusions de la pensée canadienne-française: agriculturalisme, anti-impérialisme, et canadianisme.' Several years later Brunet wrote a similar essay, 'Les trois dominantes de la pensée canadienne-française: l'agriculturalisme, l'anti-étatisme et le messianisme,' in his *La présence anglaise et les Canadiens*, 113–66.

65 Brunet, 'Agriculturalisme, anti-impérialisme, et canadianisme,' 138.

66 AUM, Brunet papers, Groulx to Brunet, 29 May 1954.

67 Brunet, *Canadians et Canadiens*, 41.

68 AUM, Brunet papers, Groulx to Brunet, 18 May 1955.

69 Ibid., Groulx to Brunet, 20 August 1957, 23 December 1958.

70 Groulx, *Notre grande aventure*, 8; Brunet, *Canadians et Canadiens*, 45.

71 Groulx, *Notre grande aventure*, 8. Groulx's backtracking from the pre-

Conquest volumes of *Histoire du Canada français* was also evident in a
pamphlet he published in 1960 entitled *Dollard est-il un mythe?* While he
had all but ignored Dollard in *Histoire du Canada français*, he was now
ready to defend the hero of the battle of Long-Sault from 'those who would
pull him down' (7).

72 Groulx, *Notre grande aventure*, 274.
73 Ibid., 8.
74 Groulx, *Mémoires*, IV, 285.
75 Ibid., IV, 293.
76 Ibid., IV, 288.
77 Ibid., IV, 295.
78 Frégault, *Lionel Groulx*, 106.
79 Ibid., 88.
80 Ibid., 108–9.
81 CRLG, Groulx papers, Groulx to Angers, 8 December 1958. At the close of
   this letter Groulx claimed that he was resigning from the Ligue d'Action
   nationale, whose journal he had once edited, presumably because of his
   inability to work with Ligue members of the younger generation. Nevertheless, his name continued to appear as a director of the Ligue.
82 Léo-Paul Desrosiers, 'Nos jeunes historiens.'
83 CRLG, IHAF papers, Groulx to Desrosiers, 8 January 1958.
84 Angers's speech was reproduced in *Le Devoir*, 13 March 1961.
85 *Le Devoir*, 20 March 1961.
86 Groulx, *Mémoires*, IV, 288.
87 *Le Devoir*, 10 April 1961.
88 Lamarre, *Devenir*, 462–3, 480.
89 *Le Devoir*, 11 April 1961.
90 Ibid., 21–22 April 1961. Genest's articles were subsequently published as
   Qu'est-ce que le 'brunetisme'?
91 CRLG, Groulx papers, Groulx to Frégault, 20 February 1959.
92 Ibid., Groulx to Frégault, 18 April 1961.
93 Falardeau, 'La correspondance Frégault-Groulx,' in Savard, ed., *Guy
   Frégault*, 61. Falardeau's point is well taken; the correspondence between
   Frégault and Groulx did largely end, but not entirely. For instance, in 1962,
   when Frégault was deputy minister, he asked his former maître if he
   would be interested in meeting with a group that was studying the story
   surrounding the heroism of Dollard des Ormeaux. Groulx, fed up at this
   point with the younger generation, showed no interest in meeting with
   those 'who would never consider a point of view different from their own.'
   CRLG, Groulx papers, Groulx to Frégault, 21 February 1962.

94 CRLG, IHAF papers, Groulx to Desrosiers, 18 August 1961.
95 Ibid., Desrosiers to Groulx, 27 August 1961. Groulx tried to sneak another hand-picked successor past the Institut's board in 1966. On this occasion, however, the effort was stymied when Frégault caught wind of it. Groulx, *Mémoires*, IV, 307. All that is known about this potential successor is that he was a priest. CRLG, IHAF papers, box 6, report of Rosario Bilodeau, 4 October 1971.
96 CRLG, IHAF papers, dossier 59.1, meeting of provisional directors of Fondation Lionel-Groulx, 6 August 1956. The other founding directors, in addition to Groulx, were Joseph Blain (lawyer), Charles Auguste Emond (notary), and Jacques Genest (doctor).
97 CRLG, IHAF papers, Groulx to Desrosiers, 18 August 1961.
98 Groulx was so sure of the treachery of his former allies that he was convinced in 1965 that they were plotting to establish 'a historical journal in opposition to ours, with the goal of replacing it.' CRLG, IHAF papers, Groulx to Léon Pouliot, 7 July 1965.
99 Ibid., dossier 59.1, Bilodeau to Groulx, 6 December 1966.
100 Ibid., dossier 59.1, 'Rapport du comité d'étude sur la fusion de l'IHAF et de la Fondation Lionel-Groulx,' 4 March 1967.
101 Ibid., dossier 59.1; memo by Groulx regarding the relationship between IHAF and CRLG. Following Groulx's death, this memo was retyped and dated 1957. It is evident from the handwritten original, however, that it was prepared for a meeting of the board of the IHAF in May 1967, the month of Groulx's death.
102 Frégault chronicled these years in his *Chronique des années perdues*. He did publish one historical volume while a civil servant, *Le XVIIIe siècle canadien*. Its essays, however, were largely written prior to his entry into the civil service; they added little to the position that he had staked out in his major works of the 1950s, discussed above. I have made no comment in this section regarding Séguin's productivity, which remained minimal.
103 Lamarre, *Devenir*, 23.
104 Ouellet, 'Review of *Les Canadiens après la Conquête*,' *CHR* 51 (1970), 310.
105 Lamarre, *Devenir*, 469–70.
106 Brunet, *Les Canadiens après la Conquête*, 13.
107 Ibid., 131.
108 Ibid., 30, 54–5. Brunet was fond of asserting that there were parallels between the English conquest of Quebec and the horrors of Nazism. In *La présence anglaise et les Canadiens*, he claimed that during the Second World War 'the Province of Quebec was under occupation. It resembled, in certain regards, the situation then being faced by the French, the Dutch, the Danes,

and the Norwegians' (247). In 1980, on the tenth anniversary of the introduction of the War Measures Act during the October Crisis, Brunet compared that particular infringement on the civil liberties of Quebecers with Nazi atrocities. It was 'another stage in the historical occupation of Quebec. It was the beginning of the end; we were entering the gas chambers. All that was left was for the gas valves to be opened.' AUM, Brunet papers, Brunet to Jean Blain, 16 October 1980. In a 1981 interview, he expressed some satisfaction with the way in which he had earlier shocked readers by arguing that 'Mackenzie King had chosen Louis St Laurent to succeed Ernest Lapointe, just as Hitler had chosen his henchmen in the countries occupied by the Germans.' SRC, *Écrire l'histoire au Québec*, Brunet interview, 7.

109   Brunet, *Les Canadiens après la Conquête*, 19.
110   Ibid., 289.
111   Ibid., 209 fn.
112   Ibid., 283.
113   Subtlety was never Brunet's strong suit. Nevertheless, he wrote to Fernand Ouellet following the latter's unkind review of *Les Canadiens après la Conquête* that perhaps the reviewer had been unable 'to understand the nuances in my thinking.' AUM, Brunet papers, Brunet to Ouellet, 16 October 1970.
114   Lamarre, *Devenir*, 476.
115   *RHAF* 21 (1967–8), 9–10, 12.
116   CRCCF, Lilianne Frégault papers, Juliette Rémillard to Guy Frégault, 25 September 1969.
117   *RHAF* 24 (1970–1), 329.
118   At a meeting of the board of the IHAF in February 1972, a report was submitted by Durocher, Linteau, and Claude Galarneau which proposed that the *RHAF* be managed by a team, not principally by a single editor. Perhaps it was a coincidence, but at the next meeting of the board Bilodeau submitted his resignation. CRLG, IHAF papers, Minutes, Conseil d'administration, 18 February 1972, 20 June 1972.
119   Harvey and Linteau, 'L'évolution de l'historiographie,' 181–2.
120   Ibid., 183.
121   See, in this regard, Behiels, *Prelude*.
122   *RHAF* 23 (1970), 666.
123   CRLG, IHAF papers, dossier 59.1, Règlements, 1947; 12.13, Règlements, 1970. In chapter 2, I suggested that the 'sections' were similar to the relatively autonomous local credit unions within the original caisse populaire structure established at the start of the century. Over time, the

autonomy of the individual caisses was whittled away through centralization of power within the Mouvement Desjardins. A similar process led eventually to the disappearance of the 'sections' from the IHAF. In several walks of Quebec life, the decades just before and immediately following the Second World War saw the growing power of bureaucratic organizations, within which authority emanated from some central headquarters. In the process, there was a comparable decline in the role of decentralized organizations, in which considerable power had resided in local communities. I have discussed this issue in *In Whose Interest?*

124 CRLG, IHAF papers, Minutes, Conseil d'administration, 18 July 1972.
125 *RHAF* 24 (1970), 79.
126 CRLG, IHAF papers, Juliette Rémillard to Brunet, 16 February 1971.
127 *RHAF* 25, no. 1 (1971), 147.
128 Lamarre, *Devenir*, 194.

4: Maybe It Was Our Fault: The Laval Approach

1 Behiels, *Prelude*, ii.
2 Trudeau, 'The Province of Quebec at the Time of the Strike,' in his *The Asbestos Strike*, trans. James Boake (Toronto, 1974), 7.
3 Ibid., 15.
4 Behiels, 'Father Georges-Henri Lévesque,' 323.
5 Fournier, *L'entrée*, 124–9.
6 Hughes, *French Canada in Transition*, 2nd ed. (Chicago, 1963), 58. Hughes formed part of a larger group of University of Chicago sociologists who had a profound interest in Quebec society. I have discussed their point of view at length in 'One Model, Two Responses.'
7 Hughes, *French Canada*, 62.
8 Ibid., 209.
9 Falardeau, 'The Seventeenth-Century Parish in French Canada,' in Rioux and Martin, eds., *French Canadian Society*, 31.
10 Falardeau, 'The Role and Importance of the Church in French Canada,' in Rioux and Martin, eds., *French Canadian Society*, 355. For more on Falardeau's career, see Fournier, *L'entrée*, 175–96.
11 Faucher and Lamontagne, 'History of Industrial Development,' in Rioux and Martin, eds., *French Canadian Society*, 268.
12 Ibid., 269.
13 Ibid., 271.
14 Lamontagne, *Le fédéralisme canadien*, 288.
15 Lamarre, *Devenir*, 23.

16 AUL, Maheux papers, Maheux to Scott Symons, 1 September 1958.
17 Trudel, *Mémoires d'un autre siècle*, 186.
18 CRCCF, Frégault papers, Trudel to Frégault, 17 February 1953.
19 Trudel, *Le régime militaire*, 213.
20 CRCCF, Frégault papers, Frégault to Trudel, 30 October 1950. In this same letter, Frégault also proposed that Trudel think about taking a job at the Université de Montréal. This matter was discussed in chapter 2.
21 CRCCF, Frégault papers, Trudel to Frégault, 5 November 1950. Also, see Trudel, *Mémoires d'un autre siècle*, 230. The Trudel review in question does not seem to have been published by the *CHR*, in either language. The first French-language review ultimately appeared in the journal in 1952, but the first full length article, Fernand Ouellet's 'Fondements historiques de l'option séparatiste,' was published only in 1962. One has to wonder if the editors decided that their clientele would be more inclined to read an article in French if it had a politically agreeable point of view. Ouellet's article had been originally published in the journal *Liberté*. I know of no other example of an article in the *CHR* previously published elsewhere. Perhaps the *CHR* was looking for a way of avoiding the editorial work that French-language publication would entail.
22 CRCCF, Frégault papers, Frégault to Trudel, 30 October 1950. On Maheux's Second World War volume, see chapter 2.
23 AUM, Brunet papers, Brunet to Trudel, 12 May 1954.
24 Ibid., Trudel to Brunet, 19 May 1954.
25 See, for instance, Ouellet, 'Lettres de Louis-Joseph Papineau à sa femme,' *Rapport de l'Archiviste de la Province de Québec* (hereafter *RAPQ*) 34–5 (1953–5), 187–442. Within a few years, following his break with the Montreal historians, Trudel would have a very positive assessment of Ouellet. In 1957, Trudel wrote to Groulx: 'Whenever Ouellet produces an article, he always has something new and interesting to say, even if he does not share the point of view of Brunet (who, between you and me, makes a mess of whatever he tries).' CRLG, IHAF papers Trudel to Groulx, 14 April 1957.
26 Desrosiers's critique (in *Notre Temps*, 21 June 1952) of *Histoire du Canada par les textes* was discussed in chapter 3.
27 Brunet, Frégault, and Trudel, *Histoire du Canada par les textes* (1963), I, 175.
28 Ibid., I, 194.
29 Ibid., I, 178.
30 Ibid., I, 231.
31 Trudel, *Le régime militaire*, 128, 133.
32 Trudel, *Chiniquy*.
33 Trudel, *L'église canadienne*, I, 114.

34 Brunet, 'Review of Trudel, *L'église canadienne*, vol. 1,' *RHAF* 11 (1957–8), 117.
35 Ibid.
36 Ibid.
37 Trudel, 'La Nouvelle France,' *Cahiers de l'académie canadienne-française*, 2 (1957), 50. Trudel's point of view was at odds with that which Frégault advanced in his *Canadian Society*, 15.
38 Trudel, 'Le séparatisme, solution de reniement,' lecture given 11 December 1961; cited in Gagnon, *Twentieth Century*, 21.
39 Trudel's correspondence with Frégault covered a period from 1948 to 1953; that with Brunet continued, but at a much slower pace beyond 1954.
40 Trudel, *Mémoires d'un autre siècle*, 238–9.
41 Frégault, *Chronique*, 46–7. In using the term 'Québécois,' Frégault was reflecting the view of many of those involved in building the new Quebec state in the 1960s. In his own memoirs, Trudel remarked: 'Frégault, as deputy minister, did not take kindly to [our] competition' (*Mémoires d'un autre siècle*, 238). Trudel's experience with the Conseil des arts was ironic in several regards. Not only was he pitted against Frégault, his old ally in cultural matters, but he was also joined in his battles against Frégault regarding the Conseil by Jean-Charles Falardeau, one of the Laval social scientists towards whom he had earlier shown so little sympathy in a letter to Brunet.
42 Trudel made the latter point in *L'esclavage au Canada français*. Trudel's role in the Mouvement laïque de langue française (MLF) affair is discussed in his *Mémoires d'un autre siècle*, 240–4.
43 Trudel, *Memoires d'un autre siecle*, 243.
44 Ibid., 244–5, 255–6. Trudel claims that Frégault was offered his old job at Laval, which Frégault allegedly 'refused because of their friendship' (ibid., 245). Given the nature of the relations between the two, this is a bit difficult to believe, and there is no evidence in the Frégault papers to indicate that such an offer was ever made.
45 SRC, *Trou de mémoire*, 26–7.
46 SRC, *Écrire l'histoire au Québec*, interview with Marcel Trudel, 7–9. The interviewer, the literary critic and historian François Ricard, seemed incredulous that Trudel could really believe that his work was value-free. Accordingly, Ricard repeatedly asked the same question in the hope that Trudel would go beyond a faith in the value of facts in their own right, but he received only Trudel's repeated denial that his work had been marked by any ideology.
47 Trudel, *Mémoires d'un autre siècle*, 191.

48 The history and geography departments became separate units in 1955.
49 AUL, History Department papers, memo from Trudel, 16 December 1963.
50 CRCCF, Frégault papers, clipping, 19 December 1946, no source.
51 Frégault, *La Guerre de la Conquête*, 321; *Le Petit journal*, 10 April 1955.
52 On Frégault's conviction that professors from France received preferential treatment, see chapter 2.
53 CRCCF, Frégault papers, Frégault to Chartier, 21 December 1959. Given his francophobia, it is ironic that Frégault, the deputy minister of cultural affairs in the 1960s, helped negotiate close links between Quebec and France. In his recollections of his civil service days, he noted that he had been able to participate in such negotiations because they were based on a certain mutual respect between two states. Frégault described Quebec's emerging relationship with France as one in which Quebecers might receive certain benefits 'without having to bow down' and might acquire 'expertise without being lectured to.' He concluded his description of his dealings with France pointing to 'how deeply I love France.' Frégault, *Chronique*, 89.
54 Lamontagne, *Le fédéralisme canadien*, 296; Brunet's review of this work was republished in his *Canadians et Canadiens*, 168.
55 Trudel, *Mémoires d'un autre siècle*, 197.
56 I am including Fernand Ouellet among the four, even though, as we shall see, he taught Quebec history as a professor in Laval's Faculty of Commerce.
57 SRC, *Écrire l'histoire au Québec*, interview with Claude Galarneau, 2–3.
58 Ibid., 6.
59 Ibid., interview with Pierre Savard, 3.
60 *Le Canada français: aujourd'hui et demain* (Paris, 1961), 11. Latreille was the co-author of *Histoire du catholicisme en France*, 3 vols. (Paris, 1957–63), and sole author of *L'eglise catholique et la révolution française*, 2 vols. (Paris 1946–50).
61 SRC, *Écrire l'histoire au Québec*, interview with Fernand Ouellet, 3.
62 Ibid., 6.
63 Ouellet also received his doctorate from Laval in 1965, thus gaining a complete set of professional credentials. As we see below, by the time Ouellet earned his doctorate he had already been a major, and highly controversial figure within the profession for some time.
64 Conversation with Fernand Ouellet, 14 November 1995.
65 Ouellet subsequently taught at the University of Ottawa and York University.

66 Galarneau and Lavoie, eds., *France et Canada français*, 299.
67 Dubuc, 'The Influence of the Annales School,' 135.
68 In chapter 2, I discussed Groulx's inquiries regarding the work of Bloch and Febvre during a visit to France between the wars. In general, however, neither Bloch nor Febvre had very much influence in Quebec prior to the Second World War.
69 Bourdé and Martin, *Les écoles historiques*, 193. Peter Burke has observed that 'given his influence on younger historians of the group, Labrousse might be said to have been absolutely central to Annales. In another sense, Labrousse might be located at the margins of the group' (*French Historical Revolution*, 54). Labrousse was far enough from the centre of the Annales establishment that the word 'Annales' is not even mentioned in Pierre Renouvin's appreciation of his career. See 'Ernest Labrousse,' in Hans Schmitt, ed., *Historians of Modern Europe* (Baton Rouge, 1971), 235–54.
70 Braudel, ed., *Conjoncture économique; structures sociales: hommage à Ernest Labrousse* (Paris, 1974), 11.
71 Lynn Hunt, 'French History in the Last Twenty Years,' 214.
72 Labrousse, *La crise de l'économie française à la fin de l'ancien régime et au début de la Révolution* (Paris, 1944); 'Comment naissent les révolutions.'
73 Labrousse, 'Comment naissent les révolutions,' 19–20, 12.
74 Burke, *French Historical Revolution*, 74.
75 Ibid., 43.
76 Ibid., 60.
77 *Le XVIII siècle: une révolution intellectuelle, technique et politique* (Paris, 1953). While Mousnier and Labrousse were listed as co-authors, they did not collaborate on writing the various parts of the volume; each assumed responsibility for particular sections.
78 Lamarre, *Devenir*, 334.
79 Gagnon, *Twentieth Century*, 164–5.
80 Regarding Groulx's embrace of Papineau in the 1930s, following an earlier coolness towards the Patriote leader, see chapter 2.
81 See *RAPQ* (1951–3), 160–229; (1953–5), 187–442; (1955–7), 253–375; (1957–9), 53–184.
82 *RAPQ* (1953–5), 187; (1957–9), 55.
83 Ouellet, 'Papineau dans la révolution de 1837–8,' 13.
84 Labrousse, 'Comment naissent les révolutions,' 16.
85 Ouellet, 'La mentalité et l'outillage économique,' 131.
86 Ibid., 135.
87 Ibid., 136.
88 Ouellet, 'Papineau dans la révolution de 1837–8,' 32.

89 Ouellet, 'Papineau et la rivalité,' 312.

90 Ouellet, 'Le destin de Julie Bruneau-Papineau,' 12.

91 Ibid., 14.

92 Ibid., 13; 28–31.

93 Ibid., 28–31, 37.

94 Ibid., 49–51.

95 As far as I can tell, this is the first extended discussion of Ouellet's unpublished book, which was ready to be distributed in 1961 with a cover page noting that it was part of the series 'Cahiers d'Institut d'histoire' directed by Marcel Trudel. It bore the imprint of Les presses de l'Université Laval, 1961. The circumstances surrounding the work's suppression are discussed below in this chapter. Since the courts ultimately ruled that this work was in certain regards defamatory, I have avoided citing directly from the manuscript, which can be found in ANQ, Cour supérieur de Québec, Box 68, dossier 110–644 (hereafter ANQ, Ouellet lawsuit). I refer below to this manuscript by its title as if it had been published.

96 For the only unambiguously positive treatment of a Papineau child, see Ouellet's discussion of the life of the eldest child, Amédée, in *Julie Papineau*, 85, 89.

97 Ouellet, 'Le destin tragique de la mère de Henri Bourassa,' *Annales de l'ACFAS pour l'année 1959–60*, 27 (1961), 84.

98 Ouellet, 'Ambitieuse et mélancolique Julie,' *Magazine Maclean*, 1 (June 1961), 19.

99 Ouellet, *Julie Papineau*, 121.

100 Ouellet's difficulties in dealing with the place of women in Quebec society became a matter of heated debate in the late 1980s. See Ouellet, 'La question sociale au Québec, 1880–1930,' *Histoire sociale* 21 (1988), 319–45; and the response from Micheline Dumont, *Histoire sociale* 23 (1990), 117–28. Ouellet's article has been translated and published in his *Economy, Class and Nation*.

101 Ouellet, *Julie Papineau*, 85, 89.

102 Groulx, 'Fils de grand homme,' 310.

103 Ouellet, *Julie Papineau*, 91, 99.

104 Groulx, 'Fils de grand homme,' 331–2.

105 Guy Frégault remarked that this section of Groulx's memoirs was written in 1955. Frégault, *Lionel Groulx*, 194.

106 Groulx, *Mémoires*, II, 267, 256.

107 Ouellet, 'Le destin tragique,' 84.

108 Groulx, *Mémoires*, II, 228.

109 Ibid., 255.

110 The three sisters were Anne, Marie, and Jeanne Bourassa. As the case continued, a brother, Jean Bourassa, associated himself with the action.

111 This is presumably Ouellet's talk regarding Azélie referred to above. It is puzzling that Anne Bourassa was seemingly unaware of Ouellet's 1958 attack against Julie Bruneau in the *BRH*.

112 ANQ, Ouellet lawsuit, 'Déclaration d'Anne Bourassa et al.,' 2 June 1961.

113 In the early 1970s, the Canadian Historical Association (CHA) tried to publish the book on its own, but it was stymied, Blair Neatby told me, when it learned that the book had been shredded. As we shall see, Neatby, by then Ouellet's colleague at Carleton, played a central role in the CHA's defence of Ouellet.

114 ANQ, Ouellet Lawsuit, Judgment, 8 January 1970.

115 Blair Neatby, personal archives, Memorandum on 'Ouellet–Bourassa case' for members of the CHA, n.d. From the context, his memo was written shortly after the Supreme Court's decision, in November 1970, not to hear an appeal of Dorion's judgment. I am extremely grateful to Blair Neatby for having allowed me to consult and cite from his files on the Ouellet case. The agreement allowing Anne Bourassa to remove some of the family's documents from the Archives nationales du Québec can be found in ANQ, Dossier de correspondance, JB 1983–31, Dossier famille Papineau–Bourassa, Contract signed by Anne Bourassa and the Quebec Ministry of Cultural Affairs, 29 January 1968. André Beaulieu of the ANQ was instrumental in directing me to this document and in securing permission for me to refer to it.

116 ANQ, Ouellet Lawsuit, 'Déclaration d'Anne Bourassa et al.,' 2 June 1961.

117 The Bourassas claimed that they were asking for $600 'in order to avoid court costs,' but they likely had another motive. When Ouellet tried to appeal the judgment, he discovered that this sum was so small as to preclude appeal. Palais de Justice (Quebec City), Cour du banc de la reine (en appel), dossier 8306, submission by Bourassas, 23 February 1970.

118 ANQ, Ouellet lawsuit, submission by Ouellet, 17 September 1963.

119 The witnesses for the defence were Ouellet's former colleagues at Laval (he was by then at Carleton) Jean-Charles Bonenfant and Jean Hamelin, and Antoine Roy, the former provincial archivist.

120 ANQ, Ouellet Lawsuit, Judgment, 8 January 1970, 26.

121 This matter was discussed at length above in chapter 3.

122 Blair Neatby, personal archives, Brunet to Neatby, 7 June 1968.

123 Numerous letters of thanks from the CHA to individual contributors to the Ouellet defence fund can be found in NA, CHA papers, Bourassa-Ouellet lawsuit, Correspondence. For instance, a letter was sent to Gérard Parizeau thanking him for a $50 contribution (6 March 1970). Parizeau was an

amateur historian and author of a number of works dealing with nine-teenth-century Quebec; he was also the father of a future premier of Quebec.

124 In fairness to the IHAF, I should add that the CHA's motives for support-ing Ouellet probably also had a political dimension. It seems highly unlikely that the CHA would have supported a more nationalistic historian who might have found himself in the same position. After all, Ouellet had been a favoured figure in the English-Canadian historical profession since at least the early 1960s, when an essay of his, critical of nationalism, became the first French article published in the CHR. In regard to this article, see the discussion above in this chapter.

125 The first reference to CHA support comes from the minutes of the CHA council of 29 October 1966. The council asked the Canadian Association of University Teachers (CAUT) to investigate the matter since 'the interests of all historians – and those from other disciplines – are involved because the legal issue involves academic freedom in the use of documents.' NA, CHA papers, Council minutes, vol. 3.

126 Blair Neatby personal archives, Neatby to Maurice Careless, 17 May 1968. The Ouellet case had cost the CHA and its members $4,500 up to February 1970, when appeals to the Quebec Court of Appeals and the Supreme Court of Canada had not yet been pursued. Neatby projected that those actions might cost another $6,000. Blair Neatby, personal archives, Neatby to A. Berland (CAUT), 10 February 1970.

127 For a biographical sketch of Dorion, see Ignace-J. Deslauriers, *La Cour supérieure du Québec et ses juges* (Quebec City, 1980), 129.

128 In the Court of Queen's Bench, even after the appeal had been thrown out on this technicality, the CHA tried, albeit unsuccessfully, to have the appeal judges change their minds in light of the significance of the case. Palais de Justice (Quebec City), Cour du banc de la reine (en appel), dossier 8306; rulings of 8 April and 8 September 1970. The Supreme Court of Canada refused to hear the case when it accepted the ruling of the Court of Queen's Bench regarding the size of the award.

129 At its annual meeting, held at McGill University in June 1972, the general assembly of the CHA asked that the Presses de l'Université Laval 'proceed as quickly as possible to put the book by Fernand Ouellet on the market.'

130 Blair Neatby, personal archives, Memorandum on 'Ouellet–Bourassa case' for members of the CHA, n.d.

131 The CHA considered publishing the book by acquiring the copies already printed and replacing the original title page with one of its own. Its council passed a resolution to this effect on 20 October 1973 (NA, CHA papers, Council minutes, vol. 26). As we saw above, however, the matter could not

be pursued when it was learned that PUL had already shredded the printed copies.

132 Ouellet, *Papineau: A Divided Soul*, 3, 20; *Dictionary of Canadian Biography* , X, 564–78.

133 See, for instance, NA, CHA papers, Bourassa-Ouellet lawsuit, Neatby to Careless, 17 May 1968. The Bourassas have had the last, or at least the most recent, word on the subject, thanks to a fictional account of the life of Julie Papineau that appeared in 1995. Micheline Lachance noted in the preface to *Le roman de Julie Papineau* (Montreal, 1995) that she owed a special debt to Anne Bourassa, 'who has dedicated her life to keeping the tumultuous history of the family alive, and who, thanks to her marvellous ability to tell a story, shared with me all of the memories that had been passed on to her' (14). Given the family's participation, it is little wonder that Julie emerged in this account as a strong woman who did what she could to attend to both the political struggles of the 1830s and the needs of the members of her family.

134 For a discussion of this literature, see Bettina Bradbury, 'Femmes et famille,' in Rouillard, ed., *Guide d'histoire du Québec*, 213–28.

135 Because the Ouellet case has not been discussed in print, only historians old enough to remember the controversy even know that it occurred. In other words, this case is not part of the collective memory of the majority of Quebec historians in the late twentieth century. Prior to doing the research for this book, my own knowledge of the episode was based on an off-hand comment made by Ramsay Cook in a graduate seminar in the early 1970s.

136 Gagnon, *Twentieth Century*, 111.

137 SRC, *Écrire l'histoire au Québec*, interview with Fernand Ouellet, 7. Hamelin has described, in a pleasantly self-effacing manner, the unrealistic expectations that he and Ouellet held at the end of the 1950s. See his preface to Hamelin and Roby, *Histoire économique du Québec*, xix–xx.

138 Hamelin, *Économie et société* 13.

139 Ibid., 34. Hamelin also took issue with Frégault in a review of the latter's *La Guerre de la Conquête*. Hamelin argued that French speakers had little reason to complain about the negative aspects of the Conquest. Rather, they had only themselves to blame for not taking advantage of the opportunities that had come with integration into the British Empire: 'In the nineteenth century, the French Canadians had the chance to settle the Canadian west and to establish their civilization and their culture in that region. They did not take advantage of this opportunity.' Hamelin, 'Review of Frégault, *La Guerre de la Conquête*,' *Culture*, 19 (1958), 114–6.

140 Hamelin, *Économie et société*, 135–7.

141 Ibid., 106–7

142 Ouellet and Hamelin, 'La crise agricole,' 17. The point of view developed by Ouellet and Hamelin was contested most vigorously by Jean-Pierre Wallot and Gilles Paquet, whose work is discussed below in chapter 5. The debate regarding the agricultural crisis has been discussed at length in articles and books, but one of the best discussions is in Greer, *Peasant, Lord and Merchant*, chap. 8.

143 *Études rurales*, no. 7 (1962), 36–57.

144 Ouellet and Hamelin, 'La crise agricole,' 19.

145 Ibid., 32.

146 Subsequent references to this work are from the English translation, *Economic and Social History of Quebec*.

147 Ibid., xvii–xx.

148 Ibid., 36.

149 The revisionists – the focus of chapter 5 – owed Ouellet a considerable debt, though they have been little inclined to recognize it. They sought to depict Quebec as a normal society partly by de-emphasizing the Conquest. As we saw above, Ouellet was the trail-blazer in developing such a perspective.

150 Ouellet, *Economic and Social History*, 463. Ouellet's view in 1966 was similar to that evident in his 'La mentalité et l'outillage économique,' discussed above in this chapter.

151 Ouellet, *Economic and Social History*, 212.

152 Ibid., 379.

153 Brunet, *Les Canadiens après la Conquête*, 109.

154 *RHAF* 20 (1966), 235.

155 Desrosiers, 'Review of *Histoire économique et sociale*,' *Québec: le Canada français d'aujourd'hui*, no. 11 (October 1967), 144–7.

156 Lamarre, *Devenir*, 468.

157 Gagnon, *Twentieth Century*. Two essays, taking up half of the volume, were dedicated to Ouellet.

158 Ibid., 82, 110.

159 Other critics, most notably Jean-Pierre Wallot and Gilles Paquet, figure prominently in the next chapter.

160 While there may have been some positive French-language reviews and some negative ones in English, the linguistic division among the reviews is striking.

161 Cook, *The Maple Leaf Forever* (Toronto, 1971), 139–40.

162 Greer, 'Postscript,' in Ouellet, *Economic and Social History*, 611. Due to the general animosity of French speakers towards Ouellet and the linguistic

obstacles that prevented most English-speakers from following up on his research, Greer stands as one of the few Canadian historians of the last twenty years to have enthusiastically picked up on the course that Ouellet traced. Berger, *Writing*, 302.

163 Ouellet and Hamelin, 'La crise agricole.'

164 Hamelin and Roby, *Histoire économique*, 375–6. My view here is at odds with two reviews written in the early 1970s. Both Paul-André Linteau and José Igartua separated the approach of Hamelin and Roby from that of Ouellet. Linteau noted that, unlike Ouellet, 'Hamelin and Roby have not ventured into the murky waters pertaining to the concept of mentalities.' *RHAF* 26 (1972–3), 591. Igartua interpreted the conclusion of the book, which I referred to above, as showing a departure from Ouellet's work. *CHR* 55 (1974, 88). Since there is such strong evidence indicating the links between Hamelin and Ouellet, one has to wonder about the motivation for dissociating the former from the latter. This was both a further effort to marginalize Ouellet and a sign of respect for Hamelin, who, by the early 1970s, had developed close ties with some of the younger historians, particularly through his interest in labour history. This regard for Hamelin, which was never extended to Ouellet, was also facilitated by the fact that the former remained in Quebec, where he served as mentor to many aspiring historians. Accordingly, even though he continued to advance the Laval view of the past, he was treated with great respect – particularly evident in the staging of a conference in his honour at Laval in the autumn of 1994. The papers from this conference have been published in Yves Roby and Nive Voisin, eds., *Érudition, humanisme et savoir: actes du colloque en honneur de Jean Hamelin* (Quebec City, 1996).

165 Hamelin and Gagnon, *Histoire du catholicisme*, I, 35. Though Nicole Gagnon was listed as a co-author, she pointed out in the preface that 'Jean Hamelin did all of the archival research and wrote the first draft' (I, 10).

166 Trudel, *Histoire de la Nouvelle-France*. Trudel was still active in the mid-1990s; see Trudel, *La population du Canada en 1666* (Sillery, 1995).

167 Trudel, *Introduction to New France*, vii.

168 Ibid., 142.

169 Ouellet, *Lower Canada*, xiv. The English version toned down some of the points that Ouellet had made in the French original. Accordingly, readers who want to see Ouellet at his argumentative best might want to look at the French version. On this issue, see Allan Greer's review in *CHR* 62 (1981), 331. Ouellet reaffirmed his faith in the points that he had made in his *Histoire économique et sociale* when an English translation (*Economic and Social History*) appeared in 1980: 'The interpretive framework put forward

in this book has been confirmed in its essential features by my subsequent research' (xi).

170 Ouellet, 'The Quiet Revolution,'322. Ouellet has advanced the same viewpoint in several essays in his *Economy, Class and Nation in Quebec*.

171 Jean-Paul Bernard, 'Review of Lamarre, *Le devenir de la nation québécoise*,' *RHAF* 48 (1995), 446.

5: Searching for a Normal Quebec: Revisionism and Beyond

An earlier version of many of the ideas in the first half of this chapter appeared in my article 'Revisionism and the Search for a Normal Society.' A slightly modified version came out in French as 'La quête d'une société normale: critique de la réinterprétation de l'histoire du Québec,' *Bulletin d'histoire politique* 3 (1995), 9–42. Some of the concepts in the second half of the chapter have appeared in 'Au-delà du révisionnisme.'

1 Bouchard, 'Sur les mutations de l'historiographie québécoise,' 262.

2 None of this is meant to ignore the rather obvious connection between the introduction of language legislation and the decline of the birth rate within the French-speaking population. Suffice it to say that if the earlier attitudes towards outsiders had still been in place, then there would have been more objection to the idea of integrating the immigrants. For a more thorough discussion of this and other matters relevant to contemporary Quebec, see Linteau, Durocher, Robert, and Ricard, *Quebec since 1930*.

3 Ricard, *La génération lyrique*, 52.

4 Ibid., 96. Ricard was one of the authors of Linteau et al., *Quebec since 1930*, which, as we shall see, constituted the second volume of the revisionist text par excellence, in which the Quiet Revolution was seen as anything but a 'radical break.'

5 Simard, *La longue marche*, 25.

6 *Montreal Gazette*, 22 October 1994.

7 Ricard, 'Remarques sur la normalisation,' 12. I am grateful to Yvan Lamonde for having brought this article to my attention.

8 Courville, who figures prominently in this chapter, was a historical geographer by training.

9 Létourneau, 'Critique de la raison technocratique,' 343, 347. Létourneau has written a number of interesting articles, which are listed in the bibliography.

10 Wallot recalled Séguin as having been 'an excellent teacher,' responsible for

the training 'of hundreds, if not thousands of students.' ('À la recherche de la nation: Maurice Séguin,' in Comeau, ed., *Maurice Séguin*, 34, 61.)

11 Wallot, *Un Québec qui bougeait*, 157.

12 Paquet and Wallot, *Patronage et pouvoir*, 138–9.

13 Paquet and Wallot, 'Crise agricole et tensions socio-ethniques dans le bas-canada, 1802–12: éléments pour une ré-interprétation,' *RHAF* 26 (1972), 204; the emphasis is mine. The same authors argued along similar lines in 'Le bas-canada au début du XIXe siècle: une hypothèse,' *RHAF* 25 (1971), 39–61. The debate on the agricultural crisis took on a life of its own in the early 1970s. See, for instance, T.J.A. LeGoff, 'The Agricultural Crisis in Lower Canada, 1802–12: Review of a Controversy,' *CHR* 55 (1974), 1–31; Paquet and Wallot, 'The Agricultural Crisis in Lower Canada, 1802–12: mise au point. A Response to T.J.A. LeGoff,' *CHR* 56 (1975), 133–61; T.J.A. LeGoff, 'A Reply,' *CHR* 56 (1975), 161–8. For the 'final' word on the debate, see Allan Greer, *Peasant, Lord and Merchant*.

14 Wallot, 'Religion and French-Canadian Mores,' 90.

15 SRC, *Écrire l'histoire*, interview with Dechêne, 2.

16 For a summary of Dechêne's master's thesis, see her 'Les entreprises de William Price, 1810–1850,' *Histoire sociale* 1 (1968), 16–52.

17 SRC, *Écrire l'histoire*, interview with Dechêne, 5.

18 Burke, *French Historical Revolution*, 38.

19 Braudel, cited in Dosse, *L'histoire en miettes*, 99. For an earlier statement of Braudel's view of history, see his 'Histoire et sciences: la longue durée,' *Annales ESC* (1958), 725–53.

20 Dosse, *L'histoire en miettes*, 98.

21 Ibid., 95–9.

22 Burke, *French Historical Revolution*, 58.

23 SRC, *Écrire l'histoire*, interview with Dechêne, 7.

24 The only book that comes even close to Dechêne's in terms of enthusiastic response was Ouellet's *Histoire économique et sociale*. However, Ouellet was also criticized quite harshly in certain quarters. In Dechêne's case, however, aside from a few grumpy comments by Ouellet, discussed below, the reviews were universally and enthusiastically positive.

25 Dechêne, *Habitants and Merchants*, 279.

26 Groulx, *Histoire du Canada français*, I, 288; Frégault, *Canadian Society*, 12; Hamelin, *Économie et société*, 49.

27 Dechêne, *Habitants and Merchants*, xiv.

28 For conflicting views, contrast Frégault, *Canadian Society*, and Hamelin, *Économie et société*.

29 Dechêne, *Habitants and Merchants*, xiv.

30 Ibid., xiv.

31 Ibid., xiv.

32 Only Ouellet managed to associate Dechêne with the much more politically explicit views of Paquet and Wallot. Simply because Dechêne was prepared to see the habitant as a reasonably rational character, he placed her on the side of his enemies in the debate over the agricultural crisis. Ouellet, 'La modernisation de l'historiographie,' 26. Similarly, because she was unwilling to see the seigneurs of the French régime as exploitative, Ouellet concluded that she was providing comfort for those who would see exploitation as having begun only with the arrival of the English. Ouellet, *Socialization of Quebec Historiography*, 18. Ouellet was not entirely off-base in looking for the political implications of Dechêne's study, but typically he saw all those who opposed his view of the past as indistinguishable from one another. Accordingly, he missed the more subtle political message implicit in her work.

33 SRC, *Écrire l'histoire*, interview with Dechêne, 12.

34 On the difficulty of making sense of Wallot's prose at times, see T.J.A. LeGoff, 'A Reply,' *CHR* 56 (1975), 161–8.

35 For an account of this conference, see Christopher Moore, 'A Light on New France,' *Beaver* 74 (1994), 53–6.

36 Linteau, 'La nouvelle histoire,' 35, 44.

37 Craig, 'Pour une approche comparative,' 262. For specific studies in this mould, see Sylvie Dépatie, Christian Dessureault, and Mario Lalancette, *Contributions à l'étude du régime seigneurial canadien* (Montreal, 1987). Dechêne conceded the point to the younger historians regarding the market orientation of the habitant in the preface to *Habitants and Merchants* (xiv). One wonders, however, if she was too quick to assume that her successors were closer to the 'truth' than she had been. Allan Greer, for instance, has largely reinforced many of her points in his own case study of three parishes in the late eighteenth and early nineteenth centuries (*Peasant, Lord and Merchant*). Because he failed to see the habitant as an entrepreneur, Greer was taken to task by Craig for insisting that the habitant was interested in 'meeting the needs of the family and guaranteeing its continuation, instead of accumulating wealth' (262). I have discussed the way in which the revisionist paradigm has marked recent writing on rural Quebec in 'One Model, Two Responses.'

38 Christian Dessureault, 'Crise ou modernisation,' *RHAF* 42 (1989), 361.

39 Linteau, 'La nouvelle histoire,' 44–5. Dechêne recognized, in an interview, that her interest in New France had by 1981 become marginal to the

concerns of most Quebec historians. See SRC, *Écrire l'histoire*, interview with Dechêne, 12.

40 *RHAF* 21 (1967–8), 526; *Annuaire de l'Université de Montréal* (1967–8), 76.

41 Létourneau, 'La production historienne,' 12.

42 CRLG, IHAF papers, Minutes, conseil d'administration, IHAF, 18 July 1972, 15 February 1974.

43 Harvey and Linteau, 'L'évolution de l'historiographie,' 181–2.

44 Ibid.; J.P. Coupal, 'Les dix dernières années de la *RHAF*, 1972–81,' *RHAF* 36 (1983), 553–67; the calculations relating to the volumes published from 1982 to 1992 are mine.

45 Linteau and Robert, 'Propriété foncière'; Linteau, 'Quelques réflexions.'

46 Linteau, 'Quelques réflexions,' 66.

47 N. Séguin, 'L'économie agro-forestière.'

48 Linteau, *Maisonneuve*; N. Séguin, *La conquête du sol*.

49 Hardy, *Les Zouaves*.

50 Gagnon and Hardy, eds., *L'église et le village*, 12.

51 Bernard, *Les Rouges*.

52 This interest of Quebec historians in the concept of liberalism will be discussed again below in this chapter.

53 Rouillard, *Histoire du syndicalisme*, 8. Also see Rouillard's *Les syndicats nationaux au Québec de 1900 à 1930* (Quebec City, 1979), and his *Histoire de la CSN* (Montreal, 1981).

54 Courville, *Entre ville et campagne*, 70–1.

55 Ibid., 254.

56 Ibid., 230.

57 Ibid., 120.

58 Ibid., 242.

59 Linteau, 'La nouvelle histoire,' 40.

60 Ibid., 41.

61 On the move towards collaborative research among American historians at the time, see Kammen, 'Clio and the Changing Fashions,' 492. In Quebec this process was also facilitated by the policies of Le Fonds pour la Formation de Chercheurs et l'Aide à la Recherche (FCAR), the Quebec counterpart to SSHRC, which provided funding only to teams of researchers.

62 The perspective of the Montreal group can be secured from Linteau and Robert, 'Propriété foncière.'

63 Courville, Robert, and Séguin, 'Un nouvel regard,' 23.

64 Ibid., 30.

65 Courville, Robert, and Séguin, *Atlas historique*, 108–9.

66 Jean-Claude Robert, Normand Séguin, and Serge Courville, 'An Estab-

lished Agriculture: Lower Canada to 1851,' in R.L. Gentilcore, ed., *Historical Atlas of Canada*, Vol. 2, *The Land Transformed, 1800–1891* (Toronto, 1993), plate 13.

67 Courville, Robert, and Séguin, *Atlas historique*, 5; the emphasis is mine. In the conclusion, the authors tried to soften their insistence on modernity (127). Such a claim was compromised, however, by their remark about the triumph of the forces of 'progress.'

68 Linteau, Durocher, and Robert, *Histoire du Québec contemporain: de la Confédération à la crise* (Montreal, 1979); Linteau, Durocher, Robert, and Ricard, *Histoire du Québec contemporain: le Québec depuis 1930* (Montreal, 1986); a new and revised edition of the two volumes was published by Boréal in 1989. All references here are to the second (1989) edition. I have translated the quotes taken from this updated version, but there is an English translation of the original editions on the market; see *Quebec: A History, 1867–1929* and *Quebec since 1930*.

69 SRC, *Écrire l'histoire*, interview with Durocher, 3.

70 Linteau, Durocher, Robert, and Ricard, *Histoire*, I, 8.

71 Ibid., I, 399.

72 Annick Germain, *Urban History Review* 10 (1982), 68.

73 Linteau, Durocher, Robert, and Ricard, *Histoire*, I, 197. In the chapter outlining 'the social structure' during this period, only five out of twenty pages focused on rural life.

74 Linteau, Durocher, Robert, and Ricard, *Histoire*, I, 181.

75 Ibid., I, 267.

76 Ibid., I, 348.

77 Ibid., I, 7.

78 SRC, *Écrire l'histoire*, interview with Bernard, 6.

79 Linteau, 'La nouvelle histoire,' 44–5.

80 Ibid., 45.

81 Linteau, Durocher, Robert, and Ricard, *Histoire*, I, 209.

82 Linteau, 'La nouvelle histoire,' 41–4.

83 Landes and Tilly, eds., *History as Social Science*, 16.

84 Ibid., 9, 72. The authors were referring probably to the work of Wallot and Paquet, discussed above in this chapter.

85 Thernstrom, *Poverty and Progress: Social Mobility in a Nineteenth Century City* (Cambridge, 1964); Higham, *History*, 247.

86 Novick, *Noble Dream*, 609. Michael Kammen makes much the same point about the 'radical' turn of some social science research in his 'Clio and the Changing Fashions.'

87 Bliss, 'Privatizing,' 6.

88 Throughout this manuscript, I have tried to avoid explicit comparisons between historical writing in English Canada and that in Quebec. I realized at the beginning of this project that such an endeavour would have required a sustained analysis of two bodies of work that rarely had much in common. Since my concern was with historical writing in Quebec, I did not want to become responsible for a reassessment of writing in English Canada. In the new fields of social history that emerged in the 1970s, however, there was the possibility that the two historical communities might have moved in the same direction. This has not proven to be the case, in part because of the strength of revisionist sentiment in Quebec. In order to reinforce my discussion of revisionist writing, I have chosen to comment on the different paths taken in English Canada and Quebec in terms of the writing of working-class and women's history. While I have concentrated on differences, I do not mean to suggest that one approach was better than the other.

89 Bryan Palmer, 'Working-Class Canada: Recent Historical Writing,' *Queen's Quarterly* 86 (1979–80), 601. For concrete examples of this approach, see, for instance, Palmer, *A Culture in Conflict* (Montreal, 1979), or Kealey, *Toronto Workers Respond to Industrial Capitalism* (Toronto, 1980).

90 Joanne Burgess, 'Exploring the Limited Identities of Canadian Labour: Recent Trends in English Canada and Quebec,' *International Journal of Canadian Studies* 1 (1990), 162.

91 I am grateful for this insight to Chantal Bertrand, who brought it to my attention in an essay she wrote for a graduate seminar that I taught in 1995–6.

92 Baillargeon, 'Des voies/x parallèles,' 148. I am grateful to my colleague Diana Pedersen, who brought this article to my notice, and to Denyse Baillargeon, who provided me with a copy when I was having some difficulty in getting hold of it. In this article, Baillargeon quite appropriately pointed out that I had ignored the writing on Quebec women's history in my earlier critique of revisionism.

93 Lavigne and Pinard, *Les femmes dans la société québécoise*, 22, 29.

94 Baillargeon, 'Des voies/x parallèles,' 148.

95 Lavigne and Pinard, *Travailleuses et féministes*, 52. The best discussion of the 'feminist' perspective on nuns is Marta Danylewycz, *Taking the Veil: An Alternative to Marriage, Motherhood and Spinsterhood in Quebec, 1840–1920* (Toronto, 1987).

96 Andrée Lévesque, *Making and Breaking*, 7.

97 Clio Collective, *Quebec Women*, 177.

98 Micheline Dumont, 'History of the Status of Women in the Province of

Quebec,' in *Cultural Traditions and Political History of Women in Canada*, Study No. 8, Royal Commission on the Status of Women in Canada (Ottawa, 1971), iii. Dumont's own contribution is dated 1968.

99 Dumont, 'Un univers inscrit dans notre mémoire collective,' in Dumont and Fahmy-Eid, eds., *Les couventines* (Montreal, 1986), 20. This study formed part of a larger project directed by Dumont and Fahmy-Eid on the history of girls' education in Quebec.

100 Alison Prentice et al., *Canadian Women: A History* (Toronto, 1988); 2nd ed. (Toronto, 1994), 3.

101 Franca Iacovetta and Mariana Valverde, eds., *Gender Conflicts: New Essays in Women's History* (Toronto, 1992) xv, xx.

102 Andrée Lévesque, 'Historiography,' 88.

103 Denyse Baillargeon found that women's historians in Quebec were unwilling to adopt the new approaches because that would have produced a 'vision of Quebec society as having consisted of many component parts.' Had they followed the lead of their English-Canadian counterparts, Quebec society would have been divided not only by gender, but also by such variables as race and sexual orientation. Baillargeon found her colleagues unwilling to move in such a direction because of 'the minority status of Quebecers in Canada and in North America'; the fragility of the Quebec nation had moulded the work of women's historians, who were unwilling to depict their nation as having been overly fragmented. This conclusion is not very convincing, because it presents Quebecers as a minority fearful for its survival. In fact, since the 1960s Quebecers have tended to see themselves as having constituted a strong majority, within their own territory. Baillargeon, 'Des voies/x parallèles, 165.

104 Moore, 'A Light on New France,' 56.

105 Courville, Robert, and Séguin, *Atlas historique*, 2.

106 Gingras, 'Une sociologie spontanée,' 41.

107 What follows is a partial list. Works in this mode were still appearing with great regularity as I completed this manuscript late in 1996. On the role of modernity, see Andrée Fortin, *Passage de la modernité*; Marcel Fournier, *L'entrée dans la modernité*; and Lamonde and Trépanier, eds, *L'avènement de la modernité*. One might add works such as Claude Couture, *Le mythe de modernisation du Québec* (Montreal, 1991). I have also been struck by the way in which Kenneth McRoberts and Dale Posgate's *Quebec: Social change and Political Crisis* was translated into French as *Développement et modernisation au Québec* (Montreal, 1983). On the role of liberalism, see Gilles Bourque et al., *La société libérale duplessiste* (Montreal, 1994); Yvan Lamonde, ed., *Combats libéraux au tournant du XXe siècle* (Montreal, 1995); Lamonde,

Louis-Antoine Dessaulles: un seigneur libéral et anticlérical (Montreal, 1994); and P.A. Dutil, *Devil's Advocate: Godfroy Langlois and the Politics of Liberal Progressivism in Laurier's Quebec* (Toronto, 1994).

108 F. Roy, *Histoire des idéologies*, 115.

109 *CHR* 61 (1980), 391.

110 *RHAF* 41 (1987), 238.

111 In a similar vein, see Gertrude Himmelfarb, *The New History and the Old* (Cambridge, Mass., 1987); or Oscar Handlin, *Truth in History* (Cambridge, Mass., 1979). For an English-Canadian perspective, see Bliss, 'Privatizing the Mind.'

112 For a discussion of the postmodernist attack on history, see Rosenau, *Post-Modernism*, chap. 4.

113 Appleby, Hunt, and Jacob, *Telling the Truth about History*, 4.

114 Létourneau, 'La production historienne,' 1.

115 Dickinson, 'Commentaires,' 23.

116 Dickinson, 'Commentaires sur la critique de Ronald Rudin,' unpublished paper presented to conference on Quebec historical writing, UQAM, 1995, 6. The published paper in the previous note constituted a slightly revised version of Dickinson's public presentation.

117 Ouellet, 'General Works,' in his *Economy, Class and Nation*, 248; Ouellet expressed the same point of view in 'The Quiet Revolution,' 314.

118 Ouellet, *Socialization*, 14. I was bemused to see that I was included among these alleged separatists because I had discussed the significant role of French speakers in the banking industry of the nineteenth and early twentieth centuries. The reader can judge the depth of my separatist leanings by looking at *Banking en français* (Toronto, 1985).

119 Ouellet, 'The Quiet Revolution,' 322–3.

120 Ouellet, 'Monographs on the Working Class: Misery and Organization,' in his *Economy, Class and Nation*, 261. He had made the same point a decade earlier in a review of Rouillard's *Les syndicats nationaux au Québec*: *CHR* 61 (1980), 388–9.

121 Ouellet, 'General Works,' in his *Economy, Class and Nation*, 248; 'The Quiet Revolution,' 331.

122 Michel Sarra-Bournet has made a similar point: 'There is no direct connection between revisionism and nationalism in Quebec ... If contemporary historians are guilty of something, it is not nationalism but a certain preoccupation with theoretical models.' These historians stayed clear of direct political involvement as part of their commitment to the 'precepts of the methods of the social sciences.' 'Pour une histoire post-révisionniste,' 27.

123 Ouellet, *Socialization*, 13.

124 Igartua, 'Review of *Economy, Class and Nation*,' *RHAF* 45 (1992), 634.

125 Courville, Robert, and Séguin, 'Un nouvel regard,' 23.

126 I have also dealt with these issues in my 'Revisionism and the Search for a Normal Society.'

127 Elsewhere I have written about the way in which historical writing in Ireland went through a long period during which the normalcy of the Irish experience was emphasized, to the exclusion of the unique aspects of the Irish past. For instance, historians minimized the extent of conflict with the English so as to make the Irish appear a normal, 'modern' people, whose history was marked by larger economic and social changes that influenced much of the Western world. Only incidentally did Irish revisionists consider Anglo-Irish conflict a factor of significance. Over the past decade or so, however, a post-revisionist interpretation has emerged in which both the 'normal' aspects of the Irish past and the legacy of such unique factors as English antipathy towards the Irish have been considered. See my 'Revisionism.'

128 Serge Gagnon, 'Le Québec au temps présent,' 25.

129 For comparative data on dropout rates elsewhere, see *L'Actualité*, 15 March 1992. In 1992, the rate was 28 per cent in the rest of Canada, 30 per cent in the United States, 15 per cent in Sweden and 2 per cent in Japan.

130 Gagnon, 'Le Québec au temps présent,' 24.

131 Linteau, Durocher, Robert, and Ricard, *Histoire*, II, 440–1.

132 Fernand Dumont, 'Idéologie et conscience historique dans la société canadienne-française du XIXe siècle,' in Galarneau and Lavoie, eds., *France et Canada français*, 269–90.

133 Dumont, *Genèse de la société québécoise; Raisons communes; L'avenir de la mémoire*.

134 Dumont, *Raisons communes*, 24.

135 Ibid., 11.

136 Dumont, *L'avenir*, 92.

137 Dumont, *Genèse*, 335.

138 Dumont, *Raisons communes*, 104–5.

139 For more on Dumont's role in defending Catholicism against the changes in post–Quiet Revolution Quebec, see Hamelin, *Histoire du Catholicisme*, II, 352–4.

140 Dumont, *Raisons communes*, 23.

141 Hardy, 'A propos du réveil religieux,' 211. In the same regard, see also Hardy, *Les Zouaves*; and Jean Roy, 'L'invention du pèlerinage de la tour des martyrs de St-Celestin,' *RHAF* 43 (1990), 487–507.

142 Gagnon, *Mariage et famille*, ix. The first two books in the trilogy were *Mourir hier et aujourd'hui* and *Plaisir d'amour et crainte de dieu*.

143 Gagnon, *Mourir hier et aujourd'hui*, 144, 151.

144 Gagnon, 'Le Québec au temps présent,' 23.

145 Gagnon, *Plaisir d'amour*, 182.

146 Gagnon, 'Le Québec au temps présent,' 17.

147 For somewhat anecdotal evidence of Quebecers' preoccupation with instant gratification, see the survey produced in *L'Actualité*, January 1992. When asked if they preferred people who fulfill their obligations or those who maximize their happiness, 51 per cent of French-speaking Quebecers opted for the latter, as opposed to 35 per cent of non-francophone Quebecers and 25 per cent of Canadians in other provinces. In line with this finding, a Statistics Canada study indicated that Quebecers were the least generous of Canadians in making charitable contributions. In 1992, Canadians contributed, on average, $130 per person, and Quebecers, only $90. Before jumping to the conclusion that Quebecers gave less because they were poorer, it should be noted that Newfoundlanders gave most generously, with an average of $240. This last finding suggests the power of communal values, which have survived reasonably intact in Newfoundland and have been decimated in Quebec. *Globe and Mail*, 6 January 1994.

148 Gagnon, 'Le Québec au temps présent,' 24, 27. A Statistics Canada report issued early in 1996 indicated the rapid decline of marriage in Quebec. 'Between 1971 and 1991, the marriage rate in Ontario fell 18%, compared with a drop of 49% in Quebec ... [Accordingly], most first births in Quebec today are to unmarried women, most of whom are in common-law relationships. In Ontario, by comparison, the proportion of first births to unmarried women is much lower. In 1982, 25% of all births were to unmarried mothers in Quebec, compared with 12% in Ontario. In 1992, the proportions had gone up to 41% in Quebec and 16% in Ontario.' Statistics Canada, *The Daily*, 19 January 1996, Cat. No. 11-001, 3–4.

149 Gagnon, *Mariage et famille*, x–xi.

150 Ibid., 282.

151 See, for instance, Brigitte Caulier, 'Review of *Mourir hier et aujourd'hui*,' *RHAF* 41 (1988).

152 Rousseau teaches in the department of religious sciences at the Université du Québec à Montréal.

153 Rousseau, 'Review of Jean Hamelin and Nicole Gagnon, *Histoire du Catholicisme québécois*,' *RHAF* 39 (1985), 89.

154 Hardy, 'A propos du réveil religieux.'

155 Rousseau, 'A propos du "réveil religieux,"' 233, 243. Rousseau has also made a similar point in his 'Crise et réveil religieux.'

156 Rousseau, 'Silences, bruits, liens, citoyenneté: l'espace de la transcendance québécoise,' in Fecteau et al., eds., *La condition québécoise*, 233, 241.

157 Ibid., 238. Over the last twenty years most Quebec intellectuals have demanded elimination of the province's system of publicly supported denominational schools. Most polls have indicated that French-speaking Quebecers would prefer continuation of a Catholic system, thus suggesting a stronger link to Quebec's Catholic past than most revisionists would allow.

158 Bouchard, *Quelques arpents d'Amérique: population, économie, famille au Saguenay, 1838–1971* (Montreal, 1996), 11.

159 Bouchard, 'Sur les mutations de l'historiographie québécoise,' 261–2. Bouchard has also discussed Quebec historical writing in 'L'historiographie du Québec rurale.'

160 Bouchard, 'Le Québec comme collectivité neuve,' 16, 32.

161 Ibid., 36.

162 Létourneau, 'Critique de la raison technocratique,' 354, 355.

163 Ibid., 347.

164 Bouchard, 'Sur la dynamique culturelle.'

165 Létourneau, 'Critique de la raison technocratique,' 348.

166 Ibid.

167 Fecteau et al. eds., *La condition québécoise*, 7, 14.

168 Rousseau, 'Silences, bruits, liens, citoyenneté.'

169 Fecteau, 'La quête d'une histoire normale,' 32–3.

170 Caillé, *La démission des clercs*, 16.

171 Ian McKay, 'Why Tell This Parable? Some Ethical Reflections on the Dionne Quintuplets,' *Journal of Canadian Studies* 29 (1995), 144. The title belies the wide-ranging nature of the issues that the article raises.

172 Comeau, ed., *Maurice Séguin*, 9.

173 Sarra-Bournet, 'Pour une histoire post-révisionniste,' 27.

174 Sarra-Bournet, 'Pour une histoire politique,' *Bulletin d'histoire politique* 3 (1995), 7. Sarra-Bournet also expressed considerable scepticism about revisionist writing in his doctoral dissertation: 'Entre le corporatisme et le libéralisme.'

175 Éthier-Blais, *Le siècle de l'Abbé Groulx*, 9. Blais was responding to the attacks against Groulx in Esther Delisle's *The Traitor and the Jew*. In a similar spirit, see Stapinsky's response in *Le Devoir*, 22 January 1992.

176 *Cahiers d'histoire du Québec au XXe siècle*, no. 1 (1994), 7.

177 Ibid., no. 1 (1994), 4, 7.

178 Ibid., no. 2 (1994), 5.
179 Ibid., no. 1 (1994), 123–31; no. 2 (1994), 183–94; no. 3 (1995), 177–87; no. 4 (1995), 168–75; no. 5 (1996), 159–69; no. 6 (1996), 166–76. The last instalment of the series, available in late 1996, promised that further ones were to come.
180 Novick, *Noble Dream*, 458, 468.
181 Ibid., 595.
182 Séguin, 'Faire de l'histoire au Québec,' *Présentations à la Société royale du Canada* (1990–1), 100.

Postscript

1 Bernard, 'Review of Lamarre, *Devenir*,' *RHAF* 48 (1995), 446.

Bibliography

Primary Sources

MANUSCRIPT COLLECTIONS

Archives de l'Université de Montréal (AUM)
Michel Brunet Papers
History Department Papers
Maurice Séguin Papers
Archives de l'Université Laval (AUL)
Thomas Chapais Papers
History Department Papers
Journals of the Superior, Séminaire de Québec
Arthur Maheux Papers
Séminaire de Québec Papers
Archives du Séminaire de Québec (ASQ)
Arthur Maheux Papers
  Correspondence
  Newspaper and journal clippings
Archives nationales du Québec (ANQM) (Montreal)
Robert Rumilly Papers
Archives nationales du Québec (ANQ) (Quebec City)
Thomas Chapais Papers
Cour supérieure de Québec, Box 68, dossier 110–644 (Ouellet lawsuit)
  Copy of Fernand Ouellet, *Julie Papineau: un cas de mélancolie et d'éducation janséniste*
  Documentation relating to the case of Anne Bourassa et al v. Fernand Ouellet

Centre de recherche en civilisation canadienne-française (CRCCF) (University of Ottawa)
Guy Frégault Papers
  Correspondence
  Miscellaneous manuscripts
Lilianne Frégault Papers
  Correspondence of Guy Frégault with various parties
Hector Garneau Papers
  Correspondence
  Newspaper clippings

Centre de recherche Lionel-Groulx (CRLG) (Montreal)
Lionel Groulx Papers
  Correspondence
  Manuel d'histoire du Canada, revisions 1913–16
  Manuel d'histoire du Canada préparé pour mes élèves de Valleyfield de 1905–1906
  Notes from Cours de vacances, Université de Fribourg, 29 July–8 August 1907
Institut d'histoire de l'Amérique française (IHAF) Papers
  Board of Directors, minutes, 1971–80
  Correspondence
  Fondation Lionel-Groulx Papers
Georges-Henri Lévesque Papers
Miscellaneous unpublished manuscripts
  Maurice Fillion, 'L'origine du Manuel'
  Giselle Huot, 'Le 'Manuel d'histoire du Canada' (1905–6) de Lionel Groulx ou l'apprentissage du métier d'historien,' unpublished paper presented to IHAF, 10–11 October 1980

National Archives of Canada (NA) (Ottawa)
Canadian Historical Association (CHA) Papers
  Correspondence relating to the Ouellet lawsuit
  Council minutes
Gustave Lanctot Papers
  Correspondence
  Newspaper and journal clippings

Blair Neatby, personal archives (Ottawa)
Correspondence and other documentation relating to the Ouellet lawsuit

Palais de Justice (Quebec City)
Cour du banc de la reine (en appel), dossier 8306 (Ouellet appeal), 1970

Société historique de Montréal, archives
Council minutes

OTHER PRINTED MATERIALS

Bibliothèque du séminaire de Sherbrooke, *Lionel Groulx: Dossier de presse, 1938–84*. 2 vols. 1981.
Centenaire de l'Histoire du Canada de François-Xavier Garneau: deuxième semaine d'histoire à l'Université de Montréal, 23–25 avril 1945. Montreal, 1945.
Groulx, Lionel. *Correspondance : 1894–1967*, ed. Giselle Huot, Juliette Lalonde-Rémillard, and Pierre Trepanier. 2 vols. Montreal, 1989–93.
– *Journal, 1895–1911*. Montreal, 1984.
Semaine d'histoire du Canada. Tenue du 23 au 27 novembre 1925. Montreal, 1926.
Société Radio-Canada. *Écrire l'histoire au Québec*. Montreal, 1981. (Transcripts of radio interviews)
– *Trou de mémoire*. Montreal, 1995. (Transcripts of radio interviews)
Université de Montréal, university calendars. (Until the 1920–1 academic year, these were calendars of the Montreal branch of Université Laval.)
Université Laval, university calendars.

Secondary Sources

Appleby, Joyce, Lynn Hunt, and Margaret Jacob. *Telling the Truth about History*. New York, 1994.
Baillargeon, Denyse. 'Des voies/x parallèles: l'histoire des femmes au Québec et au Canada anglais,' *Sextant*, 4 (1995), 133–68.
Behiels, Michael. 'Father Georges-Henri Lévesque and the Introduction of Social Sciences at Laval, 1938–55.' In Paul Axelrod and John Reid, eds., *Youth and University in Canadian Society*, 320–41. Montreal, 1989.
– *Prelude to Quebec's Quiet Revolution*. Montreal, 1985.
Berger, Carl. *The Writing of Canadian History: Aspects of English-Canadian Historical Writing since 1900*. 2nd ed. Toronto, 1986.
Bernard, Jean-Paul. *Les Rouges: libéralisme, nationalisme et anticléricalisme au milieu du dix-neuvième siècle*. Montreal, 1971.
Blain, Jean. 'Économie et société en Nouvelle-France: le cheminement historiographique dans la première moitié du XXe siècle,' *RHAF* 26 (1972), 3–31.
– 'Économie et société en Nouvelle-France: l'historiographie au tournant des années 1960: la réaction à Guy Frégault et à l'école de Montréal; la voie des sociologues,' *RHAF* 30 (1976), 323–62.
– 'Économie et société en Nouvelle-France: l'historiographie des années 1950–60: Guy Frégault et l'école de Montréal,' *RHAF* 28 (1974), 163–86.
– 'La frontière en Nouvelle-France,' *RHAF* 25 (1972), 397–407.

Bliss, Michael. 'Privatizing the Mind: The Sundering of Canadian History, The Sundering of Canada,' *Journal of Canadian Studies*, 26 no. 4 (1991–2), 5–17.

Bouchard, Gérard. 'Family Reproduction in New Rural Areas: Outline of a North American Model,' *CHR* 75 (1994), 475–510.

– 'L'historiographie du Québec rurale et la problématique nord-américaine avant la révolution tranquille: étude d'un refus,' *RHAF* 44 (1990), 199–222.

– 'Le Québec comme collectivité neuve.' In Bouchard and Yvan Lamonde, eds., *Québécois et américains*, 15–60. Montreal, 1995.

– 'Sur la dynamique culturelle des régions de peuplement,' *CHR* 67 (1986), 473–90.

– 'Sur les mutations de l'historiographie québécoise: les chemins de la maturité.' In Fernand Dumont, ed., *La société québécoise après 30 ans de changements*, 253–72. Quebec City, 1990.

– 'Une nation, deux cultures: continuités et ruptures dans la pensée québécoise traditionnelle, 1840–1960.' In Bouchard, ed., *La construction d'une culture*, 3–47. Quebec City, 1993.

Bourdé, Guy, and Hervé Martin. *Les écoles historiques*. Paris, 1983.

Brunet, Michel. *Les Canadiens après la Conquête*. Montreal, 1969.

– *Canadians et Canadiens*. Montreal, 1954.

– *La présence anglaise et les Canadiens*. Montreal, 1958.

– 'Trois illusions de la pensée canadienne-française: agriculturalisme, anti-impérialisme, et canadianisme,' *Alerte* (1954), 135–46.

Brunet, Michel, Guy Frégault, and Marcel Trudel. *Histoire du Canada par les textes*. Montreal, 1952.

– *Histoire du Canada par les textes*. 2 vols. Montreal, 1963.

Burke, Peter. *The French Historical Revolution: The Annales School, 1929–89*. Cambridge, 1990.

Caillé, Alain. *La démission des clercs: la crise des sciences sociales et l'oubli du politique*. Paris, 1993.

Carbonnell, C.-O., and Georges Livet, eds. *Au berceau des Annales*. Toulouse, 1983.

Chapais, Thomas. *Cours d'histoire du Canada*. 8 vols. Quebec City, 1919–34.

– *Discours et conférences*. 1st series. Quebec City, 1898.

– *Discours et conférences*. 2nd series. Quebec City, 1913.

– *Discours et conférences*. 3rd series. Quebec City, 1935.

– *Discours et conférences*. 4th series. Quebec City, 1943.

Clio Collective. *Quebec Women: A History*. Toronto, 1987.

Comeau, Robert, ed. *Maurice Séguin, historien du pays québécois*. Montreal, 1987.

Coupal, J.-P. 'Les dix dernières années de la *RHAF*, 1972–81,' *RHAF* 36 (1983), 553–67.

Courville, Serge. *Entre ville et campagne*. Quebec City, 1990.

Courville, Serge, Jean-Claude Robert, and Normand Séguin. *Atlas historique du Québec: le pays laurentien au 19e siècle, les morphologies de base*. Quebec City, 1995.

– 'Un nouvel regard sur le XIXe siècle québécois: l'axe laurentien comme l'espace central,' *Interface*, 14 (1993), 23–31.

Craig, Béatrice. 'Pour une approche comparative de l'étude des sociétés rurales nord-américaines,' *Histoire sociale* 23 (1990), 249–70.

d'Arles, Henri. *Nos historiens*. Montreal, 1921.

de Barbezieux, Frère Alexis. 'De la manière d'écrire l'histoire au Canada,' *La Nouvelle-France* 15 (1916), 215–20, 251–5, 302–9, 349–60, and 391–9.

Dechêne, Louise. *Habitants and Merchants in Seventeenth Century Montreal*. Trans. Liana Vardi. Montreal, 1992.

– *Habitants et marchands de Montréal au XVII siècle*. Paris, 1974.

Delisle, Esther. *The Traitor and the Jew*. 2nd ed, rev. Montreal, 1993.

Desbarats, Catherine. 'Agriculture within the Seigneurial Régime of Eighteenth Century Canada: Some Thoughts on the Recent Literature,' *CHR* 73 (1992), 1–29.

Desrosiers, Léo-Paul. 'Nos jeunes historiens servent-ils bien la vérité historique et leur patrie?' *Notre temps*, 28 December 1957.

Dickinson, John. 'Commentaires sur la critique de Ronald Rudin,' *Bulletin d'histoire politique* 4 (1995), 21–4.

Dion, Léon. *Québec, 1945–2000*. Tome II: *Les intellectuels et le temps de Duplessis*. Quebec City, 1993.

Dosse, François. *L'histoire en miettes: des annales à la nouvelle histoire*. Paris, 1987.

Dubuc, Alfred. 'L'influence de l'école des Annales au Québec,' *RHAF* 33 (1979), 357–86.

– 'The Influence of the Annales School in Quebec,' *Review* 1 (1978), 123–45.

Duchesneau, Alain. 'Le cheminement historiographique de Guy Frégault, 1936–55.' MA thesis, Université Laval, 1987.

Dumont, Fernand. *L'avenir de la mémoire*. Montreal, 1995.

– *Genèse de la société québécoise*. Montreal, 1993.

– *Raisons communes*. Montreal, 1995.

–, ed. *La société québécoise après 30 ans de changements*. Quebec City, 1990.

Éthier-Blais, Jean. *Le siècle de l'Abbé Groulx*. Montreal, 1993.

Fecteau, Jean-Marie. 'La quête d'une histoire normale: réflexion sur les limites épistémologiques du "révisionnisme" au Québec,' *Bulletin d'histoire politique*, 4 (1996), 31–8.

Fecteau, Jean-Marie, et al., eds. *La condition québécoise: enjeux et horizons d'une société en devenir*. Montreal, 1994.

Ferland, J.B.A. *Cours d'histoire du Canada*. 2 vols. Quebec City, 1861–5.

Fortin, Andrée. *Passage de la modernité: les intellectuels québécois et leurs revues.* Quebec City, 1993.

Fournier, Marcel. 'Autour de la spécificité,' *Possibles* 8 (1983), 85–117.

– *L'entrée dans la modernité*. Montreal, 1986.

Frégault, Guy. 'L'actualité de Garneau,' *Action universitaire* 11 (1945), 8–16.

– *Canada: The War of the Conquest*. Trans. Margaret Cameron. Toronto, 1969.

– *Canadian Society in the French Regime*. Ottawa, 1954.

– *Chronique des années perdues*. Montreal, 1976.

– *La civilisation de la Nouvelle-France, 1713–44*. Montreal, 1944.

– *Le XVIIIe siècle canadien*. Montreal, 1968.

– *François Bigot, administrateur français*. 2 vols. Montreal, 1948.

– *Le Grand Marquis*. Montreal, 1952.

– *La Guerre de la Conquête*. Montreal, 1955.

– *Iberville le conquérant*. Montréal, 1944.

– *Lionel Groulx: tel qu'en lui-même*. Ottawa, 1978.

– 'Souvenirs d'apprentissage,' *BRH* 51 (1945), 61–3.

Gaboury, Jean-Pierre. *Le nationalisme de Lionel Groulx: aspects idéologiques.* Ottawa, 1970.

Gagnon, Serge. *Mariage et famille aux temps de Papineau*. Quebec City, 1993.

– *Mourir hier et aujourd'hui*. Quebec City, 1987.

– *Plaisir d'amour et crainte de Dieu: sexualité et confession au Bas-Canada*. Quebec City, 1990.

– *Quebec and Its Historians: 1840–1920*. Montreal, 1982.

– *Quebec and Its Historians: The Twentieth Century*. Montreal, 1985.

– 'Le Québec au temps présent: un dieu absent sans remplaçant?' *Laval théologique et philosophique* 51 (1995), 17–33.

– *Le Québec et ses historiens, 1840–1920*. Quebec City, 1978.

Gagnon, Serge, and René Hardy, eds. *L'église et le village au Québec, 1850–1930.* Montreal, 1979.

Galarneau, Claude, and Elzéar Lavoie, eds. *France et Canada français du XVIe au XXe siècle*. Quebec City, 1966.

Garneau, François-Xavier. *Histoire du Canada depuis sa découverte jusqu'à nos jours*. 1st ed. 4 vols. Quebec City, 1845–8.

– *Histoire du Canada depuis sa découverte jusqu'à nos jours*. 3rd ed. 3 vols. Quebec City, 1859.

– *Histoire du Canada depuis sa découverte jusqu'à nos jours*. 4th ed. 4 vols. Montreal, 1882.

– *Histoire du Canada depuis sa découverte jusqu'à nos jours*. 5th ed. 2 vols. Paris, 1913–20.

– *Histoire du Canada depuis sa découverte jusqu'à nos jours.* 8th ed. 9 vols. Montreal, 1944–6.

Genest, Jean. *Qu'est-ce que le 'brunetisme'?* Montreal, 1961.

Gingras, Yves. *Pour l'avancement des sciences: histoire de l'ACFAS, 1923–93.* Montreal, 1994.

– 'Une sociologie spontanée de la connaissance historique,' *Bulletin d'histoire politique* 4 (1995), 39–43.

Godbout, Archange 'Les préoccupations en histoire et les thèses de M l'Abbé Maheux,' *Culture* 4 (1943), 28–43.

Greer, Allan. *Peasant, Lord and Merchant.* Toronto, 1985.

Groulx, Lionel. 'À l'occasion du Prix Duvernay,' *Action nationale,* 40 (1952), 170–82.

– *Le Canada français missionaire: une autre grande aventure.* Montreal, 1962.

– *La confédération canadienne: ses origines.* Montreal, 1918.

– 'La déchéance de notre classe paysanne.' In Groulx, *Orientations,* 56–116. Montreal, 1935.

– *La découverte du Canada: Jacques Cartier.* Montreal, 1934.

– *Directives.* Montreal, 1937.

– *Dix ans d'Action française.* Montreal, 1926.

– *Dollard est-il un mythe?* Montreal, 1960.

– 'Fils de grand homme,' *RHAF* 10 (1956–7), 310–32.

– *Histoire du Canada français depuis la découverte.* 4th ed. 2 vols. Montreal, 1960.

– *L'indépendance du Canada.* Montreal, 1949.

– *Lendemains de conquête.* Ottawa, 1977.

– 'Ma conception de l'histoire,' *Action nationale* 49 (1960), 603–17.

– *Mes mémoires.* 4 vols. Montreal, 1970–74.

– 'M. Thomas Chapais,' *Liaison* 1 (1947), 12–17.

– *La naissance d'une race.* 1st ed. Montreal, 1919.

– *La naissance d'une race.* 2nd ed. Montreal, 1930.

– *La naissance d'une race.* 3rd ed. Montreal, 1938.

– *Nos luttes constitutionnelles.* Montreal, 1915–6.

– *Notre grande aventure.* Montreal, 1958.

– *Notre maître, le passé.* 1st series, 3rd ed. Montreal, 1937.

– *Notre maître, le passé.* 2nd series. Montréal, 1936.

– *Notre maître, le passé.* 3rd series. Montreal, 1944.

– *Pourquoi nous sommes divisés.* Montreal, 1943.

– *Vers l'émancipation.* Montreal, 1921.

Hamel, Reginald. *Dictionnaire des auteurs de langue française en Amérique du Nord.* Montreal, 1989.

Hamelin, Jean. *Économie et société en Nouvelle-France.* Quebec City, 1960.

– *Histoire de l'Université Laval*. Quebec City, 1995.

– *Histoire du catholicisme québécois: le XXe siècle*. Vol. 2. Montreal, 1984.

Hamelin, Jean, and Nicole Gagnon. *Histoire du catholicisme québécois: le XXe siècle*. Vol. 1. Montreal, 1984.

Hamelin, Jean, and Yves Roby. *Histoire économique du Québec*. Montreal, 1971.

Hardy, René. 'À propos du réveil religieux dans le Québec du XIX siècle,' *RHAF* 48 (1994), 187–212.

– *Les Zouaves*. Montreal, 1980.

Hartog, François. *Le XIXe siècle et l'histoire: le cas de Fustel de Coulanges*. Paris, 1988.

Harvey, Fernand, and Paul-André Linteau, 'L'évolution de l'historiographie dans la *RHAF*, 1947–72,' *RHAF* 26 (1972), 163–83.

Haskell, Thomas. 'Objectivity Is Not Neutrality: Rhetoric and Practice in Peter Novick's *That Noble Dream*,' *History and Theory* 29 (1990), 129–57.

Hellman, John. *Emmanuel Mounier and the New Catholic Left, 1930–50*. Toronto, 1981.

Higham, John. *History: Professional Scholarship in America*. Baltimore, 1983.

Hunt, Lynn. 'French History in the Last Twenty Years: The Rise and Fall of the Annales Paradigm,' *Journal of Contemporary History* 21 (1986), 209–24.

Kammen, Michael. 'Clio and the Changing Fashions,' *American Scholar*, 44 (1975), 484–96.

– *The Past before Us*. Ithaca, NY, 1980.

Keylor, William. *Academy and Community: The Foundation of the French Historical Profession*. Cambridge, Mass., 1975.

Kloppenberg, James T. 'Review Article: Objectivity and Historicism: A Century of American Historical Writing,' *American Historical Review* 94 (1989), 1011–30.

Labrousse, Ernest. 'Comment naissent les révolutions, 1848–1830–1789.' In *Actes du congrès historique du centenaire de la révolution de 1848*, 1–20. Paris, 1948.

LaCapra, Dominick. *History and Criticism*. Ithaca, NY, 1985.

Lamarre, Jean. *Le devenir de la nation québécoise selon Maurice Séguin, Guy Frégault et Michel Brunet, 1944–69*. Quebec City, 1993.

– 'Entre l'histoire éclatante et l'histoire éclatée: l'école de Montréal vue sous l'angle d'une sociologie du savoir historique.' PhD thesis, Université Laval, 1992.

Lamonde, Yvan, and Esther Trépanier, eds. *L'avènement de la modernité au Québec*. Quebec City, 1986.

Lamontagne, Maurice. *Le fédéralisme canadien*. Quebec City, 1954.

Lanctot, Gustave. 'Évolution de notre historiographie,' *Action universitaire* 13 (1946–7), 3–6.

– *François-Xavier Garneau*. Toronto, n.d.
– 'Garneau, fondateur de l'histoire scientifique en Canada,' *HP* (1925), 28–33.
– *Garneau: historien national*. Montreal, 1946.
Landes, David, and Charles Tilly, eds. *History as Social Science*. Englewood Cliffs, NJ, 1971.
Langlois, Charles, and Charles Seignobos. *Introduction to the Study of History*. Trans. G.G. Berry. New York, 1898.
Lavertu, Yves. *L'affaire Bernonville*. Montreal, 1994.
Lavigne, Marie, and Yolande Pinard. *Les femmes dans la société québécoise*. Montreal, 1977.
– *Travailleuses et féministes*. Montreal, 1982.
Lemire, Maurice. comp. *Dictionnaire des œuvres littéraires du Québec*. 2nd ed., rev. Montreal, 1980– .
Le Roy Ladurie, Emmanuel. *The Territory of the Historian*. Trans. Ben and Sian Reynolds. Chicago, 1979.
Létourneau, Jocelyn. 'Critique de la raison technocratique: définir une avenue à la jeune recherche.' In Fernand Dumont, ed., *La société québécoise après 30 ans de changements*, 341–56. Quebec City, 1990.
– 'La grève de l'amiante entre ses mémoires et l'histoire,' *Journal of Canadian Oral History Association* 11 (1991), 8–16.
– 'L'imaginaire historique des jeunes québécois,' *RHAF* 41 (1988), 553–74.
– 'La nouvelle figure identitaire du québécois: essai sur la dimension symbolique d'un consensus en voie d'émergence,' *British Journal of Canadian Studies* 6 (1990) 17–38.
– 'La production historienne courante portant sur le Québec et ses rapports avec la construction des figures identitaires d'une communauté communicationnelle,' *Recherches sociographiques* 36 (1995), 9–45.
– 'Québec d'après guerre et mémoire collective de la technocratie,' *Cahiers internationaux de sociologie* 90 (1991), 67–87.
– 'La saga du Québec moderne en images,' *Genèses* 4 (1991), 44–71.
Lévesque, Andrée. 'Historiography: History of Women in Quebec since 1985,' *Quebec Studies*, no. 12 (1991), 83–91.
– *Making and Breaking the Rules*. Toronto, 1994.
Lévesque, Georges-Henri, ed. *Continuité et rupture: les sciences sociales au Québec*. Montreal, 1984.
Linteau, Paul-André. *Maisonneuve ou comment les promoteurs fabriquent une ville*. Montreal, 1981.
– 'La nouvelle histoire,' *Liberté*, no. 147 (1983), 34–47.
– 'Quelques réflexions autour de la bourgeoisie québécoise, 1850–1914,' *RHAF* 30 (1976), 55–66.

Linteau, Paul-André, and Jean-Claude Robert. 'Propriété foncière et société à Montréal: une hypothèse,' *RHAF* 28 (1974), 45–65.

Linteau, Paul-André, René Durocher, and Jean-Claude Robert. *Histoire du Québec contemporain: de la Confédération à la crise*. Montreal, 1979.

– *Quebec: A History, 1867–1929*. Trans. Robert Chodos. Toronto, 1983.

Linteau, Paul-André, René Durocher, Jean-Claude Robert, and François Ricard. *Histoire du Québec contemporain*. 2nd ed., rev. 2 vols. Montreal, 1989.

– *Histoire du Québec contemporain: le Québec depuis 1930*. Montreal, 1986.

– *Quebec since 1930*. Trans. Robert Chodos and Ellen Garmaise. Toronto, 1991.

Maheux, Arthur. *Pourquoi sommes-nous divisés*. Montreal, 1943.

– *Ton histoire est une épopée*. Quebec City, 1941.

Maier, Charles. *The Unmasterable Past: History, Holocaust and German National Identity*. Cambridge, Mass., 1988.

Marie-Victorin, Frère. *Science, culture et nation: textes choisis et présentés par Yves Gingras*. Montreal, 1996.

Mandrou, Robert. 'L'historiographie canadienne-française: bilan et perspectives,' *CHR* 51 (1970), 5–19.

Mathieu, Jacques, and Jacques Lacoursière. *Les mémoires québécoises*. Quebec City, 1991.

Mawer, Donald. 'The Return of the Catholic Past: The Debate between F.X. Garneau and His Critics, 1831–1945.' PhD thesis, McGill University, 1977.

Morissette, Napoléon. 'En marges des nouvelles éditions de Garneau,' *Canada français* 16 (April 1929), 558–67.

Novick, Peter. *That Noble Dream: The Objectivity Question and the American Historical Profession*. Cambridge, England, 1988.

Ouellet, Fernand. *Le Bas Canada*. Ottawa, 1976.

– 'Le destin de Julie Bruneau-Papineau,' *BRH* 64, no. 1 (1958), 7–31; 64, no. 2 (1958), 37–63.

– *Economic and Social History of Quebec*. Trans. Ottawa, 1980.

– *Economy, Class and Nation in Quebec*. Trans. Jacques Barbier. Toronto, 1991.

– 'L'étude du dix-neuvième siècle canadien-français,' *Recherches sociographiques* 3 (1962), 27–42.

– *Histoire économique et sociale du Québec, 1760–1850*. Montreal, 1966.

– 'Historiographie et nationalisme,' *Mémoires de la Société Royale du Canada* 13 (1975), 25–39.

– *Lower Canada, 1791–1840*. Trans. Patricia Clayton. Toronto, 1980.

– 'La mentalité et l'outillage économique de l'habitant canadien: à propos d'un document sur l'encan,' *BRH* 62 (1956), 131–9.

– 'La modernisation de l'historiographie et l'émergence de l'histoire sociale,' *Recherches sociographiques* 26 (1985), 11–83.

- 'M. Michel Brunet et le problème de la Conquête,' *BRH* 62 (1956), 92–101.
- 'Papineau dans la révolution de 1837-8,' *HP* (1958), 13–34.
- *Papineau: A Divided Soul.* Ottawa, 1961.
- 'Papineau et la rivalité Québec-Montréal,' *RHAF* 13 (1959–60), 311–27.
- 'The Quiet Revolution: A Turning Point.' In T. Axworthy and P.E. Trudeau, eds., *Towards a Just Society*, 313–41. Toronto, 1990.
- *Socialization of Quebec Historiography.* Toronto, 1988.

Ouellet, Fernand, and Jean Hamelin. 'La crise agricole dans le Bas-Canada, 1802–37,' *HP* (1962), 17–33.

Paquet, Gilles, and Jean-Pierre Wallot. *Patronage et pouvoir dans le Bas-Canada.* Montreal, 1973.

Provost, Honorius. *Historique de la Faculté des arts de l'Université Laval, 1852–1952.* Quebec City, 1952.

Ricard, François. *La génération lyrique: essai sur la vie et l'œuvre des premiers-nés du baby-boom.* Montreal, 1994.
- 'Remarques sur la normalisation d'une littérature,' *Écriture* 31 (1988), 11–19.

Rioux, Marcel, and Yves Martin, eds. *French Canadian Society.* Toronto, 1964.

Robitaille, Abbé Georges. *Études sur Garneau.* Montreal, 1929.

Rogues, Nathalie. 'L'image de l'Europe dans les écrits de Lionel Groulx (1906–9),' *RHAF* 46 (1992), 245–54.

Rosenau, Pauline Marie. *Post-Modernism and the Social Sciences: Insights, Inroads, and Intrusions.* Princeton, NJ, 1992.

Rouillard, Jacques, ed. *Guide d'histoire du Québec.* 2nd ed. Montreal, 1993.
- *Histoire du syndicalisme au Québec.* Montreal, 1989.

Rousseau, Louis. 'À propos du "réveil religieux" dans le Québec du XIXe siècle: où se loge le vrai débat?' *RHAF* 49 (1995), 223–45.
- 'Crise et réveil religieux dans le Québec du XIXe siècle,' *Interface* 11 (1990), 24–31.

Roy, Christian. 'De *La Relève* à *Cité libre*: avatars du personnalisme au Québec,' *Vice Versa* 17 (1986), 14–6.
- 'Le personnalisme de *L'Ordre Nouveau* et le Québec, 1930–47: son rôle dans la formation de Guy Frégault,' *RHAF* 46 (1993), 463–84.

Roy, Fernande. *Histoire des idéologies au Québec aux XIXe et XXe siècles.* Montréal, 1993.

Rudin, Ronald. 'Au-delà du révisionnisme,' *Bulletin d'histoire politique* 4 (1995), 57–74.
- *In Whose Interest? Quebec's Caisses Populaires, 1900–45.* Montreal, 1990.
- 'One Model, Two Responses: Quebec, Ireland and the Study of Rural Society,' *Canadian Papers in Rural History* 9 (1994), 259–89.
—'Revisionism and the Search for a Normal Society: A Critique of Recent Quebec Historical Writing,' *CHR* 73 (1992), 30–61.

Rumilly, Robert. *Histoire de la province de Québec.* 41 vols. Montreal, 1940–69.

Sarra-Bournet, Michel. 'Entre le corporatisme et le libéralisme: les groupes d'affaires francophones et l'organisation socio-politique du Québec de 1943 à 1969.' PhD thesis, University of Ottawa, 1995.

– 'Pour une histoire post-révisionniste,' *Bulletin d'histoire politique* 4 (1996) 25–9.

Savard, Pierre. 'Quart de siècle d'historiographie québécoise, 1947–72,' *Recherches sociographiques* 15 (1974), 75–96.

– 'Les rééditions de *L'Histoire du Canada* de François-Xavier Garneau devant la critique, 1913–46,' *RHAF* 28 (1975), 539–53.

Savard, Pierre, ed. *Guy Frégault.* Montreal, 1981.

Séguin, Maurice. *La 'nation canadienne' et l'agriculture (1760–1850).* Trois-Rivières, 1970.

Séguin, Normand. *La conquête du sol au 19e siècle.* Montreal, 1977.

– 'L'économie agro-forestière: genèse et développement au XIXe siècle,' *RHAF* 29 (1976), 559–65.

Shore, Marlene. '"Remember the future": The *Canadian Historical Review* and the Discipline of History,' *CHR* 76 (1995), 410–63.

Simard, Jean-Jacques. *La longue marche des technocrates.* Montreal, 1979.

Tousignant, Pierre. 'Groulx et l'histoire: interrogation sur le passé en vue d'une direction d'avenir,' *RHAF* 32 (1978), 347–56.

Trofimenkoff, Susan Mann. *Action française: French Canadian Nationalism in the Twenties.* Toronto, 1975.

Trudel, Marcel. *Chiniquy.* Trois-Rivières, 1955.

– 'Les débuts de l'Institut d'histoire à l'Université Laval,' *RHAF* 27 (1973), 397–402.

– *L'église canadienne sous le régime militaire.* 2 vols. Montreal, 1956; Quebec City, 1957.

– *L'esclavage au Canada français.* Quebec City, 1960.

– *Histoire de la Nouvelle-France.* 3 vols. Montreal, 1963–83.

– *L'influence de Voltaire au Canada.* Montreal, 1945.

– *Introduction to New France.* Montreal, 1968.

– 'La littérature canadienne et la religion: l'influence de Voltaire au Canada,' *Culture* 6 (1945), 160–1.

– *Louis XIV, le congrès américain et le Canada, 1774–89.* Quebec City, 1949.

– *Mémoires d'un autre siècle.* Montreal, 1987.

– *Le régime militaire dans le gouvernement des Trois-Rivières.* Trois-Rivières, 1952.

Wallot, Jean-Pierre. 'Groulx historiographe,' *RHAF* 32 (1978), 407–33.

– *Un Québec qui bougeait.* Montreal, 1973.

– 'Religion and French-Canadian Mores in the Early Nineteenth Century,' *CHR* 52 (1971), 51–94.

White, Hayden. *Metahistory*. Baltimore, 1973.

- 'The Politics of Historical Interpretation.' In W.J.T. Mitchell, ed., *The Politics of Interpretation*, 119–43. Chicago, 1983.

Wyczynski, Paul. *François-Xavier Garneau: aspects littéraires de son œuvre*. Ottawa, 1966.

Photo Credits

Archives du Centre de recherche Lionel-Groulx: Groulx, 1920: Lionel Groulx papers, P1/T1, 1.16, photographe: inconnu; Groulx, 1946: Groulx papers, P1/T1, 4.17, photographe: Paul Guillet; Brunet and Groulx: Groulx papers, P1/T1, 29.17, photographe: Université de Montréal, Centrale de photographe, Service des archives de l'Université de Montréal

Archives nationales du Québec à Montréal: Rumilly: P303, S1, SS12, SSS1, D1, P10

Archives nationales du Québec à Québec: Hector Garneau: Collection initiale-photo, P600, S6, PGH671-23, photographe: non-identifié; Chapais: Série documents iconographiques, P1000, S4, PC55-2, photographe: Montminy & Cie

Archives de l'Université Laval: Maheux: U506/92/2, HF30, neg. 96–55; Professors and graduates, 1950: U555/92/2, tiroir 15.2, neg. 90-119 (despite our best efforts, it was impossible to identify the photographer because the studio had burned down); Hamelin: Centre de production multimédia, 86-294 No. 6

Archives de l'Université de Montréal: Séguin: IFP 2887

Fernand Ouellet: Ouellet

National Archives of Canada: Lanctot: photograph by Blank-Stoller, PA-117415

University of Ottawa, Centre de recherche en civilisation canadienne-française: François-Xavier Garneau: Collection Alfred-Garneau, P296C, 4, Ph80-I-1; Faculty and students, c. 1948: Guy-Frégault papers, Ph95-124; Trudel: Collection Marcelle-et-Bernard Barthe, Ph33-13, photographe: Thomas Studio, Ottawa

Index